Struggles Within the Struggle

Henry Isaacs

Struggles Within the Struggle

An Inside View of the PAC of South Africa

Henry Isaacs

Zed Books Ltd.

Struggles Within the Struggle was first published by Zed Books Ltd., 57 Caledonian Road, London N1 9BU, in 1985.

Copyright © Henry Isaacs, 1985.

Cover designed by Windhorse Associates
Printed by The Bath Press, Avon.

All rights reserved

British Library Cataloguing in Publication Data

Isaacs, Henry
    Struggles within the struggle : an inside view
of the PAC of South Africa.
    1. Pan Africanist Congress of Azania
    I. Title
    322.4'2'0968   DT770

    ISBN 0-86232-260-X
    ISBN 0-86232-261-8 Pbk

US Distributor
Biblio Distribution Center, 81 Adams Drive,
Totowa, New Jersey 07512

Publisher's Note:

The delay in publishing this book is in no way the author's fault.

Developments that have taken place since the manuscript was completed and to which the author has drawn attention are as follows:

1) *Lack of organisation in the rural areas:*
   There is now evidence that the resistance has spread to some rural areas in the Eastern Cape, the Transkei and Venda bantustans.

2) *The future of the EDF, which was formed primarily to mobilise opposition to the regime's constitutional strategy:*
   This is now being debated inside South Africa; a conference to debate this question to be held at the University of Cape Town to discuss the future of the EDF was banned by the regime.

3) *The author's analysis of the resurgence of the ANC ends in 1984:*
   He points out that questions can be raised regarding the lack of credible military action during the last 15 months, if, as indicated, the ANC has successfully infiltrated an estimated 1,000 trained freedom fighters who have remained undetected for several years. Why, for instance, have no police or military patrols in the townships been attacked? The policemen and other collaborators who have been killed, and the young, white corporal who was stabbed to death, were killed by people who were largely unarmed and defenceless against the poice and army.

4) A PAC sympathiser can point out that *Pokela died on June 30 1985* and his successor has been far more skilful in handling the manipulations of individuals such as Gora Ebrahim, and the organisation has attempted to infiltrate military cadres into the country in 1985.

5) *Regarding the author's dealing with the Nkomati Accord and the implications for the ANC*, a related question arises from Zimbabwe's position vis-à-vis the ANC. Why does Zimbabwe support the PAC out of all proportion to the effectiveness of that organisation when, from their own experience — i.e. FRELIMO's support for ZANU-PF rather than ZAPU with which FRELIMO had a political alliance — one would expect them to support the ANC which, even according to the Zimbabweans themselves, is leading the struggle in South Africa?

January 1986

Contents

Acknowledgements	xi

PART I: INTRODUCTION TO THE SOUTH AFRICAN STRUGGLE

Introduction	1
The Need for Committed Writing	1
The Author	1
Why Write this History of the PAC?	3
Scope of the Book	5

1. The Nature of a National Liberation Movement	8
Nationalist and National Liberation Movements — a Distinction	8
The USA and National Liberation Movements	11
The South African Response	13
Problems within National Liberation Movements	13

2. The ANC and the PAC	17
Black Political Consciousness and the Formation of the ANC	19
The Congress Youth League (CYL)	22
The Communist Party of South Africa (CPSA)	24
Formation of the PAC	29
Sharpeville and After	32
Transition to Violence	36
White Repression and Black Consciousness	43

3. The Burdens of Exile	49
The Failure to Re-establish Structures at Home	50
Divisions within the Liberation Movement	55
The Pathology of Exile	76
Conclusion	82

PART II: THE CRISIS IN THE PAC: 1978-83   87

4. The Decline of the PAC	89
Absorbing the Soweto Youths	89
PAC Weaknesses	91
PAC Crisis of Credibility	97

5. The PAC Consultative Conference, Arusha, 1978   101
Origins of the Split   101
'Two-line Struggle' or Ethno-regional Struggle?   103
Arrests of PAC Members in Swaziland   104
Background to the Leballo/Ntantala Power Struggle   106
Outcome of the Conference   114

6. Post-Arusha Anarchy: APLA Flexes its Muscles   118
APLA High Command Demands 'Strategic Leadership'   118
Indiscipline in PAC Central Committee   121
Post-Arusha Split in Central Committee   122
Leballo/Mayekiso Alliance Falls Apart   124
Problems for the PAC in Botswana   126
Swaziland Detains and Deports PAC Members   128
Central Committee Members Held Hostage by APLA   133

7. Crisis in the PAC and Exposure of Leballo   136
The Problems   137
Appointment of Commission of Inquiry   142
Leballo: Part of the Problem   144
Enemy Infiltration of the PAC   145
In Retrospect   149

8. Leballo Ousted   150
Tanzania Warns Leballo   150
Twentieth Anniversary of the PAC — Leballo Humiliated   152
PAC Divided into Two Hostile Camps   153
Leballo Forced to Step Down   154
Reactions of the High Command and the Tanzanians   160

9. The Assassination of David M. Sibeko   168
The Central Committee's Plans   168
The High Command Plots   169
The Murder   170
The Investigation   171

10. The Consequences of the Assassination   174
Elizabeth Sibeko and Family vs. Make and the PAC   175
David Sibeko: Protege of Leballo or Victim?   178
Sibeko's Assassination Widely Publicised   180
APLA Unleashes Reign of Terror   181
OAU Threatens De-recognition   185
PAC Isolated at Non-Aligned Summit   187
UN Wary   188

11. The Emergence of Vusumzi Make as PAC Chairman   191
Make and Ntloedibe Stir up Trouble in Lesotho   191
Make on Background to the Crisis in the PAC   193
Leballo Denounced and Expelled   194

PAC's Problems Deeper than Leballo's Idiosyncrasies	195
The October 1979 Plenary	197
Make's Appointment as Chairman Problematical	198
Leballo Continues to Claim Leadership of PAC	200

12. Vusumzi Make at the Helm: the Crisis Deepens — 203

Make's Leadership Ineffective	203
Diplomatic Missions	207
Threat of De-recognition of PAC Still Lingers	208
Central Committee Lacks Control over APLA	216
Leballo's Claims Continue	217
The Problems Caused by Elizabeth Sibeko	221
Maladministration	229
Factionalism and Cliquism	232

13. Vusumzi Make at the Helm: the Crisis Continues — 236

Re-emergence of the 'Cadre Forces' Movement'	236
PAC's Inability to Respond to Political Developments in South Africa	245
Non-governmental Organisations Withdraw Support	247

14. John Nyati Pokela: Saviour of the PAC? — 252

Central Committee Meeting, January-February 1981	252
Enter John Nyati Pokela	254
Plotting, Intrigues and Power Struggles	257
The End of Leballo?	267
Pokela Takes Over but Problems Persist	271
Recent Developments in the PAC	290

PART III: THE NATIONAL LIBERATION STRUGGLE: PROBLEMS AND PROSPECTS — 307

15. The Resurgence of the ANC — 309

ANC's Military Capacity	310
Phases in ANC Guerrilla Activities	311
Public Resonance	315
Pretoria Car-bomb Attack — Phase Four?	319
Legitimacy of the ANC	323

16. Unity Within the National Liberation Movement — 328

Unity Between the ANC and PAC?	328
Super-power Rivalry and Implications for Liberation Unity	330
PAC Opportunism Retraced	334
Unity with Other Patriotic Organisations	342

17. The Enemy: Responses and Capacities — 347

The 'Constellation of Southern African States'	349
Botha's Constitutional Strategy	351
Larger Regional Role	352

Africa's Response: the Southern African Development Co-ordination Conference (SADCC)	352
Pretoria's Programme of Destabilisation	354
Conclusion	366
Implications of the Nkomati Accord	368
Lessons for South African Revolutionaries	371
18. The Home Front: What Is To Be Done?	374
The Growth of the Black Labour Movement	374
The Future	380
Dangers of Increased US Involvement	384
All Quiet on the Rural Front?	387
Conclusion	388
Acronyms	392
Bibliography	394
Index	401

Tables

15.1	316
15.2	317

Illustrations

Photographs appear on pages xiii, xiv, xv.

Acknowledgements

The first draft of the manuscript for this book was completed in New York in November 1982. It was revised and completed in California and Zimbabwe in 1983. Completion of the task, once embarked upon, would have been impossible without the assistance, advice and encouragement of numerous persons. Professor Thomas Karis drew my attention to various published sources. Dr. Alfred Moleah provided information whenever I cross-checked facts about the exiled political organisations. Toby Truell, in lively correspondence, drew out my views and analyses of the South African National Liberation Movement, offering helpful comments and criticisms in the process. Dr. Peter Molotsi provided valuable information about and insights into the early history of the PAC in exile and the problems that plagued the organisation.

Many PAC members (active and inactive) furnished information conditionally upon their remaining anonymous. I have respected their wishes, although the paradox is striking that South African exiles affiliated to an organisation professedly struggling for freedom and justice are afraid of the same harassment and victimisation within their own organisation as the harassment and victimisation from which they fled in South Africa. If there is no democracy, no free exchange of views and ideas, and intolerance of constructive criticisms within the National Liberation Movement, what chance is there of the National Liberation Movement promoting those values after liberation?

Several political activists in South Africa furnished information and documents and urged me to write the book. Their identities must necessarily be concealed, but I wish to emphasise my gratitude for their assistance, assistance that was fraught with personal risk, and appreciation for their confidence.

I have similarly concealed the identities of various government officials and other persons where this was requested.

Jan Birchfield typed the first draft of the manuscript without once complaining about all the corrections, amendments and insertions that I regularly made.

The University of California at Santa Cruz (UCSC) provided accommodation and made available library facilities during my stay there in 1983. Personnel in the office of the Academic Vice-Chancellor and the

Acknowledgements

Budget Division were very helpful and accommodating in facilitating my affiliation with UCSC, as well as addressing all my enquiries. The Academic Vice-Chancellor, Dr. John Marcum, took time off from his busy schedule to read the draft manuscript. His comments, criticisms and advice were invaluable.

Without a research grant from the Ford Foundation, through UCSC, the project could not have been completed.

Robert Molteno, despite his heavy work-load, made helpful comments and criticisms. Throughout, he maintained regular contact through the mail and encouraged the completion of the book. I could not hope for a better relationship with my editor/publishers.

I owe a debt of gratitude to my wife, Gayla, and our two sons, Ifedi and Lionel, for their support and understanding when I neglected them while conducting the research and writing the book. Gayla, in particular, endured much slander and abuse from PAC elements. A less courageous person would have pleaded for abandonment of the project.

I alone am responsible for the final product and whatever weaknesses it contains.

Henry Isaacs
Harare, Zimbabwe

Three PAC Central Committee members addressing solidarity meeting in Montreal, Canada, October 1981. From left to right: Zolile Hamilton Keke (Chief Representative to the UK, Nyati John Pokela (Chairman), and Joe Mkwanazi (Administrative Secretary).

Slain PAC leader David M. Sibeko addressing UN General Assembly, 22 November 1978.

(*UN/Sam Lwin*)

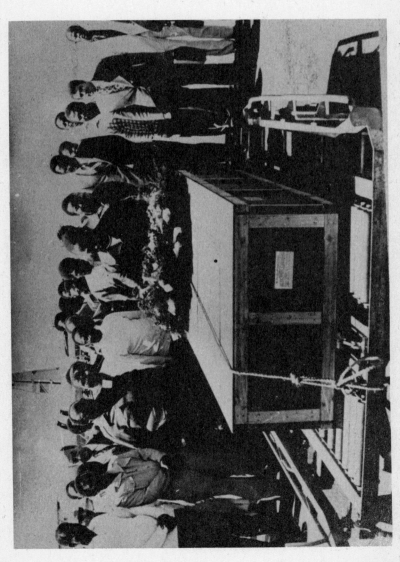

Dar-es-Salaam international airport, 17 June 1979. Casket containing Sibeko's body being loaded on aircraft for flight to Botswana for burial. Looking on are PAC members, Tanzanian officials, OAU officials and foreign diplomats.
(*Tanzania Daily News*)

Part I:
Introduction to the
South African Struggle

Introduction

The Need for Committed Writing

Participants in the South African liberation struggle should be encouraged to write, so that the history of the struggle can be accurately chronicled. One of the noticeable features of South African historiography is the dearth of literature from Black political activists and participants in the liberation struggle. For example, a number of books have been written about the Soweto uprisings, but none by the participants in these historic events.[1] Similarly, books have been written about the Black Consciousness Movement (BCM), but none by its protagonists.[2]

Many excellent publications on the situation in South Africa have appeared in recent years, many of them written by activists and committed academics.[3] Thus far, however, there has not been a systematic study of South African exile politics. The ANC and PAC both produce publications (the ANC regularly, the PAC erratically), but these often contain exaggerated claims of their 'underground activity' in South Africa, or vitriolic attacks upon each other. In addition, during intra-movement conflicts, opposing factions often engage in mutual denunciations and bitter personal attacks.[4] Consequently, it is difficult to judge the reality behind the rhetoric. Marcum's essay remains a valuable pioneering effort.[5] The book by Gibson on the national liberation struggles in Southern Africa is flawed.[6] Wilfred Burchett, the Australian-born journalist who did much to publicise the national liberation struggles of the peoples of Vietnam, Laos and Cambodia (now Kampuchea), has written a useful book.[7]

The Author

This book is an attempt to fill this gap. My qualification to do so is the fact that I have been actively involved in the liberation struggle both in South Africa and in exile. I rose through the ranks of the Black Consciousness Movement, gaining election in 1972 to the position of Vice-

2 *Introduction to the South African Struggle*

President of the South African Students' Organisation (SASO) and President in 1973. Simultaneously, I was President of the Students' Representative Council (SRC) at the University of the Western Cape where I was a law student. In May 1973, I was suspended by the University authorities after I refused, *on principle*, to pay a fine of 50 Rand imposed by them for allegedly violating the rules and regulations of the University when I performed my duties as SRC President in accordance with the SRC constitution and mandate from the student body. I had addressed student mass meetings and also had given press interviews in which I criticised security police activities on campus, including the harassment of students, and the collaboration of the university authorities. My suspension was followed by student demonstrations when the authorities refused to redress the students' grievances. During a debate in the Whites-only parliament on the closure of the University, the Minister of Coloured Affairs said that the trouble at the University began when I became President of SASO, 'a radical Black Power Movement', which was preparing for 'violent revolution' in South Africa.

On 26 July 1973, I was banned under the Suppression of Communism Act while I was giving evidence for the defence in the trial of Nyameko Barney Pityana who was charged with a violation of his banning order. Barney was the SASO General-Secretary at the time, and he was banned along with seven other leaders of the Black Consciousness Movement, including Steve Biko, Strini Moodley, Saths Cooper, Jerry Modisane, Bokwe Mafuna, Harry Nenguenkulu and Drake Koka.

I was restricted to Pietermaritzburg where I was placed under house arrest. I eventually fled the country in December 1974, during the period of intense repression that followed the pro-FRELIMO rallies organised by the Black Consciousness Movement, in solidarity with the Mozambican people when the FRELIMO-dominated provincial administration was installed on 25 September 1974 in the former Portuguese colony.

After remaining in Swaziland for six weeks, I went to New Zealand to study law at the Victoria University of Wellington, a scholarship having been offered to me by the New Zealand University Students' Association.

While studying 'down under' I was actively involved in the Liberation Support Movement and the Anti-Apartheid Movement, including the struggle against the All Blacks' Rugby Tour of South Africa in 1976. I addressed public meetings in the community, rallies at universities, colleges and schools. I undertook similar lecture tours of Australia. The aim was to heighten awareness about the liberation struggles in Southern Africa. Together with other South Africans and Zimbabwean students who were studying in the two countries under a Special Commonwealth Assistance Programme, I participated in seminars, conferences and other forums. We succeeded in raising financial, material and humanitarian support for the liberation struggles in Southern Africa.

Introduction 3

During each summer, I returned to Southern Africa and in that way maintained contact not only with the internationally-recognised liberation movements, but also with the large number of Black South African youths who fled the country in the mid-1970s, notably after the 1976 Soweto uprising.

In 1977, I was appointed PAC representative to Australasia and in mid-1978, I travelled to the United States to assist at the PAC Observer Mission to the United Nations in New York. I returned to Tanzania to participate in the second consultative conference, held in Arusha, in June–July 1978. I was appointed to the Central Committee, with responsibilities for Education and Manpower Development. While I was based in Dar-es-Salaam at the PAC external headquarters, I combined for a time the responsibilities of Director of Education and Manpower Development with those of Administrative Secretary. In October 1979, I was appointed to the position of Director of Foreign Affairs and Observer Representative to the United Nations.

During the time that I served as a representative and later a member of the PAC Central Committee, I represented the organisation in numerous meetings of the Organisation of African Unity (OAU), and at international conferences and seminars organised by the United Nations and non-governmental organisations. I have travelled extensively in Africa, Asia, Australasia, Europe, the United States, Canada, the Caribbean and Latin America, meeting with Heads of State, government officials, representatives of national liberation movements, UN specialised agencies and non-governmental organisations as well as liberation support organisations. I have lectured at universities in Australasia, Africa, the USA and Canada and have been interviewed extensively by the media in various parts of the world.

Why Write this History of the PAC?

Some critics may argue that a detailed discussion of the internal problems of an organisation with which one was associated at a leadership level is breaking faith with the organisation. I do not subscribe to that view. During my tenure in the leadership of the PAC, I consistently expressed my views forthrightly in innumerable documents (many of which are quoted in the text) and during meetings of the Central Committee. I resigned from the Central Committee on 31 March 1982 because the internal problems of the PAC had become absurd and the leaders of the organisation were neither prepared nor able to confront the problems honestly. But, I only resigned six weeks after I had presented to the Central Committee, and to all representatives and branches of the PAC, a 39-page document analysing the problems confronting the organisation and offering constructive suggestions and recommendations for the solution of some of those problems. The only response of

4 *Introduction to the South African Struggle*

the Central Committee, through the Administrative Secretary, was to write to all offices and branches of the PAC ordering the suppression of the document. Rather than address the political and ideological issues that I raised in the document, the Central Committee launched a scurrilous campaign of personal vilification.

Successive regimes within the PAC have not been able to cope with objective analysis. In a liberation movement, the truth, no matter how painful or bitter, has to be squarely faced. Genuine revolutionaries must overcome their emotional bias. The style of FRELIMO and the PAIGC as national liberation movements is a refreshing lesson in this regard. Both FRELIMO and the PAIGC demonstrated a preparedness and an ability to address their problems honestly, without blaming everybody but themselves for setbacks suffered. FRELIMO, as a Marxist–Leninist Party of workers and peasants, demonstrated a similar revolutionary candour during its fourth congress held in Maputo in 1983.

It is mistakenly believed that problems within the National Liberation Movement should not be openly discussed. Refusing or failing to discuss problems will not make them disappear. It is only through democratic debate and discussion that problems within a movement can be solved.

At this time when there are momentous developments in the politics of liberation in Southern Africa generally and in South Africa in particular, it is necessary for those who are genuinely committed to the liberation of the mass of workers and peasants in the sub-continent to engage constantly in honest criticism and self-criticism. Without such criticism and self-criticism, the liberation movements are in danger of stagnation and atrophy, or worse still, of becoming victims of their own propaganda. It can be argued that in the case of the PAC that stage has already been reached. If that be so, then, however unpalatable the fact might be, it has to be stated.

In so saying, however, several points must be emphasised. Firstly, the aim of this book is not to discredit the PAC. Instead, it examines issues and difficulties confronting the National Liberation Movement as a whole. As such, it is a contribution to the struggle. Secondly, great care has been exercised in excluding material or information that might be useful to the South African government, although this does not mean that material or information so excluded is unknown to that regime. The PAC has been seriously infiltrated by South Africa's security police. In 1982 alone, some ten PAC members, including militarily-trained cadres, returned to South Africa voluntarily. One of the returnees was a close confidante of and adviser to the PAC 'Director of Operations'. In August 1984 a leading member of the PAC's High Command returned to South Africa voluntarily.

PAC leaders have repeatedly demonstrated a disturbing lack of security-consciousness and concern for the safety of persons in South Africa.

Introduction 5

Scope of the Book

This book is an analysis of the problems confronting national liberation movements which are struggling against White minority domination in South Africa. It reviews the background to the existence of two national liberation movements from South Africa, the African National Congress (ANC) and the Pan-Africanist Congress (PAC), and explains the political and ideological differences between them. Such an historical analysis is crucial to an understanding of the current relations between the two organisations and of the problems that have plagued the PAC, problems that were inherent in its formation and have been exacerbated by the exile condition.

The book examines the international environment in which the National Liberation Movement functions and how the Movement and the environment impact upon each other. East-West rivalry, Sino-Soviet rivalry, and the ideological divisions in Africa between 'progressive' and 'moderate' or 'reactionary' regimes, affect the liberation movements and the liberation support movement around the world. The book appraises the role of the OAU and the UN, and the effects upon the ANC and PAC of continuing competition between those movements for support and influence.

Using the PAC as a case history, the book looks at the political and inter-personal relations within a liberation movement. Rather than being merely descriptive, it analyses the causes of such phenomena as intra-movement power struggles and even assassinations. This provides insight into the decline of the PAC from the time of its formation (1959) and its early organisation of the Campaign Against the Pass Laws that resulted in the Sharpeville massacre of March 1960. As a consequence of that campaign, both the ANC and PAC were banned by the South African government.

While the PAC has been in decline in recent years, the ANC has experienced a resurgence within and without South Africa. This has been particularly true since the Soweto uprising of June 1976. The book analyses and explains this change.

All national liberation movements experience problems. What is clear from an examination of the problems that have plagued the PAC, however, is that they have been recurring and persistent. The organisation has failed to work out a means for resolving its internal problems. In a sense the PAC is caught in a bind. Its persistent internal problems have eroded the credibility of the organisation. Failure to resolve the 'intra-party contradictions' and failure to establish a visible military presence in South Africa have resulted in a loss of material, financial and diplomatic support. And, without support, it cannot establish the demanded visible military presence on the ground.

Finally, the book deals with the problems faced by and future prospects for the national liberation movements in South Africa. The

6 *Introduction to the South African Struggle*

successes of national liberation movements in Angola, Mozambique and Zimbabwe have not only served to inspire the oppressed people in South Africa and their National Liberation Movement but, more importantly, the liberation of those countries has had an effect on the geo-politics of Southern Africa that greatly favours the national liberation movements. On the other hand, South Africa has embarked upon a programme of destabilisation of these countries, hoping to prevent them from providing the necessary assistance and facilities to the national liberation movements, assistance that could tip the balance in their favour in the struggle against White minority domination in South Africa. Destabilisation of the African front-line states by South Africa poses serious problems for the national liberation movements. These include problems of security, as evidenced by the assassination and kidnapping of South African exiles in a number of countries in the Southern African region, and problems of logistics, such as the necessary rear bases and supply lines for the infiltration of men and materials into the country and for freedom-fighters to retreat when necessary.

Favourable conditions exist inside the home country, however, where, despite the intensification in repression in recent years, there has been an escalation in Black mass resistance. The most notable evidence of this has been the resurgence in the Black labour movement.

Since the strikes by Black workers in 1973, there has been an increase in the organisation and strength of the Black workers' movement. The Black trade union movement has grown rapidly; strikes have been widespread. There have also been strikes by Black students protesting against the inferior education system, strikes which were sustained for a surprising length of time during 1980.

There was also evidence in 1980 that some of the mistakes made in 1976 were not repeated. Prior to the school boycott, students embarked upon an intensive campaign to obtain the support of the community for their actions. At public meetings in various parts of the Western Cape, parents expressed support for the students' demands for the abolition of the inferior education system for Blacks. As a result, there was no 'generational conflict' between parents and students, or 'hostel-dwellers' backlash' as in 1976, except in Natal where Gatsha Buthelezi's Inkatha Movement was instrumental in ordering the violent disruption of the students' school boycott. In contrast with the student demonstrations in 1976, in 1980 the students did not take to the streets in their thousands to confront the heavily-armed paramilitary forces of the South African regime. Consequently, casualties in 1980 were lower than in 1976.

More importantly, there has been an increase in military activities initiated by the National Liberation Movement, principally the ANC, in both the urban and rural areas (but more particularly in urban areas), in the period since the Soweto uprisings.

The challenge faced by the national liberation movements is

Introduction 7

precisely one of transferring the loci of their activities back into the country, so as to provide leadership and direction in the increasing mass resistance and to arm the masses for self-defence.

Notes

1. See, for example, Kane-Berman, J. 1979; Hirson, B. 1979; Herbstein, D. 1978; Brooks, A. and Brickhill, J. 1980.

2. See Woods, D. 1978; Stubbs, Aelred (ed) 1978; Arnold, M. (ed) 1979.

3. See Slovo, J., 'South Africa — No Middle Road', in Davidson, B., Slovo, J. and Wilkinson, A. 1976; Magubane, B. 1979; No Sizwe 1979; Hommel, M. 1981.

4. See, for instance, publication in *Black Dwarf* of denunciations of ANC leadership by defectors from ANC military wing, Umkhonto, quoted by Dreyer, p. 1980; also, 'An African's Story of a Terrorist Training Camp', in *Intelligence Digest* (July 1968), Cheltenham, England, Vol. 31, No. 68, pp. 17–18. See also, Nkoana, M. 1968.

5. Marcum, J., 'The Exile Condition and Revolutionary Effectiveness: The Southern African Liberation Movements', in Potholm, C.P. and Dale, R. (eds) 1972.

6. Gibson, R. 1972.

7. Burchett, W. 1978.

1. The Nature of a National Liberation Movement

Although national liberation movements occur and operate within specific geographic areas (nation-states), they are engaged in an international struggle. The South African National Liberation Movement is no exception. As Nzongola-Ntalaja points out:

> The struggle for national liberation in Southern Africa is part of a contemporary historical movement of national self-assertion involving the aspiration of millions of people in the under-developed countries of the world to emancipate themselves from foreign domination, a domination whose specific type today is imperialism.[1]

While the White-settler-colonial regime is the main internal enemy of the indigenous African people in South Africa, the main external enemy is Western imperialism. Racism and White-settler-colonial rule have been promoted to serve local and international monopoly capitalism.[2] Racism, apartheid and 'plural democracy' are all a superstructure created to serve and protect the capitalist productive economic forces at the base. In the ultimate analysis, the elimination of oppression in South Africa will be guaranteed only by the destruction of capitalist production relations.[3]

In its penetration of Africa, Asia and Latin America during the latter half of the nineteenth century, when the large-scale penetration of these continents began in earnest, capitalism was accompanied by the plunder and exploitation of the natural and human resources, and by the unleashing of social forces which were harnessed in order to entrench the capitalist system.[4] Capitalism established local agents; in the South African case, the means of production were concentrated in the hands of a single social class, namely the bourgeoisie of the White-settler-colonial national group, which in fact holds these means of production in trust for international monopoly capitalism.

Nationalist and National Liberation Movements — a Distinction

Historically, the present era of national liberation movements in Africa

The Nature of a National Liberation Movement 9

was preceded by one of African nationalist movements. Nationalist movements envisaged reform based on the existing European model. They were bourgeois movements seeking not to change the system, but to rearrange the social order, to replace the colonial ruling elite by an African elite. The bourgeois nationalists accepted and worked within a European set of values. They sought independence.

Independence in the narrow legal sense is synonymous with self-government, that is, the overt retreat of the colonial power from the governing body of the nation. Many African states have formally attained political independence, they have their own national flags and anthems as well as Black administrations. In many cases, this independence is quite nominal; in reality, they are still dependent on external economic and political interests (neo-colonialism) and the masses in these countries are still politically oppressed and economically exploited even though the colour of their immediate masters has changed. This is independence without liberation, a stratagem of imperialism against which Lenin warned in 1920:

> (Communists) need constantly to explain and expose among the broadest working masses of all countries, and particularly of the backward countries, the deception systematically practised by the imperialist powers which, under the guise of politically independent states, set up states that are wholly dependent upon them economically, financially and militarily.[5]

A new generation of liberation movements has, in consequence, emerged in several of these 'politically independent states' in Africa.[6] A genuine national liberation movement is one which has the following characteristics:

(1) It is a *revolutionary political organisation* that has as its objectives: (a) the seizure of state power; and (b) the consolidation of that power in order to effect fundamental changes in the social, political and economic institutions of a society.
(2) It places a premium upon political mobilisation of the masses, since popular support is essential for success in the struggle.
(3) It is committed to the overthrow of imperialist domination.[7]

National liberation movements are movements against external dependence (neo-colonialism) and against internal class domination (elitism). They may thus emerge in opposition to all forms of the dependent capitalist state, including states enjoying the fullest political independence,[8] and are thus of necessity anti-imperialist and committed to revolutionary change; they will, therefore, be opposed not only by the internal elites but also by the imperialist powers.

The Co-ordinating Committee for the Liberation of Africa, commonly referred to as the African Liberation Committee (ALC), states as

10   *Introduction to the South African Struggle*

its objective the attainment of formal independence for African territories still under the yoke of White minority rule.[9] The national liberation movements supported by the OAU, however, are working towards something more than formal political independence. Genuine national liberation movements seek not only political independence, but also social and economic independence for the people of their countries, the control of the natural resources of their countries, and the end of exploitation of man by man, both within the countries they seek to liberate, and internationally. The achievement of such goals requires an upheaval in the social order within the country; history shows that this is possible only through the evolution by struggle of popular mass support. Thus the reformist tactics of the bourgeois nationalists have, in the face of unyielding regimes and the development of a revolutionary ideology, progressed to armed struggle. The development of a revolutionary ideology arose from a new analysis of the situation of the oppressed and exploited people. While the bourgeois nationalists saw their situation within the context of the colonial society and its values, national liberation movements reject colonial imperialist values and seek to unite the oppressed masses in the struggle against their colonial and neo-colonial masters. After the achievement of independence by the people of Mozambique, the FRELIMO President explained:

> The struggle for the transformation of society must go hand in hand with the struggle for the transformation of man himself. But this is not an automatic process ...
>
> The New Man is born in struggle at all stages; he is dynamic, creative, capable of analysis and self-criticism, original, audacious. With a new mentality, acquired through struggle, the New Man becomes an agent of social transformation ... To create such an outlook requires internal struggle which has to be systematic and organised ... When we speak of internal struggle, this means rejecting the old values ... rejecting racism, tribalism, regionalism, egoism, elitism, all the various forms of subjectivism ...[10]

National liberation movements seek to awaken the people to the realities of their situation (conscientisation). From the awareness of a common oppression will arise support for, and then participation in, the struggle against the colonial and neo-colonial masters. Participation implies the creation of a new liberated society, the creation of new democratic procedures of government and the re-organisation of social structures on the principles of equality, as Cabral so well described.[11] After setbacks for the PAIGC in the struggle against the Portuguese in 1965, Cabral made the following point:

> With all this, as a proof of insufficient political work among our armed forces, there has appeared a certain attitude (mania) of 'militarism' which

The Nature of a National Liberation Movement 11

has caused some fighters and even some leaders to forget the fact that we are armed militants and not militarists.[12]

The situation which has given rise to the formation of national liberation movements was not created solely within the borders of the nation-states fighting for liberation. Stalin analysed the dialectical relationship between imperialism, the awakening of national consciousness and the emergence of national liberation movements in the colonial and dependent territories.[13] He showed how imperialism's endeavours to extract super-profits inevitably resulted in the growth of a proletariat and a native intelligentsia, and the awakening of national consciousness and emergence of the national liberation movement. Consequently, there emerged a 'colonial nationalism' which sought to convert these territories into autonomous economic and political units rather than areas merely for exploitation by the metropolitan capitalist nations.[14]

The USA and National Liberation Movements

In Africa, a nationalist movement challenging colonial domination emerged in the 1930s and 1940s.[15] As a result Britain implemented a policy of elective forms of government in the African colonies. World War II created contradictions among the metropolitan capitalist nations. It also expedited the break-up of the British empire,[16] and the emergence of the USA as the leader of the Western economic and political system.[17] The USA supported decolonisation, as evidenced by the Atlantic Charter signed by Roosevelt and Churchill in 1941 recognising the right of oppressed peoples to self-determination. Two factors motivated USA support for decolonisation. Firstly, the USA wished to supplant the metropolitan capitalist nations in their relations with the emerging 'developing nations'. Secondly, the USA feared that protracted liberation struggles in the colonial territories 'would provide favourable conditions for the communist-inspired, anti-imperialist forms of struggle to emerge'.[18] It was therefore necessary to entice the nationalist forces in the developing countries and the colonial territories into an alliance with the USA.

Successive administrations in the USA have expended massive financial and human resources in an attempt to suppress the growth of national liberation movements. In the 1960s President John F. Kennedy declared that wars of national liberation could not and would not succeed. The American author, David Halberstam, in his perceptive analysis of the manner in which US involvement in Vietnam escalated, has described how the Kennedy Administration was aggressively anti-communist and saw struggles for national liberation in South-East Asia as evidence of the spread of communism.[19] Following his summit meeting with Khruschev in Vienna in 1961, Kennedy was even more convinced

12 *Introduction to the South African Struggle*

that wars of national liberation, or 'brushfire wars' as they were termed, were sponsored by the Soviet Union. Because such 'brushfire wars' were perceived as being anti-American, they demanded an American response.[20] Kennedy's declaration that wars of national liberation could not and would not succeed was proved wrong by the defeat of Western imperialism, led by the USA, in Vietnam. Similarly, the victories of national liberation movements in Africa (in the former Portuguese colonies of Guinea-Bissau, Angola and Mozambique as well as the former British colony of Southern Rhodesia) disproved the thesis put forward by Dr. Henry Kissinger in NSC (National Security Council) Memorandum 39 that the only way in which change in these territories could be achieved was through the Whites who were there 'to stay'.

National liberation movements have forced the recognition that wars of national liberation are a valid category distinct from simple terrorism. The twenty-eighth session of the UN General Assembly in 1974 invited representatives of the national liberation movements recognised by the OAU 'to participate in the relevant work of the main committees of the General Assembly and its subsidiary organs, as well as conferences, seminars and other meetings held under the auspices of the United Nations which concern their countries'. This gave the African national liberation movements a status similar to that previously granted to the Palestine Liberation Organisation (PLO). It broke the monopoly of governments to be the sole representatives of the people in nation-states in international forums. The General Assembly rejected the credentials of the South African regime on the grounds that it was not representative of the majority of the population; ever since, the regime has not participated in the work of the General Assembly, although South Africa remains a member.

In an effort to forestall the victory of radical national liberation movements in Southern Africa, both Western imperialism and a number of neo-colonial African regimes attempted to manipulate the situation in their own interests. This was to be seen in Angola during the civil war on the eve of independence in 1975 when South Africa, with the blessing of the USA and a number of African governments, supported the reactionary groups, FNLA and UNITA, in an attempt to prevent the accession to power of the MPLA. The OAU was split, with half the member states recognising the government proclaimed by the MPLA in November 1975, and the other half withholding recognition, calling instead for the creation of a government of national unity. The USA lobbied extensively against recognition of the MPLA Government.

Similar manipulation was to be seen during the 'Kissinger initiative' in 1976 in Southern Rhodesia. Kissinger's proposals for the transition to majority rule, which included generous financial incentives to the colonialists, were aimed at ensuring a neo-colonial solution in Zimbabwe.[21]

LIBELLOUS

The South African Response

South Africa, the last bastion of White minority domination in Southern Africa, is attempting to combat liberation movements internally in Namibia and South Africa by increased arms expenditure and more repressive legislation, and also internationally by: building closer economic and military ties with the major Western powers, including the acquisition of a nuclear capability; attempting to build a coalition with Latin American dictatorships like Chile, Paraguay and Uruguay, as well as pariah states like Israel and Taiwan; increased and more direct interference in the affairs of neighbouring African countries, particularly the front-line states of Angola, Botswana, Lesotho, Mozambique, Zambia and Zimbabwe; attempting to gain international recognition for the Transkei and other Bantustans as justification for apartheid. The national liberation struggles in Southern Africa thus have major international implications.

Problems within National Liberation Movements

Frustrations

The frustrations of exile have been poignantly captured by the South African writer, Es'kia Mphahlele, in his recent novel, *Chirundu*. The socio-psychological problems of displacement experienced by South African exiles and refugees have not been adequately studied, nor have the national liberation movements addressed themselves to the matter. Yet, recent studies show that displacement aggravates existing emotional and behavioural problems. The psychopathology resulting from the trauma of becoming refugees has given rise to a great deal of research by psychologists in the area of *acculturation*, that is, the sociological milieu in which the refugee has to adapt.[22]

Ideological and Class Struggles

National liberation movements are not devoid of ideological and class struggles, one common example of which is opportunism.[23] Opportunism is a political attitude dispensing with a fixed moral programme and merely waiting for something to turn up to be utilised for immediate advantage. It is the opposite of principled or ideological struggle. Within the liberation movements, differences over the political line, strategy and tactics to be adopted in the struggle, as well as alliances fashioned, often reflect ideological struggles which have a class content.

Two kinds of opportunism are distinguishable, namely, rightist opportunism and leftist opportunism. An example of 'rightist opportunism' is the tendency on the part of bourgeois or petit-bourgeois elements within the national liberation movements to negotiate with, or accept any solutions offered by, the enemy that may offer immediate

14 *Introduction to the South African Struggle*

personal gain: an example is the participation of Bishop Abel Muzorewa, the Rev. Ndabaningi Sithole and other Zimbabweans in the 'internal settlement' negotiated by the White minority regime of Ian Smith in Rhodesia. Similarly, the return to South Africa of former members of the ANC and PAC to participate in politics in institutions created by the South African regime (like the Bantustans) is an example of 'rightist opportunism'. Very often, 'rightist opportunism' stems from a fear of the radicalising effect on the masses of a protracted people's war, or fear of the might of the enemy, which in turn may induce pessimism.

A further example of 'rightist opportunism' is the tendency among guerrilla leaders to promote ethno-regionalism in order to build a personal constituency or personal following within a liberation movement. The opportunism of the PAC military leaders who used Marxist rhetoric in 1977 and 1978 while promoting tribalism and regionalism falls within this category. Under the leadership of Nyati John Pokela who assumed the chairmanship in 1981, tribalism and regionalism have re-surfaced, with Xhosa-speaking Africans from the Transkei and Cape being in a dominant position in the PAC.

'Leftist opportunism' has various manifestations, including the tendency among guerrilla leaders and ultra-leftist intellectuals to be

> ... impatient with what they perceive as an overly cautious military strategy and a very slow pace in the course of the struggle. They initially tend to denounce any negotiations with the enemy, and to place an exclusive emphasis on military heroism. Their position is adventurist because it is based on a visionary type of thinking that depicts victory as being capable of being won overnight, with the probable result of crushing disillusionment when this does not happen. Left adventurism is an expression of an idealistic rather than a materialistic grasp of the situation. It is, objectively, a right-wing position, because it produces errors that weaken the struggle in the interest of the established order.[24]

The functional political line, by contrast, depends on a concrete analysis, based upon a scientific theory of revolution, placing a premium upon the interests of workers and peasants who, in the words of Amilcar Cabral, 'play the decisive role of providing the principal force behind the liberation movement'.[25]

Liberalism
Liberalism, although a phase in ideological and class struggles, is being considered separately here because of the serious problems it has caused in national liberation movements, problems which are harmful to both the liberation movement and the individual. Liberalism is the tendency to refrain from criticism of what is obviously wrong, either for, (i) fear of offending against the sensitivities of friends and colleagues, a

tendency which more often than not results in mutual 'trading off' and political blackmail ('you tell, I tell' phenomenon), or (ii) protection of personal positions which, in turn, stems from the ideologically incorrect view of a position in a liberation movement as a proprietary interest, or vehicle for self-aggrandisement (the phenomenon of careerism), rather than a means to make a contribution to the struggle. Correct leadership and revolutionary theory are incompatible with liberalism and are prerequisites for success in the liberation struggle.

Infiltration by the Enemy

Infiltration by the enemy of agents provocateurs into the national liberation movements has a disruptive effect. Sometimes such infiltration is aimed at provoking constant conflict within the liberation movements, or is aimed at the physical elimination of specific leaders or individuals. Often such agents transmit to the enemy sensitive information about the military plans and operations of the liberation movements, or the agents, acting as guides, lead the freedom-fighters into ambushes by the enemy as happened during the joint military venture by the ANC and ZAPU at Wankie in 1967.

It is not uncommon for the enemy to recruit agents from within the ranks of the liberation movements. Corruption, personal ambition, personal problems and opportunism at the individual level frequently invite exploitation by the enemy. On the other hand, militants within the liberation movements may be recruited by the enemy under duress, as for example, through threats of persecution or actual harrassment of family members or relatives.

These are merely a few of the causes of strife within the liberation movement. It has to be pointed out, however, that liberation movements do not have a monopoly on internal problems. Problems are a fact of political life; organisations differ in the extent to which they are able to contain such problems.

Notes

1. Nzongola-Ntalaja 1979, pp. 134 et seq.
2. Magubane, B.M. 1979, p. 195.
3. Shabalala, S.R. 1978.
4. See Dube, E.M., 'Relations between Liberation Movements and the OAU', in Shamuyarira, N. (ed) 1975, p. 25.
5. Quoted by Dube 1975, p. 136.
6. See Nzongola-Ntalaja 1979, footnote 11, p. 147.
7. Ibid., p. 136. See also the Introduction by Turok, B. (ed) 1980. See also the important essay by Ahmad, E., 'Revolutionary Warfare and Counter-insurgency', in Miller, N. and Aya, R. (eds) 1971, pp. 137–213.

16 *Introduction to the South African Struggle*

8. Nzongola-Ntalaja 1979.
9. See Dube 1975.
10. Quoted by Burchett, W. 1978, p. 173.
11. Africa Information Service 1973, pp. 54–5; see also McCulloch, J. 1983 for an incisive analysis of the revolutionary thought of Cabral.
12. Quoted by Davidson, B.1976, p. 59.
13. Stalin, J.V. 1970, pp. 5–6.
14. Dobb, M. 1963, p. 373.
15. See Simpson, H. 1980, pp. 130–1.
16. Ibid.
17. Dobb 1963, p. 385.
18. Simpson 1980, p. 131.
19. Halberstam, D. 1969, p. 152.
20. Quoted by Johnson, D. 1973, p. 22.
21. See Bratton, M., 'Structural Transformation in Zimbabwe: Some comparative notes from the Neo-colonisation of Kenya', in Wiley, D. and Isaacman, A. (eds) 1982, pp. 83 et seq.
22. Smither, R. 1981.
23. See Nzongola-Ntalaja 1979, p. 237, for what follows.
24. Ibid.
25. Africa Information Service 1973, p. 54.

2. The ANC and the PAC

We, the people of South Africa, declare for all our country and the world to know that South Africa belongs to all who live in it, Black and White, and that no government can justly claim authority unless it is based on the will of the people, that our country will never be prosperous or free until all our people live in brotherhood enjoying equal rights and opportunities; that only a democratic state, based on the will of all the people, can secure to all their birthrights without distinction of colour, race, sex, or belief.

The Freedom Charter

We aim politically, at government of the Africans, by the Africans, for the Africans, with everybody who owes his only loyalty to Africa, who is prepared to accept the democratic rule of an African majority being regarded as African. We guarantee no minority rights, because we think in terms of individuals, and not of groups.

Mangaliso Robert Sobukwe

This section traces the origins of the two internationally-recognised national liberation movements, the ANC and the PAC. Such an historical analysis is crucial to an understanding of the reasons for the existence of two rival organisations from the same country, the relations between them, their present fortunes and the prospects for unity between them. Although the two organisations were formed to fight against White minority domination in South Africa, the ANC (formed in 1912) and the PAC (formed in 1959) represent two variants of African nationalism which had already become manifest by the end of the nineteenth century, namely an inclusive South African nationalism and an exclusive African nationalism.

The ANC, formed in 1912 through an alliance of an African educated elite and traditional chiefs, was a reaction to the exclusion of Africans from franchise rights in the newly created Union of South Africa. Although the ANC was an African organisation, pursuing the interests of the African majority, it co-operated on an organisational basis with the other oppressed minorities, the Coloureds and Indians, through the

18 *Introduction to the South African Struggle*

Coloured Peoples' Organisation (CPO) and the South African Indian Congress (SAIC) respectively. As No Sizwe writes, these organisations were at one only in demanding the extension of the franchise to the oppressed.

> The petit-bourgeois leadership of these organisations consisting in the main of teachers, preachers, doctors, chiefs and small businessmen, articulated the demands of the oppressed people in a populist but caste-divided manner.[1]

The ANC also sought the co-operation and support of sympathetic and progressive Whites.

The PAC, whose leaders were the remnants of the more radical wing of the ANC, opposed the multi-racial alliances pursued by the ANC during the 1950s. It also opposed the adoption of a Freedom Charter in 1955, particularly its proclamation that South Africa belongs to all who live in it, both Black and White. Whereas the ANC strove after the advancement of the Africans within the existing system, the PAC was committed to the destruction of the existing system and its replacement by the rule of the African majority.

Both the ANC and PAC adopted non-violence in the pursuit of their political objectives.

After the banning of the ANC and PAC in April 1960, following the Sharpeville massacre of 21 March that year, the two organisations reconstituted themselves as movements in exile, and the distinctions between them were blurred. The leaders of both the ANC and the PAC were convinced of the ineffectualness of non-violence; both movements established military wings and embraced the armed struggle as the principal method of struggle. Both organisations would also express themselves in favour of the establishment of socialism in South Africa in the post-liberation period. The PAC remains highly critical of the multi-racial alliances pursued by the ANC, just as it had been in the fifties, but has called for the creation of a united front with the ANC.[2]

The PAC is not genuinely in favour of unity with the ANC, but adopts the posture of calling for a united front between the two organisations because of the demands that are made in the OAU and other forums for unity in the National Liberation Movement. By echoing the demands for unity, the PAC hopes to appear reasonable and 'progressive', in contrast with the ANC. Privately, PAC leaders are emphatic that they will not enter into an alliance with the ANC, arguing that the latter organisation is 'controlled by Whites', or 'communists', or 'by Moscow'. The two movements have been kept apart and at odds as a result of internal disputes, competition between them for influence and support among the African member states of the OAU and internationally, and the Soviet and Chinese connections cultivated by the two movements.

The history of the ANC as an organisation that enjoyed an overt legal existence of 50 years in South Africa provides a partial explanation for its durability and stronger ties internationally. The PAC, on the other hand, had not had the time to smooth out the weaknesses in its ideological formulations, still less to develop an organisational infrastructure in the country or to build a tried and tested leadership and membership.

We turn now to the history of the two organisations.

Black Political Consciousness and the Formation of the ANC

In the period before Union, two influences were most important, namely the Cape 'liberal tradition' with its non-racial franchise and the impact of Christian mission education.[3]

> The Cape franchise by its educational and property requirements ruled out many Blacks but it did not rule virtually all out, as did the Natal franchise. Indeed, in some electorates in the Eastern Cape Blacks were ten per cent of the total and could with considerable political sophistication play off the opposing white candidates.[4]

In the two Boer republics of the Transvaal and the Orange Free State, where it was decreed that there would be no equality between Black and White, in either church or state, the Blacks were excluded from the franchise. Moreover, the Boer republics demanded of Britain as a condition for the formation of Union in 1910 the exclusion of Blacks from the franchise. The importance of the colour-blind Cape franchise is that it represented, in the view of the African intelligentsia, the 'ideal' Native policy. The modus operandi, from the perspective of liberal African nationalism, would be for the Blacks to improve themselves within the existing socio-economic and political structures.

Christian missionary education instilled in the Black intelligentsia the liberal values of individual justice and human equality. Political matters, too, assumed a moral dimension and they embraced the principles of brotherhood and a shared society. These were the foundations of the developing ideology among the burgeoning Black educated elite.

In succeeding years other influences would be added, for instance, the awareness and influence of the Black American struggle, through the writings of Booker T. Washington and W.E.B. DuBois as well as through visits to the United States by Black South Africans. In the early years such visits were for religious or study purposes, notably through the African Methodist Episcopal (AME) Church. Rev. John Dube, the first president of the ANC, visited the United States where he was so impressed with the Tuskegee Institute established by Booker

20 *Introduction to the South African Struggle*

T. Washington that upon his return to South Africa, he established the Ohlange Institute in Natal, a vocational school modelled on Tuskegee. Another founder of the ANC, Pixley ka Seme, had studied at Columbia University. In this way, the Black American struggle had an impact upon Black political consciousness in South Africa. To this was added heightened awareness that the rapid development of South Africa was leading inevitably to economic integration and this enhanced the need for inter-racial co-operation as contacts increased across the colour line.[5]

In the twentieth century African nationalism would be influenced by the ideas of Marcus Garvey (an influence which was to be seen in the Congress Youth League), World War II and the ideals expressed in the Atlantic Charter (the latter providing inspiration for 'African Claims', a Bill of Rights drawn up by a committee of the ANC in 1945). Other strands of influence which had an indirect impact upon Black political consciousness were the Industrial and Commercial Workers' Union (ICU) and the South African Communist Party (SACP), formed in 1919 and 1921 respectively. But throughout, the outlook of the Black educated elite remained liberal and moderate. The strongest influence on the content and direction of African nationalism was the continued denial by the White authorities of freedom and justice to the Black majority, the institutionalisation of that denial in law and the steady increase in repression, which had a radicalising effect on the ideology in that the Black elite ultimately realised the inefficacy of non-violence as a strategy for liberation.

Before tracing this progression in political consciousness and the effect upon ideology, strategy and tactics, it is necessary to point out that in the latter two decades of the nineteenth century, there emerged within the church, a strand of Black political consciousness which was at variance with the liberal ideology which was prevalent at that time. Black clergy used religion as a unifying force and recruited members without regard to tribal or ethnic origins.[6] In addition, very many of the Black clergy broke away from the established churches; the independent African churches which emerged became powerful vehicles of political protest. Ethiopianism questioned many of the assumptions of a common society and encouraged the formation by Blacks of their own institutions.

Karis and Carter contend that by the end of the nineteenth century there had emerged two approaches to politics among the Africans in South Africa.[7] What they term the 'dominant approach' was the tendency for Africans to organise themselves but to work with Whites. Their goal was the eventual integration of the Africans, Coloureds and Indians (that is, those classified as non-Europeans) into a non-racial society with full participation in the body politic. The other approach was that of Ethiopianism, which, although initially a movement fostering religious separatism, translated into political terms, rejected co-operation with Whites, and White definitions of 'civilisation' and argued instead for Africans to pursue their goals through their own organisations. They argue that 'Ethiopianism can be seen as the forerunner of subsequent African philosophies and groups whose main thrust was to challenge white power through Black unity'.[8] Historians have come to term these two strands of Black political consciousness the liberal and the Africanist.[9] Gerhart distinguishes between liberal or non-racial nationalism and orthodox nationalism.[10] This distinction is crucial to an understanding of the differences between the ANC and the PAC:

> The founding of the African National Congress is generally regarded as the earliest manifestation of African nationalism in South Africa, yet the type of nationhood to which the ANC aspired did not make them nationalists in the full sense since they did not seek to create a state based on their prospective nation ... Thus the ANC has been less an African nationalist movement in the strict sense of the term than a movement to win democratic rights for Africans.[11]

By contrast, orthodox African nationalist movements are movements which aim to create in South Africa an 'African nation-state' with a government of Africans, by Africans, for Africans.[12] 'To the orthodox nationalist, the white man is a guest in the African house and should be permitted to remain in Africa only on terms set down by his indigenous hosts'.[13]

The ANC was for the major part of its legal existence, elite-led and reformist, working for the advancement of Africans within the existing socio-economic framework, campaigning for the extension of political and legal rights within the existing system. For the first three decades after its formation, the organisation adopted resolutions, presented petitions and led deputations to the White authorities, all to no avail, as Walshe points out.[14]

This liberal ideology was reflected in the first constitution of the ANC which stated as a fundamental goal of the organisation, 'enlisting the sympathy of whites and educating Blacks'.[15] Without a programme of its own, the ANC reacted to the repressive legislation enacted by the White regime in respect of franchise rights, land division and influx control. Walshe defines the period 1912 to 1936 as the 'reactive phase' of the ANC.[16]

The exclusion of Blacks from the franchise at the formation of Union in 1910, was followed by the enactment of the Natives' Land Act in 1913, in terms of which approximately 8% of the land was set aside for the African majority, the remainder being for the Whites. Africans were prohibited from purchasing land outside the 'scheduled areas', nor could Whites purchase land in the 8% set aside for Africans. The Natives' Land Act also abolished the practice outside the Cape Province whereby Africans had worked on

22 *Introduction to the South African Struggle*

White-owned land, in return for which they either paid rent or shared crops. The effect of this legislation — as was the intention — was that Africans were driven off the land and without any alternative means of income had to seek employment in the cash economy in order to live and to pay a cash poll tax. In this way a large supply of labour was released to meet the demands of mining and agriculture.[17]

The amount of land set aside for Africans was slightly increased to 13.7% under the provisions of the Hertzog Bills of 1936; as a quid pro quo, however, the Africans had to agree to the removal of their franchise rights in the Cape, and were left with only a separate voters' roll for Africans who could elect three White representatives to the central parliament and Africans to a powerless Natives' Representative Council (NRC).

The Urban Areas Act applied the principles of the 1913 Natives' Land Act to the towns which were deemed to be the creation of the White man; Blacks would only be admitted as long as they ministered to the needs of Whites. After 1919 the towns, described by one White member of parliament as the 'front trenches of our position in South Africa', became the centre of the extension of influx control under the Pass Laws.[18] Black opposition to these measures enacted by the White regime took the form of deputations, petitions and appeals to both the government as well as sympathetic Whites. There was, however, no redress for Black grievances.

During this period the ANC was eclipsed by the Industrial and Commercial Workers' Union (ICU) which had been formed in January 1919 by Clemens Kadalie with the assistance of a White Labour Party member, A.F. Batty. The direct action and militancy of the ICU contrasted strongly with the 'prayers and deputations' of the ANC.[19] The ICU organised a major strike by African dockworkers in December 1919 at the request and with the support of White trade unions. Under the leadership of Kadalie, Black dockworkers stayed at home for three weeks, 'then, without strike funds, they returned to work without having bettered their wages although they had stopped the export of food'.[20] By 1928, the ICU had declined to the point of disintegration. A number of factors can be cited for the demise of the ICU, including government action, personality conflict and leadership struggles, 'lack of clarity over organisational goals', as well as 'corruption and anti-communism'.[21] But the lesson of direct mass action was not lost upon some members of the ANC.

The Congress Youth League (CYL)

There emerged within the ANC a school of thought that was opposed to what was felt to be an attitude of supplication on the part of Congress, and felt that the African majority should assert themselves. This school of thought came to be termed Africanism, which rejects the idea that the Africans should be subordinated to Whites. Instead the Africanists sought 'to stimulate a sense of African self-confidence and self-reliance in seeking both an end to colour discrimination and a positive role in the moulding of South African society'.[22]

Exponents of Africanism formed themselves into the Congress Youth League (CYL) in 1944, which has been seen as the commencement of the 'real history of the contemporary liberation movement'.[23] Ideologue of the Africanists was the young intellectual, Anton Muziwakhe Lembede, who defined Africanism as the specific African view of man, politics, culture and society in general.[24] He deserves credit for the earliest development and clarification of the South African Black ethos by anticipating the fundamentals of Black Consciousness. Ever since, a positive identity has been developed by Blacks.

Africanism was seen by Black intellectuals as more than a philosophy. Its task was national liberation (the 'nation' being to them the community of indigenous Africans), its ultimate end the establishment of 'African socialism'.[25] The content of that socialism, however, was not defined; nor were the means to achieve the political objective of establishing socialism spelt out. Nevertheless, Lembede was far more advanced ideologically than his nationalist contemporaries in other parts of Africa.[26]

There were two streams of African nationalism of which the CYL took cognisance. Garveyism, with its slogan of 'Africa for the Africans', thus implying that the Whites had to leave Africa, was rejected as being 'extreme and ultra-revolutionary'.[27] Although there were individuals who were attracted to and influenced by Garveyism, the CYL itself recognised the historical development of White settlement in South Africa and accepted future White participation in the country, rejecting 'White domination' rather than White persons. Although there was this tension between an awareness of the need for an assertive nationalism and the dangers of a narrow exclusivism (in fact a struggle between liberal or non-racial nationalism and Africanism), the CYL succeeded in committing Congress to a more activist programme and the slogan 'Africa for the Africans' increasingly came to mean (and to be accepted) as an accommodation with those Whites prepared to accept majority rule.

The CYL did not aim to create a mass movement but remained a pressure group within the ANC with a hardcore membership of about 60. The CYL had its own basic policy — overthrowing foreign domination and foreign leadership and implementing the fundamental right of the African people to self-determination.

The decade between 1936 and 1946 was a period of rapid urbanisation in South Africa, spurred by the revival of the economy under the impetus of devaluation and subsequently World War II. Output in the manufacturing sector rose by almost 100% in the period

24 *Introduction to the South African Struggle*

1939 to 1945; the resultant demand for skilled as well as unskilled labour led to massive urbanisation and also threatened the job colour bar under which certain categories of skilled labour were reserved for Whites only. The cities became the 'centres of race conflict and African nationalism'.[28] This was to be seen in the strike by Black mineworkers in August 1946 organised by the African Mineworkers' Union in demand for higher wages and better living conditions, 'in accordance with the new world principles'. The Smuts government had hurriedly promulgated War Measure 145 which outlawed all strikes by Black workers; now, police and troops moved in to crush the strike by the mineworkers, nine of whom were killed and some 1,200 injured.

The accession to power in 1948 of the Nationalist Party, which had based its election campaign on the dangers of the 'black peril' and Smuts' liberalism (for which no evidence was produced), had, according to Walshe, three important effects on the CYL: it led to a wider acceptance of the League's ideology of African nationalism; opposition to apartheid brought the CYL and Communist Party into a common radicalism of method, that is, a willingness to co-operate in the development of mass action; willingness to co-operate on the basis of mass protests against apartheid led to increased personal contact between members of the CYL and Communist Party.[29]

The Communist Party of South Africa (CPSA)

A little historical detail is necessary in view of the indirect impact of the Communist Party upon Black political consciousness. The Communist Party of South Africa (CPSA) was formed in 1921 by White socialists who in 1922 supported the White miners' strike when White miners opposed attempts by the mine owners to cut the White wage bill by substituting Black labour. In the 'Rand Revolution' as it came to be known, White trade unionists took control of the Rand, terrorised Black workers and fought the police and troops. Approximately 230 people were killed in violence which resulted in the defeat of the White workers. The Smuts government, however, was identified with the mining interests and two years later was defeated in the White elections which brought the Pact government of the Labour Party and the Hertzog Nationalists to power.

> The new government carried into effect its policy of civilised labour by favouring whites in government controlled occupations. Blacks employed on the railways fell from 75 per cent of the labour force in 1924 to 58 per cent in 1936. It confirmed and strengthened the job colour bar by reserving skilled work in mining and heavy engineering for whites.[30]

The CPSA first concerned itself predominantly with White trade union matters; in the 1930s it adopted the Black Republic thesis and took up the question of Black liberation which resulted in bitter internal struggle. The CPSA had been critical of the ANC, whose leaders it dismissed as petit-bourgeois reformists, so that its influence on the ANC during the 1920s and 1930s was only indirect. Even though it was clear that in South Africa race, not class, was the determinant of status it organised on the basis of class. In the post-World War II period, the Party devoted its energies to the organisation of Black trade unions. Harsch explains the antipathy among members of the CYL towards the CPSA:

> The CPSA . . . tried to moderate the League's militant nationalism, accusing its members of 'racialism' and 'chauvinism' and claiming that African domination would lead to 'endless wars between black and white'. Some leaders of the Youth League responded to these attacks by the CPSA with red-baiting diatribes, and at one point even pressed for the expulsion of communists from the ANC. But their reaction was more against the specific policies of the CPSA than against socialist ideas in general.[31]

The election victory of the Nationalist Party under Malan in 1948, with its declared aim to perpetuate White supremacy and its threats to stamp out communism (by which it meant all opposition), caused alarm and drew the members of the CYL and the CPSA into closer co-operation, which led to moderation in the intense anti-communism of some leaders of the CYL. The exchange of ideas and personal contacts between the members of the two groups also increased the content of Marxist analysis in the liberation movement.[32] Some members of the CYL, however, remained implacably opposed to the communists' involvement in the liberation movement, and this opposition would be one of the reasons for the split in the Congress, as will be shown later.

The Programme of Action
The other consequence of the Nationalists' victory in 1948 was that it fuelled the public sentiment for mass action. The militancy urged by the CYL was adopted in December 1949 as the programme of the ANC. After a comprehensive analysis of African politics, the 1949 annual conference of the ANC concluded that from the outset the African Liberation Movement had not followed a definite programme of liberation. Instead, the activity of the African Liberation Movement had been a reaction to measures taken by the White parliament in execution of the programme of the White ruling party. The conference decided that henceforth the liberation movement should draw up its own programme of action, to be followed resolutely, regardless of the activity of others, especially the government of the day.

The Programme of Action proposed by the CYL and adopted by the 1949 conference aimed at the attainment of national freedom, which was defined as:

26   *Introduction to the South African Struggle*

freedom from white domination and the attainment of political independence. This implies the rejection of the concept of segregation, apartheid, trusteeship, or white leadership, which are all in one way or another, motivated by the idea of white domination or the domination of white over black.

The question of the seizure of state power was not addressed, while the concept of 'political independence' contained contradictions. It connoted the desire for freedom for the African majority, but within the existing framework. There was, therefore, no difference between this formulation and previous formulations which embodied the liberal ideology of African nationalism.

The Defiance Campaign

The CYL did, however, succeed in rejuvenating the ANC, as was demonstrated in the Defiance Campaign Against Unjust Laws, a campaign of passive resistance based on the Gandhian philosophy of non-violence. It had been planned in 1951 by a Joint Council of the ANC and the South African Indian Council and was directed at six specific laws, namely the Pass Laws, the Group Areas Act, the Separate Representation of Voters Act, the Suppression of Communism Act, the Bantu Authorities Act and the compulsory cattle culling policy.[33] The Defiance Campaign proved to be a 'test of strength', between the ANC and its allies on the one hand and the government on the other.[34] The ANC and its allies had abandoned the tactics of the previous four decades of deputations, petitions and protest, embarking instead upon the defiance of the regime.

The response of the regime to the Defiance Campaign was an intensification in repression. Draconian legislation was enacted in the form of the Public Safety Act of 1953 and the General Laws Amendment Act. The Public Safety Act empowered the regime to declare a state of emergency in any part of the country and issue emergency regulations. The General Laws Amendment Act provided for the imposition of three years' imprisonment, or fines of up to R600 or ten lashes, or a combination of any two. In addition, the regime banned individual leaders of the ANC. Nelson Mandela, Transvaal President of the ANC, was banned; Walter Sisulu, the General-Secretary was first banned and then forced to resign from the ANC.

Although forced to abandon the Defiance Campaign in the face of the regime's intransigence and repression, the ANC could claim that the campaign was successful in two respects: it resulted in an increase in ANC membership, particularly in the Eastern Cape, giving the ANC, for the first time in its history, a mass base; and it attracted international support. Benson, reflecting the view of the leadership of the ANC, describes the Defiance Campaign as an 'amazing success',[35] although in his analysis of the Defiance Campaign, Harsch is more critical.[36]

The ANC and the PAC 27

Harsch, however, ignores the difficulties posed for the organisers of the campaign by the different social situations of the various racial groups; for example, Whites, Coloureds and Indians were not affected by the Pass Laws while Indians only were affected by the prohibition on inter-provincial travel. Kuper, who made a detailed study of the Defiance Campaign, has written:

> Different targets had to be selected for each of the racial groups — Pass Laws for Africans, provincial barriers and segregation for Indians, and segregation for Coloureds. In consequence, membership of each volunteer corps of resisters was limited to members of a particular racial group, racially mixed units being permitted only where the law or regulation applied in common to all groups.[37]

The combined effects of the repression and the banning of some of the most effective leaders of the time cannot be under-estimated.

The 'Congress of the People' Campaign

Thereafter, the leadership of the ANC organised a 'Congress of the People' campaign under which the people were requested to submit their grievances as well as suggestions on the kind of society they wished to establish.

Meanwhile, Congress was strained by a fierce ideological struggle which had its origins in the role of Indians as well as White radicals who had formerly belonged to the Communist Party. Among the members of Congress who had been active in the CYL there was tremendous resentment of what was perceived as the dominant role being played in the ANC by Indians as well as by White members of the Communist Party. Before the Suppression of Communism Act became law in 1950, the Central Committee of the CPSA voted in favour of voluntary dissolution of the Party, after which its members formed the Congress of Democrats and began to play an increasingly active role in the ANC.[38] Many of the Africanists charged that the ANC was being used as a front by the members of the Communist Party.

The final split was preceded, if not precipitated by, the 'Congress of the People Campaign' in 1955–56. By 1953, the ANC was nominal leader of several other congresses with which it had forged an alliance, the 'Congress Alliance', comprising the ANC, the Congress of Democrats (White), the Coloured Peoples' Organisation (later Coloured Peoples' Congress), the South African Indian Congress and the non-racial South African Congress of Trade Unions. It was a shaky alliance, which aroused fears and provoked protests of a White take-over of the ANC leadership.[39]

At the 'Congress of the People' on 25–26 June 1955, the Freedom Charter was adopted. The Freedom Charter, a liberal policy statement, reiterated the ANC demand for 'one man, one vote', as well as the

28 *Introduction to the South African Struggle*

nationalisation of banks, mines and industry. One analyst has termed the Freedom Charter 'a curious mixture of nineteenth century liberal aspirations and twentieth century socialist aims'.[40] Another has described it in the following terms: 'The Freedom Charter was a document for liberal revolution drafted in the spirit of 1776 and 1789 not 1917'.[41]

The Freedom Charter omitted references to 'national independence and self-determination' for the African people. Instead, it stated that 'South Africa belongs to all who live in it, both Black and White'. As had been the case with the 1949 Programme of Action, the Charter did not address itself to tactics to be employed in the liberation struggle in order to achieve the objectives set out in the document. The liberal tone of the Freedom Charter did not, however, save the ANC from attack by the regime. 156 Congress leaders were charged with treason after the ratification of the Charter; the trial lasted five years but ultimately resulted in the acquittal of all those on trial.

The ANC Splits

Attacks also came from the Africanists, led by Potlako Leballo, Mangaliso Robert Sobukwe and others. The Africanists charged that the adoption of the Freedom Charter, with its omissions of African nationalism, Pan-Africanism and inter-African co-operation, was tantamount to treason. In particular they objected vehemently to the statement that 'South Africa belongs to all who live in it, both Black and White'. The Africanists argued that the land belongs to the indigenous African people; the objectives of the ANC, they argued, should be the overthrow of White domination and the restoration of the land to the Africans who were regarded as the rightful owners.

As a result of the bitter wrangling between the 'Charterists' and the 'Africanists', as the two opposing sides came to be known, and the effects of the Treason Trial, the ANC was immobilised and could offer neither direction to nor support for the mass struggles in other areas, for example the Alexandra Bus Boycott and the women's struggles in Sekukhuniland, Zeerust and Harding. In the Bahurutshe reserve in the Zeerust area, women protested against regulations extending the Pass Laws to women. For almost a year there were violent clashes between chiefs and headmen (appointed by the regime) and their supporters, and those opposed to them. Police intervened, violently breaking up demonstrations and arresting hundreds of people. Similar police violence was used against Blacks in Sekukhuniland in May 1959 when they demonstrated against the introduction of the Bantu Authorities Act (which established the Bantustans) and cattle-culling schemes. In 1959 in the rural areas of Natal in places like Harding violence flared up, as hundreds of women opposed to the extension of influx control to women were arrested and there was trouble over dipping tanks. In Pondoland there was bitter fighting during 1959–60 when Blacks revolted against the imposition of Bantu Authorities. There were clashes between government-appointed chiefs and headmen who attempted to implement the policies of the regime and Blacks opposed to them.[42]

These struggles took place in the countryside, and their extent and significance were largely lost on the urban-orientated political movements. In addition, press coverage of the resistance was meagre, if not deliberately suppressed. The political nature of the resistance was concealed, the press simply describing the clashes between pro- and anti-government groups as 'tribal faction fights', echoing the police slant. This concealment facilitated the brutal suppression of the resistance by the police and military.[43]

In the meanwhile, the final split between the 'Charterists' and the 'Africanists' was occasioned by the failure of the 1958 'stay-at-home' strike called by the Congress Alliance to protest against the Whites-only general election. Initially the proposal was rejected by the ANC because its provincial divisions were opposed to the strike. As the Africanists, who urged Africans to disregard the call for a strike, described it:

> It was conceived in a tepid multi-racial conference at the Gandhi Hall. It was launched by a rash and impetuous SACTU, popularised by a mysterious 'one-pound-a-day' committee and called by a panic-stricken ANC.[44]

Following the failure of the strike there was a purge of Africanists within the ANC, with expulsions and walk-outs (depending on the point of view of the 'Charterists' or 'Africanists') all acrimonious, the wrangling widely publicised by the press.

Formation of the PAC

Finally, on 6 April 1959, at Orlando in Johannesburg the Pan-Africanist Congress (PAC) was formed by the Africanists under the presidency of Mangaliso Robert Sobukwe. The formation of the PAC occurred during the period of decolonisation in Africa. In 1957, Ghana had gained its independence under the energetic leadership of the African visionary, the late Dr. Kwame Nkrumah, who advocated the unity of Africa. Ghana hosted the All-Africa Peoples' Conference and became the leading protagonist of Pan-Africanism. The Blacks in South Africa were not unaffected by these developments which were reflected in the resurgence of Africanism and the formation of PAC.

In his presidential address, Sobukwe paid tribute to Ghana's policy of non-alignment, or 'positive neutrality', by which was meant, 'independent in everything and neutral in nothing that concerns the destiny of Africa'.[45] PAC's commitment to African unity and the creation of a 'union of free, sovereign, independent and democratic states of Africa' was pledged.

30   *Introduction to the South African Struggle*

What of the charges made (and still frequently made) that the PAC is racist? In his presidential address Sobukwe explicitly rejected any and all theories of racial superiority, stressing that 'the Africanists take the view that there is only one race to which we all belong, and that is the human race'.[46] While this has continued to be the fundamental policy of the PAC, there have been and continue to be individuals within the PAC who believe that racial (African) exclusiveness should be maintained not only organisationally but also in struggle.

The concept of multi-racialism was unequivocally rejected:

> Against multi-racialism we have this objection, that the history of South Africa has fostered group prejudices and antagonism, and if we have to maintain the same group exclusiveness, parading under the term of multi-racialism, we shall be transporting to the new Africa these very antagonisms and conflicts. Further, multi-racialism is in fact pandering to European bigotry and arrogance. It is a method of safeguarding white interests irrespective of population figures.[47]

Sobukwe here was confusing means with ends. Clearly, the Congress Alliance was not committed to multi-racialism as a political objective. All the constituent organisations in the Alliance envisaged the elimination of racism and racial discrimination in an independent South Africa. In other words, they were committed to the creation of a non-racial society. They were nationally-specific organisations, linked through structures like the Joint Planning Council during the Defiance Campaign, and joint campaigns (again like the Defiance Campaign). But the statements of their political objectives emphasised the need for the organisation of society without regard to race, colour or creed. It can be argued that the nature of the Congress Alliance was determined by the manner in which the society was organised. The ANC, although an *African* organisation, had from the outset condemned racism and racial discrimination and in later years, the objectives of the organisation were articulated in terms of 'equal rights for *all*' South Africans, irrespective of race. The Congress Alliance was multi-racial in form, but non-racial in perspective and goals. In exactly the same way, the PAC emphasised African exclusiveness but pursued non-racial goals. Sobukwe repeatedly stated that in the society envisaged by the PAC, the colour of the individual's skin would be as irrelevant as the size or shape of the nose.

Whereas Lembede spoke of socialism, Sobukwe spoke of an 'Africanist Socialist Democracy' being the ultimate political objective of the PAC. In his presidential address, Sobukwe cited China as an example.[48] What Sobukwe envisaged was the development of an authentic application of socialism to the particular needs of the South African people. There are contradictions in Sobukwe's thinking on 'democracy'. At times, he seems to equate socialism with totalitarianism; at the same time, he rejects the system of capitalism because of its exploitative nature yet lauds the system of parliamentary democracy of the advanced capitalist societies (the West). In this regard, Sobukwe exhibits the liberal bias of the Black petit-bourgeoisie, the foundations of which, in the South African context, are traceable to the Cape 'liberal tradition' and the impact of mission education. Liberal Western political values were values to which the Black petit-bourgeoisie aspired. But the mistaken view held by Sobukwe here is that such freedoms are only permitted in bourgeois democratic societies. Yet, in an article written in May 1959, Sobukwe analysed the relationship between White minority rule in South Africa (where the Black majority were denied basic freedoms) and Western imperialism (which espoused certain fundamental freedoms in the name of democracy). Given his understanding of the role of Western imperialism in the maintenance of the system of White domination in South Africa and his understanding also that genuine liberation for the oppressed population would require the destruction of the system of capitalism, it is strange that Sobukwe could identify the PAC with Western concepts of democracy. These were some of the weaknesses in the theoretical formulations of the PAC which were not addressed during the short time of its overt legal existence in the country and which were to plague the organisation into its life in exile.

The PAC was emphatic that the Africans should provide their own leadership in the liberation struggle. Sobukwe wrote in May 1959:

> We want to make the African people conscious of the fact that they have to win their own liberation, rely on themselves to carry on a relentless and determined struggle instead of relying on court cases and negotiations on their behalf by 'sympathetic' whites. We have admitted that there are Europeans who are intellectual converts to the African's cause, but because they benefit materially from the present set-up, they cannot completely identify themselves with that cause.

Several years later the Black Consciousness Movement was to make the same argument.

The founders of the PAC emphasised the need for the psychological liberation of the Black masses. In his 'State of the Nation' address of 30 August 1959, Sobukwe stated:

> For over 300 years, the white foreign ruling minority has used its power to inculcate in the African a feeling of inferiority. This group has educated the African to accept the status quo of White supremacy and Black inferiority, as normal. It is our task to exorcise this slave mentality and to impart to the African masses that sense of self-reliance which will make them choose 'to starve in freedom rather than have plenty in bondage'; the self-reliance that will make them prefer self-government to the good government preferred by the ANC's leader ... We are calling on our people to assert their personality.[49]

Introduction to the South African Struggle

Sharpeville and After

At its first and only national conference held in Johannesburg on 19 and 20 December 1959, the newly-formed PAC resolved to launch its Positive Action Campaign, details of which were announced by Sobukwe at a press conference in Johannesburg on 18 March 1960. First target of the campaign was the hated pass system. Under the Pass Laws every African person above the age of 16 years has to carry on his or her person at all times a document known as a pass; failure to produce such a pass on demand results in immediate arrest. The frequent house-to-house searches, the total lack of respect for personal privacy, the frequent harassment of Africans in buses, on trains, in beer halls, everywhere, were (as they still are) a constant reminder to the people of their de facto status as 'temporary sojourners' in their own country. Central to the whole system of apartheid aimed at preventing the emergence of a settled urban African proletariat and scourge of the people, the Pass Laws were the ideal immediate target.

The aim was that on 21 March 1960, all African males would refuse to carry passes; instead they would offer themselves up for arrest at police stations throughout the country. The slogan was to be 'No bail, no defence, no fine', and in the spirit of non-violence they would disperse in orderly fashion if ordered by the police to do so. The police were informed of this decision, as also were the PAC cadres. Sobukwe wrote: 'My instructions, therefore, are that our people must be taught *now*, and *continuously*, that in this campaign we are going to observe absolute non-violence'. (His emphasis.) The rationale was that if the men were arrested then the White economy would be deprived of that which it needed most — Black labour.

There was no basis for such optimism; successive governments had reacted brutally to Black protests and strikes in the past; each campaign was followed by more draconian legislation and harsher measures (as had happened in 1953 when the Public Safety Act and the General Laws Amendment Act were promulgated following the Defiance Campaign). There was no reason to believe that the regime would react any differently to the PAC anti-pass campaign. One explanation for the optimistic assessment is to be sought in the fact that the two organisations, the ANC and PAC, were competing for the 'hearts and minds' of the masses. It was therefore necessary for the PAC leaders who had criticised the ANC as ineffectual and denounced its leaders as cowards, to demonstrate that the new organisation was different, hence the promises of independence by 1963 with exhortations to the masses to move 'forward now to independence, tomorrow the United States of Africa', in the words of a PAC lyric. It would also explain the PAC decision that in the anti-pass campaign the leaders would be up front; the ANC leaders, on the other hand, had been pilloried for shielding behind the masses.

The ANC, which had prepared its own anti-pass campaign,

The ANC and the PAC   33

scheduled for 30 March, refused to co-operate with the PAC on the grounds that the PAC campaign was sensational and insufficiently prepared.

The PAC went ahead with the campaign on 21 March, with demonstrators offering themselves up for arrest at police stations in several centres. At Sharpeville, near Vereeniging in the Transvaal, the police fired on a crowd of peaceful demonstrators, killing 67 and wounding 186, mostly in the back as they fled. At nearby Van der Bijl Park two Africans were fatally shot, while at Langa and Nyanga, more than a thousand miles away in the Cape, five people were killed by police gun-fire. Following the Sharpeville massacre, Sobukwe and Albert Luthuli (President of the ANC) called for the observance of 28 March as a stay-at-home day of mourning. The stay-at-home proved very successful.

On 30 March, a peaceable march on Cape Town by 30,000 people from Langa, organised by the Western Cape branch of PAC was led by the young student, Phillip Kgosana, then 19 years old. The crowd, however, dispersed on the instructions of Kgosana who accepted a false promise of a meeting with the Minister of Bantu Affairs. In an interview with the author, Kgosana explained that the massacre at Sharpeville less than ten days earlier was still fresh in his mind; he was afraid that if the crowd did not disperse peacefully there might be a repetition of Sharpeville.[50]

The Repression

At that stage public meetings had already been outlawed. Now the regime reacted ferociously, declaring both the ANC and PAC unlawful organisations. A state of emergency was declared, followed by the arrest and detention of approximately 2,000 of the regime's active opponents (including those still on trial for treason) and about 18,000 others. The state of emergency lasted until 13 August (except in the Transkei) when the last of the detainees was released. Robert Sobukwe was sentenced to three years' imprisonment on Robben Island, but on expiry of his term he was reimprisoned annually by special Act of Parliament. When eventually he was released in 1969, he was immediately restricted to Kimberley in the Northern Cape where he died of cancer on 26 February 1978, during his second five-year term of banning and house arrest.

The PAC had repeated in its Positive Action Campaign tactics which had been employed during the Defiance Campaign, with consequences which were far more tragic and grave for the liberation struggle. Neither the ANC nor PAC was prepared for the events which followed the Sharpeville massacre; the problems which have bedevilled the PAC from the time that it set itself up as a movement-in-exile are traceable to Sharpeville and its aftermath. At the time of the anti-pass campaign, the organisation was less than one year old. It had not yet developed a tried and tested leadership and was competing with an older established

34 *Introduction to the South African Struggle*

organisation, the ANC, for membership. The policy of 'leaders in front', as a demonstration of the courage of the leaders of the new organisation, resulted in the removal, through the arrests of Sobukwe, Leballo and others, of the leadership. The rank-and-file were left without direction and leadership. Even though the leaders of the PAC in the period leading up to the anti-pass campaign conveyed the impression that they had a plan for a sustained struggle it was clear in the wake of the Sharpeville massacre and the subsequent banning of the organisation that there was no such plan. Harsch, in his analysis, refers to a 'lack of any real strategic orientation' in the organisation.[51] One of the leaders of the PAC during that period has informed the author that he learned several months after the Sharpeville massacre and the banning of the organisation that the President, Sobukwe, had issued written instructions to one of his lieutenants who had not been arrested (and to whom the conduct of the affairs of the organisation had been entrusted) to recruit people for military training abroad, but that he was not shown such written instructions and hence could not verify firstly whether such instructions existed and secondly whether they had been issued by Sobukwe. Sobukwe at that time was already in prison.[52] Two members of the PAC had been sent out of the country prior to the Sharpeville massacre, but their mission had been to explain the PAC position and the rationale behind the anti-pass campaign to the international community.

Apart from the declaration of a state of emergency and the banning of the ANC and the PAC, an attempt was made on the life of the Prime Minister. The White would-be assassin later told a magistrate that he shot the Premier because he was 'leading the country into darkness'.

White South Africa suffered what Johnson calls a 'severe crisis of confidence'.[53] The Pass Laws were temporarily suspended, which led to a short-lived and strangely optimistic belief that the system would be abolished. There appeared to be intense soul-searching among Whites of all shades of opinion. They called for an inquiry into the underlying causes of the disturbances and a reassessment of policies towards the Blacks. Acting Prime Minister Paul Sauer spoke of the need for a 'new chapter in race relations' and, in a speech at Humansdorp in the Cape on 21 May, said:

> The old book of South African history was closed a month ago, and, for the immediate future, South Africa would reconsider in earnest her whole approach to the Native question. We must create a new spirit which must restore overseas faith — both white and non-white — in South Africa.

This hint of liberalisation was, however, short-lived. Verwoerd recovered (attributing his 'miraculous escape' to divine intervention) and with messianic zeal re-affirmed the whole policy of apartheid.

The Sharpeville massacre brought home to the international community the horrors of South Africa's racial policies, earning her

The ANC and the PAC 35

widespread and sustained condemnation. But while condemning the apartheid policies of the White minority regime on moral grounds, the West proceeded to provide the financial and military support which enable the regime to perpetrate these sanguinary crimes.

The Economic Consequences
Sharpeville was to have grave economic consequences for South Africa. The massacre seriously undermined the confidence of foreign investors as a result of which there was a flight of capital.

> In the six months that followed Sharpeville foreign capital fled from South Africa at the rate of $17 million a month . . . By the end of 1960, $207 million had left the country. South Africa's foreign reserves which had totalled $425 million in December 1959, had been cut to $240 million. The flight continued into 1961, and by June reserves were down to $215 million. Government officials publicly expressed their deep concern about the damage done to the economy by the loss of 'investor confidence.[54]

After the regime had imposed stringent foreign exchange control regulations in 1961 and had by 1963 crushed the last remaining pockets of resistance, investors, satisfied with the political stability, virtually fell over one another in their haste to invest in apartheid:

> A decade later foreign reserves had risen to a record level of $864 million. American and British investors were competing to find new industries in which to invest in South Africa and the annual net inflow of capital had risen to an average of more than $43 million, six times the level of the pre-Sharpeville figure . . . Foreign investment, which is particularly important to South Africa's peculiar economy and strategic position, began to return to the Country *only after the bite of the harsh repression that followed Sharpeville began to be felt* . . . Stability as the investors saw it was the most important point, not the form it took or the morality of it.[55] (Emphasis added.)

The injection of foreign capital into the South African economy was important for a variety of reasons. It enabled the regime to weather the storm and thereafter facilitated economic growth which in the decade after Sharpeville was phenomenal, averaging 5% annually. Western corporations, through their subsidiaries in South Africa, made available their discoveries in research and development so that the country was provided with advanced technology from the developed Western countries. In turn the regime began to promote a diversification in the economy and to encourage self-sufficiency in order to stave off economic sanctions which were being advocated by the Afro-Asian bloc of countries, supported by the socialist states. The theory advanced by foreign investors that increased economic involvement in South Africa would

36 *Introduction to the South African Struggle*

have an erosive effect on apartheid was disproved by the fact that in the decade 1961–71, which were years of economic boom, some 94 new repressive laws were passed, among them the Terrorism Act which provides for indefinite incommunicado detention without trial. On the contrary, foreign investment has strengthened the regime and enabled it to reinforce the system of apartheid. Ruth First and her co-authors pointed out the crucial role of such investment:

> The psychological value of that investment to South Africa cannot be measured. It provided the capital without which the economy could not have grown. It staved off the recurring danger of balance-of-payments crises by ensuring the country a ready source of foreign exchange. It gave South Africa access to advanced technology as leading Western corporations passed on their findings in research and development to their South African subsidiaries.[56]

Transition to Violence

Sharpeville was neither the first nor the last massacre of Blacks in South Africa. Between 1919 and 1960 there were approximately 21 massacres; for example, the Bulthoek massacre in 1920 when members of a religious sect were gunned down, leaving 163 killed and 129 wounded; in 1946 thirteen Black miners were fatally shot by the police of the internationally-acceptable government of the seemingly benign General Smuts.

The significance of the Sharpeville massacre, however, is that it convinced many Blacks (and some Whites) of the inefficacy of non-violent resistance in South Africa. In keeping with its declaration of 1963 as freedom year, the PAC began to make preparations for violent struggle. The ANC had its final attempt at legal protest when, under the banner of the 'All-In' Africa Convention it called for a national convention to draft a new constitution for the country. Mandela warned that if the regime failed to heed the call for such a national convention then a three-day general strike would be called to coincide with the establishment of the Republic on 31 May 1961. The response of the regime to Mandela's threat was to issue a warrant for his arrest (after which he went underground); public meetings were banned and legislation was enacted empowering the regime to detain persons without trial for a period of twelve days.

The regime mobilised its armed forces to crush the strike which had to be called off on the second day. Mandela hinted at the new forms of struggle being planned by the ANC which had maintained, under difficult conditions, the skeletal framework of an organisation after the declaration of a state of emergency and the subsequent outlawing of the ANC and PAC.[57]

The ANC and the PAC 37

Subsequently there emerged three main underground movements: Umkhonto we Sizwe (Spear of the Nation) POQO and the African Resistance Movement. Membership of Umkhonto was drawn largely from the Congress Alliance and the Communist Party which had been resurrected in 1960. Membership of POQO was drawn largely from the PAC. There was neither co-operation nor co-ordination of efforts between the two; instead, the feuding which had characterised the parent bodies was taken up by the new underground movements, with POQO accusing Umkhonto of diluting African nationalism by admitting into its ranks non-Africans. Membership of the African Resistance Movement consisted largely of White intellectuals and disillusioned members of the Liberal Party.

Umkhonto we Sizwe

Umkhonto we Sizwe was founded by Nelson Mandela and other ANC leaders with the intention of disrupting communications and destroying government buildings in the hope that public order would gradually collapse, guerrilla warfare would begin and White supremacy would be overthrown. A symbolic day (Dingaan's Day, 16 December, when White conquest was finally established) was chosen for the start of the campaign of selective sabotage. A leaflet distributed by Umkhonto said:

> We of Umkhonto we Sizwe have always sought — as the liberation movement has sought — to achieve liberation without bloodshed and civil clash. We do so still. We hope even at this late hour that our first actions will awaken everyone to a realisation of the disastrous situation to which the Nationalist [government's] policy is leading. We hope that we will bring the government and its supporters to their senses before it is too late, so that both government and its policies can be changed before matters reach the stage of civil war.[58]

The leaflet itself is revealing. Despite the banning of the mass organisations, the massacres and the sheer ruthlessness of the White minority regime, Umkhonto still hoped that the new tactic of sabotage would strike a responsive chord in White ears. Sabotage was a new form of *protest*, rather than the initiation of a protracted struggle, involving the masses, aimed at the seizure of state power and social transformation. Gwendolen Carter wrote in 1958:

> The dilemma of Non-European [sic] leaders in the Union lies in the fact that their aims are not revolution, though European [sic] South Africans seldom seem to recognise this fact . . . In South Africa, in contrast, Non-European [sic] political organisations seek changes within the existing system, not its overthrow. They want a share in political power, not to oust Europeans . . .[59]

38 *Introduction to the South African Struggle*

In 1961, the ANC and its allies, operating as an underground organisation, were still adopting the same approach. There is also to be detected in the Umkhonto leaflet, an attitude of 'look-what-you've-made-me-do', of placing moral responsibility on the regime for the transition to revolutionary violence by the liberation movement. This, too, reflects the lingering influence of Christian liberalism.

The decision to resort to violence was made without prior analysis of the earlier methods of struggle and the reasons for their failure. There seems to have been optimism that the majority of Whites, or a substantial proportion of Whites, were opposed to apartheid. Yet there was no difference in reaction to Black protest from the White establishment, regardless of the government of the day. Individual Whites, or even a body of White opinion might express concern about 'race relations' or oppose the regime's apartheid policies or condemn police excesses, but in the final analysis the state apparatus was the custodian of White interests. The campaign of sabotage, even though it did cause alarm among Whites, had the more important effect of rallying the White populace behind the regime. By 1963, however, the tone of Umkhonto propaganda had changed, the focus being levelled upon the *White* state and the *African* character of the organisation.[60] The effect of the acts of sabotage, combined with the acts of violence by the other organisations, was to polarise loyalties of Blacks and Whites.

White fears were further reinforced by the sensationalised media reports of the imperialist-inspired confusion in the newly-independent Congo.[61]

After the Sharpeville massacre there was a tremendous amount of bitterness and anger (as well as fear) among the Black masses, yet there was a failure on the part of Umkhonto to harness and channel this bitterness and anger in a revolutionary direction. By the time that preparations were made for widespread armed action, which would entail the mobilisation of the masses, the plan could not be put into effect because the leaders of Umkhonto were arrested soon after, in 1963.

On the contrary, Umkhonto had selected an elite corps which was responsible for the perpetration of the acts of sabotage. The black masses were left as spectators in what was essentially a contest between the elite of Umkhonto and the White regime. Besides there not having been preparation of the masses for the new forms of struggle, the masses were not incorporated in the programme once embarked upon, hence they could not participate, even if they were enthusiastic about the sabotage campaign. We must agree with Turok when he says: 'The sabotage campaign failed on the main count — *it did not raise the level of action of the masses themselves.*'[62] (Emphasis added.)

To be fair, the difficulties under which activists had to operate have also to be appreciated. The political socialisation of most of the activists had taken place during an era when, despite the repression and harassment by the regime's uniformed police and the Special Branch (as it then was), legal political activity was permitted. The majority of them were people who had spent all their politically active lives in overt legal activity. Suddenly they had to transform themselves into security-conscious freedom-fighters. Fatima Meer, in her instructive critique, writes:

> Reports of trials of persons now suffering severe penalties make sad reading. The so-called cell meetings appear in evidence to have been no more than haphazard encounters on street corners, badly arranged car rides, or careless academic discussions in flats. There was far more talking than doing, and the doing often proceeded with gross carelessness so that explosives would be transported in broken-down cars.[63]

The leaders were all known to the police, as were the majority of leaders at regional levels. As a result of the arrests during the various passive resistance and defiance campaigns police libraries were well-stocked with photographs, finger-prints, etc., while the Treason Trial had provided police with a comprehensive history of the ANC and its allies through the documents and correspondence which were confiscated.

Those whose identities were unknown to the police were quickly betrayed by their comrades under pressure and threats of torture, which became routine and was effectively used to extract information. The regime had sent military and police officers to Algeria where they learned the interrogation methods used by the French against the Algerian freedom-fighters. Suddenly the 'fascism' and 'gestapo tactics' of the secret police, so long spoken about, were actually experienced by activists, very many of whom broke under the strain; some committed suicide while others were murdered in detention. Again the lack of preparation of the liberation movement was exposed: it had no reply to the 'brutal wave of terror', to borrow a phrase from Turok, unleashed by the regime.[64] Meer speaks of the lack of an 'esprit de corps in the underground', attributing this to the fact that the 'underground was new, inexperienced and desperate'.[65] All of these may be true but the overriding factor was the failure to analyse the new objective and subjective conditions before embarking upon a course of action. That failure proved costly, because the new methods of struggle adopted 'had the effect of isolating the organised movement from the mass who felt unable to join in this new phase or even to defend the actionists when they were seized'.[66]

During the era of its legal existence the liberation movement could always rely on the masses when they were involved, as during the Defiance Campaign of the fifties. The masses not only participated but provided invaluable moral support for the activists and for their families during times of arrest. Yet during the sabotage campaign there

40 *Introduction to the South African Struggle*

was a noticeable lack of such support. Again Meer is instructive:

> When political activity had been legal, political prisoners had enjoyed the status of martyrs, the community had rallied around them, and publicly-organised funds had cared for their families. Persons working underground retained the same expectations for their sacrifices. Thus many became disillusioned and embittered and, in that state, susceptible to becoming witnesses against their fellows.[67]

While Meer's observation is valid, the deterrent effect on the community (especially when the masses had not been mobilised) of the intense repression and extensive harassment by the regime cannot be underestimated. The repression and harassment, which increased sharply as the sabotage campaign mounted, were directed also at the community, so as to cut off the activists from the support of the community.

Admittedly, the activists of Umkhonto had had no experience in underground revolutionary work, still less successful models of revolution which they could adapt to their own situation. After Mandela went underground in 1961 following the failure of the three-day general strike, he began to read Von Clausewitz *On War* and other works, in an attempt to work out a strategy and tactics for revolution in South Africa. But he was under constant harassment by the police. He left the country secretly and undertook a tour of the newly independent and emerging African states in order to canvass support for the liberation struggle in South Africa. Back in South Africa, he was captured by the police in August 1962, after having eluded them for over a year. He was sentenced to five years' imprisonment for having left the country without a passport.

Umkhonto we Sizwe continued its campaign of selective sabotage throughout 1962 and early 1963. Simultaneously recruits were leaving the country for military training while other established missions abroad where they engaged in petitioning the United Nations and soliciting international support. Oliver Tambo, the ANC Vice-President, had secretly left the country shortly before the banning of the ANC and PAC, and became the 'roving ambassador'. After being joined by other ANC exiles, Tambo established ANC missions in various countries.

In July 1963 the security police achieved one of their biggest successes. Acting on a tip-off from an informer, they discovered the headquarters of Umkhonto at Lilliesleaf Farm in Rivonia, near Johannesburg. The farm had been secretly purchased by the South African Communist Party. There they arrested Govan Mbeki, Walter Sisulu, Ahmed Kathrada, Bob Hepple, Denis Goldberg, Lionel Bernstein, Harold Wolpe and Arthur Goldreich. Wolpe and Goldreich escaped from detention while awaiting trial after offering to bribe a prison warden. Bob Hepple was also released from detention after agreeing to become a state witness, but subsequently fled the country. Nine persons were

The ANC and the PAC 41

eventually convicted and sentenced to long terms of imprisonment in what has come to be termed the 'Rivonia trial' in 1964. Nelson Mandela at that time was already serving a five-year prison term; he was now implicated in 250 documents seized by the police, including the diary of his secret tour, recklessly left at the homestead. Mandela, Sisulu, Mbeki, Kathrada and three other Umkhonto leaders were sentenced to life imprisonment on Robben Island.

The capture of the Umkhonto leadership and the seizure of incriminating documents at Rivonia reflect the lapses in security and the lack of vigilance which characterised the early operations of the underground movement in South Africa. Rather than being dispersed, all the top leaders of the movement were assembled in one place, with the result that when the security police discovered their hideout, they were all captured. Decisions to decentralise the operations had been taken but never implemented. Umkhonto operatives and recruits who visited the hideout saw the leadership there, which also increased the risks of detection, largely through divulgence by such operatives under torture. In later years, some of these mistakes were acknowledged by ANC leaders.[68]

For some time afterwards there were sporadic explosions for which Umkhonto claimed credit. But these explosions were of little more than nuisance value. The Rivonia debacle was a serious setback for the liberation movement and it would take the movement more than a decade to recover.

The African Resistance Movement (ARM)

ARM, a multi-racial body of young students, actually committed the first act of sabotage in October 1961. Thereafter, they committed several acts of violence in the hope of frightening the government into making concessions. One disillusioned member of ARM, John Harris, a former member of the Liberal Party, placed a time bomb in a suitcase in the Whites-only concourse of Johannesburg's Park Station on 24 July 1964. An elderly White woman was killed and a child maimed. Harris was executed on 1 April 1965.

Black membership of ARM was token. Most of its originators, White liberals, fled to Britain while their fellows faced the music. The one Black member, Edward Daniels, was sentenced to fifteen years' imprisonment after his conviction on charges of sabotage. The White members on the other hand received sentences of between two and ten years for their parts in various acts of sabotage or conspiracy.

An offshoot of ARM was the Yu Chi Chan Club led by a brilliant Black graduate of a German university, Dr. Neville Alexander. He and a group of Black leaders from the Cape were sentenced to ten years' imprisonment. During his trial, Dr. Alexander revealed that the group had neither had plans nor taken any action although they had studied and discussed ways of overthrowing the regime.

POQO

POQO (meaning 'pure [Africans] only'), the military wing of the PAC, was launched shortly after the banning of the ANC and PAC. POQO militants armed with pangas, axes, home-made bombs and a few stolen guns and pistols engaged in several clashes with the police and with pro-apartheid chiefs and their supporters. The most serious clash was the Paarl uprising, an attack upon the Paarl police station, apparently in an attempt to capture arms. In the ensuing struggle, two Whites were killed and several policemen injured. This alarmed the regime which set up a one-man Commission of Inquiry. The Commissioner, Mr. Justice Snyman, found that:

> the POQO organisation consisted of a network of cells or groups, the members of each group not knowing more about the organisation as a whole than what each had been told, to prevent information leaking about its activities.[69]

He went on to warn the Whites that unless they appreciated the 'message of Paarl', their future was bleak: 'We must not only change our attitude, but we must also find what is acceptable to the African, or to find a way to make our policies acceptable to him'.[70]

Julius Lewin, former Professor of African Studies at the University of the Witwatersrand, expressed the view that the country 'would pay a high price for apartheid', according to the people with whom he had discussed the 'Paarl Tragedy'. He expressed the view that:

> Events at Paarl marked the entry of South Africa into a phase which the forces of security would have constantly to be on the alert to cope with the forces of discontent. We must try to perceive what lies beneath the tragedy. At the bottom is the moral and social problem created by our political policies. And merely to increase the strength of the police or even to call the aid of the military, will not alter the nature of the situation.[71]

On 4 February 1963, at Bashee Bridge in the Transkei five Whites were reportedly killed with home-made bombs, causing consternation among Whites in the country who feared a Mau-Mau type revolt in South Africa. The regime denied that the killings were politically motivated but official reports were contradicted by newspapers which revealed that POQO was responsible. There were a number of uprisings and media-suppressed clashes between POQO militants and White police. Black informers and spies were killed.

Several analysts termed POQO a 'terrorist organisation'.[72] Certain of the organisation's activities merit the description. Terror and coercion were used in efforts to recruit members as well as to levy a head 'tax' of 25 cents; persons who refused to join the organisation or to contribute financially to its activities, were assaulted and in some cases murdered.

The ANC and the PAC 43

In the Western Cape, a number of Coloured women were crippled as a result of physical attacks by POQO militants because they allegedly seduced African migrant-labourers who were potential recruits.[73]

There is little doubt, however, that the PAC and POQO, through their rhetorical militancy, gained considerable support among the Black masses. Thus Feit, a hostile commentator, writes that growing African discontent was evidenced 'by the mounting support for PAC and its terrorist wing POQO'.[74]

One Black academic has analysed the support for the PAC in the early 1960s in terms of the political economy of the country. He argues that modern capitalist industry in South Africa has widened the contradiction between the oppressive conditions under which Blacks work and live, and the heightened consciousnes and awareness of this oppression by the average worker among the Black masses. Consequently not only do the Black masses voice their views and feelings more articulately and self-confidently, but their children also grow up in a community environment that is more articulate and self-confident. He explains:

> The ideas and forces of the PAC . . . which sprang up in 1959, and gained momentum in the early 1960s, were an expression of this new historical situation. *It was a reflection of the higher level of impatience with white domination among the masses of urban African workers*, who were being awakened to political consciousness by modern industry and modern education. It was an expression of the quite legitimate and progressive hatred to whites *as oppressors*, among the masses of these urban industrial workers, who in their day-to-day lives, never receive even a modicum of that white liberal kindness, friendship and favours, which sometimes fall upon highly educated Blacks. The day-to-day experience of the masses of urban Blacks has taught them that they do not owe whites any favours, in return; and that the emancipation of Blacks from white supremacy can only be brought about by the efforts and struggles of the masses of Blacks themselves. Hence the initial displeasure of white liberals and members of the old Black elite with the ideas of the PAC . . . This new historical situation, plus the ideas of the PAC, which acted as fertiliser, was the soil upon which the Black Consciousness Movement grew in the late 1960s.[75] (Emphasis added.)

White Repression and Black Consciousness

After three years of sabotage, killings and attacks, the regime outlawed Umkhonto we Sizwe, the African Resistance Movement and POQO under the General Laws Amendment Act of 1962–63. By 1964, the remaining pockets of resistance were wiped out. The transfer to violence had not produced the desired result. Instead it provided the justification

44 *Introduction to the South African Struggle*

for the regime to unleash a reign of terror. Legislation was enacted to enable the government to detain its opponents for periods of 90 days, then 180 days, during which the systematic use of torture became routine. The Sabotage Act was passed, the Suppression of Communism Act was amended to enable the Minister of Justice to detain any person upon completion of his prison sentence 'till this side of eternity'. This particular clause was used to detain Sobukwe in solitary confinement on Robben Island annually for six years after completion of his three-year sentence for incitement. The security branch of the police was expanded, as also was the informer network. Defence spending was substantially increased.[76]

By 1965 the White regime was confident that it had crushed the Black resistance. On the surface all was calm. All that remained to remind the complacent White community of the turbulence of the previous four years which had posed the most serious challenge to their privileged position were the regular trials of individuals charged with furthering the aims of the banned organisations. Occasionally pamphlets of the ANC would be discovered. Repressive legislation introduced during the 'crisis' and justified on the grounds of the extraordinary situation facing the country, acquired a certain normality and permanence, rationalised in terms of the 'communist threat'. Apart from a few academics and clergymen, there was little protest; White South Africans regarded the deprivation of basic civil liberties as a necessary but lesser evil. A greater evil would be the loss of the opulent and affluent lifestyle to which they had so grown accustomed as to regard it as a God-given right.

For the Black majority, the post-Sharpeville period was one of hope, but hope was gradually superseded by a gloomy atmosphere of hopelessness, fear and defeatism. The major mass movements had been banned; those organisations that were not banned were rendered inactive through the decimation of their leadership by bannings, house arrest and banishment. All the known leaders were either in prison or in exile. The reign of terror for Blacks did not end with Rivonia but was sustained and intensified, varied in form and substance. The expanded security branch informer network infiltrated many Black organisations, from Christian youth clubs to women's guilds. Budding leaders were intimidated and harassed.

Between 1963 and 1968 mass resistance was crushed; the bannings of the ANC and PAC resulted in a leadership vacuum in the politics of resistance. The regime attempted to promote ethnic functionaries of apartheid-created institutions, the Bantustan leaders and leaders of the Coloured Persons' Representative Council and the South African Indian Council, to fill the vacuum.

The Black Consciousness Movement
Resistance outside the framework of apartheid was revived in the late 1960s and during the 1970s by the Black Consciousness Movement

The ANC and the PAC 45

(BCM), a conglomeration of organisations subscribing to the philosophy of Black consciousness. The South African Students' Organisation (SASO) was formed in 1969 by Black (that is, African, Coloured and Indian) students from the University of Natal Medical School, the Federal Theological Seminary and the segregated universities following their breakaway from the National Union of South African Students (NUSAS). SASO rejected co-operation with White liberals, arguing that such co-operation inhibited Black initiatives. SASO was instrumental in the formation of a number of other organisations encompassing a wide range of activities in the political field, labour, youth, arts and culture. These included the Black People's Convention (BPC), the Black and Allied Workers' Union (BAWU), the National Youth Organisation (NAYO) and the South African Students' Movement (SASM) (which played a leading role in the youth township rebellion in 1976 and 1977), the Black Women's Federation and the South African Black Theatre Union.

These organisations, which have come to be termed the Black Consciousness Movement, emphasised the principles of Black pride, self-reliance, self-confidence and the need to rid Blacks of the feelings of inferiority which have been the result of centuries of White supremacy and paternalism. Psychological as well as physical liberation were stressed in all the writings and programmes of the Black Consciousness Movement.

Because of the Black exclusivity that SASO and other organisations espoused, the BCM was for a while tolerated by the South African authorities who thought that the Black students were seeing the virtues of 'separate development'. As from 1973, all the top leaders of the BCM were banned, while others were forced into exile. In September 1977 the charismatic leader of the BCM, Steve Biko, was murdered by his security police interrogators and on 19 October 1977, SASO, BPC, the Black Women's Federation and other organisations were banned. The BCM survived the bannings, however, as evidenced by the emergence of other organisations like the Azanian People's Organisation (AZAPO), the Azanian Students' Organisation (AZASO) and the Media Workers' Association of South Africa (MWASA), all of which are committed to Black Consciousness. Whereas at its formation in 1969, SASO had a membership of about 30, by the time that the regime banned the organisation and 17 others (one of which was the multi-racial Christian Institute), the BCM had struck deep roots among the Black urban youth and intelligentsia. The 'politicisation and conscientisation' which had been done by SASO and other organisations, the organisational infrastructure which they had established, the layers of leadership which had been trained and the ideas of self-help which had been propagated in a practical manner through various community development programmes, enabled the BCM to survive the repression of the seventies.

Probably because they saw the BCM as a competitor, the ANC and

46 *Introduction to the South African Struggle*

PAC (functioning as movements in exile) were initially hostile to the BCM.[77] The Communist Party of South Africa (CPSA) has been persistent in its criticism of the BCM. The PAC, on the other hand, once the BCM gained increasing support inside the country, hailed Black consciousness as 'the ideology with which the PAC burst forth upon the Azanian political scene and rallied the African masses'.[78]

In the mid-seventies, particularly after the pro-FRELIMO rallies organised by the BCM in September 1974, many of the activists of the BCM upon fleeing the country joined either the ANC or the PAC, while others remained non-aligned. The BCM has now also constituted itself as a movement in exile, although at this stage it does not enjoy recognition by the Organisation of African Unity (OAU).

Notes

1. No Sizwe 1979, pp. 46–7.
2. See for instance interview with Edwin Makoti, PAC Director of Publicity and Information, *The Herald* (Zimbabwe), 6 December 1982.
3. See Walshe, P. 1979.
4. Trainor, L. 1975, p. 13.
5. Walshe, P. 1979, pp. 609–10.
6. Hull 1980, pp. 101–4.
7. Karis, T. and Carter, G. 1973, Vol. 1, p. 8.
8. Ibid.
9. Collins, C.B. 1976. This paper was read at the Comparative Education Conference at the University of New England. I am indebted to the author for having made the paper available to me.
10. Gerhart, G. 1978.
11. Ibid., pp. 12–13.
12. Ibid., p. 13.
13. Ibid.
14. Walshe, P. 1970, pp. 349–50.
15. Meer, F., 'African Nationalism — Some inhibiting factors', in Adam, H. (ed) 1971, p. 126.
16. Walshe 1970.
17. Trainor 1975, p. 13. The formation of the ANC has to be viewed against the backdrop of the South African political economy. For an expansion of this view, see Magubane, B.M. 1979.
18. See Trainor 1975, p. 13.
19. The phrase belongs to No Sizwe 1979, pp. 43 et seq.
20. Trainor 1975, p. 14.
21. No Sizwe 1979, pp. 43 et seq.
22. Carter, G., 'African Concepts in Nationalism', in Adam, H. (ed) 1971, p. 105.
23. Gibson, R. 1972, p. 44.
24. See Walshe, P. 1970, p. 355.
25. See Karis and Carter 1973, Document 53, 'Policy of CYL', article by A.M. Lembede in *Inkundla Ya Bantu*, May 1946.

26. Hirson, B. 1979, p. 314.
27. Walshe 1970, pp. 358-9.
28. Laurence, P. 1976, p. 47.
29. Walshe, P. 1970, pp. 358-9.
30. Trainor, 1975,p. 14.
31. Harsch, E. 1980, p. 227.
32. Walshe, P. 1970, pp. 358-9.
33. See Feit, E. 1962, p. 27.
34. See Laurence, P. 1976, pp. 46-8.
35. Benson, M. 1966, p. 159.
36. Harsch 1980, p. 229.
37. Kuper, L., 'African Nationalism in South Africa, 1910-1964', in Wilson & Thompson (eds) 1971, p. 462.
38. The CPSA resurfaced many years later. The Central Committee of the Party criticised itself severely for its decision to dissolve voluntarily — see Turok, B. 1974, p. 23.
39. This is a point made by both Feit, E. 1962, p. 16 and Gibson, R. 1972, pp. 54-5. Turok, B. 1974, pp. 32-3 presents an opposing view.
40. Quoted by Laurence, P. 1976, p. 48.
41. Johnson, R.W. 1977, p. 18.
42. Horrell, M. 1971, p. 32. See also Mbeki, G. 1964; Turok, B. 1961.
43. Turok, B. 1974, p. 38.
44. 'Africanists: Kick the Europeans out of ANC', *The Bantu World*, 21 June 1958, quoted by Feit, E. 1962, p. 17.
45. Basic documents of the PAC, published by the External Mission of PAC, Dar-es-Salaam. All quotations and excerpts from the *Speeches of Mangaliso Sobukwe*.
46. Ibid.
47. Ibid.
48. Ibid.
49. Ibid.
50. Interview with Phillip Kgosana, New York, 8 May 1982.
51. Harsch 1980, p. 241.
52. Interview with Phillip Kgosana, New York, 8 May 1982.
53. Johnson, R.W. 1977, p. 19.
54. Hoagland, J. 1973, pp. 338-9.
55. Ibid.
56. First, Steele and Gurney 1973, p. 25.
57. See Davis, J.A. and Baker, J.K. (eds) 1966, p. 258.
58. Quoted by Turok, B. 1974, p. 44.
59. Carter, G. 1962, p. 378.
60. On this point see Turok, B. 1974, pp. 44-7.
61. For a brilliant analysis of the role of the Western powers in the Congo, see Kalb, M. 1982.
62. Turok, B. 1974, p. 45.
63. Meer, F., in Adam, H. (ed) 1971, p. 149.
64. Turok, B. 1974, p. 45.
65. Meer, F., in Adam, H. (ed) 1971, p. 149.
66. Turok, B. 1974, p. 45.
67. Meer, F., in Adam, H. (ed). 1971, p. 149.
68. See Slovo, J., 'South Africa — No Middle Road', in Davidson, Slovo and Wilkinson 1976.

48   *Introduction to the South African Struggle*

69. Quoted in Norman Bethune Institute 1976, p. 24.
70. Ibid.
71. Ibid.
72. See for instance Turok, B. 1974, p. 44: 'POQO was primarily active as a terrorist organisation'.
73. See 'The Birth Pangs of POQO', *Drum*, February 1963.
74 Feit, E. 1971.
75. Vilakazi, H. 1978.
76. Meer, F., in Adam, H. (ed) 1971, p. 149.
77. See Stanbridge, R., 'Contemporary African Political Organisations and Movements', in Price, R.G. and Rosberg, C.G. (eds) 1980, p. 87.
78. Ibid.

3. The Burdens of Exile

This chapter aims to analyse the environment in which the South African National Liberation Movement functions, and its impact. How far, in particular, has over-dependence on external relationships and aid enhanced or, alternatively, impeded the achievement of the revolutionary goals of the Liberation Movement?

Although international support for the National Liberation Movement has been important, it has had a number of negative effects. It has resulted in the Liberation Movement concentrating upon international solidarity at the expense of establishing revolutionary structures in South Africa. This was particularly the case in the period after the banning of the ANC and the PAC when the two organisations established external missions; it has exacerbated existing divisions within the National Liberation Movement; and it has encouraged 'exile tendencies towards debilitating over-dependence and malfunction'.[1]

We examine the political developments internally and internationally, to demonstrate that while the National Liberation Movement was instrumental in the campaigns in the early 1960s to isolate the apartheid regime, it was alienated from political developments in South Africa. The outlawing of the ANC and PAC had created a vacuum in the politics of resistance, which was exploited by the ethnic functionaries of apartheid-created institutions, like the Bantustan leaders and the leaders of the Coloured Persons' Representative Council as well as the leaders of the South African Indian Council. In the late 1960s the Black Consciousness Movement emerged, pursuing a policy of non-collaboration with the regime and a programme aimed at the unity of the oppressed Black population and its psychological and physical liberation. A wave of strikes by Black workers in Natal in 1973 was followed by the revival of an independent Black trade union movement which was to grow in strength and organisation in the late 1970s. These political developments occurred independently of the ANC and PAC.

Hostility between the ANC and PAC was exacerbated by the external relationships which the two organisations had forged, as well as by the competition between them for support and influence. An examination

50 *Introduction to the South African Struggle*

of the relations of the National Liberation Movement with the United Nations, the Western powers, the socialist countries and the Afro-Asian nations reveals the extent to which the Liberation Movement has been affected by East-West rivalry.

While the hostility between the two organisations has been exacerbated by the external relationships which they have forged, they are at the same time almost totally dependent upon these external relationships. Hostility between the ANC and PAC, and internal dissension within each organisation, are part of what has been termed the 'exile syndrome'. One aspect of the existential situation of the South African Liberation Movement which has not been adequately addressed is the effect of frustration upon the behaviour of individuals — which in turn affects the performance of the organisations. It is suggested that this is an area which requires attention not only by the Liberation Movement but also by those agencies which are involved in work with liberation movements.

The Failure to Re-establish Structures at Home

Successes Abroad

If the ANC and PAC were not prepared for revolutionary underground activity in South Africa after the banning of the two organisations in 1960, they were even less prepared for the transformation from political organisations with deep roots among the Black masses in the country to pressure groups operating in a highly manipulative external environment. Both organisations had despatched representatives abroad prior to Sharpeville, but their mission was one of public relations and subsidiary to political activity in the country. Gradually, however, public relations and international solidarity superseded the primary function of the National Liberation Movement which was (and still remains) to wage revolutionary armed struggle in South Africa.

After the Sharpeville massacre the representatives abroad of the ANC and PAC formed a united front, but it lasted scarcely two years. The South African United Front collapsed as a result of the mutual hostility and suspicion between the two organisations and the external alliances which they had forged. Reports filtered back to South Africa of the bitter hostility between the ANC and the PAC, and of internecine strife within the individual organisations; occasional deserters would, upon capture (or surrender), testify in court to the 'dog eats dog' life in exile, all of which were given prominence in the White establishment media. Not unnaturally, the reports had the effect of demoralising Blacks in the country while at the same time provoking scepticism about the intentions of the exiles.

The two organisations were active in the 1960s in mobilising world opinion in support of the struggle against apartheid. It is no exaggeration

The Burdens of Exile   51

to say that the National Liberation Movement was successful in keeping the issue of apartheid high on the agenda of the international community and also in isolating the apartheid regime. The year 1960 was the year of Sharpeville: it was also the year of General Assembly Resolution 1514 on the Granting of Independence to Colonial Peoples and Territories. The emerging Afro-Asian nations were strident in their demands for decolonisation. That same year Ethiopia and Liberia instituted legal action against South Africa in the International Court of Justice challenging the legality of Pretoria's mandate over the territory of Namibia.

In succeeding years the Pretoria regime was either expelled or forced to withdraw from a number of international and regional organisations. Pressure from the Afro-Asian members of the Commonwealth forced the withdrawal of Premier Verwoerd's application for membership of the Commonwealth when South Africa became a Republic in 1961.[2] South Africa was forced to withdraw from the International Labour Organisation (ILO), the Committee for Technical Co-operation in Africa (CCTA), the Scientific Council for Africa (CSA) and the Economic Commission for Africa (ECA). Anti-Apartheid Movements emerged in many parts of the world, very many of them under the inspiration of the hundreds of South Africans forced into exile after Sharpeville. In many countries, the ANC and PAC established offices. All these efforts succeeded in keeping the issue of apartheid in the consciousness of the world community, while simultaneously sustaining the pressure for the diplomatic and cultural isolation of the Pretoria regime.[3]

Time, resources and personnel had to be expended on diplomatic work in independent Africa and internationally, (a) to ensure continued support for the National Liberation Movement, and secure material assistance and facilities, and (b) to frustrate the efforts by the Pretoria regime to undermine the National Liberation Movement by improving relations with independent Africa. In 1969 for example, Pretoria embarked upon a policy of 'dialogue' with independent Africa, a policy which received a favourable response from several conservative African states. Both the ANC and the PAC lobbied extensively against Pretoria's 'dialogue' policy. Plans by the Ivory Coast for a summit meeting with Pretoria were defeated at the OAU summit of Heads of State in Addis Ababa in 1971 by progressive African states such as Tanzania, Zambia and Nigeria, which supported the National Liberation Movement. The fact that Pretoria's overtures received a favourable response from a number of African countries (conservative though they might be) meant that the National Liberation Movement could not take for granted its support by independent Africa.

Loss of Contact at Home
Involvement in international solidarity resulted in the National Liberation

52   Introduction to the South African Struggle

Movement being alienated from political developments in South Africa from the mid-1960s into the early 1970s. The Bantustan leaders, together with Coloured and Indian leaders who had opted for participation in the political institutions created by the Pretoria regime became increasingly vocal and were given liberal publicity in the White-owned media.[4] Because such leaders were in positions of influence *created for them* rather than by them, their capacity to mislead the Black masses could not be under-estimated. The impression created by these leaders was reinforced by the regime (through its bannings and harassment of opponents) and by the White institutions such as the media (through their self-imposed censorship of news or information about Black resistance outside the framework of apartheid) was that political activity outside the framework of official policy was illegal.[5]

An argument advanced by the ethnic functionaries of apartheid institutions was that they were using the platforms created by the regime because of the limited immunity they offered from arbitrary restrictions and detention. But the apartheid regime, in its propaganda, used such vociferous criticisms by the Bantustan and other ethnic leaders to demonstrate that there was freedom of speech for 'responsible Blacks' in South Africa.

Bantustan and other leaders were used by the apartheid regime in its efforts to undermine the National Liberation Movement by portraying them as the authentic representatives of the Black masses in South Africa. While the National Liberation Movement argued that armed struggle was the only means to achieve liberation, the Bantustan and other ethnic leaders argued that peaceful solutions and a negotiated settlement of the problems in South Africa were possible. While the National Liberation Movement called for the imposition of mandatory economic sanctions against the Pretoria regime, the Bantustan leaders opposed sanctions on the ground that the Black masses would be hurt most by such measures.

The other major political development in South Africa from which the externally-based Liberation Movement was alienated was the emergence of the Black Consciousness Movement in the late 1960s and early 1970s, which was outlined above.[6]

The absence of any revolutionary structures in the country meant that the National Liberation Movement had no control or influence over these political developments. The ANC, at its conference in Morogoro, Tanzania, in 1969, recognised that political organisation and the establishment of underground machinery in South Africa to facilitate the execution of armed struggle had suffered, firstly by the events leading to the Rivonia trial in 1964 and secondly by the excessive involvement in international mobilisation.[7] Despite the statements of intent to re-orient the activities of the ANC 'homeward', the objective was still difficult to achieve.

Problems of Logistics

The difficulties experienced by the National Liberation Movement have to be appreciated because while there were subjective factors (such as the lack of preparation, lack of security-consciousness and internal dissension) to which the failure to establish an underground in the country can be attributed, there were also objective factors. In the first place, the euphoria ushered in by the 'winds of change' north of the Zambezi in the early 1960s was tempered by political reality. Condemnations of apartheid at conferences and summit meetings are one thing, commitment to action towards the overthrow of White supremacy quite another. South African exiles arriving in many parts of Africa soon discovered that the 'struggles for independence' had been led by bourgeois nationalists whose ambitions were to replace the former colonial masters, and were somewhat lukewarm in their attitude to the struggles in the south.[8]

The OAU seemed prepared to postpone the question of South Africa to some never-never date. The 'Ben Bella strategy' decided upon by the OAU in 1963 envisaged the tackling of the White-ruled territories in the following order: the territories under Portuguese rule (Angola, Guinea-Bissau and Mozambique) followed by Zimbabwe and Namibia and, finally, South Africa. The rationale was that the weakest should be tackled first. But the weakness of this strategy was that it afforded Pretoria sufficient time to build up a massive military capability which enabled that regime to underpin for a time the other two pillars of White supremacy in the sub-continent. Pretoria invested in Angola and Mozambique and deployed troops there to assist the Portuguese. Similarly, Pretoria maintained a military presence in Southern Rhodesia and gradually acquired a status akin to that of a metropolitan power vis-a-vis Salisbury. The apartheid regime eventually became the greatest military power in sub-Saharan Africa, enabling it to threaten and intimidate Black Africa, should the latter harbour freedom-fighters. P.W. Botha, while still Defence Minister, boasted that should Black Africa attempt 'aggression' against Pretoria, then the latter would whip all the African states before breakfast.

The above factors highlight the problems of logistics faced by the National Liberation Movement in the early years of exile. Both the ANC and the PAC realised that the liberation struggle would be a protracted one. The PAC, under the influence of the Chinese, committed itself to a strategy of people's war. But for successful people's war a rear base and supply lines are crucial. South Africa was separated from 'radical' Black Africa by Angola, Mozambique and Rhodesia. Trained freedom-fighters would have to travel thousands of miles, through unfamiliar terrain, in territories controlled by colonial regimes allied to Pretoria.

Despite these difficulties, both the ANC and the PAC attempted to infiltrate trained freedom-fighters into the country. The ANC entered

54 *Introduction to the South African Struggle*

into an alliance with the Zimbabwe African People's Union (ZAPU) and in 1967–68 freedom-fighters from the two movements made abortive attempts to launch armed struggle in Zimbabwe and South Africa. The ANC was adamant that its forces were en route to South Africa. The ANC/ZAPU freedom-fighters engaged Rhodesian and South African forces at Wankie: Pretoria had deployed troops (euphemistically called 'security police') to assist the forces of the Smith regime.

The Wankie debacle was caused by a lack of political work among the Zimbabwean masses who were not prepared to receive the freedom-fighters. Moreover, the ANC freedom-fighters were operating on foreign soil, in conditions with which they were not familiar. ZAPU had also been infiltrated by the Smith regime and some of the guides turned out to be enemy agents. The mobility of the guerrilla forces was impeded by their large numbers and the heavy weapons (more suited for conventional warfare) with which they were armed.

The PAC, not to be outdone by the ANC which it vehemently criticised for the Wankie incursion, in 1968 forged an alliance with the Mozambican splinter group, COREMO, with whose help it attempted to infiltrate freedom-fighters into South Africa through Mozambique. Several hundred miles inside the territory, they were discovered by Portuguese troops. In the ensuing battle several of the freedom-fighters were killed or captured, while several escaped to Zambia.

Apart from the military encounters there were several court cases involving individuals charged with furthering the aims of the ANC and PAC in South Africa; other individuals were charged with recruiting personnel for military training abroad, or of having undergone military training in various countries. In 1969, PAC activists in Graaff-Rienet in the Western Cape and Mount Coke in the Eastern Cape were charged with having co-ordinated their activities and politicised the broad masses under the cloak of religion. In 1970, alleged PAC activists were arrested in the Orange Free State and charged with recruiting people for military training. Alleged activists of the ANC and the Unity Movement were also arrested in the early 1970s and charged under the Terrorism Act. In most cases they were sentenced to long terms of imprisonment. During the early 1970s ANC pamphlets began to appear in Johannesburg and other centres, but it was only in 1975 after the independence of Mozambique that the ANC and PAC attempted to establish structures in the country.

To sum up, in the period after the Rivonia trial in which the top leaders of the ANC were sentenced to life imprisonment, the underground organisations established by the ANC and PAC were smashed. The National Liberation Movement concentrated on international mobilisation at the expense of establishing organisational machinery and networks in the country for the purpose of recruiting cadres for military training, infiltration of freedom-fighters and equipment and setting up

The Burdens of Exile   55

lines of communications as well as caches of arms. While part of the reason for this failure has to be sought in the lack of preparation on the part of the National Liberation Movement which had to transform its external mission from one of public relations to one of being planning headquarters for armed liberation struggle, and in the internal dissension within the Movement, there were objective conditions which made this task difficult.

Within the Liberation Movement there was a recognition that excessive concentration on international mobilisation had retarded the tasks necessary for the launching of revolutionary armed struggle. Early efforts aimed at rectifying the situation met with little success. Favourable conditions for the South African Liberation Movement arose as a result of the changes in the geo-politics of the region following the collapse of the Portuguese empire in Africa and the resultant independence of Mozambique. For the first time, there was a country contiguous to South Africa under the control of a revolutionary government sympathetic to the aspirations of the South African Liberation Movement.

Divisions within the Liberation Movement

Meanwhile, East-West rivalry as well as Sino-Soviet rivalry also affected the Liberation Movement in a variety of ways, not least among them being the intensification of the conflict between the already quarrelsome organisations. Early in their history as exiled organisations, the ANC and PAC forged alliances with other African national liberation movements. The ANC was allied with SWAPO, ZAPU and the movements fighting against Portuguese colonialism, namely, the PAIGC, MPLA and FRELIMO. The PAC was allied with SWAPO, ZANU, COREMO and the FNLA. On the advice of Holden Roberto, leader of the FNLA, the latter grouping, known as the 'Congo Alliance', was granted politico-military facilities and financial assistance by the Adoula regime in the Congo. SWAPO belonged to the two 'rival leagues' of liberation movements because it was the pre-eminent liberation organisation in Namibia. The ANC and the PAC fashioned these alliances not only because of the opportunities presented by these other liberation movements, as for example, the possible infiltration of men and material into South Africa through joint ventures like the ANC/ZAPU incursion into Rhodesia in 1967 and the PAC/COREMO one into Mozambique in 1968, but also because of certain shared affinities. The ANC and allied organisations (with the exception of SWAPO) tended to be multi-racial, with well-educated leaders and militants drawn from the urban elite. The PAC, COREMO and FNLA tended to be uniracial, were less well-educated (except for some of the top leaders) with most of their membership drawn from rural and labour protest

56 *Introduction to the South African Struggle*

experiences. The ANC, SWAPO, PAIGC. MPLA and FRELIMO were endorsed by the Soviet Union as 'authentic' liberation movements; the PAC, ZANU, UNITA and COREMO on the other hand, received Chinese support. Even though ZANU belonged to the 'Congo Alliance' the organisation had many well-educated leaders and militants, which was a noticeable feature throughout the armed struggle for liberation in Zimbabwe.

The National Liberation Movement and the UN

The attention of the UN was drawn to the racial policies of the South African regime from as early as 1946 when the Government of India brought a complaint to the world body regarding the treatment of persons of Indian origin in South Africa. Initially, opinion in the world body was divided between two contradictory principles enshrined in the Charter, namely (i) concern for human rights, and (ii) non-interference in the internal affairs of member states. For many years the argument of the Pretoria regime that discussion of apartheid, as its racial policies came to be known, constituted interference in its internal affairs which was beyond the jurisdiction of the UN was supported by the major Western powers. Following the massacre of unarmed Blacks at Sharpeville in March 1960, however, the Security Council, without objection from the major Western powers, discussed the situation in South Africa. That argument is no longer heard and the apartheid policies of the South African regime have become a permanent item on the agenda of the UN. A permanent committee was appointed by the General Assembly in 1962 to 'monitor developments in South Africa'. That Committee, since known as the Special Committee Against Apartheid, reports directly to the General Assembly.

Since 1974 the national liberation movements recognised by the OAU — that is the ANC and PAC — have been granted observer status by the UN General Assembly. That same year the General Assembly rejected the credentials of the Pretoria regime on the ground that the regime was not representative of the majority of the population. This rejection has been challenged by a number of Western countries through a narrow legal interpretation of the principle of universality.

Observer status entitles the National Liberation Movement to participate in the work of the General Assembly and all its organs, although it does not have the right to vote. Each year during regular sessions of the General Assembly when the question of the 'apartheid policies of the Government of South Africa' is debated, normally over a period of approximately ten to fourteen days, the ANC and PAC are invited to participate and to make statements.

During the regular sessions of the General Assembly a number of agenda items are delegated to various committees. The UN has designated 1985 'International Youth Year'; the questions of activities relating to youth, the role of youth in building peaceful societies and the

The Burdens of Exile 57

preparations being made for 'International Youth Year' have been discussed in the Third Committee. Similarly, the programme of the International Decade for Women, under which women in Southern Africa have been singled out as a special category requiring special measures of assistance to promote equality of women in society as well as enhance the role of women in decision-making, has been discussed in the Third Committee. The Fourth Committee of the General Assembly has discussed 'The Activities of Foreign Economic and Military Interests which Impede Decolonisation'.

Participation by the National Liberation Movement in these committees enables the representatives of the ANC and PAC to make statements on all these issues. The PAC presented statements in 1980 and 1981 in the Third and Fourth Committees on the questions of Youth, Women and Foreign Economic and Military interests in South Africa.

Such activities, however, are only marginally related to the revolutionary goals of the National Liberation Movement. They enable the liberation organisations to provide information on the various issues, including their own policies and programmes, if any. But there is a danger of wasted motion; liberation organisations can be distracted by an excessive involvement in the UN bureaucracy. What is required is for the liberation movements to cultivate skills in determining the amount of time and energy to devote to those activities which are most important for the achievement of the goals of the liberation struggle. The ANC has demonstrated far greater skill in this regard than has the PAC. The ANC does not participate in every meeting within the UN system, but selects those which are of importance to the organisation and to the objectives of the liberation struggle. The PAC, on the other hand, attends even the most insignificant meetings, to compensate for the organisation's lack of a military programme for armed struggle.

The Special Committee Against Apartheid: As a sub-organ of the General Assembly, the Special Committee Against Apartheid meets throughout the year, and also holds meetings to commemorate events which have special significance in the national liberation struggle, such as 21 March (International Day for the Elimination of Racial Discrimination, to coincide with the anniversary of the Sharpeville massacre) and Soweto Day (16 June). The Special Committee also organises conferences and seminars on various aspects of apartheid with a view to heightening public awareness internationally about the inequalities of apartheid, and attempts to mobilise international support for the liberation struggle. Very often the Special Committee co-sponsors conferences and seminars jointly with Anti-Apartheid Movements in various countries or provides financial and material support for conferences which, in the opinion of the Special Committee, genuinely promote the struggle against apartheid.

Problems have arisen where financial and material support have

58   *Introduction to the South African Struggle*

been requested from the Special Committee by Anti-Apartheid groups for conferences or seminars from which certain liberation movements recognised by the OAU have been excluded. Theoretically, the Special Committee is committed to a policy of even-handedness vis-a-vis the ANC and PAC, but it has participated in or been represented in or provided financial support for conferences from which the PAC has been excluded. Because of the hostility between the ANC and PAC, the Special Committee decided in 1979 that it would provide financial and material assistance for conferences which are organised or co-sponsored by the liberation organisations recognised by the OAU, that is, the ANC and PAC, whether or not one of them is excluded from participation in such conferences.

One of the problems is that even within the Special Committee, as in the United Nations, there are a number of countries which recognise and support the ANC exclusively. Consequently, even though theoretically both the ANC and PAC enjoy UN support and have status as observers, in practice the ANC is in a stronger position because of its bilateral relations with a greater number of governments (and parties), particularly of the Eastern Bloc. In this way, the hostility between the ANC and the PAC is fuelled by the competition between them for support within the Special Committee Against Apartheid and within the UN system as a whole.

The UN has, since 1979, provided financial assistance from the regular budget, for the ANC and PAC to maintain offices in New York. This followed a resolution adopted by the OAU Council of Ministers in Nairobi in February of the same year calling upon the UN to provide such assistance.

At the UN the National Liberation Movement also participates in an observer capacity in the meetings of the African Group of countries as well as the Movement of Non-Aligned countries. Within the African Group (which comprises all member states of the OAU), there is a smaller contact group on Southern Africa whose function is to deal specifically with matters relating to the African sub-continent. The role of the National Liberation Movement in this group is an important one: very often the political positions urged by the National Liberation Movement are ultimately adopted by the African Group as a whole. Draft resolutions on Southern Africa, for either the Security Council or the General Assembly, are first discussed in the contact group. Similarly, press statements on various issues such as South Africa's aggression against the People's Republic of Angola, or the 'tilt' in United States policy towards South Africa under Reagan are first hammered out in the contact group.

The Security Council
The Security Council meets from time to time to discuss the situation in

The Burdens of Exile 59

Southern Africa and in South Africa, as for example, following the Soweto uprising of 16 June 1976, when South African policemen fired upon unarmed Black schoolchildren who were demonstrating against forced instruction through the medium of the Afrikaans language. In October 1977, following the murder of the Black Consciousness Movement leader, Steve Biko, by South Africa's security police and the bannings by the Pretoria regime of 18 organisations and two Black-run newspapers, a meeting of the Security Council was convened to discuss the situation. In June 1980 a meeting of the Council was convened once more to consider the deteriorating situation in South Africa following escalating Black resistance, provoked by a boycott of schools by Black students, and police brutality. A resolution condemning the killings by the regime's police was adopted by the Security Council.

Following the conviction and sentencing to death of three ANC freedom-fighters by the Pretoria regime in August 1981, the Security Council, at a meeting convened at the request of the African members of the Council, condemned the death sentences which were handed down by the Supreme Court and called upon the Pretoria regime to exercise clemency.

Unlike in the General Assembly, the National Liberation Movement does not have observer status in the Security Council. Participation of the National Liberation Movement is by invitation of the President of the Security Council to whom one or other African member (usually) addresses a written request.

Repeated efforts of the African nations to persuade the Security Council to adopt measures against the Pretoria regime other than more resolutions of condemnation, have been frustrated by the Western powers who are the major trading partners of the apartheid regime, through the exercise of their right to veto. Attempts to secure the imposition of mandatory economic sanctions under Chapter VII of the UN Charter have been frustrated even though a case can be argued that the continued enforcement of the racial policies of apartheid by the Pretoria regime constitutes a threat to international peace and security. Firstly, through the persistent denial of fundamental human rights to the Black majority in South Africa, the regime has created an explosive situation with ominous consequences for the entire region; secondly, the regime has committed acts of aggression against and violated the territorial integrity of the independent African states in the subcontinent; thirdly, it has persistently flouted resolutions of the UN calling for the abolition of the policy of institutionalised racism as well as the termination of the illegal occupation of Namibia.

In 1977, however, the Security Council adopted Resolution 421 imposing a mandatory arms embargo against the Pretoria regime. Pursuant to the resolution, a sub-committee was established to monitor the arms embargo; although the sub-committee had, by the end of 1981, prepared a report on the implementation of the embargo, it was not debated

60 *Introduction to the South African Struggle*

in the Security Council. No satisfactory explanation was offered for this.

UN Agencies and Their Assistance
A number of UN agencies have programmes of assistance for the non-military activities of the liberation movements recognised by the OAU.

THE United Nations Educational, Scientific and Cultural Organisation (UNESCO): UNESCO provides assistance to the National Liberation Movement on a bilateral basis for projects which have an educational, scientific or cultural content. The agency has encouraged the liberation organisations to establish structured education departments so as to provide academic training and opportunities for students and refugees from South Africa. Institutions established by the National Liberation Movement, such as schools or colleges, receive support from UNESCO. Thus the Solomon Mahlangu Freedom College established by the ANC in Morogoro, Tanzania, is supported by UNESCO; similarly, when the PAC proposed the establishment of an Institute in the Sudan, the project was sponsored by UNESCO .Fellowships are also provided for students upon the recommendation of the National Liberation Movement.

UNESCO has also sponsored seminars for the National Liberation Movement. At the end of 1979, the agency sponsored a month-long seminar on textbook writing at the University of Dar-es-Salaam for all the national liberation movements of Southern Africa. The purpose of the seminar was to train the liberation movements in the preparation and production of their own textbooks. UNESCO also commissions experts to assist the national liberation movements at their request.

World Health Organisation (WHO): WHO has programmes of assistance to the national liberation movement in the field of health. These range from expert advice regarding the health projects of the liberation organisations such as the establishment of clinics to the training of medical personnel. UNESCO, the UNDP, the Tanzanian Government and the Executive Secretariat of the OAU Liberation Committee have established at Morogoro in Tanzania, a health training centre for the national liberation movements of Southern Africa. All the national liberation movements in the region have sent personnel to the centre to be trained as medical assistants who have played an important role in the liberation struggles, attending to the health needs and problems of refugees in the camps as well as freedom-fighters on the battlefield as has been seen during the liberation struggle in Zimbabwe and in the current struggle of the Namibian people led by SWAPO.

The United Nations High Commission for Refugeess (UNHCR): The UNHCR has representatives in the African front-line states who play an

The Burdens of Exile 61

important role in the protection of refugees in the countries of asylum. They provide humanitarian assistance, assist in securing scholarships for refugees and their placement in educational institutions in independent Africa and abroad. Apart from such general assistance the UNHCR has programmes of assistance to the national liberation movement, including the provision of ambulances for use at refugee camps run by the Movement, medical supplies and, in co-operation with the World Food Programme, the provision of food supplies.

Food and Agriculture Organisation (FAO): Since agriculture and related activities are the field of competency of FAO, projects of the national liberation movement related to agriculture and food production (including fisheries and dairy farming) are supported. When the PAC established a transit centre in the Pongwe District of Tanzania, FAO made available the services of experts to conduct soil surveys in order to determine the suitability of the site for crop production.

International Labour Organisation (ILO): The ILO has instituted a programme under which individuals nominated by the National Liberation Movement are placed at institutions in the host countries to undergo vocational training. The programme is aimed at meeting the manpower needs of the national liberation movement during this stage of the liberation struggle and also to plan for the future manpower requirements of South Africa upon the achievement of liberation.

The United Nations Development Programne (UNDP): The UNDP is the funding agency: all the UN agencies which have programmes of assistance to the national liberation movement are financed by the UNDP, which has resident representatives in all the African front-line states. In recent years, as a result of the decline in the contributions from member states, the UNDP has experienced serious financial difficulties.

In December 1981, the UNDP convened a meeting in Dar-es-Salaam, Tanzania, of the UN agencies, the Executive Secretariat of the OAU Liberation Committee, the Tanzanian Government and the national liberation movements, ANC, PAC and SWAPO. The purpose of the meeting was to evaluate programmes of assistance to the national liberation movements so as to facilitate a rationalisation of the available financial resources in terms of the stated priorities of the movements. Greater co-ordination among the UN agencies was another objective.

In all the programmes sponsored by the UN agencies there is no co-operation between the ANC and PAC; instead each of the agencies has had to conclude bilateral agreements with each organisation. Competition between them has resulted in a waste of resources since each organisation has presented grandiose projects to the UN agencies for

62 *Introduction to the South African Struggle*

sponsorship, each of which has required separate funding as well as implementation. In the case of the PAC, plans for the establishment of an Institute in the Sudan were abandoned after UNESCO had financed a feasibility study and had earmarked funds for the project. Similarly, four years after the plans for the establishment of a transit centre in Tanzania were announced by the PAC, no discernible progress had been made in either the construction of the buildings or the development of agriculture and fisheries production. This resulted in a waste of financial resources.

Apart from the programmes of assistance, the UN agencies are mandated by the General Assembly to invite the liberation movements recognised by the OAU to participate as observers in all conferences, seminars and meetings organised by the agencies. Consequently, representatives of the liberation movements spend much time on the conference circuit in various capitals of the world. Very often the conferences have little relevance to the liberation movements; however, they feel compelled to utilise the round-trip air-tickets and the daily subsistence allowances which are provided. To persons having to endure the hardship — and, to many, the monotony — of life in Africa, the attraction of travel to Europe or the United States, and possible shopping is often irresistible. In certain instances, nomination of delegations to conferences is used as political patronage by the leadership in the liberation movement. One of the complaints made by PAC cadres in September 1980 when they demanded the dismissal of the then Administrative Secretary was that individuals who challenged his decisions were threatened with denial or withdrawal of 'the privilege' of attending international conferences.

Representation of the National Liberation Movement at the UN and its support by the UN agencies raises a number of questions. Does this blunt the effectiveness of the National Liberation Movement? The danger does exist that the National Liberation Movement can place too much hope in the UN and the international community whose record on questions of 'peaceful transition to majority rule' in Southern Africa has not been very successful.

In the aftermath of the Sharpeville tragedy the South African National Liberation Movement, probably deceived by the volume and intensity of verbal support for the morality of the cause, believed in the possibility of deliverance by the UN. One of the contentious issues in one of the PAC disputes in the mid-1960s centred around the question of UN intervention in South Africa, apparently urged by one of the factions at the UN conference in Brazil.[9]

Apart from the relief of 'psychic tensions', participation by the National Liberation Movement in the work of the UN and in international conferences has afforded the Movement a high level of visibility as well as legitimacy. The questions of apartheid and White minority rule in South Africa and Namibia have been kept under the international spotlight. As the isolation of the White minority regime in South Africa has increased, the status of the National Liberation Movement has been enhanced, and increasingly in the Third World it has come to be recognised as the legitimate representative of the oppressed majority.

There have also been negative effects of UN assistance on the National Liberation Movement. In the case of the PAC, ever since the decision by the General Assembly in 1979 to provide financial assistance to the ANC and PAC to maintain offices in New York, the position of Observer Representative to the UN has been viewed as a 'plum' post. As a consequence the position has been coveted by numerous individuals; plots and intrigues, smears and slanders, which are the stock-in-trade in the politics of exile, have greatly increased since 1979 and the organisation has experienced endless problems at its Observer Mission to the UN. The ANC and SWAPO have also experienced problems of a similar nature, although not of the same degree as those of the PAC. This phenomenon is partially explicable in terms of the psychology of oppression. To many individuals who have been born and raised in the South African society where Black people are subjected to devastating humiliations in the social, political and economic spheres, it is prestigious to be in the company of diplomats, to socialise with them in the UN delegates' lounge — even if only to gossip. The South African writer Es'kia Mphahlele has described this phenomenon, 'the exile's private world':

> You move in with a sense of belonging, you have an international status. You are being noticed by the international community. Being there makes you a 'legitimate' exile, and exile justifies your being there. Who of your political enemies back home would dare cross that threshold to be graciously received by the ambassador and his wife, and still maintain a normal flow of adrenalin, sail in, and assert a cosmopolitan presence — who?[10]

A number of diplomats remarked to the author about the social habits of PAC members who would sit in the delegates' lounge of the UN until the bar closed, engaging in loud chatter and raucous laughter. While such deportment on the part of individuals representing or associated with the National Liberation Movement certainly creates a poor image, many of the individuals in question earnestly believe that they are 'lobbying'.

The National Liberation Movement and the West
Although many writers on Southern Africa often refer indiscriminately to the 'Western countries', or 'the West', it is important to note that these countries do not represent a monolithic entity. Differences are discernible in their attitudes towards Southern Africa in general, and towards the National Liberation Movement in particular.

64 *Introduction to the South African Struggle*

The major Western powers (Great Britain, the USA, West Germany, France — before the election of a socialist President — and Canada) have traditionally refused to recognise the National Liberation Movement or to provide any support on a bilateral basis. Wars of national liberation which have been endorsed by the Soviet Union or the People's Republic of China, or both, have been regarded as part of a carefully orchestrated communist conspiracy.

Despite their professed abhorrence of the Pretoria regime's racial policies of apartheid, the major Western powers have established a relationship with Pretoria that is anti-revolutionary. Through their supplies of military hardware to the Pretoria regime, the transfer of scientific and industrial technology, the provision of bank loans and credits, as well as direct and indirect investments in the South African economy, the major Western powers have strengthened the industrial-military complex of the regime and its apartheid system.[11]

In considering the operations of the National Liberation Movement in the West, it has to be borne in mind that there are many counter-revolutionary forces ranged against the national liberation movements. These range from well-planned, well-organised, heavily-financed campaigns of disinformation and propaganda aimed at undermining the National Liberation Movement, to sophisticated surveillance and infiltration of the national liberation movements by intelligence agencies. Transnational corporations, Western intelligence agencies and, often, governments constitute a complex network working against the National Liberation Movement.

Western governments often work through proxies in Africa to undermine the National Liberation Movement. Francophone Africa, under pressure from France, was in the forefront of the campaign for 'dialogue' with Pretoria, against the wishes and protestations of the National Liberation Movement. The Ford Administration in the US exerted enormous pressures on African countries against recognition of the MPLA Government in Angola in 1975, actually splitting the OAU. The Reagan Administration, after having expressed its displeasure at the decision of the OAU in 1981 to hold its next summit of Heads of State in Libya because of US antipathy towards Colonel Gaddaffi, actively disrupted two OAU summits in Libya in 1981 by manipulating a number of African countries. The OAU, through the Liberation Committee, remains a principal source of diplomatic, political and material assistance to the National Liberation Movement. Collapse of the OAU would thus deny the National Liberation Movement continental and international recognition and support.

In response to pressures for disinvestment, US corporations have formulated the 'Sullivan principles' to guide the operations of their subsidiaries in South Africa. The 'Sullivan principles' call upon US corporations with investments in South Africa to adopt fair employment practices, provide equal pay for equal work, provide training for

The Burdens of Exile 65

Black employees and encourage trade unionism among Black workers.[12] Similarly, the European Economic Community (EEC) has formulated a 'code of conduct' for British and European corporations operating in South Africa.

Although the major Western powers have refused to recognise the ANC and PAC, or to provide military and economic assistance to them, they have contributed to the UN Trust Fund for Southern Africa, established by the UN to provide assistance for education of refugees from South Africa as well as legal assistance for political prisoners. They also contribute to the budget of the UNDP which funds the non-military programmes of the ANC and PAC.

The Nordic countries (Sweden, Denmark, Norway and Finland), on the other hand, have recognised the national liberation movements from Southern Africa and have provided humanitarian assistance to them. In Sweden, the ANC and SWAPO have official representatives. In Norway, the PAC was represented by Count Pietersen from 1978 to 1980; he was recognised by the Norwegian government as the official representative of the organisation. The governments of these countries provide humanitarian assistance to the liberation movements on a bilateral basis. They also contribute generously to the UN Trust Fund for Southern Africa. In addition, the Nordic countries have been major donors to the International Defence and Aid Fund for Southern Africa which provides legal assistance for defendants in political trials as well as assistance for families and dependents of political prisoners in South Africa and Namibia.

The Swedish Government in 1979 enacted legislation prohibiting new investments by Swedish companies in South Africa. All the Nordic countries participated in an 'International Conference on Sanctions Against South Africa', held in Paris in May 1981, under the auspices of the UN and the OAU.

While the governments of the Nordic countries have adopted policies vis-a-vis the National Liberation Movement which may be termed 'progressive' relative to the major Western powers, there is evidence that East-West rivalry has been a consideration in the attitudes of the Social Democratic Parties in these countries towards the liberation struggle in South Africa. This has emerged from the spy scandal in the largely Scandinavian-sponsored International University Exchange Fund (IUEF). Craig Williamson, a captain in South Africa's security police, had infiltrated the IUEF which, among other things, provided scholarships for South African refugees as well as financial assistance to organisations in South Africa affiliated to the BCM. From documents stolen by Williamson and published in South Africa by the Johannesburg *Sunday Times*, it would appear that the Social Democrats wanted to finance a liberation movement that was anti-Soviet (to counter the ANC) but more dynamic than the PAC which was regarded as being politically unstable.[13] The BCM was chosen as an alternative with the

66 *Introduction to the South African Struggle*

objective of promoting that movement as a 'third force' to the recognised liberation organisations. A combination of lobbying by the ANC, together with the influence of Williamson (by then he claimed ANC/SACP membership, his bona-fides vouched for by ANC leaders when suspicions about him were expressed) resulted in a decision by IUEF in 1978 to recognise the ANC as the 'sole and authentic liberation movement' in South Africa.

The Government of The Netherlands similarly provides humanitarian assistance to the National Liberation Movement on a bilateral basis, contributes generously to the UN programmes from which South African refugees benefit and subsidises the activities of anti-Apartheid groups in The Netherlands. In recent years, The Netherlands Government has enacted legislation requiring visas for South African passport-holders wishing to enter The Netherlands, a measure which has been used to prevent South African sports teams from visiting the country. In addition, the Government in 1981 abrogated a cultural exchange programme between The Netherlands and South Africa.

Certain other middle Western powers like Australia have adopted policies towards South Africa which also differ in tone and substance from those of the major Western powers. The former Australian Prime Minister, Mr. Malcolm Fraser, for instance, was vocal in his condemnation of apartheid. He prohibited the Australian national airline, QANTAS, from flying to South Africa (instead encouraging the airline to explore the possibilities of routes to independent African countries, like Zimbabwe) and actively discouraged Australian sporting contacts with South Africa. During the controversial visit to New Zealand by a South African rugby team in 1981, the Australian Government denied transit facilities to the team. More recently, Mr. Fraser announced a life-long ban on entry to Australia on the West Indian 'rebel' cricketers who toured South Africa. The Labour Party Government of Mr. Bob Hawke invited the ANC and SWAPO to open information offices in Australia.

The World Council of Churches (WCC): A major breakthrough for the national liberation movements of Southern Africa was the decision in 1970 by the WCC to grant financial assistance out of its Programme to Combat Racism (PCR) for the non-military activities of the national liberation movements. As a result, many other non-governmental organisations were challenged to progress beyond moral protest and condemnations of apartheid, to actual support for the liberation struggle. While many non-governmental organisations in Western countries proceeded to support the national liberation movements, the decision provoked a controversy as a result of which many churches criticised the decision on the grounds that the WCC was supporting 'marxist terrorists' in Southern Africa. Some members, like the Salvation Army, disaffiliated from the WCC. The controversy was exploited by the

Pretoria regime, which secretly financed the Christian League of Southern Africa, established to counter the South African Council of Churches (SACC), which had close relations with the WCC.

The decision of the WCC provoked an intense debate within theological circles about the attitude of Christians towards 'violence'. The concept of oppression as 'institutionalised violence' directly related to institutionalised racism owes much to this debate as also does much of the moral justification for armed struggle.

Ever since the decision by the WCC to grant financial assistance to the national liberation movements for humanitarian purposes, the ANC and PAC have been regular beneficiaries of such assistance. The WCC has attempted to provide assistance to the national liberation movements recognised by the OAU. An exception was in 1981 when assistance was granted only to the ANC and SWAPO. Although no official reasons were given for the exclusion of the PAC, various unofficial explanations were offered. One was that a particular PCR staff member had succeeded in convincing the PCR that the internal problems of the PAC were such as to make the organisation unworthy of support. Also, prior to the decision, Gora Ebrahim, the PAC's delegate to the consultations held in Nairobi and Amsterdam, succeeded in antagonising many of the delegates. In Amsterdam, according to one person present, when all Third World delegates called for a 'Black Caucus' to discuss various issues of common concern to them, Ebrahim insisted that the only issue worth discussing was racism in South Africa. Later, PCR personnel would attribute the exclusion of PAC from assistance to Ebrahim's 'arrogance'.

Liberation Support Organisations: Within most Western countries, there have emerged private organisations which support the National Liberation Movement. They argue the collective cause of and serve as publicists for the National Liberation Movement, often challenging the official policies of their governments and the practices of corporations investing in South Africa. They raise funds for the occasional land-rover or ambulance, collect used clothing and medical supplies for use in the refugee and military camps, but in no instance has support from such organisations been crucial or decisive for any National Liberation Movement in Southern Africa.

In many instances these liberation support organisations and anti-Apartheid movements choose between the ANC and PAC. The London-based British Anti-Apartheid Movement supports the ANC to the exclusion of the PAC; similarly the Irish Anti-Apartheid Movement and many others in Continental Europe support only the ANC. To counter such organisations a number of rival organisations have emerged. Thus Azania Solidarity in London is committed to supporting not only the ANC and PAC but also the BCM; Azania Komittee in The

68   *Introduction to the South African Struggle*

Netherlands has adopted a similar policy. Kampfendes Afrika in Switzerland supports the PAC exclusively. In the United States, organisations like the American Committee on Africa (ACOA) have attempted to maintain a policy of even-handedness vis-a-vis the ANC and PAC. The New Zealand Anti-Apartheid Movement, arguably the most effective of all the anti-Apartheid movements in the West, has similarly adopted a position of support for the two internationally-recognised liberation movements. In Australia, the Adelaide-based Campaign Against Racial Exploitation (CARE) supports the ANC, while the Sydney-based Southern Africa Support Campaign (SASC) supports the PAC.

In this way the liberation support organisations and anti-Apartheid movements have not only become embroiled in the feud between the ANC and the PAC, but have themselves been divided by the conflict between the two liberation organisations.

The National Liberation Movement should constantly distinguish between the various Western countries and the policies which they adopt towards the liberation struggle in South Africa and seek to exploit differences in policy which either exist or arise between them. In the same way, distinctions should be made between the people in the Western countries and the governments and corporate interests whose relationships with the Pretoria regime are anti-revolutionary. The National Liberation Movement must realise that governments do not have mandates from all their people for all the policies which they pursue; not all Americans, for example, support the policy of 'constructive engagement' with Pretoria pursued by the Reagan Administration. Such distinctions would enable the National Liberation Movement to build bases of support among the people even in those Western countries which are the major allies of the Pretoria regime.

The National Liberation Movement and the Afro-Asian Countries
Article II of the Charter of the OAU declares one of the objectives of the pan-African organisation to be the elimination of 'all forms of colonialism from Africa'.[14] In this way, the OAU from its inception established the principle of 'collective responsibility' for the liberation of the territories still under colonial and White-minority rule. The 'strategy for liberation' formulated by the OAU at its inauguration had three elements.

The first involved isolating the colonial and White-minority regimes (Portuguese, and Rhodesia and South Africa) by discouraging diplomatic relations and restricting economic and other ties between member states of the OAU and such regimes. The only African country which has openly defied the OAU ban on diplomatic relations is Malawi. Various efforts by Pretoria to break this diplomatic isolation in Africa have failed. Although there are economic and commercial ties with independent African countries, other than those which are Pretoria's immediate neighbours, these are shrouded in secrecy.

The Burdens of Exile 69

The second element involved isolating the colonial and White-minority regimes internationally, by appealing directly to the Western powers and major trading partners of these regimes to support the policy of isolation and by seeking support in various international bodies. As early as 1962, the General Assembly supported the call by African states for economic sanctions against the Pretoria regime. Demands for mandatory economic sanctions have been repeatedly frustrated by the Western powers in the Security Council. Following the unilateral declaration of independence (UDI) by the Smith regime in Rhodesia in 1965, the OAU was instrumental in securing the imposition by the UN the following year of mandatory economic sanctions against the rebel British colony. In 1977, the OAU succeeded in securing the imposition of an arms embargo against the Pretoria regime.

Within the Commonwealth several countries, notably Ghana and Nigeria, supported by other Third World nations, forced the withdrawal by Pretoria in 1961 of its application for membership of the Commonwealth. In the same way, the OAU prevented a settlement by Britain with the Smith regime 'without the approval of all the peoples of Rhodesia'.[15] In 1977, the African members of the Commonwealth, supported by other Third World nations, urged the adoption of the Gleneagles Agreement which obliges member states to discourage sporting links with South Africa. In 1979, the OAU member states within the Commonwealth scored a significant victory in Lusaka, Zambia, when the Commonwealth Heads of State and Government decided that Britain should convene an all-party conference to resolve the problem of Rhodesia. This led to the Lancaster House Conference and ultimately the independence of Zimbabwe under Prime Minister Mugabe following free and fair elections.

The third element in the OAU 'strategy for liberation' entailed supporting the armed struggles for liberation in the Portuguese-ruled territories, Rhodesia, Namibia and South Africa. At its inauguration the OAU established a Co-ordinating Committee for the Liberation of Africa (commonly referred to as the Liberation Committee) in order to channel material and financial assistance to the national liberation movements from these territories.

In addition to the 'strategy for liberation', the Lusaka Manifesto (1969) has guided the OAU in its approach to the problems of Southern Africa, including the question of apartheid in South Africa.[16] The Lusaka Manifesto stresses Africa's preference for peaceful solutions: only if these fail is armed struggle endorsed. That has been the approach of the OAU towards the liberation struggles in the former Portuguese colonies, Zimbabwe, Namibia and South Africa. While the OAU has supported the armed struggle for liberation, it has also co-operated at all times with the rest of the international community in trying to negotiate peaceful solutions to the conflicts in the Southern African region.

National liberation movements aspire for recognition by the OAU

70 *Introduction to the South African Struggle*

because it affords them *legitimacy* as well as access to support from Africa and the rest of the world community. Public and private international organisations tend to provide assistance to those liberation movements recognised by the OAU. Although there are no specific criteria for recognition, the OAU tends to recognise as National Liberation Movements those movements which have opted for armed struggle. Movements which have either ceased to be involved in armed struggle, or which have adopted a policy of collaboration with the enemy have been denied recognition.[17]

Even though a liberation movement may be recognised as such by the OAU, it may still be denied support by individual member states that refuse to recognise such movements. Although the PAC enjoys OAU recognition, it has been banned by the Government of Zambia since 1968 and is not recognised by the Governments of Angola and Mozambique. The PAC therefore lacks diplomatic support as well as facilities in those countries. This greatly affects the ability of the PAC to operate inside South Africa; if facilities were available to the PAC it might be able to infiltrate freedom-fighters into the country. It has also greatly eroded the credibility of the PAC.

Just as the ANC and PAC compete for support and influence internationally, they also do so within the OAU and the Movement of Non-Aligned Countries. Thus far, attempts at reconciling the two movements have not been successful. Instead, supporters of the ANC have been campaigning for the de-recognition of the PAC as a liberation movement by the OAU. These include influential and radical member states like Algeria, Angola, Benin and Mozambique. The more conservative member states like Liberia, Senegal and Sudan have opposed the de-recognition of PAC.

In an attempt to minimise external interference in and manipulation of differences between the liberation movements, the OAU has insisted that all aid to the liberation movements be channelled through the Liberation Committee. This has proven well-nigh impossible to enforce in view of the inadequacy of aid provided by the OAU. The national liberation movements have independently negotiated assistance from friendly countries on a bilateral basis.

The OAU must examine ways and means of enforcing the requirement that all material assistance to the national liberation movements be channelled through the Liberation Committee. This would have to be contingent upon *reforms* within the Liberation Committee, inter alia:

Professional Efficiency: Since assuming the position of Executive Secretary of the Liberation Committee, Brigadier Hashim Mbita has improved the professional efficiency of the Secretariat. A professional soldier, he has been sensitive to the needs of the freedom-fighters. Not only has he been conscientious about the prompt disbursements of

The Burdens of Exile 71

financial allocations to the national liberation movements for administration, publicity and information, but also about the logistical support for the fighters in the field — equipment, transportation and medical supplies.

Despite the improvements which have already been made, more can be done, especially to reduce the administrative budget of the Liberation Committee so more would be available to the liberation movements for prosecution of armed struggle.

Effective Monitoring: The Liberation Committee should assess on a regular basis the revolutionary performance of national liberation movements recognised by the OAU so as to determine whether or not they merit continued support. In the case of the national liberation movements fighting against the Portuguese, the Liberation Committee was able to undertake tours of the liberated zones created by the PAIGC in Guinea-Bissau, FRELIMO in Mozambique and the MPLA in Angola. In the case of the South African National Liberation Movement the Liberation Committee relies almost exclusively on media reports (which are not always accurate) and on reports by the liberation organisations themselves, which often tend to be exaggerated claims of their successes. This partly explains why the PAC, for example, continues to receive financial and material assistance from the Liberation Committee even though it has not infiltrated a single freedom-fighter into South Africa since December 1978. Independent assessments of the revolutionary performance of the South African National Liberation Movement have revealed the growing support for the ANC among the country's Blacks as a result of that organisation's military activities in the country.[18]

Greater efficiency should also be demanded of the National Liberation Movement by the Liberation Committee, particularly in the area of administration. At present, the liberation organisations are not obliged to account to the Liberation Committee for financial allocations received or for material assistance. If a satisfactory system of accountability could be devised it would ensure that the resources placed at the disposal of the national liberation movements are properly utilised, while at the same time offering protection to leaders of the liberation movements against charges of corruption and improper use of resources — frequent sources of conflict within the movements.

National liberation movements are not governments. Often they lack human and physical resources, and operate under various constraints so that stringent standards of administrative performance cannot always be expected of them. However, they do present themselves as alternatives to the ruling authorities in their countries of origin. Their performance therefore should be assessed to determine whether they fulfil their obligations towards their members and people as well as their supporters.

72 *Introduction to the South African Struggle*

The National Liberation Movement and the Socialist Countries
The socialist countries have consistently supported the struggles for national liberation in Southern Africa and have been the principal source of arms for the liberation movements. By far the greatest support has come from the Soviet Union and the People's Republic of China. At the same time other socialist countries — Cuba, the German Democratic Republic, Romania, Yugoslavia and North Korea — have all provided material and financial assistance.[19] This has included military training as well as educational and vocational training.

The Soviet Union has had close relations with the South African Communist Party since the formation of the latter in 1921. Through its alliance with the SACP, the ANC has had access to material and financial support from the Soviet Union which has also provided diplomatic support in international forums and propaganda in its media. Scholarships have been provided for members of the ANC to study in the Soviet Union where they are encouraged to maintain an active interest in the affairs of the organisation.

In 1969 the Soviet-aligned World Peace Council (WPC) and the Afro-Asian People's Solidarity Organisation (A-APSO) organised an International Conference on Southern Africa in Khartoum, Sudan, to which were invited only those Southern African liberation movements endorsed by the Soviet Union, including the ANC and SWAPO. Those liberation movements endorsed by the Chinese, including the PAC and ZANU of Zimbabwe, were excluded from participation. The conference re-affirmed support for the six 'authentic' liberation movements from Southern Africa and adopted a programme aimed at maximising international support for the six.[20]

In 1977 a conference organised by the Afro-Asian People's Solidarity Organisation in Lisbon declared exclusive recognition of and support for the ANC of South Africa, SWAPO of Namibia and the Patriotic Front (in reality ZAPU) of Zimbabwe as the 'sole and authentic liberation movements' from their respective countries. The conference set up a permanent committee — the International Committee Against Racism, Colonialism and Apartheid in Southern Africa (ICSA) — to accelerate the campaign for international support for the three national liberation movements. Working in conjunction with local committees and organisations in a number of countries, ICSA has already organised conferences 'in solidarity with the peoples of Southern Africa' in New York (October 1981), Frankfurt, West Germany (November 1981) and Ottawa, Canada (May 1982). The purpose of the conferences has been to raise material and diplomatic support for the ANC and SWAPO.

The Soviet Union places a premium upon external aid. The People's Republic of China, on the other hand, emphasises the need for self-reliance in the liberation struggle. The Southern African national liberation movements have been drawn into the Sino-Soviet conflict.[21]

The Burdens of Exile 73

As the Sino-Soviet rivalry intensified, it exacerbated the cleavage between the ANC and the PAC, with the ANC being supported by the Soviet Union to the exclusion of the PAC. China, for its part, recognised the PAC as the 'authentic' liberation movement in South Africa. During a tour of ten African countries in December 1982 and January 1983, the Chinese Premier, Zhao Ziyang, met with the leaders of the ANC in Lusaka and called for unity between the ANC and PAC.[22] This reflects not only the Chinese desire for unity — on the lines of the Patriotic Front between ZANU and ZAPU in Zimbabwe — between the ANC and PAC, but also the Chinese policy of not cold-shouldering the liberation movements supported by the Soviet Union. In the same way, although the PAC has been recognised by the Chinese as the 'authentic' liberation movement, the ANC has received much media publicity in China as a result of its increasing military activities in South Africa. On the other hand, the PAC has received little support from the Chinese in recent years: a PAC delegation, led by former Chairman of the Central Committee Vus Make visited Beijing in October 1980 — the first in three years — and was given a cash sum of US$ 20,000. Although Pokela has since visited Beijing, Chinese assistance to the PAC has been considerably scaled down. While the Chinese have not completely ignored the ANC, the Soviet Union has refused to recognise the PAC so that the latter receives neither assistance from the Soviet Union nor publicity in the Soviet media.

The fortunes of the PAC have been affected by the rivalry between the Soviet Union and the People's Republic of China in other ways. Firstly, its diplomatic isolation among the African front-line states is a result of the political alliance among the Southern African liberation movements prior to the independence of Angola, Mozambique and Zimbabwe. The PAC was excluded from the grouping of the 'authentic six'. On the contrary, the PAC found itself lumped with UNITA in Angola and COREMO in Mozambique, movements which were discredited. Since their accession to power as the Governments of Mozambique and Angola, FRELIMO and the MPLA support the ANC to the exclusion of the PAC.

Communist Parties in many countries similarly support either the ANC or PAC, depending on the orientation of such parties, whether pro-Soviet or pro-Chinese. Thus in the USA while the Communist Party–USA supported the ANC, the Communist Party (Marxist–Leninist) supported the PAC. The developments in China following the death of Mao have resulted in the pro-Chinese Communist Parties in many countries being in disarray, with splits and dissolutions as a result of the passionate debates about whether or not China has turned 'revisionist', or whether 'the gang of four' were the 'authentic' leaders of the Chinese revolution. Because many of these 'Maoist' groups supported the PAC, the fortunes of the organisation have been affected also by these political developments. For example, the Communist Party

74 Introduction to the South African Struggle

(Marxist–Leninist) in the USA, which had been a staunch supporter of the PAC, is, to all intents and purposes, defunct.

Revolutionary Models: In addition to military and economic support, the socialist countries have also provided the South African Liberation Movement with revolutionary models. Soviet writers on revolution advance the proposition that 'there are not and cannot be universal forms of struggle suitable in all conditions'.[23] They stress the need to alternate between various forms of struggle, legal and illegal, violent and peaceful. Soviet theorists also emphasise the need for thorough planning and political preparation.[24] Soviet revolutionary theory has had a great influence on the SACP, described as the most orthodox pro-Soviet Party, and thereby indirectly on the ANC with which it has been allied.[25]

The writings of Mao-Tse-Tung and Lin Piao on 'people's war' have been particularly attractive to South African revolutionaries. Mao-Tse-Tung and Lin Piao both emphasise that a revolutionary war is a war of the masses who must be mobilised in support of the guerrillas. Even though the guerrillas face a formidable enemy equipped with superior and sophisticated weaponry, that is no deterrent, since the crucial factor is the extent to which the guerrillas succeed in mobilising the people so that they become full participants in the revolutionary struggle.

Three important additions to Marxism–Leninism by Mao have been identified:

(1) He elevated the struggle against imperialism in the colonial periphery to a level of historical significance in its own right, and not simply a blow struck at the European imperialist powers through the 'weakest link' in the system.

(2) He always insisted that the party build its own army and keep that army exclusively under party control (although he was not opposed to a united front with national non-communist organisations).

(3) [He was] drawn to the necessity of armed struggle and to the fact that guerrilla warfare requires a mobilised and sustaining population behind the guerrilla activists.[26]

So attracted to the teachings of Mao were some of the PAC activists that during the power struggle at the PAC external headquarters in Tanzania in 1977, the leader of one of the factions urged his followers to 'bombard the bourgeois headquarters', by which he meant that the political centre, controlled by the Leballo faction, should be attacked.

Another model whose applicability to the South African situation has been debated by South African freedom-fighters is the Cuban revolution, especially the ideas of Regis Debray.[27] Debray, developing on the theory of Che Guevara, advanced the proposition that the military foci

The Burdens of Exile 75

are the nucleus of the party and not vice versa. The foci need not necessarily wait for the maturation of a revolutionary situation, but can themselves create one by launching attacks on government targets. Such attacks would have a mobilising effect, but initially the foci do not make contact with the peasants for fear of betrayal.[28]

Both the ANC and PAC emphasise the need for political control over the activities of their military wings, to avoid an attitude of militarism towards the liberation struggle which is primarily a political struggle. Both organisations also stress the necessity for mobilisation and involvement of the masses in the liberation struggle since the survival of the guerrilla depends on the extent to which he can be integrated among the masses. In their earlier formulations of strategies for liberation, both the ANC and PAC emphasised the need to mobilise the masses in the countryside and to launch armed struggle in the rural areas first.[29] In recent years, however, the ANC has concentrated predominantly on attacking economic and military installations in the urban areas.[30]

Both the ANC and PAC stress the importance of learning from the experiences of other revolutions, both successful and unsuccessful, while creatively formulating a theory of revolution for South Africa based on their knowledge and experience of the concrete conditions prevailing 'at home'.

To sum up, we have examined the relations of the South African National Liberation Movement with the UN, the West, the Afro-Asian countries and the socialist countries to assess the support received from these quarters and the effects upon the Movement, both of the support and the relationships. Competition between the ANC and PAC for international support has had the effect of worsening the cleavage between the two organisations which have found themselves involved in conflicts not of their making. The ANC has been able to mobilise far greater support and resources in exile than has the PAC, principally as a result of the relationships established with the Soviet Union and the other socialist countries. As a consequence, the PAC has been eclipsed by the ANC in the international arena. The fortunes of the PAC have been further affected adversely by the developments in the People's Republic of China following the death of Mao.

In Southern Africa, the influence of the Chinese suffered a setback when the organisations supported by the Chinese, namely the FNLA and UNITA, were defeated by the MPLA which received Soviet and Cuban backing during the Angolan civil war in 1975–76. The victory of the MPLA in Angola has meant that the ANC has the support of the Governments of Angola and Mozambique. The victory of ZANU-PF in Zimbabwe in the elections in March 1980 was a victory for the Chinese who had endorsed that liberation movement during the liberation struggle. It was also the liberation movement with which the PAC had forged a political alliance. However, the government of Zimbabwe is not

76 *Introduction to the South African Struggle*

in a position to offer the PAC any military facilities in the country.

There is a need for the South African National Liberation Movement to diminish its reliance upon external aid as well as its involvement in international mobilisation. The breadth of international support enjoyed by the South African National Liberation Movement is not matched by its effectiveness, politically and militarily. The challenge confronting the ANC and PAC is to build a base in the country and to mobilise the resources of the broad masses of the people. In this way, external interference in and manipulation of the Liberation Movement would be decreased.

It is suggested that one way in which external interference in the Liberation Movement may be reduced is through a reinforcement by the OAU of the directive that all assistance to the Liberation Movement should be channelled through the Liberation Committee. The enforcement of the directive, however, would necessitate reforms within the Committee, including an improvement in its professional efficiency and the constant assessment of the revolutionary performance of the Liberation Movement. Material and financial assistance from the OAU would also have to be increased since without such an increase the Liberation Movement would be forced to supplement the material and financial assistance from the Organisation through bilateral arrangements with friendly countries.

While the operations of the South African Liberation Movement in a highly manipulative environment explain to a large extent the internal dissension which has plagued the Movement in exile, it has to be borne in mind that exile is an abnormal condition which, by affecting the way individuals behave, affects in turn both the performance and the cohesion of the organisations to which they belong. Displacement aggravates existing emotional and behavioural disorders. One cluster of problems with which the leaders of the liberation organisations have to deal, has been defined as the 'existential'.[31] It is that aspect to which we now turn.

The Pathology of Exile

Exile is an important theme in Black South African literature. Poets and writers have attempted to convey the trauma experienced by Black South Africans who have been displaced from their country.[32] Nat Nakasa, a prominent Black South African journalist living in New York, and Arthur Nortje, a poet studying at Oxford, committed suicide during fits of depression.[33]

Es'kia Mphahlele poignantly captures the frustration of exile in the introduction of his recent novel, *Chirundu*.[34] Here, he explains the reasons for his decision to return to South Africa after twenty years of self-imposed exile, during which he lived in Africa (Nigeria, Kenya and

The Burdens of Exile 77

Zambia), Europe (France) and the United States where he spent several years teaching Black literature at a university in Denver, Colorado. He writes of the frustrations of teaching Black literature in the USA and of not really being accepted in some African countries: 'I had learned enough about Kenya and Zambia to realise that foreign Africans are welcome in only very few African countries'. He describes how in Kenya, South African refugees arriving at Nairobi airport were often despatched on the first available flight out; in some instances, they were given a stay of deportation through ministerial intervention. In Zambia, refugees from South Africa (as well as the other unliberated territories) were detained unless they were affiliated to a recognised liberation movement from their country of origin. One theme which Mphahlele does not develop in *Chirundu* is the fate of two refugees, Chieza from Zimbabwe and Pitso from South Africa, who are in detention resumably because they have not been 'cleared' by their liberation movements.

Critics may argue that Mphahlele is merely justifying his decision to return to South Africa, a decision which some would regard as 'selling out'. However, many South African exiles have had similar experiences in a number of African countries — whether it be difficulty in securing employment, problems with immigration, being made to feel unwelcome or constantly being reminded of being a mere *mkimbisi* (refugee) who should be grateful for the sanctuary which has been offered. There are reasons for many of the measures which independent African countries have enacted.

An example is Tanzania which was one of the first independent African countries to accept refugees from South Africa. Most of these refugees were of urban origin, educated or semi-skilled. However, as the burden increased, the Tanzanian Government insisted that the Liberation Movement — the ANC and PAC — assume responsibility for these refugees: asylum was made contingent upon affiliation to either of these two organisations.[35]

Some of the problems faced by South African refugees and exiles in Africa can be listed: (i) most employment in the public sector is open primarily, if not only, to nationals of the host countries;[36] (ii) some of the newly independent countries are still coping with the problems of illiteracy inherited from the colonial regimes, and have to ensure that their educational programmes first cater for their own nationals;[37] (iii) some of the refugees find themselves in difficulty because the OAU and individual governments such as Tanzania and Zambia have made it a condition of asylum that such refugees be approved by one or other of the exiled political movements from their countries of origin;[38] (iv) some of the African countries fear that the refugees will create a political disturbance and constitute a security problem;[39] (v) many of the refugee settlements are funded by the UN, hence the income is minimal since the host countries have their own economic priorities for their own

78　*Introduction to the South African Struggle*

countries; (vi) with the passage of time many refugees become apathetic, bitter or disillusioned since they are inactive.

It is not only in Africa that South African refugees have experienced problems, but probably what has accentuated the problems is the mistaken belief by many South Africans that they merely have to cross the borders into independent African countries and all doors will be open to them. Very many Black South Africans believe that the world owes them a debt because they are Black and have been oppressed under the system of apartheid, that they are 'victims of apartheid'. In many cases, the goodwill shown and hospitality accorded to South African refugees by many independent African countries have been dissipated as a result of the arrogance of South Africans who regard themselves as being 'better' than other Africans; hence, in the wake of the Soweto revolt of 1976 many of the students who were offered scholarships in various African countries to complete their education, abandoned their studies, demanding to be repatriated to their countries of asylum because they could not eat the food in West Africa.[40] Benjamin Mkapa, the Tanzanian Foreign Minister, often related the story of the Soweto youths who came to Tanzania under the auspices of one of the liberation movements: upon arrival in Dar-es-Salaam, they asked, 'where is the city?'

The problem, however, goes much deeper than mere arrogance. South African refugees, exiles and emigrants have experienced difficulties in adjusting not only in Africa, but also in Australia, North America, Europe and Scandinavia.[41] In recent years, as a result of the emotional and behavioural disorders among Cuban and Indochinese refugees in the USA, much research is being done in the area of *acculturation*, that is, the social environment in which the refugee has to adapt.[42]

Unfortunately, little, if any, research has been done in the field of psychology of the South African refugee and exile. However, by using the findings of clinical researchers on frustration, several types of dysfunctional behaviour can be anticipated.[43] The effects of frustration which have been identified by clinical researchers are: restlessness and tension, aggression and destructiveness, apathy, fantasy, stereotypy and regression.

Restlessness and Tension: When the individual achieves desired goals or stated objectives, the result is satisfaction and calm. Frustration, however, can cause restlessness and tension which may manifest themselves in fidgeting, sullenness and complaining. Within the liberation movement such restlessness may be exhibited by freedom-fighters who, after completion of their military training, are forced to spend long periods of time in either military or refugee camps. The restlessness may be expressed in complaints about the failure, or refusal, of the military commanders or political leaders to provide them with a programme to

The Burdens of Exile 79

return 'home' to fight, or complaints about the alleged high living of their leaders. This, in turn, can cause friction between cadres and leaders, especially where there are no democratic structures and procedures for the discussion and resolution of problems. Very often the frustrations of the cadres, especially those who have to endure the hardships and deprivation of the camps, are exploited by individuals for their personal interests, the chief of which are leadership ambitions.

Aggression and Destructiveness: Frustration may manifest itself in aggression and destructiveness. The aggression may be verbal or physical. In the liberation movement cadres may be involved in brawls among themselves, or in physical clashes with local populations of their host countries. The aggression may be displaced, a common example of which is the practice of 'scapegoating', or blaming innocent victims for one's troubles. Such victims are made the targets of aggression. Very often physical brutality is inflicted upon innocent victims rather than being directed against the real enemy. Or, such aggression may find expression in destruction of the property belonging to the liberation organisation. Alcoholism, drug abuse and other forms of self-destructive behaviour are also forms of displaced aggression. Among South African exiles excessive use of alcohol is common.

Another form of indirect aggression in the liberation movement, particularly, but not necessarily only, in instances where there is strict discipline or where channels do not exist for the airing of grievances is gossiping and griping.[44] Even where the controls within an organisation are not authoritarian, individuals may still gripe about alleged ill-treatment they experience at the hands of their superiors, or gossip in a derogatory manner about their leaders. Probably such forms of indirect aggression serve as a catharsis for individuals who can engage in gossiping and griping with their 'fellow sufferers' who are subjected to the same types of restrictions or discipline. But, there is no doubt that the effects upon such organisations are disruptive.[45]

A very good example of the disruptive effects of such behaviour in the liberation movement is provided by the PAC office in New York. Functionaries would expend an inordinate amount of time gossiping and griping about their former Chief Representative not only among themselves but also to representatives of political organisations and liberation support groups; consequently, very little work was done whenever the Chief Representative was out of the office. The Chief Representative would have to undertake all the tasks in the office, ranging from the production of a journal to routine correspondence.

Apathy: Apathy, withdrawal, indifference, inattentiveness and inactivity are other effects of frustration.[46] In the liberation movement this type of response may occur among individuals who are convinced of the might or invincibility of the enemy, or it may stem from such individuals'

80 Introduction to the South African Struggle

estimation of their own weaknesses. It is not uncommon to find such individuals seeking refuge in alcohol, or seeking solace in the bars of Dar-es-Salaam and hotels in Lusaka or the delegates' lounge of the UN, or writing long plaintive letters home to family and friends, which, when intercepted by the Pretoria regime's security police, provide valuable information not only about such individuals but also about the liberation movement. Such lapses of security can prove costly to a liberation movement. Alternatively, such frustrated individuals may decide to return voluntarily to their country of origin and trade off their information about the liberation movement for their liberty.

Fantasy: Often when an individual is faced with what may appear to be insurmountable problems, he may seek escape in flights of fantasy. Within the liberation movement a common example of fantasy is the individual exaggeration of personal involvement in the liberation struggle. Thus, individuals whose political involvement in their country of origin was peripheral at best, claim to have 'known Mandela personally', to have 'walked with Sobukwe', or to have been 'lieutenants of Steve Biko'. If they cannot be as great as such well-known leaders, then they should at least be identified with them.

One South African attached to one of the liberation movements, claims to have 'saved the Government of President Kaunda' of Zambia in the mid-1960s (without really explaining how); to have launched the Angolan revolution by providing houses in Zambia in turn to the MPLA, FNLA and UNITA (without distinction, it should be noted). Her ultimate revolutionary deed was to 'warn' the Third World of the dangers of Depo-provera in 1980 at the International Women's Conference in Copenhagen, organised by the UN, 'after which the contraceptive was banned by most Third World countries'. Perhaps the saddest part of all is the fact that she actually believes that she has accomplished all these feats.

Another exile, attached to the same liberation organisation, claims to have 'lobbied the UN' to provide financial assistance to the ANC and PAC to maintain offices in New York. Needless to say, he was not at the OAU Council of Ministers in Nairobi in February 1979 when a resolution was adopted calling upon the UN to make such assistance available to the two liberation movements.

A South African exile who has lived in the Ethiopian capital, Addis Ababa, for more than a decade and who has never travelled out of the country during that time, claims to have only recently returned from one or other exotic capital each time that he speaks to his fellow-exiles, even though he must be aware that they do not believe him but humour him by requesting details of his most recent travels. In January 1979, after having met with the author the previous day, he claimed the following morning to have returned that very moment from Moscow where the late President Leonid Brezhnev had personally assured him of the full

The Burdens of Exile 81

support of the Soviet Union in the liberation struggle in South Africa and for the PAC. It is common knowledge, of course, that the Soviet Union neither recognises nor supports the PAC.

Yet another South African exile, living in Geneva, claims credit for the 'reforms' implemented by the Pretoria regime. He alleges that the desegregation of park benches and the other cosmetic changes in South Africa in recent years have been the result of memoranda and personal correspondence which he has directed to P.W. Botha. Following the Lancaster House conference on Zimbabwe, he submitted a lengthy, incoherent memorandum to the Queen of England, copied to P.W. Botha, urging the British Crown to convene a similar conference to resolve the problem of White minority rule in South Africa.

Exiles may also enter into their own fantasy world of dancing, partying, fast cars, constant sexual play and womanising, etc., in order to forget their frustrating circumstances.

Stereotypy: Frustration may result in stereotypy, that is, 'a tendency to blind, repetitive, fixed behaviour'.[47] The ability to solve problems efficiently requires flexibility and the ability to branch out in new directions once the realisation dawns that no progress is being made in the solution of a problem or problems. 'When repeated frustration baffles a person, some of his flexibility appears to be lost, and he stupidly makes the same effort again and again, though experience has shown its futility'.[48] Stereotypy may manifest itself in the blind pursuit of a single strategy which results in the capture or death of guerrillas of the liberation movement by the enemy when repeated failure should cause the authors of the strategy to pause, reflect and re-assess the strategy and tactics. In the Liberation Movement, where the leaders have to deal with environmental, existential and technical problems, innovative and imaginative thinking are required, rather than attempting to deal with the complexities of the liberation struggle on an ad hoc basis or on the basis of expediency.[49]

Regression: Frustration may induce feelings of insecurity which in turn may lead to an individual exhibiting more primitive modes of behaviour, or behaviour which is associated with a younger age.[50] In the abnormal conditions of exile, where an individual or a group of individuals, exhibits such regressive tendencies, such as a need for individual attention or pampering, stress may be placed upon the organisation causing conflict and tension. It can be argued that in the circumstances of exile, greater demands are placed upon the individual to demonstrate independence and maturity in order to ensure adjustment in the new and difficult environment outside of the country of origin.

82 *Introduction to the South African Struggle*

Conclusion

Frustrations of individuals affect the functioning of the organisations to which they belong. Although there has been a realisation among South African exiles of the stresses and strains caused by their displacement, perhaps most eloquently expressed by writers like Mphahlele and poets like Brutus and others, there has been little research on the psychology of the South African exile. The liberation organisations have not yet begun to address themselves to the problem, yet the psychology of exile would help to explain much of the internal dissension which has plagued the Liberation Movement. Addressing the problem would not only assist the Liberation Movement in producing more effective revolutionaries, but would contribute in no small measure to the overall effectiveness of the Liberation Movement.

Psychology alone, however, does not provide a complete explanation for the problems and ineffectiveness of the South African Liberation Movement. Rather the explanation has to be sought in the total environment in which the Liberation Movement operates and the impact that this has had. Operating in a highly manipulative environment has not only exacerbated the cleavages within the liberation movement, but has also increased the dissension within each of the liberation organisations. Exile has had a more devastating impact upon the PAC, which in the two decades and more that it has operated as a movement-in-exile, has been wracked by splits, power struggles and expulsions; it has not been able to mobilise, or sustain, the broad support in exile which the ANC has been able to do. Its role and relevance in the liberation struggle are increasingly questioned as its international isolation becomes more acute. East-West rivalry, Sino-Soviet rivalry and the exile tendencies towards over-dependence and malfunction have had a debilitating effect upon the Liberation Movement as a whole, but on the PAC more particularly.

Apart from taking urgent steps to minimise its dependence on external relationships and aid, the Liberation Movement has to concentrate on establishing both a presence and a political constituency inside the country. Self-reliance has to be translated into a reality if the revolutionary objectives of the Liberation Movement are to be achieved.

Notes

1. This phrase has been taken from Marcum, J., 'The Exile Condition and Revolutionary Effectiveness: Southern African Liberation Movements', in Potholm, C.P. and Dale, R. (eds) 1972, pp. 262–75.
2. See generally, Barber, J. 1973. Also Barratt, J., 'South Africa's Outward Policy: from isolation to dialogue', in Rhoodie, N. (ed) 1970.
3. See Alfred Nzo, 'Ten Years of Armed Struggle, 1961–1971', January

The Burdens of Exile 83

1972, quoted by Stanbridge, R. 'Contemporary African Political Organisations and Movements', in Price, R. and Rosberg, C. (eds) 1980.

4. See Laurence, P. 1976.

5. See Dugard, J., 'Political Options for South Africa and Implications for the West', in Rotberg, R.I. and Barratt, J. (eds) 1981, pp. 17–31.

6. See Schlemmer, L., 'Inkatha and other Black Political Movements', in Price and Rosberg (eds) 1980, p. 101.

7. See Johns, S. 1973.

8. This is a view shared by many of the older South African exiles. See also the essay by Es'kia Mphahlele 1982, pp. 29–48 in which he recalls some of his experiences in Africa in the early 1960s.

9. See Nkoana, M. 1969; and Gibson, R. 1972 for details of earlier power struggles within the PAC. Nkoana puts across the views of the anti-Leballo faction, while Gibson is sympathetic to the Leballo faction.

10. Mphahlele 1982, p. 34.

11. See First, Steele and Gurney 1973.

12. See Schmidt, E., *Decoding Corporation Camouflage: U.S. Business Support for Apartheid* (1980), Institute for Policy Studies, Washington, D.C. for a critique of the 'Sullivan Principles'.

13. See series titled, 'War in the Shadows', *Sunday Times* (Johannesburg), 12, 19 and 26 October 1980.

14. See Tandon, Y., 'The Organisation of African Unity', in Potholm and Dale (eds) 1972, pp. 245–61 for a general analysis; also Legum, C., 'The African Dimension', in Carter, G. and O'Meara, P. (eds) 1982, pp. 122–7.

15. See Legum , in Carter and O'Meara 1982.

16. Ibid., p. 125.

17. Movements which were de-recognised by the OAU include the South West African National Union (SWANU) in Namibia, COREMO in Mozambique, Bishop Muzorewa's UANC and Rev. Sithole's ZANU in Zimbabwe. In South Africa, the Unity Movement (UMSA) and the Black Consciousness Movement are not recognised by the OAU.

18. See Stanbridge, R., in Price and Rosberg 1980.

19. See Albright, D.E., 'The Communist States and Southern Africa', in Carter and O'Meara (eds) 1982, pp. 3–44.

20. The 'authentic six' as they came to be called, were the PAIGC, FRELIMO, MPLA, ZAPU, SWAPO and ANC. See generally Marcum, in Potholm and Dale (eds) 1972, and Johns 1973 for details of the conference and the effects.

21. Marcum, in Potholm and Dale (eds) 1972.

22. See *Africa Now*, February 1983, for a report on the Chinese premier's African tour. The report contains an inaccuracy where it states that the Chinese instructors are presently training 5,000 PAC guerrillas in Tanzania. The PAC has never had such a large number of guerrillas under its command; a liberal estimate of the present number is about 150. Moreover, there are no Chinese instructors providing any training for them in Tanzania. See also Legum 1983, pp. 20–22, for an explanation of the Chinese position on support for the South African Liberation Movement.

23. Leibson, Boris, *Petty-Bourgeois Revolutionism* (1970) Progress Publishers, Moscow, p. 73. Quoted in Johnson, C. 1973.

24. Krason, Y., *Lenin, Revolution and the Third World Today* (1971) Progress Publishers, Moscow, p. 106, quoted in Johnson 1973.

84 *Introduction to the South African Struggle*

25. Lenin's definition of a 'revolutionary situation' is contained in *Left-Wing Communism: an infantile disorder* (n.d.) Foreign Language Publishing House, Moscow, p. 81. On the Soviet influence on the SACP and the ANC, see Callinicos, 1981. See also *Towards Azania: the liberation movements* (1982) ABOSA, New Zealand, p. 14.

26. Johnson, C. 1973, p. 13.

27. See Johns 1973, pp. 281–2.

28. See Johnson 1973, pp. 89–90. Debray's ideas can be found in Debray 1967, pp. 106, 109, 116.

29. See for instance ANC 'Strategy and Tactics', adopted at the Morogoro Conference in 1969; Johns 1973 contains a useful analysis of the document. The PAC strategy is outlined in *The New Road to Revolution* (1975) PAC external mission, Tanzania. The latter publication is, however, an unashamed plagiarism of Mao-tse-Tung, Lin Piao and other Chinese theorists.

30. The ANC refers to these attacks as 'armed propaganda attacks', for an exposition of which see *Moto* (Zimbabwe), February 1983, pp. 23, 26, interview with John M. Makathini, ANC representative to the UN.

31. Marcum in Potholm and Dale 1972.

32. See Mphahlele 1982; also Mphahlele 1971; also Couzens, T. and Patel, E. (eds) 1982, pp. 272–88.

33. See the excellent autobiography of Richard Rive 1981, pp. 113–14 and pp. 126–8, for details of the suicides of the two men. Rive also describes the effects of exile on the state of Black literature in South Africa, listing names of the well-known writers and poets who were forced to leave the country.

34. Mphahlele 1979. The book was first published in South Africa by Ravan Press, Johannesburg, but the South African edition does not have the introduction.

35. Holborn 1975.

36. Hamrell 1967.

37. Ibid.

38. Rubin 1974.

39. Ibid.

40. In 1978–79, as Director of Education in the Central Committee of the PAC, this writer had personal experience of South African refugee students who had been placed in educational institutions in Nigeria, Sierra Leone, Guinea and Liberia. Many of them complained about the food, about the language, about the competence of their instructors and various other things; they demanded to be repatriated to their countries of asylum. To be fair, though, it has to be pointed out that many others persevered and have acquired various qualifications. Another observation made by this writer at that time was that most of the refugees seeking scholarships, expressed as their first preference, to be placed in schools and colleges abroad, with the USA and the UK being top of the list.

41. See Rive 1981, pp. 195–7 for an excellent analysis of the distinction between South African *exiles*, that is, those who have been forced to leave the country, normally as a result of their political activities and concomitant harassment, and *emigrants*, or persons who have left the country legally in search of greener

The Burdens of Exile 85

pastures. He points out that while most exiles have gone abroad to assert their basic humanity and remain almost fanatical in their commitment to the destruction of the apartheid system in South Africa, emigrants in the main have left to entrench their middle-class positions free of colour discrimination and its impediments. He discusses the problems of adjustment experienced by South African emigrants in Canada, Australia and other countries.

42. See Padilla 1980; also Smither 1981.
43. See Janis et al. (eds) 1969, p. 152; Hilgard and Atkinson 1967, p. 590.
44. Janis, et al. 1969, p. 163.
45. Ibid.
46. See Hilgard and Atkinson 1967, p. 590.
47. Hilgard 1967.
48. Ibid.
49. Marcum in Potholm and Dale (eds) 1972.
50. Hilgard 1967; Janis et al 1969.

Part II:
The Crisis in the PAC:
1978–83

4. The Decline of the PAC

In an assessment of the PAC in the mid-seventies, Colin Legum wrote:

> In exile, the PAC ... has declined in strength, largely because a series of splits robbed it of its ablest leaders. Its exile leader [until May 1979 was] Potlako Kitchener Leballo, around whose personality many of the debilitating quarrels have swirled. Although the PAC has flirted with Peking, it has received only token support from the Chinese. It has very few armed guerrillas in its training camps in Tanzania, and its ability to survive in exile is due entirely to the strong support of the ALC which, inexplicably, favours it with funds out of all proportion to the movement's effective strength.[1]

The crises and internal strife within the PAC over the years have weakened the organisation to the point where: (i) it has several scores of militarily-trained cadres in Tanzania where its external headquarters are located (a liberal estimate would be in the region of 150 to 200), *but it has no liberation army*, that is, an organised body of highly-motivated, disciplined, politicised, armed and ideologically-grounded cadres who constitute the vanguard of the revolutionary struggle; (ii) it lacks functional organisational structures and procedures that are revolutionary goal-oriented; (iii) it lacks revolutionary leadership of the calibre of Amilcar Cabral, Samora Machel or Robert Mugabe (and their lieutenants) all of whom led successful armed struggles for liberation, during which they demonstrated profound intellectual, political and organisational ability.

Absorbing the Soweto Youths

South African intelligence sources estimated that of the approximately 4,000 youths who fled the country after the Soweto uprising of 1976, 75% joined the ANC.[2] Of the remainder, many joined the PAC, while others remained aloof from the two movements, attempting instead to form

90   *The Crisis in the PAC: 1978–83*

their own organisations, the Black Consciousness Movement of Azania (BCM-A) and the South African Youth Revolutionary Council (SAYRCO).

Organisationally, the PAC was ill-equipped to cope with the influx of young recruits after the Soweto uprisings for a number of reasons. Firstly, the organisation lacks facilities in countries contiguous to South Africa. This meant that after the youths who had fled the country had remained in Botswana or Lesotho or Swaziland for a considerable length of time, they were sent to Tanzania where, again, they waited for a considerable length of time before being sent for military or academic training. The youths spent almost one year living in over-crowded conditions in cheap hotels in Dar-es-Salaam, because the organisation lacked sufficient accommodation. It was only in late 1977 that the PAC actively pursued the idea of a transit centre which would serve as sanctuary for the mass of people living in Dar-es-Salaam. Boredom and frustration in turn created disciplinary problems for the organisation.

Secondly, the recruits who joined the PAC after the Soweto uprisings of 1976 did so at a time when the organisation was in crisis, when there was a power struggle between two factions in the leadership, one led by P.K. Leballo (and including, inter alia, David Sibeko, Elias Ntloedibe, Vusumzi Make and others) and the other led by Templeton M. Ntantala (and including other military leaders of the organisation). The recruits were thus placed in a position where they had to choose between the two factions. As a consequence, the new recruits were involved in the physical clashes which occurred in Dar-es-Salaam in November–December 1977 between the two factions, as a result of which a number of persons were stabbed and assaulted.

Thirdly, there was an inter-generational conflict between the older exiles, particularly those who had left the country in the early sixties, and the new recruits who tended to be more educated than the older exiles and less amenable to discipline. The older exiles regarded the new recruits as young upstarts (and at worst, 'Soweto stonethrowers') while the younger recruits were contemptuous of the earlier generation of exiles. They regarded them as having 'grown old in exile', or alternatively, of not having been in Soweto and other Black townships when they faced the armed might of South Africa's paramilitary forces. In a sense this was understandable. The new recruits had little idea of the history of the older movements, or appreciation of the difficulties faced by these older movements in exile. They were merely determined that they were not going to spend the rest of their lives in exile.

Moreover, given the fact that the new recruits were mainly former students who had defied the South African police and paramilitary forces, and defied their parents and teachers, they were not going to adopt attitudes of obeisance towards their elders in exile. This was to manifest itself in the remark frequently heard among the young exiles: 'Here, we are all comrades'.

The inter-generational conflict exacerbated the problems in the PAC in 1977; the new recruits complained that the older exiles did not regard them as members of the PAC yet expected them to be prepared to die in the name of the PAC. Leballo accused the Ntantala faction of refusing to integrate the new recruits into the organisation's military leadership and programme so as to utilise their fresh experiences. The Ntantala faction accused Leballo of trying to create a 'private army' out of the new recruits.

Fourthly, after the completion of their military training in various countries, the guerrilla recruits returned to Tanzania where, once more, they spent a considerable length of time in the camp at Ithumbi in southern Tanzania made available by the Tanzanian Government to the PAC. All the members of the organisation who had completed military training (identified in the text as the 'military cadres') were expected to live at the camp located several hundred miles away from Dar-es-Salaam. The lack of facilities in the countries contiguous to South Africa meant that the organisation could not embark upon the infiltration of its freedom-fighters immediately after completion of their military training. The organisation also lacked arms, ammunition and other equipment necessary for the launching of armed struggle. The organisation was, however, able to infiltrate a small number of cadres into the country briefly in 1978, after the Arusha consultative conference. Jimmy Kruger, the former Minister of Justice, referred in a South African Broadcasting Corporation radio programme on 19 November 1978 to two PAC military operations, flamboyantly code-named 'Operation Home-coming' and 'Operation Curtain-raiser'. He announced also that a band of 28 PAC 'terrorists' had been apprehended, five of them in the Transkei.[3] The figure of 28 guerrillas captured was grossly exaggerated; the number infiltrated was considerably less than that. By December 1978, however, the curtain went down on both operations. Thereafter, internal problems completely immobilised the PAC military programme.

PAC Weaknesses

The death of Mangaliso Robert Sobukwe, founder-President of the PAC, of cancer in February 1978 had serious repercussions for the PAC. It removed an influential rallying figure; as long as Sobukwe was alive, the PAC could point to him as a national leader of stature to balance Nelson Mandela. The death of Sobukwe also fuelled an intense power struggle for the succession. These struggles and problems became manifest in the period before and after the consultative conference.

Leadership Instability
During the period between July 1978, when the PAC concluded its

92   The Crisis in the PAC: 1978–83

consultative conference at Arusha in Tanzania, and July 1983, three different persons held the position of Chairman and leader of the organisation; three different individuals held the position of Director of Publicity and Information; and, similarly, the position of Director of Education and Manpower Development was held by three different persons. The organisation has had three different Directors of Finance and four different Administrative Secretaries. Of the thirteen persons who were appointed to the Central Committee at the consultative conference, only two are still in the leadership. The two are Edwin Makoti (Director of Publicity and Information, formerly Secretary for Defence) and Vusumzi Make who, while theoretically still the Deputy Chairman of the PAC, has for intents and purposes, been excluded from the leadership. He was the subject of an investigation by a Commission of Inquiry, appointed in March 1981 following allegations of 'factionalism, cliquism and splittism' against him and three other members of the Central Committee by the rank-and-file members of the organisation living in Dar-es-Salaam and at the transit centre at Pongwe in the Bagamoyo district (members identified in the text as 'untrained cadres' to distinguish them from the 'military cadres'). The findings of the Commission had not, at the time of writing, been disclosed.

Changes in personnel in any organisation are often essential in order to enhance effectiveness by maximising productivity, since it is not uncommon for individuals to be appointed to positions for which they are not suited or qualified. In a national liberation movement this problem is even more pronounced since the movement, more often than not, lacks the machinery to test the quality or competence of its personnel before they are appointed to office. Appointments often depend upon personal allegiances, factional, tribal and regional affiliations, or individual manipulability. In the PAC, elections were held for the first and last time at the inaugural conference, held in Orlando, Johannesburg, in April 1959. Ever since, all office-bearers have either been appointed or co-opted.

Lack of Democracy
With the banning of the PAC by the Pretoria regime in April 1960, the members of the organisation also lost their democratic right to question the performance of the 'leaders'. Since the 'leaders' were not elected by the members, they felt no obligation to account to the members for the actions carried out in the name of the members, or of 'the people at home'. Various 'leaders' have at various times claimed immunity from censure by the members on the ground that they were elected by 'the people at home'. A situation has thus arisen, and has been perpetuated, where a lack of democracy exists within an organisation which, theoretically, is engaged in a struggle for democracy for twenty-four million people.

There is democracy in an organisation when the views and feelings of the members are not merely embodied in the policies but when the leaders take their input into consideration, either in policy-formulation or in decision-making. The concept of democracy implies the power of the members, through peaceful means, to remove their leaders if in the performance of their duties they do not measure up to expectations, or if they violate established policy, or deviate from established procedures. The need for democracy within the revolutionary collective was spelt out by Mao Tse-Tung.[4]

One of the problems faced by the PAC at the present time is precisely one of effecting democratic centralism and promoting a climate of democracy within the organisation which would enable the leadership to harness the enthusiasm of the many disenchanted members in various parts of the world. There is a need for the effective establishment of democratic centralism in the organisation. Democratic centralism refers to the political and ideological processes within an organisation, centralism being first of all a centralisation of *correct ideas*, on the basis of which unity of understanding, policy, planning, command and action are achieved. In the words of Mao Tse-Tung: 'This is called centralised unification'.[5] The Central Committee is the organ which implements, or should implement, *centralised leadership*.

Lack of Organisational Infrastructure

The fact that the PAC was banned barely one year after its formation meant that it had not had the time to consolidate an organisational infrastructure throughout the country, nor been able to develop a tried and tested leadership.[6] In this regard, the history of the ANC was to stand that organisation in better stead in terms of continuity, durability, and stability. Consequently, whereas today the PAC appears to be in disarray, weak and ineffectual, the ANC appears to be stronger, more organised and certainly more effective, both politically and militarily.[7] This superficial comparison says nothing about the ideological strengths and weaknesses of the two national liberation movements, but merely reflects the present objective reality.

In recent years the PAC has not been overtly involved in, nor has it been identified by independent observers, analysts and activists (including individuals and organisations in South Africa) as being part of the mass resistance to White minority domination and exploitation. Eighteen leading activists of the PAC were arrested in South Africa in 1977; sixteen were subsequently sentenced to long terms of imprisonment in 1979 in a marathon political trial, dubbed the 'PAC Bethal 18 Trial', after the small town in the Orange Free State where it was held. (Alfred Mtshali-Mtshali, a Swazi national, was acquitted. Hamilton Zolile Keke was convicted but given a five-year suspended sentence. Keke subsequently fled the country; he was appointed a member of the PAC Central Committee and Chief Representative to the UK in December

94 The Crisis in the PAC: 1978–83

1981 and has served in London since that date.) One state witness testified during the trial that the first defendant, Zeph Mothopeng, the 67 year-old former National Executive Member of the PAC, had informed a meeting in the township of Kagiso in May 1976 that there would be riots, led by students who would burn and destroy government property.

The arrests and subsequent trial were a godsend to the PAC. The exiled organisation launched an international propaganda campaign, using the indictment and the charges against the defendants as evidence of PAC's political presence in South Africa and the efficacy of its 'underground network'.[8] The organisation even claimed credit for the planning of the Soweto uprisings of June 1976.[9] While it is true that members of the PAC, or more accurately, *former members*, since it is a banned organisation in South Africa, were actively involved in various parts of the country prior to the uprisings of 1976, it is certainly not true that the organisation had planned and orchestrated the township revolt. Moreover, given the blatant coaching of state witnesses in political trials in South Africa and the general unreliability of evidence produced in such trials, it smacks of desperation on the part of a national liberation movement to cite such evidence of its underground activities in the country.[10] For the PAC, the implications of the arrests and imprisonment of Mothopeng and others, the effects of its continued influence on political developments in the country, were not analysed.

In April 1983, four persons, including the banned former vice-president of the Media Workers' Association (MWASA), Joe Thloloe, were convicted on charges of possessing PAC literature. Thloloe and another were sentenced to two and a half years' imprisonment each for possessing a single copy of a PAC publication entitled *The New Road to Revolution*. Two others, who had each had boxes of PAC literature, were sentenced to three years' imprisonment each. Considerable pre-publicity was given to the trial in which there were originally nine accused persons. The South African media predicted that it would be a major PAC trial. The PAC, too, geared itself for a major publicity campaign. In a surprise move, however, the state dropped charges against five of the accused and all but one charge against the other four. The PAC carefully pointed out the political affiliations of the nine, in order to 'prove' its links with the organisations still active in South Africa. But the acquittal of the five, among them a prominent Black trade unionist, dashed to pieces the PAC's hopes to make political capital out of the trial. Nevertheless, it was the first major PAC trial since the 'Bethal 18 Trial'.

Since December 1978 not a single militarily-trained freedom-fighter of the PAC has been infiltrated into South Africa, nor has a single one of its freedom-fighters been intercepted by the regime's security forces. The military programme of the organisation was immobilised by the internal problems which plagued it. The Tanzanian Government decided in February 1979 that the PAC would be prohibited from bringing into the country any new recruits until 46 militarily-trained cadres who had been involved in various acts of indiscipline were removed from the country. The organisation failed to find a country or countries prepared to accept them. After being detained at a military camp in Southern Tanzania for several years, the 46 were emphatic that they rejected the PAC leadership. They were subsequently moved to a refugee camp at Tabora. By April 1984 the number of former PAC members living as refugees under the care of UNHCR in Tanzania rose to approximately 70. Of this total, 13 were resettled in Canada by the UNHCR and 13 joined the ANC.

Hostility from Front-line States

Hostility of several front-line states towards the PAC created added difficulties for the organisation. Both Zambia and Angola deny facilities to the PAC. The Governments of both Angola and Mozambique have close relations with the ANC. Gora Ebrahim, a member of the PAC Central Committee, in a newspaper interview in Zimbabwe in August 1983, claimed that his organisation was in the process of normalising relations with Angola and Mozambique and that the Chairman, Nyati Pokela, was going to lead delegations to the two countries before the end of the year.[11] Yet, a few weeks earlier, the delegates of both Angola and Mozambique, threatened to leave the meeting of Southern African information ministers, held in Kadoma, Zimbabwe, if the PAC participated.

Since the arrests and deportation of PAC members in Swaziland in 1978 (engineered by the Leballo faction) the PAC has been excluded from that country. Botswana and Zimbabwe, although recognising both the ANC and PAC as national liberation movements and offering moral and diplomatic support, do not permit South African freedom-fighters to operate from their territories against the White minority regime. In effect, this means that the PAC, with its external headquarters in Tanzania, lacks rear bases and supply lines, which are essential for the launching of armed struggle. Except for a presence in Lesotho, an enclave completely within South Africa, the PAC remains cut off from the people and political developments in South Africa.

Loss of International Support

Within Africa and internationally, the diplomatic isolation of the PAC has increased, while its image and prestige have been seriously tarnished and eroded by the seemingly endemic instability within the organisation and its ineffectiveness on the ground. The continued recognition of the PAC as a national liberation movement by the OAU is under constant threat. At the OAU Council of Ministers in Nairobi in June 1981, a number of delegations, including Nigeria and Zambia, referred to the continuing internal problems of the PAC and called upon the organisation to solve them once and for all. In the resolutions on South Africa, the Council of Ministers singled out the ANC for special commendation for having 'intensified the armed struggle'. At a summit meeting of leaders of the African front-line states, held in Maputo in March 1982, the PAC was not invited — which was not surprising, given the hostility of the Mozambican Government towards the PAC. However, in the communique that was issued in the names of the leaders of the front-line states, no reference was made to the PAC. The communique stated that the leaders of the African front-line states decided:

> to intensify their material and diplomatic support for the liberation movements of SWAPO of Namibia and ANC of South Africa, so that they can intensify the armed struggle for the attainment of national independence for their peoples.[12]

Gora Ebrahim, in a letter to a New York radical newspaper, explained that despite the omission of the PAC in the communique, he had been privately assured by the Foreign Ministers of Tanzania and Zimbabwe that there was no change in the policies of their respective governments vis-a-vis the PAC.[13] That may be so, but, as a journalist subsequently pointed out, it was the public declaration of the leaders of the African front-line states, rather than the private assurances given to individual representatives of the PAC, that was likely to be quoted by observers and analysts of developments in the Southern African liberation struggle.[14] The ANC certainly interpreted the Maputo declaration of the African front-line states as recognition (perhaps exclusive recognition?) of the ANC and SWAPO.[15] What is probably more accurate, however, is that it reflects a recognition by the African front-line states of the primacy of the ANC in the national liberation struggle in South Africa at this stage. In February 1983, the ANC was represented by its President at a meeting of leaders of the front-line states in Harare while the PAC was not represented. The communique issued at the conclusion of the meeting did not refer to the ANC and the PAC but stated that the leaders of the front-line states 'pledged their fullest support to the people of South Africa in their gallant struggle against apartheid and for the creation of a non-racial and democratic state'.[16]

In April 1984 the PAC was again excluded from a meeting of the leaders of the front-line states held in Arusha to discuss the situation in Southern Africa after the Nkomati Accord between Mozambique and South Africa.

The danger for the PAC would be if the position adopted by the leaders of the front-line states in Maputo in March 1982 were to be endorsed by the Heads of State and Government of the OAU. If that were to happen, it would mean the de-recognition of the PAC by the OAU. The collapse of two OAU summits in Tripoli in 1982 prevented any serious scrutiny by the African Heads of State of PAC's continued recognition.

Within the Movement of Non-Aligned Countries, the PAC has faced a similar erosion of its credibility and prestige. A declaration issued by the Co-ordinating Bureau of the Movement of Non-Aligned Countries in 1981 endorsed the resolutions of the OAU Summit and similarly singled out the ANC for special commendation. In 1982, the PAC did not participate in any of the meetings of the Movement of Non-Aligned Countries.

Following a visit to India by ANC President Oliver Tambo early in 1983, it was rumoured that the ANC would apply for full membership of the Movement of Non-Aligned Countries at the Summit in New Delhi in March. Prior to the Summit, the PAC announced that it had applied for full membership of the Movement of Non-Aligned Countries, a move clearly calculated to block the ANC application for membership in the event of such an application being submitted since the Movement only permits one member per country. The New Delhi Summit did not, however, pronounce itself on the separate applications of the ANC and PAC for membership. Prominence was given in the media to the address made by ANC President Oliver Tambo to the Summit. There was no mention of the PAC, even though the leader of the organisation was present in New Delhi.

PAC Crisis of Credibility

At the present time, the PAC faces a crisis of credibility. There is a tendency within the organisation to dwell on the past, glorifying historic achievements while at the same time trying to convince a cynical world that the lack of media coverage of PAC political activity in South Africa is because the organisation is pursuing its programme of 'politicisation and mobilisation of the masses'. The salient issue in the national liberation struggle is the relationship between the externally-based movement and the internal resistance, the Black workers' movement, the mass organisations, the student movement and the community-based organisations. Even though the military programmes of the PAC have been seriously affected by the debilitating internecine strife that the organisation has experienced since the Soweto uprising, it has claimed credit for the escalation in Black mass resistance in the country. In a memorandum to the OAU member states, dated 30 December 1981, the Administrative Secretary, Joe Mkwanazi, claimed that the resistance, including industrial strife, was the result of the implementation by the PAC of the second phase of its programme. The memorandum stated:

In this phase of the programme the PAC leadership is fully in contact with

98 The Crisis in the PAC: 1978–83

the underground movement at home through whom it continues to recruit cadres for military training abroad and to infiltrate those who are already trained and to integrate them, in conjunction with the home leadership, with the activities of the broad masses of the people.

Not surprisingly, an official of the OAU Liberation Committee, in response to such claims of infiltration of PAC freedom-fighters into South Africa, remarked that the PAC could not even infiltrate its publication, *Azania News*, into the country yet expected people to believe that the organisation could infiltrate persons into the country to wage armed struggle. If the PAC had infiltrated freedom-fighters into South Africa at the rate at which its leaders claimed, then the organisation would have had no military cadres left in Tanzania. It was not without good reason that Amilcar Cabral enunciated the principle, 'Claim no victories, tell no lies'.

The PAC can point to a number of former members of the organisation who have risen to prominence in the trade union movement or in the mass organisations which are engaged in overt legal activity in South Africa. But it would not be accurate or true to attribute their roles to a specific PAC programme of action. The late Joseph Mavi, leader of the Johannesburg Black Municipal Workers' Union which, in August 1980, organised a strike involving 10,000 Black municipal workers who were ultimately dismissed by the Johannesburg City Council, rounded up by the police and the majority deported to the Bantustans, was one of the alleged co-conspirators in the PAC 'Bethal 18 Trial'. His trade union activities, however, were not in pursuit of a PAC programme.

The objective reality of the lack of influence over current political developments in the country is one to which the PAC will have to face up if it ever hopes to achieve relevance in those political developments. The organisation will also have to restructure itself totally, including fundamental changes in leadership and, more importantly, in the concepts of leadership and organisation in revolutionary struggle. Otherwise, as the pace of the liberation struggle accelerates in South Africa, the PAC will increasingly become irrelevant and will be a perfect tool for imperialist interests. That danger will be discussed later.

What makes an analysis of the crisis in the PAC imperative is the danger the organisation poses for the liberation struggle in South Africa. The PAC has all the makings of another FNLA or UNITA, that is, a moribund organisation, characterised by personality conflicts and power struggles, ineptitude and corruption, not involved in the liberation struggle and without any programme for armed struggle, yet enjoying recognition as a national liberation movement. It is led by a small core of individuals, concerned merely about *political survival*, and who will accept assistance from *any quarter* in order to survive. The PAC has the capacity to play as reactionary a role in the South African liberation struggle as the FNLA and UNITA did in Angola.

The Decline of the PAC 99

This study enables those genuinely committed to the liberation of South Africa, indeed all of Southern Africa, to examine the PAC on the basis of its actions, rather than on what its leaders say they are doing, or want to do. It is appropriate to begin the study, therefore, with an analysis of the consultative conference, held in June–July 1978.

Notes

1. Legum, n.d., p. 18.
2. Kane-Berman, J. 1979, pp. 144–5.
3. South African Broadcasting Corporation Week-end Newsroom, 19 November 1978.
4. Schram, 1974, p. 164.
5. Ibid.
6. Taped interview with Phillip Kgosana, New York, 8 May 1982. See also in this regard, Karis, Carter and Gerhardt 1977, Vol. III, p. 341.
7. This is a view held by most academic analysts on South Africa.
8. See Sibeko 1978. The booklet was published while the trial was in progress, so that the defendants' plea of not guilty could not be sustained. In addition, one of the accused in the trial, Johnson Nyathi, smuggled out a letter to Sibeko in February 1977 while recuperating in hospital after he had sustained severe physical injuries following attempts by the security police to throw him out of a window at security police headquarters in Johannesburg where he was being interrogated. Sibeko despatched the letter to Gordon Winter, the BOSS spy, with a request that he publicise the charges of torture made by Nyathi in the letter. Winter gave a copy of the letter to BOSS, as a result of which Nyathi faced an additional charge of attempting to escape. This account is given by Winter in Winter 1981, pp. 583–6.
9. PAC memorandum to OAU member states, dated 30 December 1981. See also letter to New York *Guardian*, 25 August 1982 by Gora Ebrahim, PAC Observer Representative to the UN. According to a reliable source, the same claim was made by a member of the PAC delegation to the *International Conference on Women Under Apartheid*, held in Brussels, 13–15 May 1982.
10. See Brooks and Brickhill 1980, p. 137 for further evidence from Bethal 18 trial of PAC involvement in 1976 uprisings. See also Hirson 1979, p. 202, for a critical view of the PAC role.
11. *The Herald*, 22 August 1983. A member of the PAC informed the author in Harare on 23 August 1983 that in response to questions by PAC members in Dar-es-Salaam about similar claims made by Ebahim in another interview, Pokela (the PAC Chairman) claimed that Ebrahim's assertions about a normalisation of relations with Angola and Mozambique were 'a mistake'.
12. Communique of Heads of State and Government of Front-Line States, Maputo, Mozambique, 6–7 March 1982, published by the UN Centre Against Apartheid, New York.
13. Ebrahim, in *The Guardian* (New York), 25 August 1982.
14. James Khatami, 'PAC: A Movement in Disarray', *The Guardian* (New York), 2 September 1982.

15. *Sechaba*, June 1982. The cover carries the caption, 'Front-line States support ANC and SWAPO'.

16. *The Herald*, 21 February 1983.

5. The PAC Consultative Conference, Arusha, 1978

The PAC held a consultative conference in Arusha, Tanzania, from 27 June to 2 July 1978, ostensibly to renew the mandate of the liberation struggle and to review the strategy and tactics as well as combat methods of the revolution. Such a conference was essential, it was argued, in order to reach unanimity over: (i) determination of the targets of the revolution; (ii) formulation of an elaborate programme of action for the recruitment, training and deployment of the forces of the revolution; (iii) a clear articulation of the strategic role of leadership in the struggle; and (iv) the actual fight that has to take place in the implementation of that mandate.

The conference was also supposed to isolate the main contradiction that had arisen within the organisation in respect of the military line that flows from the political line. The two had become incompatible and the military leaders had used squabbling at the personal level to cover up their deviations and limitations, and their positions in the Central Committee to obstruct appropriate investigation and disciplinary action.

Many of the members of the PAC who went to Arusha had gone in the hope that the consultative conference would establish a machinery of accountability and responsibility for the leaders, machinery that the organisation abroad lacked as it functioned over the years on the basis of emergency measures prescribed for internal use but inappropriate for the situation in exile where the members of the organisation can meet freely to discuss matters, resolve problems and devise operational plans.

Origins of the Split

Unknowingly, the majority of the participants at the conference were caught between two opposing factions in a power struggle that had developed in the preceding months. Its origins could be traced back several years, more particularly to 1977 when the infusion of younger

102 The Crisis in the PAC: 1978–83

members who had joined the organisation following the 1976 Soweto uprisings created tensions between young and old. The tensions had resulted in violence, and the splitting of the organisation into two factions — one led by Potlako Kitchener (P.K.) Leballo (then acting President) and the other by Templeton M. (T.M.) Ntantala, then deputy Chairman and Commander-in-Chief of the armed wing of the PAC. Among the members of the Central Committee who belonged to the Leballo faction were David Sibeko, Vus Make, Victor Mayekiso, Elias Ntloedibe, Edwin Makoti, Mogale 'Jimmy' Mokgoatsane and Esrom Mokgakala. In the Ntantala faction were P.Z. Mboko (political commissar), Theo Bidi (chief of staff), Gasson Ndhlovu and others who constituted the military leadership. The split had tribal and regional dimensions also in that the Leballo faction was drawn largely from the Sotho linguistic group from the Transvaal region, while the Ntantala group comprised a majority of Xhosa-speakers from the Transkei and the Cape.

Both factions attempted to deny the tribal-regional dimensions of the power struggle and attempted to advance political and ideological explanations. The Ntantala faction, for example, argued that there was a 'two-line struggle' between Marxists and anti-Marxists, with his group being victimised by the Leballo faction because of their Marxist persuasions. The Leballo faction argued that the problems had arisen when the young cadres who had joined the PAC after the Soweto uprisings expressed their lack of confidence in the organisation's military leaders whom they accused of cowardice and a failure to implement an effective military programme.

Ntantala argued that the PAC Central Committee had adopted Marxism–Leninism–Mao-Tse-Tung thought and, through its adoption of the document *The New Road to Revolution*, had transformed the PAC into a Marxist–Leninist Party. In pursuit of this argument, Ntantala's faction rejected the idea that the new recruits who joined the PAC after the 1976 uprisings were members of the PAC. They were merely members of the military wing of the PAC, the Azanian People's Liberation Army (APLA). This seemed to place the PAC in the same category as communist parties, such as those of the People's Republic of China and the Soviet Union, where membership of the Party and the Army are not synonymous.

Leballo and his faction argued that the members of APLA had sworn an oath of allegiance to the PAC. Consequently, they had rights and duties as members of the PAC.

At the beginning of 1978 the Tanzanian Government appointed a reconciliation committee, under the chairmanship of the principal secretary in the Ministry of Foreign Affairs, Mr. Nyaki, to mediate between the two factions. Right up until the time of the consultative conference, the reconciliation committee was seized of the matter. Both factions had to agree on the list of conference participants. Since numbers would be crucial to the outcome, each faction tried to ensure participation by the maximum number of its supporters — or neutral persons. For almost two days after the opening session of the conference, the reconciliation committee attempted to resolve a dispute that had threatened to cancel the conference. Both factions objected strenuously to the participation in the conference by a number of persons alleged not to be bona-fide members of the PAC. Among those who were excluded were individuals who had been sent as delegates by the PAC branches in their countries of exile.

The atmosphere was extremely tense in Arusha. A large Tanzanian military contingent was assigned to maintain the peace and to prevent any possible physical clashes between the two opposing groups. Throughout the proceedings of the conference, representatives from the OAU Liberation Committee, the ruling party in Tanzania, Chama Cha Mapinduzi, and representatives of the diplomatic corps were present.

'Two-line Struggle' or Ethno-regional Struggle?

The conference was characterised by acrimonious debate, with accusations, counter-accusations, charges and counter-charges levelled. For many conference participants, like the present writer, who had no knowledge of the history of the antagonisms, decisions had to be made on the basis of what was presented there. With hindsight, one could argue that, if the entire history of the PAC abroad during the previous eighteen years had been known by the rank-and-file members, then the decisions that were taken at the consultative conference would not have been supported by the majority of the participants, whose sole interest was in the emergence of a strong, viable organisation. For example, this writer fully supported the motion for the expulsion of the military leaders of the organisation on the basis of the evidence provided of their activities in promoting factionalism, regionalism and tribalism. Numerous delegates, principally from the military wing of the PAC, testified that the military leaders within the Central Committee questioned them closely as to their 'tribal' and regional background; those who were 'Xhosas' were recruited into the faction, especially if they had originally come from the Cape or the Transkei.

The military leaders did not refute any of the allegations levelled against them. In his four-hour speech their spokesperson, T.M. Ntantala, did not address himself to these charges. Throughout the debate and argument that followed the political report presented by Leballo, there was no evidence of a 'two-line struggle' between 'Marxists and anti-Marxists'. It was clear that Marxist rhetoric was simply used to camouflage activities that were contrary to the basic tenets of the National Liberation Movement. Tribalism, on which the South African regime has based its Bantustan policy, was revived by the regime

104 *The Crisis in the PAC: 1978–83*

because of the threat posed to White minority domination by the unity of the oppressed masses.[1] The founders of the ANC were similarly aware of the divisive nature of tribalism. The Congress Youth League (CYL) had advocated the adoption of 'African Nationalism' by the national organisation — which it did at its annual congress in 1949. Yet in 1978, the leaders of a national liberation movement were promoting tribalism once more.

In considering the power struggle between the two factions, which also had tribal connotations, the historical rivalry between the 'Reef' and the 'Cape' in Black political activity in South Africa cannot be ignored. Gerhardt has explained the regional variations in Black politics in South Africa by pointing out that Johannesburg has traditionally been the headquarters of the ANC, but the Eastern Cape has been the region where political consciousness at the mass level was highest in the fifties, and where the greatest support for the ANC's political campaigns was registered.[2] Gerhardt goes on to explain that the politically-conscious Africans on the Reef looked down upon the Africans in the Eastern Cape as being 'conservative', meaning that they were moderate or cautious, while the Africans from the Eastern Cape responded to such attitudes with criticisms of parochialism on the part of the Transvaal in the planning of national political campaigns.[3]

After the formation of the PAC, the organisation enjoyed much support in the Western Cape where it succeeded in organising the migrant workers, many of whom had come from the Transkei and Ciskei in the Eastern Cape.[4] The rivalry between the two regions , the 'Reef' and the 'Cape', continued even after the establishment of a mission in exile. As will be explained in a later section, this ethno-regional conflict was a contributory factor in the collapse of PAC's 'Operation Tape-recorder', a joint politico-military venture with the FNLA in the Congo in 1963.

Arrests of PAC Members in Swaziland

Ntantala failed also to explain to the delegates at the consultative conference the circumstances surrounding the detentions of the PAC representative in Swaziland, Joe Mkwanazi, his assistant, Joe Moabi, and other members of the organisation resident in that country. Yet, he had been in contact with them as well as with others in Swaziland. When David Sibeko challenged him in the meeting by stating that Mkwanazi and others had been arrested by the Swaziland authorities for allegedly supporting and providing military training for a faction which was opposed to the King, Ntantala did not refute the allegation.

The truth of the matter, as this writer established a few months later, was that Mkwanazi and those detained in Swaziland (and subsequently deported) were the victims of the power struggle between the Leballo and Ntantala factions. Their detentions were engineered by the Leballo faction which believed that the people in Swaziland, arguably the most viable and active unit of the PAC, who maintained close contact with activists inside the country and who had been responsible for the larger proportion of the recruitment of young people after the Soweto uprisings, supported the Ntantala faction.

In April 1978, Leballo and David Sibeko visited Swaziland. In the presence of the Swaziland authorities at a meeting in Siteki, Leballo accused Mkwanazi and Moabi of active collaboration with a faction that was opposed to the King. Leballo made the accusations; Sibeko was present but remained silent. Leballo denied that a small quantity of arms or ammunition which had been procured by the Swaziland unit belonged to the PAC, even when asked three times and even when he was assured that if he indicated that the arms belonged to the PAC they would be released to the organisation. Had Leballo acknowledged PAC ownership of the arms and ammunition, then perhaps the Swaziland authorities would not have taken action against the members of the organisation.

Immediately after that meeting in Siteki, Joe Mkwanazi and Joe Moabi were taken into custody by the Swaziland police. Sibeko wept; he told Mkwanazi that they (Mkwanazi and others) were the victims of something that they did not understand and promised to assist in finding countries which would be prepared to grant them sanctuary as refugees. The other members of the PAC resident in Swaziland were detained pending deportation.

The effect of the arrests and subsequent deportation of Mkwanazi and others was that the PAC was excluded from Swaziland; since that time the organisation has been without representation in that country. Attempts to normalise relations with the government of Swaziland thus far have been unsuccessful.

The human tragedy of the arrest and deportation of the PAC members was devastating. Families who had fled the repression of apartheid and who had found sanctuary in Swaziland were uprooted once more. They had to start afresh in distant foreign lands — England, Denmark, Canada. Several of them spent several months in a refugee transit camp in Greece. Their travail was visited upon them by the leaders of their own organisation. Throughout the history of the PAC in exile the leaders have not hesitated to use the state power of host countries against their own members. Each crisis, each power struggle, has thrown up its own crop of victims, people who have been detained, declared prohibited immigrants or deported. They are today to be found scattered throughout the world.

The truth of what actually happened in Swaziland was known to both factions who were involved in the power struggle at the consultative conference, as well as to Mkwanazi, Joe Moabi, Dan Mdluli, Gilbert Sifuba, Pitika Ntuli and others. All of the latter, however, were in prison in

106 *The Crisis in the PAC: 1978–83*

Swaziland. The majority of the delegates had no idea of the events that led to their arrest. This writer, although doubtful of the allegations against them since most of them were well-known to him, was also unaware. The full details of the detentions were revealed to this writer during a visit to Swaziland in November 1978, and subsequently during discussions with the victims themselves.

Background to the Leballo/Ntantala Power Struggle

What has become very clear is that the PAC consultative conference, rather than providing the members of the organisation the opportunity to sum up experiences of the years in exile and to chart a new course for the future conduct of its work, was an act of political axe-grinding. The members had been summoned to join in settling scores which had their origins in events concerning which the majority of the conference participants were ignorant. To this writer, the deep personal enmities and the webs of conspiracies only became clear long after the consultative conference.

While still PAC's chief representative to West Africa, based in Monrovia, Liberia, Vus Make wrote to David Sibeko who was based in New York as the PAC observer representative to the UN:

> I have just received communication from Gqobs giving all kinds of directives on the control of finances. I will be pleased to learn your comments. It would seem to me that there is the usual attempt to tie P.K.'s hands. Unless they have changed they will use this procedure to make sure that only those operations which enhance their positions are financed.
>
> I was very disturbed lately, during the visit here by Putuse Appolus, that they are still fomenting their Xhosa moves to oust P.K. She indicated that she was in Dar and she learnt that they are trying to 'put P.K. under control'. It would seem that they are still communicating with the Makiwanes as part of this strategy. The people she mentioned by name were Gqobs and T.M., together with Mgweba. Is there no end to this stupidity? It is clear that 'Grays' still have a lot of work to do. How is the London situation? I hope their man there has been contained. You must, of course, have seen the latest from Bolofo concerning the name Azania. Even the latest issue of *Africa* has given respectability to that garbage. I hope that Makoti will deal with this situation and expose Bolofo and his Mhlongos and Mngazas.[5]

It was, therefore, no coincidence that Make, Sibeko, Makoti and Leballo were ranged against the persons named in the letter quoted above.

The alliances, of course, were not based on any principles. For example, David Sibeko and Victor Mayekiso, although personally antagonistic to each other, supported Leballo against Ntantala. Each would nevertheless try to jockey for influence with Leballo who, in turn, exploited the situation to his own advantage. A communication to David Sibeko from Victor Mayekiso on 21 April 1976 is instructive. The letter concerned a 'Research Centre' which the PAC proposed to establish, with the support of the late President Tolbert of Liberia. The letter demonstrates very clearly the bitter disagreement between Mayekiso and Sibeko over the control of the Centre. Mayekiso writes:

> As to the personnel of the Board, we had discussed it earlier in Tripoli with P.K. and later mentioned it to you;[6] Dick Gibson, Ras Makonnen, an appointee of the Liberian President, yourself and myself. P.K., who suggested some of the names, particularly emphasised that his name should not appear as it may militate against the setting up of the Board that [sic] should have a semblance of independence . . .
>
> The suggestions that I made as to the drawing up of the Articles were to accommodate your fears and were still not even final yet until, in your presence, they are ratified . . .
>
> It is obvious that if the Centre is going to serve the revolution it has to be a co-ordinated effort of various departments. Apparently, you have long come to your decision alone and will not be deterred by collective effort but would rather have a Centre which is your private domain.[7]

Mayekiso goes on not only to attack bitterly Sibeko's conception of the proposed Centre, but to accuse Sibeko of being no different from the Ntantala group in Dar-es-Salaam which had been pursuing its own programme:

> In my letter from Nairobi telling you about the arrangements for the two cadres Travel Documents I mentioned that Gqobs and T.M. went to Addis for a camp and funds but failed on both counts. This they kept to their vests but Ellie [Elias Ntloedibe], whom I met in Nairobi attending the U.N. Environment thing, told me. How different is your position from that of the fellows in Dar who also have their own private things going?
>
> I would like to mention again that this Centre has nothing personal for me but there has to be a serious effort concerning the cadres, what they have to study, what equipment they need in relation to what South Africa has and is doing. The question ᴗf mass involvement is a highly relevant question. How will they be mobilised through their various institutions or those to be created? A Centre under [the Department of] Foreign Affairs only can satisfy the needs of conferences and will end up being an exclusive club of the elite which has nothing to do with the masses and the struggle on the home-front.

108 The Crisis in the PAC: 1978–83

Mayekiso then returns to the 'private doings' of Sibeko to which he made reference earlier:

> I noticed that you also have [sic] your own private doings when you had the discussions with the Churchman out there and particularly asked that I should absent myself even over my protestations. Even thereafter you kept mum about it. We try as much as possible to channel funds to the project while Dar tries as much as it can to do its own private thing. *Perhaps you cannot mention what the cheque was because that is private.* I am caught at the cross-roads of individual privacies.

Apart from demonstrating the fact that even within the Leballo faction, there were personal contradictions, jealousies and power struggles among his inner circle, the letter also sheds light on the divisions which were playing themselves out as far back as early 1976. Each faction tried to strengthen its position. Appointments of representatives, the co-optation of members to the Central Committee, the projects initiated and programmes pursued have to be seen in this light. Leballo, Sibeko, Mayekiso and Make were determined to pursue their own military training programme, independent of the military leadership under Ntantala. Victor Mayekiso and David Sibeko had been close associates ever since the latter had been chairman of the Transvaal region of the PAC in the early 1960s. Ten years later, Mayekiso was co-opted to the Central Committee to bolster the Leballo-Sibeko faction in its struggle with the Ntantala faction. As representative in the Middle East, based first in Cairo and then in Tripoli, he was in a strategic position to negotiate financial and military assistance for the PAC from various quarters in that region, including the Libyan government.

When the Libyan government offered to provide military training for PAC cadres, Leballo and his lieutenants initially concealed the offer from the military leaders of the organisation. For this reason, the first recruits sent to Libya for military training by the PAC were not PAC cadres, but members of the Basutoland Congress Party (BCP), led by Ntsu Mokhehle, who was a close associate of Leballo. This was to create serious difficulties for the PAC in the OAU where the Lesotho government threatened to expose the PAC for interfering in the internal affairs of a member state. Make and others later denied any knowledge of the arrangement, claiming that it had been one of Leballo's unilateral actions in the course of which he betrayed the faith of both the Libyan government and his colleagues in the Central Committee. Leballo's inner circle knew of the arrangements, so did the Ntantala faction. Upon completion of their military training, the BCP cadres shared a camp with the PAC military cadres in Ithumbi, Tanzania, until early 1980 when the last of them were evacuated.

Vus Make, who was also co-opted to the Central Committee and appointed Director of Pan-African Affairs (a post which was specifically revived for him) in the mid-seventies, was appointed because of his influential position in Liberia where he served as a political adviser on Southern Africa to President Tolbert. Because of this position, Make was able to secure substantial assistance for the PAC from the Liberian Government which also provided diplomatic support in the OAU and other international forums. Tolbert was attempting to atone for his 'sins' (in the eyes of radical African governments opposed to any form of dialogue with the South African regime) by offering the PAC financial and material assistance. Make, who was previously at odds with Leballo, was brought back into the fold. Thereafter, he was appointed to various leadership positions and, together with David Sibeko, became one of the pillars of the Leballo faction.

The Ntantala faction, for its own part, was also determined to match the scheming and manoeuvring of the Leballo faction. This it sought to do by placing stringent controls on the use of funds by Leballo and others, a measure which it could enforce since the acting Treasurer-General was Mfanayasekaya Pearce Gqobose (referred to as 'Gqobs' in correspondence between Make and Sibeko and between Mayekiso and Sibeko). At the same time, they attempted to make their own representations to various governments for financial and material assistance, hence the mission to Ethiopia by Ntantala and Gqobose to request military training facilities and financial assistance, which, according to the letter to David Sibeko from Victor Mayekiso, was not successful. Temba Lawrence Mgweba visited Nigeria, but according to a report submitted to Leballo by David Sibeko on 4 September 1976 following a visit to that country by Sibeko, Make and Elizabeth Sibeko, he succeeded only in annoying the officials he met. Sibeko stated in his report:

> 10. The only stain on the excellent rapport between PAC and Nigeria are Mgweba's activities. Quietly but firmly the Director of the Africa Division of the Ministry of External Affairs told the Director of Foreign Affairs of the PAC that his country is not amused by such antics. He made the following points:
> (i) Mgweba had descended on Lagos without proper arrangements and this had embarrassed his Ministry (especially himself as a long-standing supporter of the PAC from his days in the U.N. Secretariat when he fought against Reddy's sectarian bias in favour of the ANC).
> (ii) 'The Man', in Blankson's own words, 'came without a scrap of paper from either Comrade Leballo, the Chairman of your Central Committee, or from you, the Director of Foreign Affairs'.
> (iii) He stressed that continuity is of the essence with Nigeria in its dealings with liberation movements, meaning that proper procedures in the delegation of responsibilities must be followed if PAC expects to be taken seriously.
> (iv) Mgweba had rambled on in his interviews with the Director's subordinates and the transcript thereof left him wondering if the man had PAC's mandate at all.

110   *The Crisis in the PAC: 1978–83*

(v) This was compounded by impertinent cables offending to the Nigerian Government and Head of State.[8]

There is no reason to doubt the accuracy of Sibeko's report, since Mgweba had a history of such behaviour. According to a former PAC activist, he and Mgweba were part of a group of PAC members who were severely censured by the Nigerians in 1963 following offensive telephone messages conveyed to the former Nigerian Foreign Minister, Jaja Wachuku, by Mgweba demanding that a limousine be sent to transport the group from a Nigerian border post where they were stranded following a dispute among the PAC members in Accra.[9] In June 1981, Mgweba, in his capacity as Director of Finance in the Central Committee, acted in exactly the same manner as that complained of by Sibeko in his report. At two OAU meetings he button-holed delegates, requesting financial assistance for the PAC; at the OAU Ministerial Council in Nairobi, for instance, he even made such a request to the Mozambican Foreign Minister after the latter had left the conference hall where he had just bitterly attacked the PAC. Sibeko's report demonstrates that while each faction attempted to enhance its own position, the PAC was harmed.

The harm that was done to the PAC in the period leading up to the consultative conference would be seen in the area of solidarity work internationally. Each faction attempted to capture a section of the international liberation support movement; in the process, each faction tried to discredit the other in the eyes of supporters of the national liberation struggle. The Ntantala faction succeeded in convincing a number of organisations in West Germany that they were the 'progressive forces' in the PAC while the Leballo faction was 'reactionary', comprising as it did 'personally ambitious' and 'petit-bourgeois' elements like Sibeko who were determined to crush the 'communist spectre in the PAC'. In this way, supporters of the national liberation struggle were encouraged to take sides and interfere in the internal affairs of the organisation.

The Ntantala faction, however, lacked the broad contacts which had been built up by the Leballo faction, largely as a result of the latter's control of the strategic Department of Foreign Affairs through which they were able to appoint their supporters to crucial positions and to monopolise the PAC delegations to international conferences (where valuable contacts were made) as well as missions to various countries in quest for material, financial, military and political support. In this regard, David Sibeko, in his capacity as Director of Foreign Affairs, recommended the appointment of Winston Mvusi as representative to the United Kingdom and Continental Europe, to replace Vuyani Mngaza who was regarded as a Ntantala supporter. But, Mngaza had incurred Sibeko's wrath for another reason, namely, that when he took up the position of representative to the UK to succeed Sibeko who had been appointed Observer Representative to the UN, he discovered that there had been financial mismanagement on the part of his predecessor. He carefully prepared a dossier which he despatched to the PAC headquarters in Dar-es-Salaam. The dossier, however, was removed by Elias Ntloedibe, then the Administrative Secretary based at the organisation's headquarters. Ntloedibe despatched the dossier to Sibeko in New York, thereby earning the undying gratitude and eternal support of Sibeko. Thereafter, Sibeko did not criticise Ntloedibe's political actions or performance, even when Ntloedibe was the organisation's representative in Botswana where his performance drew criticism from the members of the PAC as well as the authorities in that country, nor ever censured him.

Mvusi was subsequently removed as representative and replaced by Ngila Michael Muendane, formerly representative to Egypt. Muendane proved himself to be a trusted supporter of Sibeko.

When the military government of the Federal Republic of Nigeria, under the leadership of the late General Murtala Mohammed and General Olusegun Obasanjo, committed themselves to an active role in the national liberation struggles in Southern Africa, supporting the liberation movements from Zimbabwe, Namibia and South Africa materially, financially and diplomatically, the Leballo faction strove to consolidate its position in that country. A number of delegations of the Central Committee, personally led by P.K. Leballo, visited Lagos in 1976, to apprise the Nigerian government of political developments in South Africa, particularly after the Soweto uprisings, and to outline the requirements of the PAC to enable the organisation to perform its tasks in the country. One such delegation, led by Leballo and including David Sibeko, Vus Make and T.M. Ntantala, visited Lagos in October 1976. The delegation submitted a memorandum containing requests for material and financial support. On 12 October 1976, Leballo and Sibeko wrote to the Permanent Secretary (Political) in the Cabinet Office informing him of the appointment of Vus Make as Chief Representative to the Federal Republic of Nigeria.

Through the appointment of Make as representative based in Nigeria, the Leballo faction created a fairly strong network, controlling the following points: the UN and North America (David Sibeko), the UK and Continental Europe (Ngila Muendane), the Middle East (Victor Mayekiso), West Africa (Vus Make). In East Africa, they could count on the allegiance of the representatives to Idi Amin's Uganda (Benedict Sondlo) and Tanzania (Moses Dhlamini). At the PAC headquarters in Dar-es-Salaam, individual members of the Central Committee like Elias Ntloedibe and, later, Mogale 'Jimmy' Mokgoatsane (appointed Director of Education and Manpower Development upon the recommendation of David Sibeko) also supported them. Through their control of these various centres, the Leballo/Sibeko faction controlled the PAC's access to financial assistance from and politico-military facilities in those countries that supported the organisation. In their struggle with

112 *The Crisis in the PAC: 1978–83*

the Ntantala faction, they denied the latter access to such financial and material assistance, without which the military leadership was immobilised.

The Ntantala faction attempted to challenge the dominance of the Leballo/Sibeko faction by despatching their own delegations to a number of countries in quest of financial and material assistance. They also appointed their own supporters in different centres to undertake diplomatic work on their behalf. Thus, there was a duplication of PAC representation in various centres. A salient example was the UK where the Leballo/Sibeko faction was represented in 1977–78 by Ngila Muendane, while the Ntantala faction was represented by Vuyani Mngaza. Mngaza accompanied Mfanayasekaya Pearce Gqobose on fund-raising tours of Western Europe and Scandinavia where they convinced a number of liberation support organisations that they represented the 'progressive' faction of the PAC.

The Ntantala faction also established its own bank accounts (in the name of PAC) in Dar-es-Salaam. Funds destined for the PAC ended up in these accounts and were used to promote the activities of the Ntantala faction. At the consultative conference in 1978, Gqobose was unable to present a financial report. He gave as an excuse the fact that during the physical clashes between members of the two factions in Dar-es-Salaam, he had been physically prevented from performing his duties as treasurer and that subsequently the Leballo faction appointed Reggie Xoxelelo to handle the organisation's financial affairs. At the conference a number of delegates reported that funds had been collected in their centres and transferred to Dar-es-Salaam, for which no account was ever given. Count Pietersen, then the PAC Chief Representative in the Nordic Countries, reported that Gqobose, during a tour of Scandinavia, had raised a sum of approximately US$35,000, ostensibly for the maintenance of student refugees who had joined the PAC after the Soweto uprisings. There had been no official acknowledgement of receipt of the funds in spite of several requests by Pietersen. A non-governmental organisation in New Zealand, CORSO, had sent a bank draft for US$48,000 for the PAC's publicity and information programme, a request for which had been made by this writer. After several enquiries had been made by CORSO and this writer, a cable was sent by the PAC headquarters acknowledging receipt of the funds, but there was never any record of the funds or an account of the expenditure — nor was there any improvement in PAC's publicity effort.

The Ntantala faction also strove to tighten its grip on the military. The military, including the military camp in Ithumbi, Tanzania, and the 'operational areas' were declared to be out of bounds for the political leaders (essentially the Leballo faction). The 'operational areas' were defined as the Southern African region, encompassing Zambia, Botswana, Swaziland and Mozambique. In Botswana, the political commissar, P.Z. Mboko (alias Dimitrov), was stationed in Francistown where, together with an ANC member, Baldwin Hlanti, he was involved in certain business ventures. Hlanti owned a liquor retail business; he and P.Z. Mboko also purchased a number of luxury automobiles out of funds that, ostensibly, were 'for operations'.

The 'operations' of Mboko and Hlanti in Botswana had all the ingredients of comic opera. They were supposed to have been involved in serious military operations in Francistown, activities which were strictly prohibited by the Botswana government. For transportation they used a Mercedes-Benz sedan, a Range Rover (of which there were only five in the entire country, one of them owned by the late President Khama) and a new Ford Granada sedan. To complete their cover, each had a nom de guerre, Mboko being 'Japie Belgeveer' (an uncharacteristic but conspicuously Boer name for an African revolutionary), and Hlanti being 'Spooky'. The two of them regularly received cables from Leballo in Dar-es-Salaam, with Leballo signing himself as 'Ado'. This writer suspects that one reason why Pretoria's security forces did not take Mboko and Hlanti seriously, was because all this was too amusing even for the regime. When, at the end of 1979, Hlanti was deported from Botswana, he returned to South Africa where the regime's security forces did not even bother to apprehend him.

The independence of Mozambique in 1975 opened up an access route to Swaziland from Tanzania. The PAC's military leaders, seeing the prospects for recruitment and infiltration through Swaziland, began to work closely with Joe Mkwanazi who had been the de facto representative there since the early 1960s. Mkwanazi and others in Swaziland had been cut off from the PAC headquarters in Tanzania, and were thus largely ignorant of the power struggles and conspiracies going on at the level of leadership, a fact for which they were to pay dearly in 1978. The level of Mkwanazi's ignorance could be seen in December 1974 when, during a conversation with this writer who had recently arrived in Swaziland after fleeing from South Africa, he informed the writer that the PAC had 20,000 militarily-trained men in camps in Tanzania. He was not lying; he really believed that, probably because that was the information he had been given by the PAC leaders in Dar-es-Salaam. This writer was to learn later that at that time the PAC had a mere twenty-two old men at its camp in Tanzania. They were quietly engaged in poultry-farming and other activities of a non-military nature.

Mkwanazi visited the PAC headquarters in Dar-es-Salaam for the first time in early 1975, en route to Europe, after winning a competition for recording the highest sales for the Coca-Cola Bottling Company by which he was employed in Swaziland. During that short visit it was impossible for him to get a clear and complete picture of what was *really* happening, as opposed to what he was told was happening. This fact is important to note, because Mkwanazi and others who were later detained and deported by the Swaziland authorities, following

114   *The Crisis in the PAC: 1978–83*

representations made to the government by Leballo and Sibeko, were caught up in a power-struggle of whose depths and complexity they were ignorant, just like the majority of the participants in the consultative conference.

In the circumstances, one of the two factions had to come out on top, by any means necessary. The Leballo faction had, in the months preceding the conference, elbowed out the military leadership of Ntantala and others, appointing in their place a high command personally selected by Leballo from among the new recruits who joined the PAC in 1975 and in the post-Soweto period. Leballo justified this action (termed a 'coup d'etat' by the Ntantala faction) on the ground that the military leadership had walked out of a meeting of the Central Committee on 22 January 1978 when they were called upon by their colleagues to account for their failures.

Outcome of the Conference

From the point of view of the Leballo faction, the consultative conference was successful in that it resulted in the expulsion of the Ntantala faction. The consultative conference was publicised as a 'Conference of Unity and Progress'. The PAC emerged from Arusha neither united nor stronger, but emaciated. Eight members of the Central Committee were immediately expelled at the conference; approximately 60 other rank-and-file members were expelled a week later after their refusal to dissociate themselves from the expelled leaders. Among those who were expelled were the most disciplined members of the organisation.

A Central Committee of thirteen members was *appointed* by Leballo, presumably after consultation with some of his lieutenants, *not elected* by the conference participants. The members appointed to the Central Committee were the following:

1) Potlako Kitchener Leballo — Chairman of the Central Committee and leader of the PAC;
2) Mogale 'Jimmy' Mokgoatsane — Administrative Secretary;
3) David Maphumzana Sibeko — Director of Foreign Affairs and Observer Representative to the UN;
4) Vusumzi Linda Make — Director of Pan-African Affairs;
5) Elias L.M. Ntloedibe — Director of Publicity and Information;
6) Edwin Makoti — Secretary for Defence;
7) Erret V. Radebe — Director of Finance;
8) Henry E. Isaacs — Director of Education and Manpower Development;
9) Victor Mayekiso — Member of Central Committee (and Member of the Military Commission);

10)	Esrom Mokgakala — Member of the Central Committee (and Member of the Military Commission);
11)	Elizabeth R. Sibeko — Member of the Central Committee;
12)	Gertrude Deliwe Mathutha — Member of the Central Committee;
13)	Reginald Xoxelelo — Special Assistant in the office of the Chairman.

The appointment of thirteen members was anomalous since the document approved by the conference for the restructuring of the PAC, provided for a Central Committee of twelve members. The appointment of Reginald Xoxelelo as the thirteenth member caught even Leballo's lieutenants, Sibeko and Make (who had drawn up the document) by surprise.

It was decided that the consultative conference would be the highest organ of the PAC. It would meet every three years. Between conferences, the Central Committee would be the highest organ and would meet twice yearly, once in plenary when all the representatives would partcipate equally with members of the Central Committee. The importance of this decision is that it laid down the principle of accountability. Henceforth, the 'leaders' would report and account to the members in conference every three years.

The conference also established a chain of command and defined the relationship between the 'Party' and the 'Army'. The Military Commission, comprising the Chairman of the Central Committee (also Chairman of the Military Commission), the Secretary for Defence (Edwin Makoti) and two members of the Central Committee (Victor Mayekiso and Esrom Mokgakala) would be the sub-organ of the Central Committee which would liaise with the military wing of the PAC, that is, APLA, through the high command.

Clear-cut directives were issued to the re-organised military leadership. It was impressed upon them that the national mandate of the liberation movement and its programme of action had short-term as well as long-term plans; that the armed struggle must take place according to those plans and must consequently break out when the motive forces of the revolution have been mobilised and built into a revolutionary force and when the armed forces of the masses have been strategically deployed around the country.

At the same time, the leadership stated its intention to strengthen the central organs of the PAC and to unite the cadres around the political tasks of the struggle. The rallying point of this activity had been to impress upon the cadres in particular, and the membership in general, the fact that in a revolutionary war the key to the liberation struggle is the underground movement among the people; that the trained political cadre is the leading factor in the process and directs it through guerrilla activity to achieve the political tasks of the revolution. The underground

116 *The Crisis in the PAC: 1978–83*

movement must, therefore, take root in the villages and towns, in accordance with the defined military strategy and tactics of the PAC, in the form of cells from which the guerrilla must learn to live and fight. It was emphasised that these activities should not be dampened by, or deferred through, lack of facilities required for use in enemy-occupied territory; the aim is to foster a spirit of self-reliance and develop the resourcefulness of the masses.

One of the power struggles deferred at Arusha, was the struggle for a successor to the late President Mangaliso Sobukwe. In this regard, there had been speculation in the media that Leballo, because he was acknowledged to be a liability to the PAC, was not likely to be elected President even though he had been Acting President in the external mission. David Sibeko was said to be a strong contender in view of the fact that he was probably the best-known member of the PAC leadership in exile. The PAC members in the USA recommended to the Central Committee that Zephaniah Mothopeng, then on trial at Bethal on charges under the Terrorism Act, should be elected the successor to Sobukwe so that he could serve to focus attention upon the trial and also serve as a rallying figure for the PAC members in South Africa and in exile. That idea was not even considered by the Central Committee, or discussed at the conference. Certain members of the organisation felt that the election of Mothopeng to the presidency would merely invite retribution from the South African regime which would use his election to that post as evidence of the charges he faced.

Leballo was adamant that since he had been Acting President, he should be confirmed as President of PAC by the conference. This was resisted by most people, both privately and during the debate in plenary when the document outlining the new structure of the PAC was tabled. The compromise that was agreed upon was the use of the nomenclature, 'Chairman of the Central Committee and Leader of the PAC'. It was clear, though, that Leballo was not satisfied with this title. By that time, of course, he had identified Sibeko as a possible challenger for the leadership; that struggle was to be played out in the ensuing months and was to culminate in the assassination one year later.

The members of the Central Committee appointed at the conference dispersed to undertake various assignments, including participation in the OAU Summit in Khartoum and a visit to Baghdad, the PAC having established, through Fezile Nhlapo (subsequently appointed representative to Egypt), relations with the Arab Ba'ath Socialist Party. The Arusha consultative conference and the decisions (which drew negative media publicity) were to be packaged and sold as a great development in the history of the PAC. The organisation was, according to these optimistic assessments, on the threshold of great achievements. As we shall see, however, this was not to be; the problems which led to Arusha were to manifest themselves in the months ahead.

Notes

1. Van den Berghe 1967, p. 106.
2. Gerhardt 1979, p. 136.
3. Ibid.
4. Tape recorded interview with Phillip Kgosana, New York, 8 May 1982.
5. Letter not dated, but written at the time that Make was based in Liberia.
6. The name of the person mentioned in the letter is omitted here because the person is presently in South Africa and the author is not certain whether he had permitted his name to be put forward as a candidate for the Board of Trustees of the proposed Centre. In the circumstances, his safety cannot be jeopardised.
7. Copy in author's files.
8. Copy in author's files.
9. Kgosana, interview, 8 May 1982.

6. Post-Arusha Anarchy: APLA Flexes its Muscles

It would be fallacious to argue that the consultative conference solved the problems of the PAC. In fact, the problems which had partially led to the conference being held, re-surfaced shortly after it had closed. A few days after Arusha, a delegation of the militarily-trained cadres who were in Dar-es-Salaam in large numbers (having been brought by Leballo and his faction to maintain 'security'), threateningly demanded money from the Administrative Secretary, Mogale 'Jimmy' Mokgoatsane, and the Director of Publicity and Information, Elias Ntloedibe. Their spokesperson, the deputy political commissar, Mzwandile Ngqotjane (called 'Zwai Maglas' because he wore spectacles, although he used the nom de guerre, Zola Zymba), informed the two members of the Central Committee that 'the army' could not be expected to 'mount security operations' on 'empty stomachs', and that they would have to be provided with cash on a daily basis for their maintenance.

The matter was resolved amicably, but the point was made. Henceforth, the militarily-trained cadres would coerce the Central Committee. The chain of command and the procedure defined at Arusha were ignored. Rather than channel their grievances or requests through the high command to the Military Commission, the militarily-trained cadres, relying on their superiority in numbers, would make direct approaches to the Central Committee, employing threats and pressure, if necessary.

In September 1979 the Director of Finance, Erret Radebe, was forced by the high command, led by their commander, the late Edgar Phiri (alias Lancelot Dube), to take them to the bank where they scrutinised the PAC bank accounts.

APLA High Command Demands 'Strategic Leadership'

What emerged at a very early stage after the consultative conference was that the members of the high command were extremely bitter about their exclusion from the Central Committee. They argued that the

Post-Arusha Anarchy 119

military leaders who were expelled at Arusha had been in the Central Committee, which they regarded as the 'strategic leadership', since it was the decision-making body of the PAC. They felt that they, too, should have been integrated in the Central Committee rather than having to liaise with the Central Committee through the Military Commission, a sub-organ of the Central Committee.

The high command also argued that the commander of the Azanian People's Liberation Army (APLA), Edgar Phiri, should have been appointed Secretary for Defence. In this regard, they pointed out that in ZANU (later ZANU-PF), the commander of the Zimbabwean African National Liberation Army (ZANLA), the late General Josiah Tongogara, held the position of Secretary for Defence in the Central Committee of that organisation.

Members of the high command also felt betrayed by Leballo and his lieutenants. Promises had been made to certain members of the high command that in return for their support in the struggle against the Ntantala faction, they would be appointed to the Central Committee. This, however, was not done, and the highly ambitious deputy political commissar, 'Zwai Maglas', was extremely bitter. At the conference in Arusha, he assumed all the duties of the camp commander, regularly organising the parades and drilling of the APLA cadres outside the conference hall, as well as assigning tasks to those responsible for the 'security operations'. All this was done with a view to impressing the conference participants. David Sibeko was so impressed by Zwai Maglas's performance that while still in Arusha, he thanked the latter in the presence of a number of members of the newly-appointed Central Committee for all that he had done, adding that his 'good work' had not gone unnoticed. Ironically, Zwai Maglas would later leave Dar-es-Salaam for Lagos two days before the assassination of Sibeko and would circulate a document explaining the situation in the PAC, speculating how an event like the murder of Sibeko could have taken place.

The high command later presented to the Central Committee a document outlining their views on the relationship between the Central Committee and APLA. In essence, what they proposed was that the latter should be completely autonomous. The sole function of the Central Committee should be to provide the finances for the 'operations' of APLA, the leadership of which would be provided by the high command. The high command would not be accountable to the Central Committee. The proposal was rejected by the Central Committee. It was pointed out to the high command that the chain of command and the procedure established at Arusha for liaison between the Central Committee and APLA was devised after careful study of the problems that had arisen with the erstwhile military leadership. The latter had used their superior numbers in the Central Committee to prevent any investigation into or punitive measures for their deviations and failures.

120 *The Crisis in the PAC: 1978–83*

Whenever the question of the failure of the military leaders was raised in the Central Committee, they would argue that 'military matters' could not be discussed by the Central Committee for 'security reasons'. The procedure established at Arusha was to enable the Central Committee to hold the military leaders of the organisation accountable.

At the beginning of November 1978, a truck-load of the APLA forces left the military camp at Ithumbi for Dar-es-Salaam, several hundred miles away. They planned to abduct this writer (then Director of Education and Manpower Development) and force him to surrender an amount of US$5,000,000 he allegedly had. The writer was tipped off by one of the cadres who had travelled with the group and that same evening surprised them at one of the PAC residences in Upanga, Dar-es-Salaam, where they had gathered. When confronted by the writer about the allegations of $5 million, the APLA cadres were taken aback and denied that they planned any abduction. This incident has been cited here to demonstrate that problems of indiscipline continued to bedevil the PAC but it also demonstrates the manner in which the ordinary members were manipulable. At that time a report appeared in the Tanzania *Daily News* announcing the grant by the Norwegian Government of 4.2 million Tanzanian shillings (approximately US$500,000) to the PAC for humanitarian purposes, in particular for the maintenance of refugees at the transit centre in the Bagamoyo district. Since the transit centre was under the jurisdiction of the Department of Education and Manpower Development, it was assumed that the director of that department had control over the reported grant from the Norwegians.

What was ignored (or unknown to them) was that it was not a cash grant. Strict control over expenditure was exercised by the Norwegian embassy in Dar-es-Salaam. This had not been explained to the military cadres. They were simply informed by a mischief-maker that they were unable to return 'home' because the Director of Education and Manpower Development was hoarding $5 million.

The PAC had no structures to facilitate the flow of information from the leaders to the rank-and-file. There were no organised discussions or political education classes, thus further widening the gap between the leaders and the rank-and-file. In such a situation rumour-mongering was endemic and the rank-and-file manipulable, especially when there appeared to be disparities in life-styles and living conditions of the leaders and the ordinary members, especially the military cadres who lived in the bush camp in Ithumbi. In the PAC, the alienation was exacerbated by the bitterness among the militarily-trained cadres in particular who believed that the older leaders had abandoned any desire to fight and that the youth would have to sacrifice their lives in the armed struggle while being excluded from any real power in the organisation.

Leballo was able to exploit the alienation between the other members of the Central Committee and the rank-and-file by portraying himself as the only leader who really cared for their welfare. He dismissed the other members of the Central Committee as 'cowards' who lived only for comfort and high living in exile. This was very appealing to young people who were forced to endure conditions of hardship and deprivation as refugees or freedom-fighters to whom the prospect of 20 years or more in exile (like the older members in the organisation) was a frightening one. These were some of the causes of the tension and frustration underlying the continued instability and internal dissension in PAC.

Indiscipline in PAC Central Committee

It would, however, be entirely wrong to view the problems in the PAC during that period as being entirely due to indiscipline among the cadres. The conduct of members of the Central Committee, or certain of them, served also to fuel the tensions. For example, shortly after the consultative conference, the Administrative Secretary, Mogale Mokgoatsane, without having consulted the Central Committee, travelled to Lusaka from Dar-es-Salaam in a Scania truck belonging to the PAC. The truck, which had in fact been given to the PAC by the OAU Liberation Committee for the work of the organisation, was to be sold in Zambia, or to be exchanged for four land-rovers. Mokgoatsane took a sum of approximately $4,000, ostensibly for his subsistence and other expenses in Zambia. This hair-brained scheme to dispose of the truck failed. The Administrative Secretary was away from the headquarters for four weeks. Rumours of the trip to Zambia reached the cadres, with certain embellishments, naturally. Although the Central Committee reprimanded the Administrative Secretary for his poor judgement and indiscretion, its failure to adopt any punitive measure against him appeared to many of the cadres as weakness on the part of the Central Committee, or, at worst, an example of mutual political blackmail in practice, the Central Committee being unable to take disciplinary action against one of its own members for fear that he would expose certain other indiscretions of which others were guilty. Leballo was able to use the incident of the trip to Zambia to blackmail Mokgoatsane.

Another reason why Mokgoatsane was vulnerable to pressure from Leballo was that he had, without having informed the Central Committee, secured from Unesco a sum of US$5,000 and a return airticket from Dar-es-Salaam to Khartoum prior to the conference. While still Director of Education and Manpower Development, Mokgoatsane was to have accompanied Dr. Hubert Dyasi, an educational consultant, to the Sudan to conduct a feasibility study, preparatory to the establishment of a PAC 'June 16 Azania Institute'. The Institute was to have been an academic as well as military institution, staffed

122 *The Crisis in the PAC: 1978–83*

by South Africans recommended by the PAC, with curricula specifically designed to meet the needs of the liberation struggle and post-liberation South Africa. For various reasons, the mission was postponed. The Central Committee decided that the Director of Education and Manpower Development should travel to Khartoum to explain the reasons for the postponement of the feasibility study to the authorities there, and impress upon them the continued interest of the PAC in the project.

The PAC provided Mokgoatsane with funds for his subsistence as well as a return air-ticket. Yet, he secretly secured from Unesco, through the project co-ordinator in Dar-es-Salaam, Awad Idris, a sum of US$5,000 for his daily subsistence allowance and an additional return air-ticket. This was discovered later when the Unesco project co-ordinator, in the presence of Mokgoatsane and Vus Make, pointed out that since the PAC had already used half the amount allocated for the feasibility study, the organisation would have to pay the travel expenses as well as the subsistence allowance for its Director of Education and Manpower Development when the feasibility study was to be undertaken. When this writer assumed the position of Director of Education and Manpower Development he was able to secure funding for the mission. The feasibility study was completed in April 1979.

Each time that Mokgoatsane attacked or criticised Leballo in meetings of the Central Committee, Leballo reminded him of the US$5,000 from Unesco and the attempted sale of the Scania truck. Leballo also cited these examples of indiscipline among members of the Central Committee to the militarily-trained cadres at the camp in Ithumbi when he explained to them that they could not return to South Africa 'to fight' because there were 'vultures squandering money'.

Other members of the Central Committee also gossiped about Mokgoatsane, and about one another, to the cadres, but in meetings of the Central Committee there was no honest discussion or debate of these matters.

Post-Arusha Split in Central Committee

Another problem that affected the organisation immediately after the consultative conference was the division in the leadership. According to reliable sources, Leballo and David Sibeko quarrelled bitterly in Khartoum during the OAU Summit of Heads of State in July 1978, over Leballo's lack of sophistication. Leballo attempted to draw the attention of an African Head of State by shouting at him in the corridor of an hotel. When Sibeko pointed out to him that such behaviour was unbecoming of a leader of a national liberation movement, Leballo angrily replied that Sibeko and Make thought that they were 'indispensable' to the PAC. When this writer visited Baghdad in January 1980 as

Post-Arusha Anarchy 123

part of a delegation led by Vus Make, the latter explained to the leaders of the Arab Ba'ath Socialist Party the circumstances surrounding the assassination of Sibeko and the circumstantial evidence pointing to Leballo's complicity. An official of the Africa Bureau of the Party indicated that when Leballo and Sibeko visited Baghdad in 1978 after the OAU Khartoum Summit, relations between the two appeared strained.

Leballo moved away from Sibeko and forged a closer alliance with Victor Mayekiso. The two of them went to Libya where they spent a considerable length of time together, making representations to the government for financial and material assistance for the PAC. The Libyan government provided Leballo and Mayekiso with a quantity of arms and ammunition for the execution of the armed struggle by APLA. Mayekiso was held personally responsible for the safe transport and delivery of the arms and ammunition. En route, Mayekiso and Leballo visited Lagos where they held discussions with certain officials in the military government of the Federal Republic of Nigeria. Vus Make, at that time PAC's chief representative to Nigeria, was not in Lagos but in the USA at the invitation of David Sibeko.

Leballo and Mayekiso successfully smuggled the arms and ammunition into Tanzania early in November 1978, by which time the alliance between the two of them was quite firm. But then two things occurred. Firstly, at a meeting of the Central Committee at which Leballo and Mayekiso reported on their missions, the two of them engaged in a strong denunciation of Make and Sibeko. According to them, there were complaints from the Nigerian authorities about the PAC representative (Vus Make) who had spent very little time in Nigeria since his appointment to that office; even when he was in Lagos they said, he spent all his time visiting and socialising with the Liberian Ambassador. According to Leballo and Mayekiso, the Nigerian authorities requested that Make be recalled and that he be replaced by a military cadre in order to facilitate liaison with the Nigerian military leaders. Leballo and Mayekiso also alleged that the Nigerian authorities complained about Sibeko who behaved as though he were a foreign minister; he 'wore three-piece suits' and was 'arrogant'. At the meeting, Ntloedibe, who was one of Sibeko's praise-singers, did not question any of the accusations levelled against his two associates. Instead, he supported the suggestion made by Leballo that Make be recalled from Nigeria.

Admittedly, given the fact that Leballo and Mayekiso were the only two persons who were present during the discussions with the Nigerian officials, it was difficult to challenge the report. It was, however, clear that Leballo was preparing the ground for action against Make and Sibeko.

124 *The Crisis in the PAC: 1978–83*

Leballo/Mayekiso Alliance Falls Apart

The second development was that the alliance between Leballo and Mayekiso came apart within a few days of their arrival in Dar-es-Salaam. Mayekiso would learn that to Leballo there were no permanent alliances, only permanent interests. Leballo, in attempting to impress the members of the high command, informed them about the arms and ammunition procured from the Libyan government, but took personal credit for the negotiations and the carriage of the arms and ammunition. The high command wanted to inspect the weapons which at that time were kept by Mayekiso in his luggage in his hotel room; as has been indicated already, the weapons were released into his custody by the Libyans on the understanding that he would accept personal responsibility to ensure that they were used for the intended purpose. Leballo sent the members of the high command to Mayekiso, who was representing the PAC at a meeting of the OAU Ad Hoc Committee on Unity between the ANC and PAC, to demand the keys to his luggage. After Mayekiso refused to surrender the keys to the high command, Leballo personally went to him to demand the keys. Mayekiso, aware of the consequences of a breach of the agreement with the Libyans, tendered his resignation with immediate effect from the Military Commission, but not from the Central Committee. He departed for Nairobi — and was never to participate in the work of the Central Committee again.

After various plans had been devised by the high command to transport the arms and ammunition overland to Botswana, the weapons were returned to the military camp at Ithumbi where they were concealed. They were used several months later in the assassination of David Sibeko.

With Mayekiso removed from the scene, Leballo proceeded to tackle what he knew was inevitable, the showdown with Make and Sibeko, whom he regarded as contenders for the leadership. He had already poisoned the minds of the militarily-trained cadres against the two whom he accused of high living and corruption. Sibeko was accused of 'hoarding money in New York', and thus obstructing the military programme of infiltration of the cadres into South Africa after completion of their military training.

At the meeting of the Central Committee in November 1978 at which Leballo launched a scathing attack on Make and Sibeko in their absence, he had also prepared the Central Committee psychologically for any changes or reshuffle.

Rather than inform Make that he was being recalled from Lagos because of complaints about his performance from the Nigerian authorities, Leballo complained to him about the breakdown in administration at the organisation's headquarters, a breakdown he attributed to the incompetence of Mokgoatsane, the Administrative

Secretary. He then informed Make that in order to strengthen the administrative machinery at the headquarters, he wanted Make to assume the position of Administrative Secretary. Make at that time was still in the USA. In a letter dated 21 November 1978 and addressed to the 'Chairman and Members of the Central Committee', Make wrote:

> I have today received a cable from the Chairman informing me of my having been appointed Administrative Secretary of the PAC, in addition to my present portfolio. From the onset, I wish to express my thanks for the confidence reposed in me by appointing me to this high office in our vanguard movement. This is even more so, since our organisation is in the threshold of intensifying the struggle to which we are all so dearly committed. I will, to the best of my ability, try to live up to that confidence by fulfilling my new duties with all the resources at my command. To effectively do this, I will need the support and assistance of my colleagues as, in keeping with the policies of our organisation further reinforced at the historic Consultative Conference, collective responsibility is the cornerstone of our party with the leadership acting as a 'collective'.

From the letter it is very clear that Make was concerned as to whether or not consultations had taken place among the members of the Central Committee before the appointment had been made; he also sought clarification as to the new department to which Mokgoatsane had been assigned. Finally, he was concerned about the interpretation which might be read into the new change, so soon after the consultative conference. His letter continues:

> I wish to request that this appointment be effective after a full discussion at the forthcoming meeting of the plenary session of the Central Committee to be held in January 1979. It is my view that this and all future appointments should first be discussed by the Central Committee. I wish to state that this does not imply my refusal to take up the appointment, far from it, what I wish to underline is the need for proper consultation with the pros and cons of every major change in the composition and personnel of key appointments fully considered before a final decision is taken. In this particular case, I would wish to know whether any such consultation did take place. Ideally, the views of all those, like myself, who could not be at Headquarters should have been solicited prior to this appointment.
>
> If I have been seen to belabour this point it is for the fact that we should be seen to be implementing the mandate of the Consultative Conference in good faith. Further, any changes should not be likely to result in the belief that so soon after the Conference we are already forced to make drastic changes in the composition so recently approved by the Conference.
>
> Finally, I hope that we will [be] informed quite shortly which Department Comrade Mogale Mokgoatsane has been re-assigned to.

126 *The Crisis in the PAC: 1978–83*

It is very clear from Make's letter that he was suspicious of Leballo's motives and sought assurances that he was not being 'promoted' at the expense of Mokgoatsane, since he was fully aware of Leballo's antipathy towards Mokgoatsane and the effort a few months earlier to remove him from the position of Administrative Secretary following the Scania truck fiasco.

Without consultation with other members of the Central Committee at the PAC headquarters and without even informing Sibeko, the Director of Foreign Affairs, Leballo appointed 'Zwai Maglas' as Chief Representative to Nigeria, in a move clearly aimed at ingratiating himself with the high command. The high command had its own schemes to appoint its own candidates to key positions. Nigeria, which provided substantial financial assistance in 1976 and 1977 and indicated a preparedness to provide further financial and material assistance, was regarded by the high command as a strategic post. Together with Leballo, the high command rationalised the appointment of 'Zwai Maglas' on the grounds that the Nigerian authorities suggested the appointment of a person from the military wing of PAC because of the necessary negotiations and liaison which would have to be conducted with the Nigerian military leaders in power at that time.

Problems for the PAC in Botswana

While these problems existed at the leadership level, more serious problems surfaced within APLA, particularly in Botswana; despite the policy of the government of prohibiting freedom-fighters from both the ANC and PAC from operating in the country, the high command (without the approval of the Military Commission), had despatched large numbers of militarily-trained cadres to Botswana in pursuit of a 'home-going programme' worked out jointly by the high command and Leballo. A number of cadres were arrested in South Africa in the latter half of 1978 after having been infiltrated into the country.

The problems that were created by the presence of large numbers of militarily-trained cadres in Botswana were made known to this writer during a visit to that country in November 1978. He submitted a report to the Central Committee on 18 December 1978. After eight days in Botswana, it was clear to the writer that the state of affairs of the PAC there left much to be desired. The report to the Central Committee stated as much:

> The representative and the APLA cadres appeared to be functioning as two separate entities, even though sharing accommodation. At the meeting I attended (at which the APLA cadres were not present although in the house) dissatisfaction was expressed with the behaviour and attitudes of the high command and APLA cadres by the members present. Various

Post-Arusha Anarchy 127

individuals also reported of private or informal discussions with locals as well as persons in authority who expressed displeasure [with] and concern about the behaviour of our cadres.

At the meeting the representative reported the theft of approximately R2,175.00 and 17 air-tickets from his brief-case and wardrobe respectively during his absence. Apparently the high command has admitted to the use of the money and ten of the tickets.

My assessment of the situation (which was reflective of the general situation among South African exiles there), was that the differences and divisions have no ideological basis, nor do they centre around the programme of action, but around personalities, with the usual gossiping and rumour-mongering, slanders, etc. This has been aggravated by the tendency, conscious or unconscious, of certain members of the Central Committee during visits to the region to either deal with or fraternise with certain individuals or even assign them certain tasks. In some instances this has fueled inter-personal rivalries and friction. During informal discussions with a few highly placed officials I was informed of the concern in Botswana at the conspicuous presence of large numbers of APLA cadres. This sensitivity was heightened by Pretoria's threats against Botswana for allegedly 'harbouring terrorists'.

Media reports at that time about the arrests in South Africa of 23 PAC guerrillas and activists, five of them in the Transkei, and the flight of six guerrillas into Botswana increased sensitivity even further. A decision was taken at the highest level to refuse entry into Botswana to Edgar Phiri and Edgar Nqolase. The two of them, travelling by road in a Mercedes-Benz sedan belonging to the high command and driven by an APLA cadre, were turned back at Gazankulu. Unknown to the Botswana authorities, the vehicle was being used to transport the arms and ammunition smuggled into Tanzania by Leballo and Mayekiso. It was hoped that if the weapons could be infiltrated into Botswana, it would facilitate the military programme then being implemented by the high command, with the approval of Leballo.

Early in the morning of Thursday, 23 November 1978, the PAC representative in Botswana at that time, Douglas D.D. Mantshontsho, was summoned by the Special Branch and the Immigration Department to be informed of the decision that was taken, and approved by the late President Seretse Khama, to deny entry to the three PAC members who were travelling by road. They had not informed Mantshontsho of their travel plans. Instead, upon arrival at the Botswana border post at Gazankulu, they had indicated to the immigration officials that they had an arrangement with a senior official in the Special Branch under which they were cleared for entry into the country without complying with the normal procedures. Upon enquiry, the Special Branch official denied knowledge of such 'arrangement'. The following morning, the

128　*The Crisis in the PAC: 1978–83*

Special Branch visited the PAC residence where they requested from the representative a list of names of all the persons living there. In addition, he was instructed to present immediately to the Commissioner of Police for interview three PAC military cadres who had arrived in the country the previous day. (One of them was Thobile Gola, at the time of writing a member of the Central Committee and Chief Representative to Tanzania.) The three cadres were detained pending deportation from the country.

This writer regarded the situation in Botswana as being extremely grave and on 24 November 1978 from Lusaka telephoned the PAC headquarters in Dar-es-Salaam to inform the Central Committee of the developments and spoke on the telephone to the deputy Political Commissar, at that time 'Zwai Maglas'. He was requested to convey to the Chief Representative the suggestion that 'no technicians should be sent to Pitso until the programme has been re-evaluated'. The gravity of the situation was fully explained to him. In addition, the writer also explained fully to Edgar Phiri and Edgar Nqolase in Lusaka (where they had returned after being denied entry into Botswana), the problems that existed in Botswana.

Swaziland Detains and Deports PAC Members

This writer then proceeded to Swaziland. He discussed with the then Deputy Prime Minister, Dr. Mzonke Khumalo, and various officials the question of the PAC's representation in the country in the light of the arrests and deportation of the members. The officials suggested that despite the detentions and deportations of the PAC members, the organisation was permitted to appoint another representative to the country.

Following the visit to Swaziland, the writer reported to the Central Committee:

> There is a tremendous amount of bitterness against the [PAC] as a result of the detentions in Swaziland. The bitterness is not restricted to the immediate families and friends of those detained and subsequently deported — for both of which they hold what they term the 'Leballo faction' responsible — but I also encountered it among locals in Swaziland.

It has already been stated that this writer learned the truth about and the full details of the arrests of Mkwanazi and others in Swaziland during that visit. They had not been involved in the internal politics of Swaziland in any way. Their arrest was engineered by Leballo and Sibeko: they were the victims of the futile power struggle between the factions at the PAC headquarters.

Surprisingly, the writer discovered intense bitterness and anger

Post-Arusha Anarchy 129

among Swazi nationals towards the PAC. They expressed anger that a national liberation movement could use the state machinery of Swaziland against its own members. In this regard, it has to be borne in mind that individuals like Mkwanazi and Pitika Ntuli had lived in Swaziland for many years and built up friendships and relationships with the local population. Pitika Ntuli, for example, was a well-known sculptor who had exhibited in the country, drawing the attention of foreign artists also. All that would be destroyed by the internecine strife within the organisation they served and whose interests they believed they promoted. There were emotional scenes at the Matsapa airport in Swaziland on 12 December 1978 when families and friends bade farewell to several of the deportees.

One person who was left behind and still detained at that time was an old woman, Mrs. Ndziba. This writer reported to the Central Committee:

> The UNHCR asked me whether we could not prevail upon the Botswana government to grant asylum to Mrs. Ndziba. Apparently she is old, was not actively involved in politics and has said that she does not want to be released if she would have to leave Africa. UNHCR expressed the view that she would never adjust outside of Africa: her two children are working in Swaziland and if she could be granted asylum in Botswana they could travel there to see her.

While in Swaziland, the writer also met a number of political activists from South Africa who had travelled specially to see him. The writer, in the report to the Central Committee, dated 18 December 1978, stated:

> While in Swaziland, I was visited by activists from the home-front who briefed me on developments there, particularly on the intensified repression. They were also very critical of our home-going programme and even bitterly suggested that there were no differences between our programme and that of the ANC. They complained that some of the cadres who were captured by the enemy had gone directly to their home areas where they contacted friends to whom they boasted about their being trained (militarily) and showed off their materials. According to these sources, the number of arrests reported in the media was deflated: not only were trained cadres arrested but their contacts detained and in some cases even family members [were detained].

The problems of the PAC continued to escalate. Further arrests of militarily-trained cadres in South Africa were reported in the media, including the arrest of Justice Nkonyane, the deputy commander of APALA. The Military Commission had to all intents and purposes ceased to function; the Central Committee thus had no control or

130 *The Crisis in the PAC: 1978–83*

influence over the military programme of the organisation being implemented by the high command. The military programme that resulted in the arrests (and later in December in the police killing of one freedom-fighter, Kenny Mkwanazi, in Soweto), was agreed upon by Leballo and the high command. Within six months of the Arusha consultative conference, therefore, the problem of the relationship between the 'political' and the 'military' had resurfaced.

Mantshontsho and a number of other cadres (both military and untrained) were deported from Botswana. Elias Ntloedibe was despatched by Leballo to Botswana in an effort to smooth relations with the government and the ruling party, a decision that was made on the false premise that he was held in high esteem by the government and people of that country, a view later revised by the Central Committee.

The crackdown in Botswana had its ramifications in Dar-es-Salaam where the arrival of a sizeable number of South African refugees, not all of them members of the PAC, who had been promised scholarships by the members of the high command and others associated with them, seriously strained the available resources and facilities of the organisation such as housing, food and medical supplies.

There was a noticeable hostility towards education among many of the militarily-trained cadres. This attitude was reinforced by the irresponsible actions and utterances of P.K. Leballo. Shortly after his return from a mission in mid-December when a large number of refugees arrived in Dar-es-Salaam from Botswana, Leballo visited the PAC residence, where he addressed the members of the organisation and the new arrivals living there. He told them flatly that nobody was going to be allowed to study and that everybody was to undergo military training. A week later he repeated the warning when a group of female recruits and refugees arrived from Botswana. A day after their arrival in Dar-es-Salaam, Leballo summoned them to his apartment, where he informed them that there were no scholarships available for people wishing to pursue academic careers, that he did not know why they had been brought to Dar-es-Salaam and that they would be sent for military training.

But perhaps the crowning act of irresponsibility occurred shortly before Christmas 1978, on the day that Ngubeni April (who had served a prison term on Robben Island in the early sixties) and twelve others arrived from Botswana from where they had been deported. Leballo met them at the airport where he fired off his usual anti-education fusillade. He went a step further and declared that all those who had come to Tanzania could go to Bagamoyo, the transit centre, 'to starve'.

The cumulative effect of Leballo's statements was to create the impression among the new arrivals (many of whom were not members of the PAC) that they had been recruited for military training under false pretences. Many of them reported the matter to the Prime Minister's office, indicating that they wished to be repatriated to Botswana whence they had come. This created problems for the PAC with the Tanzanian authorities who demonstrated a certain degree of sympathy for the prospective students. The office of the UNHCR assisted in the maintenance of the refugees after they had severed their links with the PAC. A number of those whose travel documents were still valid and included a right of return to Botswana were repatriated.

The hostility demonstrated towards those who indicated an intention to pursue their educational careers engendered acute feelings of insecurity among the new and prospective recruits. For example, after returning from Addis Ababa on 19 January 1979, this writer was confronted by a number of new recruits who sought explanations about their future with the PAC. Early the following morning, the writer went to the PAC residence in Ilala to see the students, only to discover that for the previous two nights they had gone into hiding, having heard the rumour that Leballo was threatening that those members of the PAC living in Dar-es-Salaam would be forcefully removed to the transit centre at Pongwe by the high command and that all the persons at the centre would be forced to undergo military training. As a result of the prevailing fear, uncertainty and confusion, the writer summoned a meeting of the students at Ilala on Saturday, 20 January 1979. At the meeting the students repeated the statements and threats made by Leballo that they would not be permitted to pursue educational training.

The hostility towards education has to be viewed within the context not only of the developments in the period after the Arusha conference, but in the context of the development of the PAC as a national liberation movement. The anti-intellectualism that Leballo and his personally-nominated high command encouraged was an integral part of the militarism that was promoted. The idea that was propagated was that education and the armed struggle were mutually exclusive, which they clearly are not. In the PAC, anti-intellectualism not only resulted in talented individuals being driven out of the organisation but also contributed to the perpetuation of the mediocrity and disarray within the organisation. Individuals who have no formal educational qualifications or vocational training have no alternative means of livelihood; they thus ensure that their positions in the organisation are not jeopardised, either by opposing the leaders or asserting political independence. Successive PAC leaders have used this to perpetuate themselves. The fear of suddenly having to earn a livelihood at an advanced age, in a foreign country where opportunities are limited anyway, without any training, is quite a daunting one, the writer discovered repeatedly during discussions, particularly with those who had fled South Africa in the early sixties and who after completing their military training spent the ensuing years in camps in various parts of Africa.

PAC's Educational Programme Overhauled
In September 1978 this writer prepared a critical evaluation of the PAC's

132 The Crisis in the PAC: 1978-83

educational policy and programme for presentation at the plenary meeting of the Central Committee in January 1979. Various independent African countries offered places to PAC cadres in their educational institutions following the 1976 township uprisings. UN agencies and other non-governmental organisations, notably the IUEF, the African-American Institute (A-AI), the World University Services (WUS) and the Phelps-Stokes Fund, had offered scholarships to South African refugees. The PAC failed to take advantage of the offers. Between 1976 and 1978, the organisation sent only six female students to The Gambia to complete their high school education and to pursue a secretarial training course. Two other female cadres were sent to Geneva for in-service training with the UNHCR, the idea being that upon completion of their six-months' training course they would serve as counsellors to the young recruits and refugees in the care of the PAC. After the two young females completed their training and returned to the PAC headquarters, however, they were victimised by the Central Committee which decided at a meeting in August 1978 (at which the writer was not present), that they would not be provided with any assistance by the PAC because they lived with a PAC sympathiser in Dar-es-Salaam rather than with other PAC members. (That was one example of the pettiness within the organisation and how the Central Committee wasted time discussing trivia. More importantly, it was reflective of the victimisation to which females in particular were subjected. One Tanzanian official once remarked to the author that the only time that the PAC Central Committee was decisive was when it was called upon to take punitive measures against women. Allegedly, the two young women in question were victimised because of the personal antipathy of a female member of the Central Committee towards them.)

In creating a department which actually functioned rather than existing in name only, the writer appointed a staff of three persons, each of whom had specific responsibilities, namely, (i) project administration and liaison with UN agencies and non-governmental organisations; (ii) scholarship administration and placement of students; (iii) office administration and typing. Apart from the formulation of a substantive educational policy and programme, the Department was responsible for the administration and development of the transit centre in Pongwe. Later, the Department also assumed responsibility for Women's Affairs since the question of the status of women and their role in the national liberation struggle had not been addressed by the exiled organisation.

As a result of negotiations conducted by the Department with the Tanzanian authorities, a number of students who had been idle in Tanzania since 1976 and 1977 were placed in high schools in Dar-es-Salaam, under the sponsorshp of UNESCO. Under a pilot scheme sponsored by the ILO, a number of students were placed at the Changombe Institute in Kurasini (a suburb of Dar-es-Salaam) for vocational training as motor mechanics, electricians and fitters and turners. Twelve students were sent to West Germany for vocational training under a programme sponsored by the Otto Benecke Foundation. The objective was that the PAC should begin to train skilled manpower both for the liberation struggle and also for the stage of national reconstruction. In this regard, the ANC had embarked upon such an educational programme from as early as 1962; by the mid-1970s therefore, the organisation did not have the problem that the PAC had of a lack of qualified or educated personnel.

The writer also reversed the previous practice whereby only PAC leaders' children benefited from the educational assistance programmes offered by the UN specialised agencies and non-governmental organisations. The practice of victimising PAC members, or the children of members, who were regarded as 'dissidents' because they were critical of the leadership was also abandoned. The revamped Department adopted a policy of providing educational assistance for all South African refugees, not merely those affiliated to the PAC. If the organisation claimed to be a national liberation movement, then it had to assume national responsibilities.

The Department encouraged the active participation of women in the affairs of the organisation, an aspect that had been neglected. A seminar on *The Role of Women in the Liberation Struggle*, sponsored by UNESCO, was held in June 1980 and brought together PAC women from different parts of the world, Tanzanian women from the ruling party, Chama Cha Mapinduzi, the ruling party of Guinea-Conakry (the Democratic Party of Guinea), and the Black Consciousness Movement. Despite the obstructive and negative attitudes of certain members of the Central Committee, who saw in the progress of the Department, an attempt by 'SASO to take over the PAC', the seminar proved to be a great success. The PAC women in particular benefited from the experience which enabled them to participate effectively in the International Women's Conference in Copenhagen in 1980 and subsequent international conferences and seminars concerned with the issues of women and their role in the liberation struggle and in decision-making in society.

Throughout the writer's tenure as Director of Education and Manpower Development, there was much interference in the Department by other members of the Central Committee, as well as petty envy and jealousy. In some instances the interference was malicious, in others it was occasioned by the general confusion within the organisation.

Central Committee Members Held Hostage by APLA

The tension between the high command and the militarily-trained cadres on the one hand, and the Central Committee on the other, erupted into violence on 26 December 1978 when a group of some 40 cadres

134   The Crisis in the PAC: 1978–83

from the military camp at Ithumbi held several members of the Central Committee hostage at the PAC residence in Kijitonyama, outside Dar-es-Salaam. Edwin Makoti, then Secretary for Defence, was abducted from his PAC residence in the morning and taken to Kijitonyama several miles away. The Central Committee members were held for several hours, during which time a number of them were assaulted, threatened with knives and interrogated. Mantshontsho, who by then was in Dar-es-Salaam following his deportation from Botswana, was also interrogated, particularly regarding his alleged role in the arrests of APLA cadres and the decision by the Botswana Government to deny entry to Edgar Phiri and Edgar Nqolase, as well as the deportation of three cadres who had been sent to Botswana without prior notice to Mantshontsho.

The siege ended that same afternoon following the 'intervention' of Leballo, whose complicity in the attack upon the Central Committee members was betrayed by one of the cadres, Trofomo Sono, a former president of the Soweto Students' Representative Council (SSRC), who joined the PAC after fleeing to Swaziland in 1977. Directing an appeal to Leballo to permit the detention and interrogation of the Central Committee members, Sono said, 'Mookameli [a Sotho word meaning "President" or "He who presides over"] you have told us that there are vultures squandering money, so we have come to rectify the situation'. The cadres were to lay siege to the residence of the Central Committee for approximately two days, even though the captivity and interrogations ended on the first day. Thereafter, they agreed to return to the military camp at Ithumbi only on condition that six members of the Central Committee be immediately dismissed. The six whose dismissals were demanded were: Mogale 'Jimmy' Mokgoatsane (Administrative Secretary), Erret Radebe (Director of Finance), Reggie Xoxelelo (Special Assistant in the office of the Chairman), Edwin Makoti (Secretary for Defence), Victor Mayekiso (Member of the Military Commission) and Esrom Mokgakala (Member of the Military Commission).

After consultations among members of the Central Committee living in Dar-es-Salaam and also with David Sibeko in New York (by telephone), it was decided that the matter should be reported to the Tanzanian authorities in view of the gravity of the situation. Firstly, the militarily-trained cadres had left the camp without the authority of the Special Defence Unit (SDU) of the Tanzanian People's Defence Forces (TPDF), which had special responsibility for security at the camp. Secondly, they assaulted members of the Central Committee, which was clearly a violation of the law of Tanzania.

There was also serious concern for the safety of Mantshontsho whom Leballo instructed to accompany him to the camp with the APLA cadres when they returned so they could continue to interrogate him about the developments in Botswana up to and including the detentions and deportations of the PAC members, as well as the arrests in South

Africa of a number of PAC freedom-fighters. In view of the hostility that had been shown towards Mantshontsho by the high command and the accusations that had been levelled against him, virtually holding him responsible for both happenings, there was a real danger of his being physically harmed or even killed.

The SDU intervened after Mantshontsho and the others had arrived at the camp and he had been interrogated; he was not allowed to remain at the camp but was accommodated instead by the SDU. According to Mantshontsho, reporting to the Central Committee members living in Dar-es-Salaam upon his return, Leballo and the APLA cadres at the camp were 'taken by surprise' by the intervention of the SDU.

When questioned by the SDU about the unauthorised movement of the APLA cadres from the camp, Leballo informed the officer in charge, Colonel Matiko, that they had merely gone to play soccer after which they had had a 'braaivleis' (barbecue). He had, he informed the Colonel, purchased an ox for them for this purpose. Given the fact that these cadres were guilty of a breach of military discipline and also violated the laws of Tanzania as well as the disciplinary code of the PAC by assaulting members of the Central Committee, the actions of Leballo could only be construed as condoning their indiscipline.

The siege of Kijitonyama and the assaults upon Central Committee members further strained relations between the Central Committee on the one hand and the high command on the other, and between the Central Committee and Leballo. It also provoked the wrath of the Tanzanian government.

By January 1979, it was clear that the PAC was experiencing serious internal problems once more, and that the consultative conference had not solved the problems of the organisation. Negative references to the internal problems of the PAC were contained in the report of the Executive Secretary of the OAU Liberation Committee, Brigadier Hashim Mbita, who caustically stated that the PAC should not think that it could 'thrive on crises'.

As if to underscore the crisis in the organisation, early in January 1979, the commander of APLA, Edgar Phiri (alias Lancelot Dube) and Edgar Nqolase were fatally injured in a road accident. Two passengers in the vehicle, Esrom Mokgakala (a member of the Central Committee) and an untrained cadre, escaped with minor injuries.

It was against this background of crisis that the first plenary meeting of the Central Committee was held in Dar-es-Salaam from 22 to 27 January 1979. At the plenary meeting, the representatives participated on par with members of the Central Committee, a decision reached in Arusha the previous year.

7. Crisis in the PAC and Exposure of Leballo

The 1978 consultative conference established two important principles: *accountability* and *collective leadership and consultation*. The conference established procedures aimed at facilitating consultation and collective leadership, rather than the arbitrary actions of Leballo who justified all his actions on the basis of clause 14(b) of the PAC constitution. That section provides for the suspension by the president of the constitution during times of emergency and rule by decree. However, it was difficult to justify the many arbitrary actions of Leballo, like the suspensions and expulsions of members, including members of the central organs, when the organisation operated in exile in conditions which could in no way be termed 'a state of emergency', and members could meet freely and discuss problems. When it suited the leaders, it was argued that the PAC constitution and basic documents were inoperative since they were devised for totally different conditions in South Africa when overt political activity was still legally permissible. Certain shortcomings in the constitution and basic documents, for example, omission of provisions for a military wing, were frequently cited to support this argument. Yet, arbitrary actions taken by Leballo, often in concert with or on the advice of others around him, were always justified on the basis of the emergency powers provided for in the PAC constitution. In other words, whether or not the constitution was operative depended solely on the whims of the person or persons in the leadership at any given time. The consultative conference, through defining the principles of collective leadership and consultation, aimed to restrain the leaders and to protect the members of the organisation from arbitrariness.

The conference did not, however, deal with *all* the issues involved in the liberation struggle and the process that had begun at Arusha should have been continued. But, in the period after the conference there was little, if any, analysis of past mistakes and failures, or evaluation of the progress and achievements of previous years. This process was made difficult by the dispersion of the appointed leaders immediately after the consultative conference. Each leader continued to do as he or she wished, which was not always in the best interests of the organisation or of the liberation struggle.

The Problems

Three major problems were discernible, namely lack of organisation, lack of effective leadership, and lack of authority. From these three flowed other problems, notably, lack of direction and co-ordination, fiscal irresponsibility and mismanagement, and lack of discipline.

Lack of Organisation
The existence of an organisation implies an orderly structure, for the smooth functioning of which there must necessarily be co-ordination. It is, however, an open secret that after Arusha there was a collapse in administration, fiscal irresponsibility and mismanagement and an almost total breakdown in discipline within the PAC.

The Administrative Secretary: The breakdown in administration was due in large measure to the incompetence, lethargy and lackadaisical attitude of the Administrative Secretary appointed at Arusha. Correspondence went unattended to, or it would not be passed on to the relevant departments for attention, to cite but two examples. Part of the problem was that the functions of the Administrative Secretary were not properly defined. There was a need after the consultative conference for the Central Committee to lay down clear job descriptions for the holders of the various posts.

The position of Administrative Secretary is crucial in a national liberation movement. The Administrative Secretary has to co-ordinate the relationships among the various departments of the organisation, monitor developments within the organisation, ensure the implementation of the decisions of the Central Committee and ensure the flow of information between the central organ and the various centres. The Administrative Secretary is in a very real sense the lynchpin of the organisation.

There was general agreement among the members of the Central Committee *before* the consultative conference that Mogale Mokgoatsane failed in his previous position as Director of Education and Manpower Development. Yet, he was appointed at Arusha to the crucial position of Administrative Secretary. The reason was that he had to be rewarded for his support for Leballo against Ntantala. As noted above, when, a few weeks after the conference, Leballo proposed that he be removed from the position of Administrative Secretary and given another portfolio, the proposal was opposed by Sibeko and others. Sibeko was committed to Mokgoatsane because the latter was

138   *The Crisis in the PAC: 1978–83*

co-opted into the Central Committee on his recommendation in the first place. Mokgoatsane had been one of the victims of the earlier power struggles within the PAC when he and others, regarded by Leballo as 'dissidents', were declared prohibited immigrants by the Tanzanian authorities, after which they were bundled off into the area on the border between Tanzania and Kenya known as 'No Man's Land'. After spending several years in Ethiopia he went to the USA where he lived in Atlanta, Georgia, with his wife and family. He was brought back into the fold by Sibeko in the mid-seventies when the power struggle between the Leballo/Sibeko and Ntantala factions developed, each side striving in the process to strengthen its position. The background to Mokgoatsane's appointment is important to an understanding of the dynamics involved in the PAC, where personal allegiances and antagonisms have been important factors in the political careers of many an individual, a point that has to be borne in mind in attempting to understand the struggles-within-the-struggle.

Financial Control: Another area where a lack of organisation was manifest was finance management. For example, purchases of food for the various PAC residences in Dar-es-Salaam were made on a daily basis, while supplies for the transit centre were made twice weekly. Budgeting was non-existent, nor was there any long-term planning. Instead, whenever financial grants were received, the manner in which funds were disbursed conveyed the impression that the Director of Finance and his associates regarded money as a commodity that was going out of fashion.

Along with the lack of financial management, were inadequate financial controls. It is no exaggeration to say that the organisation lost control of the number of creditors it had. It owed hotels for accommodation for the conference delegates as well as for previous bills. At the height of the physical clashes between the two factions in Dar-es-Salaam in 1977–78, members of the Central Committee based in Dar-es-Salaam (and also those who visited the PAC headquarters from their various stations) lived in local hotels rather than the organisation's residences, accumulating substantial bills. The PAC owed doctors, businessmen, private individuals, travel agents and airlines, from all of whom bills were received regularly.

The Transit Centre: In October–November 1978 this writer attempted to prepare a report on the progress of the Bagamoyo project, as the transit centre was termed. The effort was hampered by the fact that the Department of Finance was unable to furnish the required information about all the financial contributions that had been received for the project since its inception in 1977. Further problems were caused by the fact that in most cases there was no evidence that the funds were used for the project. The Royal Netherlands Embassy in Dar-es-Salaam, for

Crisis in the PAC and Exposure of Leballo 139

instance, had advanced an amount of money (as part of a grant from the government of The Netherlands) for the completion and repairs of the existing buildings on the site. Yet those buildings were not completed. After assuming the position of Director of Education and Manpower Development, with responsibility for the project, this writer engaged a building contractor to complete the construction of the buildings, comprising a hall and three dormitories.

Mismanagement of the funds solicited specifically for the transit centre hampered development of the project. Conditions at the transit centre in 1978 were depressing. There was a lack of basic furniture, despite the fact that the government of The Netherlands had contributed a significant sum of money for the purchase of basic furniture and cooking utensils. Donors frequently requested to visit the centre to see the progress and were not impressed by the lack of it despite the contributions they had made towards the project. Donor agencies consult with one another, even if informally; similarly, 'cocktail diplomacy', in an influential front-line state like Tanzania meant that even without the PAC being aware of it, developments within the organisation, at all levels, were monitored.

The view of Leballo and others was that the transit centre could be used to raise funds for other activities of the organisation, including its military activities. To them, the development of the centre into an institution which, among other things, would provide the opportunity for the PAC members to manage an organised community and the attendant social services was not the objective.

A further factor in the lack of progress at the transit centre was the attitude of the persons living there. They were reluctant to engage in physical labour. A contradiction between the PAC theory of self-reliance and the practice was exposed; Tanzanian peasants were hired as labourers to work in the construction of the buildings. Even when the UNDP provided a consultant to provide training in low-cost technology specifically road construction at the site, the PAC members living at the centre were unco-operative.

The lack of progress at Bagamoyo had the effect of undermining the confidence of donors, and seriously eroding the credibility of the PAC. Within circles of the UN specialised agencies which provide humanitarian assistance to the national liberation movements, the PAC acquired the reputation of showing the least development in its projects of all the national liberation movements in Southern Africa. As a consequence, the PAC experienced difficulties in 1978 and 1979 in securing substantial financial assistance. This was further aggravated by the crisis that culminated in the assassination of David Sibeko in June 1979.

The lack of development at the transit centre in turn created further problems, the most discernible of which was the constant drift of the persons from the centre into Dar-es-Salaam because of the poor living

140 *The Crisis in the PAC: 1978–83*

conditions and inadequate medical services there. As a result, the PAC residences in and around Dar-es-Salaam at Upanga, Ilala, Mwananchi and Senegal were constantly over-crowded, creating health problems.

The Department of Education and Manpower Development in September 1978 took certain initiatives to improve conditions at the transit centre. Approaches were made to the Tanzanian Christian Refugee Services for material assistance. From them were received clothing, shoes, medical supplies, food and agricultural equipment. The Tanzanian Christian Council donated radios and indoor games. Towards the end of 1978 the UNDP commenced the implementation of its programme of assistance to the PAC for the development of the transit centre, the agreement having been signed with the UNDP officials in New York by this writer in July 1978. In January 1979, the UNDP purchased a twelve-seater land-rover for use at the centre. The PAC was in dire financial straits after the consultative conference which was financed by the OAU Liberation Committee through a surplus in its funds for assistance to the national liberation movements; it was decided that the surplus should be divided among the movements. The amount allocated to the PAC was used to defray the costs of the conference.

The Director of Finance, Erret Radebe, reported to the plenary meeting of the Central Committee on 21 January 1979:

> Decentralisation of funds has not been effectively implemented due to the lack of funds. We have been receiving small amounts and because of the high expenditure in Dar-es-Salaam, some departments have not received their appropriate shares.
>
> The Norwegian Government has contributed to the Party ONE MILLION KRONERS, 5% of [which] is for administration but it has since been given to the OSLO OFFICE. The balance is 950,000 Kroners, which can only be released for projects.
>
> From the financial statement it will be discovered [sic!] that some outstanding accounts arise from the ARUSHA CONSULTATIVE CONFERENCE. The OAU has been approached and statements rendered but Comrade Metterden declined stating that the OAU never undertook to meet such expenditure.
>
> Due to the serious financial position of the Party, the Director has made initial preparation for a fund-raising tour, starting in AUSTRALIA. Because the Director of Education and Manpower Development was a representative in this region his assistance has been solicited.
>
> Due to congestion in Dar-es-Salaam and with a desire to uphold the Arusha declaration, the Party purchased two houses in ILALA and KIJITONYAMA for 140,000 T.Shs. and 136,000 T.Shs. respectively. Payments made to date on account in respect of the said houses is 70,000 T.Shs. and 36,000 T.Shs. respectively.

Crisis in the PAC and Exposure of Leballo   141

I am told that the owner of the ILALA house was at the office demanding payment of the balance of the purchase price, failing which she threatened to take immediate repossession of the house without further warning.[1]

Because of the bad financial position in which we find ourselves today, *we are unable to pay office and house rents, water bills and other rates, more especially the telephone account.* We are unable to meet our debts and creditors are pressing. Only yesterday, the STATE TRAVEL AGENCIES were at the office demanding payment of the 20,000 T.Shs. The position is really bad.[2] (Emphasis added.)

The Director of Finance, however, failed to make the connection between the parlous state of the PAC's finances and the continued internal problems the organisation experienced. Governments and non-governmental organisations were reluctant to support the PAC because of what was perceived as continued turmoil in the organisation. The PAC was kept afloat during that difficult period by the quarterly allocations from the OAU Liberation Committee (amounting to about US$25,000 for administration, publicity and information), grants from the Norwegian government for humanitarian purposes, the programme of assistance from the UNDP for the transit centre, and financial assistance negotiated by the Department of Education and Manpower Development. As a result of requests made by this writer non-governmental organisations in Australia and New Zealand made financial contributions amounting to approximately US$32,000 in 1978; among the organisations were Australian Freedom From Hunger, Community Aid Abroad, AUSTCARE, CORSO and the Catholic Commission on Justice, Peace and Development. The World Council of Churches, through the Tanzanian Christian Council, granted the equivalent of US$30,000 in 1979 specifically for the maintenance of the PAC members living at the transit centre.

Lack of Effective Leadership: Lack of Authority
The consultative conference did not resolve the problem of *leadership* in the PAC, but merely deferred it. In the post-Arusha period the different interest groups within the Leballo faction (the victors at Arusha) began to compete once more for control of the levers of power within the PAC, namely the Central Committee and APLA. As a result, there was a lack of cohesion among the members of the Central Committee and a lack of effective leadership. One of the questions to which the plenary meeting had to address itself was that of the extent to which the Central Committee was rendered ineffective by the usurpation of power by the Chairman, Leballo. The latter interfered in every department. Worse still, he concerned himself with the sordid details of every bit of tavern gossip.

142   *The Crisis in the PAC: 1978–83*

In such circumstances, the Central Committee lacked authority. Because it lacked machinery to impose its authority or exert discipline, decisions of the Central Committee were flouted with impunity. The high command refused to co-operate with the Military Commission to which it was answerable, but the Central Committee could not bring the members of the high command to book. Similarly, the Central Committee decided (and repeatedly stated) that all the PAC members who had no valid reason or official permission to remain in Dar-es-Salaam should return either to the camp at Ithumbi if they were militarily-trained, or to the transit centre in Bagamoyo if they were not militarily-trained. It was, however, unable to enforce the decision. The problem was further aggravated by the inability of the Central Committee to discipline its own members. Many cadres felt that there could not be one standard by which to judge the behaviour and actions of the leaders and another by which to judge the behaviour and actions of the ordinary members. An untrained cadre assaulted a member of the Central Committee, Reggie Xoxelelo, in 1979 after Xoxelelo without explanation squandered several thousand Tanzanian shillings at a time when the organisation lacked funds for basic needs like medical attention for the sick. Xoxelelo had demonstrated such irresponsibility on numerous occasions, often disappearing in the suburbs of Dar-es-Salaam for several days at a stretch, without any disciplinary action by the Central Committee.

Appointment of Commission of Inquiry

The plenary meeting was confronted with all these problems, problems that should have been examined in depth at the consultative conference. As a consequence, the plenary meeting decided to appoint a Commission of Inquiry to investigate every aspect of the organisation and activities of the PAC, with a view to improving its overall performance.

The motivation for the appointment of the Commission of Inquiry, proposed by David Sibeko, however, has to be seen in the context of the power struggles at the time. The Tanzanian authorities had identified Leballo as being largely responsible for the indiscipline within the PAC through his incitement of the militarily-trained cadres; in his opening speech to the plenary meeting, Leballo reported that he had been warned of dire consequences for his person should there be any repetition of indiscipline within the PAC such as the siege of the Central Committee's residence at Kijitonyama and the assault upon members of the Central Committee by the cadres from the camp at Ithumbi. He went to the extent of offering to step down, adding that he did not want 'to go down with the Party'. Apart from the warning from the Tanzanian authorities, Leballo was also isolated within the leadership. Of the 23 members of the Central Committee and representatives who participated

Crisis in the PAC and Exposure of Leballo 143

in the plenary meeting, Leballo had the support only of 'Zwai Maglas', then the Chief Representative to Nigeria.

There was a possibility at that meeting of a motion of no-confidence in Leballo's leadership being successful. Ngila Muendane (former Chief Representative to the UK), Edwin Makoti and this writer were among those in favour of this course of action. So was Elizabeth Sibeko. Others like Erret Radebe, Reggie Xoxelelo and Esrom Mokgakala, although they expressed strong condemnation of Leballo's actions during the private consultations that took place among the Central Committee members, were very unreliable. It was assumed that they would support any position which they believed would win majority support. David Sibeko, Elias Ntloedibe and Vus Make indicated that they would not support the move for fear that Leballo would be vindictive if it failed. Since they had families to maintain, they could not jeopardise their positions in the leadership of the organisation. Sibeko proposed instead the appointment of a Commission of Inquiry; privately, he rationalised this on the grounds that the findings of the Commission would very clearly demonstrate Leballo's misdeeds and that action against Leballo on the weight of the report of the Commission would be easier to justify internationally, as well as to the general membership of the PAC.

The Commission of Inquiry was duly appointed, comprising three representatives (at that time) namely, Ngila Muendane, Mosebjane Malatsi (Representative to The Gambia) and Fezile Nhlapo (Representative to Egypt). The Commission conducted a lengthy and costly investigation, financed in part by the OAU Liberation Committee, but its report was never tabled. The Commission travelled to the camp at Ithumbi, to the transit centre in Bagamoyo, to Botswana and Zambia, and interviewed PAC members. They also communicated in writing with PAC members in various countries inviting them to submit evidence to the Commission about their grievances as well as suggestions and recommendations of improvements that they wanted implemented by the Central Committee in the functioning of the organisation. The Commission of Inquiry was a costly exercise in futility.

The appointment of the Commission and the failure of the plenary to take action against Leballo was testimony to his political skill. Leballo realised that he needed the political support of Make and Sibeko against the other members of the Central Committee who had been at the PAC headquarters in Dar-es-Salaam continuously and who had been victimised by the APLA cadres as a result of his incitement. He was aware of the hostility and opposition he faced from these members. Whereas in November 1978 he had singled out Make and Sibeko for criticism, in January 1979 he singled them out for lofty praise. This writer pointed out this contradiction, in the process accusing Leballo of dishonesty and unequivocally charged him with responsibility for the siege of the Central Committee's residence at Kijitonyama in December

144　*The Crisis in the PAC: 1978–83*

and the assaults upon the members. Make and Sibeko also challenged Leballo to substantiate the allegations he made against them in their absence but he was unable to do so. He only cited the name of one Nigerian official attached to the military who had been critical of Make. Mayekiso, of course, was not present, following his resignation from the Military Commission in November after his quarrel with Leballo over the question of the arms from Libya.

Leballo: Part of the Problem

It was not really necessary to appoint the Commission of Inquiry. The plenary meeting in January 1979 clearly exposed the fact that most of the PAC's problems since the consultative conference were inter-woven with the personality of Leballo. Immediately after the conference Leballo violated the very principles established at Arusha. Without consulting other members of the Central Committee, he made important appointments, by-passing the established structures and ignoring the established procedures. He appointed Vus Make to the crucial position of Administrative Secretary, without consulting other Central Committee members. He appointed 'Zwai Maglas' as Chief Representative to Nigeria without reference to the Director of Foreign Affairs who was, technically, responsible for the recom-mendations of representatives to the Central Committee for appoint-ment.

But that was vintage Leballo — indisciplined, deceitful, divisive, and disloyal to his own colleagues. His sole pre-occupation was to maintain personal power. He even succeeded in converting a small core of the militarily-trained cadres into a private army of auxiliaries paying allegiance only to himself, and then used this 'private army' to subject loyal PAC members and leaders to a reign of terror.

Leballo propagated the idea and encouraged the attitude among the militarily-trained cadres that 'the army' (APLA) was an independent organ, which was both ideologically incorrect and in breach of the decisions of Arusha. The PAC maintained that 'politics must direct the gun', that a guerrilla is a political fighter bearing arms and is thus an embodiment of the political and the military. He has not only the will to fight and die for the liberation of his country but also to work with and teach the people: that is the essence of politicisation and mobilisation aimed at maximising the participation of the people in the struggle for liberation. At the Arusha conference, it will be recalled, it was argued by many participants, including this writer, that advancing the idea that there existed a political wing and a military wing of the PAC was not only dangerous for the future but was counter-revolutionary. The erstwhile military leadership argued that the cadres who joined the national liberation movement after 1976 were not members of the PAC.

In collaboration with his personally-nominated high command, Leballo frustrated the functioning of the Military Commission, the sub-committee of the Central Committee established at Arusha and entrusted with liaison between the militarily-trained cadres and the leadership, and the implementation of the programme of action, particularly the 'home-going programme'. Hiding behind the smokescreen of 'security', they embarked upon a programme of action contrary to that adopted at Arusha, a programme that called for careful political preparation inside the country before the infiltration of trained freedom-fighters. Rather than use established contacts inside the country, such as known sympathisers and former members of the PAC, the high command decided against working with such contacts. They argued, spuriously, that such contacts were untrustworthy, many of them having become informers. They failed to engage in criticism and self-criticism, or to review the strategy and tactics they had adopted. Even when APLA cadres who were infiltrated into the country were captured by the South African security forces, the high command failed to evaluate their programme, or to change their strategy and tactics in case those captured divulged information under torture.

Lack of Security Consciousness in the PAC

Another serious problem during this period, one ignored or under-estimated by Leballo and the high command, was the PAC's lack of security consciousness, and on occasion its infiltration even by the South African regime's agents. It is necessary to examine this question of infiltration in greater detail.

The exodus of large numbers of people fleeing the brutal repression that followed the 1976 township uprisings created favourable conditions for infiltration of the National Liberation Movement by the agents of the South African regime. Elements of the 'underclass', that is, those not involved in production, and those who had not been politically active in South Africa, were able to claim upon leaving the country that they had been involved in the uprisings. Competition between the ANC and PAC for members during this period was also accompanied by a relaxation in vigilance; new recruits were not thoroughly screened. In this way enemy agents infiltrated the liberation organisations. Among the state witnesses in the PAC Bethal 18 trial, for instance, were informers and agents provocateurs who had actually gone to the PAC head-quarters in Dar-es-Salaam as well as to Botswana and Swaziland where several PAC members lived.

The lack of security consciousness was demonstrated in the evidence against John Ganya, one of those tried in Bethal and subsequently

146 *The Crisis in the PAC: 1978–83*

sentenced to ten years' imprisonment. When Ganya denied that he had been to Tanzania the state produced as exhibits in court 43 letters purportedly written by former Soweto students who joined the PAC. The letters were addressed to families and relatives but they contained incriminating evidence against Ganya: for example, that he had been in Tanzania, that they would be undergoing military training after which they would return 'home', etc. Moreover, one agent who had been as far as Dar-es-Salaam identified Ganya in court and stated that he had seen him at the PAC headquarters.

The same agent, Philemon Moema (also known as 'Nkie') also led the police to the house in Soweto where Kenny Mkwanazi, a PAC freedom-fighter later killed by the police in December 1978, was in hiding. He also gave evidence for the state against three PAC freedom-fighters convicted in June 1979 on charges under the Terrorism Act.

Lack of security consciousness was also reflected in the events of January 1979 when two PAC freedom-fighters (one of them the deputy commander of APLA, Justice Nkonyane) who had been arrested in South Africa in November 1978, were alleged to have escaped from custody together with a Black policeman who was said to have assisted them.[3] The circumstances surrounding the arrest, detention and escape of the freedom-fighters were extremely strange. Firstly, although they were militarily-trained freedom-fighters — and, therefore, in the eyes of the South African regime, 'dangerous terrorists' — they were not detained in a maximum security prison but in the Jeppe police cells, where drunks and 'vagrants' are kept. Secondly, Justice Nkonyane had arranged to meet another APLA cadre at an agreed rendezvous. Unaware that Justice had been arrested, this cadre kept the appointment but when he arrived at the meeting place, there were several White policemen in the vehicle in which he expected Justice. The cadre was shot and wounded in the arm but managed to escape. This raises the question as to who informed the police about the rendezvous when, according to the wounded cadre, only he and Justice as deputy commander of APLA knew of the mission and the arrangements. Thirdly, at the January plenary meeting, Leballo informed the meeting that a letter written by Justice Nkonyane on a toilet roll had been smuggled out of the police cells. In that letter, Justice was alleged to have named Central Committee members identified by his captors as being on the payroll of South Africa's Bureau of State Security (BOSS), as it was then known. Again, this raises questions about a detainee like Justice being able to write letters while in police custody. Also, could this naming of certain members of the Central Committee as BOSS agents be an attempt to draw red herrings across the trail? Alternatively, even if such vital information was divulged to him by his captors, was that not a ploy to sow suspicion in the minds of PAC members, an example of divide and rule in the best tradition?

The mysterious letter was never shown to the Central Committee

Crisis in the PAC and Exposure of Leballo 147

members. Supposedly, this was also for security reasons. But even assuming that one or more members of the Central Committee were identified by South Africa's security police as informers or agents (and the possibility cannot be excluded), why would they choose to blow the cover or covers of their agent or agents, or reveal their identities? It would be thought that such 'agents' would be more useful if their identities were kept secret. South African security police spy Gordon Winter has revealed that one of the 'dirty tricks' employed by BOSS was to smear individuals as BOSS agents.[4]

In January 1980, Baker 'Basie' Metsa, another APLA cadre who drove the cadre who was shot and wounded by the police when they went to the rendezvous, during a conversation with this writer in Botswana confirmed that a letter was received from Justice Nkonyane after his arrest in South Africa in November 1978. He denied, however, that it named certain Central Committee members as BOSS agents. According to him (he claimed to have personally received and read the letter), the letter was an appeal to the Central Committee for greater assistance for APLA and detailed the difficult conditions under which the APLA cadres had operated, with meagre financial resources and military hardware.

It is also perhaps relevant to note that Justice Nkonyane and another cadre who was arrested with him, Tshepiso Gumede, were reported in late January 1979 to have escaped from police custody with the assistance of a Black policeman, one Samuel Ngubeni. Ngubeni was reported to have fled with them. Not only did they escape with the keys to the police cells but they even had transportation awaiting them. They were alleged to have escaped to Mozambique via Swaziland. From Mozambique they cabled the PAC headquarters in Dar-es-Salaam requesting that they be cleared with the Tanzanian authorities for entry into the country.

Upon their arrival in Dar-es-Salaam, Justice Nkonyane bore no trace of assault or ill-treatment. Tshepiso Gumede, on the other hand, required medical treatment and subsequent hospitalisation because of the serious injuries sustained after being assaulted while in detention in South Africa. The widely-publicised injuries sustained by the late Steve Biko who was assaulted and tortured while in police custody are an indication of the treatment meted out to detainees in South Africa. Steve Biko was, by admission even of the South African regime, a 'moderate'. Justice Nkonyane was a militarily-trained freedom-fighter, the deputy commander of PAC's military wing — a prize-catch by any standard. Yet, he escaped without even a scratch! That was understandable, because shortly after his arrest, Justice Nkonyane transmitted a message to David Sibeko, then based in New York as the PAC Observer Representative to the UN, that he had broken down during interrogation, and that Sibeko should arrange legal defence for him. This was reported to the Central Committee by Sibeko.

At the time of the alleged escape, all these suspicions were voiced. It

148   *The Crisis in the PAC: 1978–83*

was suggested that the Tanzanian authorities should be requested to interview all three escapees — Nkonyane, Gumede and Ngubeni — when they arrived in Dar-es-Salaam because the PAC lacked facilities. Leballo vehemently opposed this suggestion. He and the high command subsequently obstructed, physically, the possibility of screening the three by removing them to the camp at Ithumbi immediately after their arrival in Tanzania. The purpose of screening would have been to try to determine whether or not their escape was genuine, or whether it was contrived by the South African security police in order to destabilise the PAC even further, and to assess the extent of the disclosures made by Justice Nkonyane and Tshepiso Gumede about the PAC's operations during interrogation. The logical thing to have done would have been for them to be interviewed by the Military Commission, if not by the Central Committee. The presence of a Black South African policeman, whose character was unknown to the PAC leaders, within the ranks of the organisation, had security implications for Tanzania as well, a fact that made the screening all the more imperative.

After they had been removed to the camp, Leballo did two things. Firstly, he decorated the three escapees. Justice Nkonyane was awarded a non-existent 'Lembede Medal' for bravery; Tshepiso Gumede was awarded a non-existent 'Sobukwe Medal' and the policeman a yet-to-be-named award for 'patriotism'. Secondly, without reference to the Central Committee, he appointed Justice Nkonyane commander of APLA to succeed Edgar Phiri (alias Lancelot Dube) who was killed in a road accident en route to Dar-es-Salaam in January 1979. Nkonyane and the policeman were among the 19 detained by the Tanzanian authorities in connection with the murder of David Sibeko in June 1979.

One of the ironies is that when suspicions were voiced by several persons about Nkonyane's escape in January 1979, David Sibeko hailed the escape as the work of a fictitious 'PAC underground'. He undertook personal responsibility to discuss the matter with the Mozambican authorities in Maputo where he attended a meeting of the Co-ordinating Bureau of the Movement of Non-Aligned Countries. There he, Ngila Muendane and Donald Morwatsehle (the former Assistant Representative in Dar-es-Salaam and also one of the nineteen detained in connection with the murder of Sibeko) represented the PAC. Upon his return to Dar-es-Salaam after the Maputo meeting, Sibeko reported to the Central Committee that in the view of the Mozambican officials with whom he discussed the matter, the escape was 'genuine', and the three escapees genuine 'patriots'. Nkonyane was later one of those accused of the plot to eliminate physically the PAC leaders, including Sibeko who was the first victim.

In Retrospect

It is open to conjecture, and beyond the purview of this work, what the consequences might have been had the Central Committee taken action against Leballo in January 1979 when the weight of evidence against him was so overwhelming. He had been identified by the Tanzanian authorities as the prime cause of the problems within the PAC, and warned personally of dire consequences in the event of a repetition of indiscipline among the organisation's cadres. That he was shaken by the warning was clear; at the opening of the meeting he indicated that rather than 'go down with the Party', he would leave Tanzania. It should be added, however, that after the luncheon recess, Leballo returned to the meeting bellicose, and maintained that posture throughout the remainder of the plenary. The speculation among Central Committee members at that time was that Leballo was advised, or warned, by the members of the high command with whom he conferred after each adjournment, not even to entertain the idea of abdicating the leadership of the Central Committee. He vigorously defended all his actions, even in the face of overwhelming evidence of his personal wrongdoing. He accused the Central Committee and the representatives of having forged a 'united front' against him. His continued leadership of the PAC after that plenary meeting cost the organisation dearly.

Notes

1. Both the Ilala and Kijitonyama houses were subsequently repossessed because the PAC had failed to pay the purchase price.
2. Report in author's files.
3. *The Star* (Johannesburg), 29 January 1979.
4. Winter 1981. Care has to be taken in the use of the material in this book because apart from the unscrupulous character of the author who was a common criminal turned journalist and security police informer, when referring to a number of individuals as either agents or informers in the employ of South Africa's security police, he quotes Van den Berghe, the former head of BOSS as his source. In the circumstances, it is difficult to check the authenticity of some of his allegations.

8. Leballo Ousted

Tanzania Warns Leballo

It was patently clear that Leballo was incorrigible and that no amount of discussion or persuasion, or criticism and condemnation could change him from his set ways. As a result of his leadership the continued existence of the PAC in Tanzania was in jeopardy. He had inspired and condoned indiscipline among the militarily-trained cadres; he had presided over acts of thuggery and gangsterism which brought the organisation into disrepute.

On 14 February 1979 Leballo summoned an impromptu meeting of the Administrative Committee (which is responsible for the daily management of the affairs of the organisation, empowered to take decisions binding on the Central Committee) at 12.45 p.m. in order to report on a meeting he and Elias Ntloedibe had had with the Junior Minister of Home Affairs of Tanzania on 12 February. In addition to the Junior Minister of Home Affairs, also present at the meeting were the Permanent Secretary in the Ministry of Home Affairs, the Commissioner of Police, a security officer from the President's office and an official from the Ministry of Foreign Affairs. Leballo was summoned to the meeting to be informed by the Junior Minister of Home Affairs of the Tanzanian government's decision that the 40 militarily-trained cadres who were involved in the invasion of the Central Committee's residence at Kijitonyama and the resultant violence had been declared prohibited immigrants. As such, they were to be removed from Tanzania within two weeks: the authorities, on a request from Leballo, reluctantly agreed to extend the period to three weeks. Until such time that all these cadres were removed from Tanzania the PAC would be prohibited from clearing for entry into the country any new recruits. Leballo was warned to ensure that there was no repetition of indiscipline in the PAC. The fact that Leballo was personally summoned to the meeting demonstrated not only the grave light in which the Tanzanian authorities viewed the turmoil within the PAC, especially the indiscipline among the APLA cadres, but it was also a personal humiliation for him. Under normal

Leballo Ousted 151

circumstances, such a decision would be communicated to the Chief Representative of the organisation through the Prime Minister's office. This was not lost on Leballo.

Leballo and Ntloedibe felt that this grave new turn of events had to be explained to the cadres at the military camp at Ithumbi. For this reason, it was decided that Leballo should proceed immediately to the camp. When Ntloedibe, supported by this writer, recommended that Edwin Makoti as Secretary for Defence should accompany him, Leballo strongly advised against this, pointing out the hostility towards him among the militarily-trained cadres at the camp and the consequent risks to his personal safety. Later, the Central Committee learned from Thobile Gola and others who were then at the camp that when Leballo reported to the cadres the decision of the Tanzanian authorities, he held Edwin Makoti responsible for the expulsion order against the 40 cadres. He informed them that Makoti had reported the incident at Kijitonyama to the Tanzanian authorities.

During the discussion that followed the report of the Tanzanians' decision, the options available to the Central Committee were assessed. One possibility was for the expellees to be sent to Libya for further military training. Another option that was considered was for the expelled group to be sent to Nigeria for a crash course in advanced military training. Neither option was feasible and the failure of the Central Committee to remove the expelled cadres from Tanzania seriously restricted the functioning of the PAC. More of that later.

At that meeting of the Administrative Committee, note was taken of two Central Committee members who had declared themselves refugees without informing their colleagues of their intentions. One was Esrom Mokgakala, a member of the Military Commission; the other was Mogale Mokgoatsane who had failed in each of the leadership positions to which he had been appointed — Director of Education and Manpower Development first and, in the post-Arusha period, Administrative Secretary and Director of Labour. At the January plenary meeting, the Central Committee endorsed the appointment of Vus Make as Administrative Secretary; upon the recommendation of David Sibeko, Mokgoatsane was appointed to the hastily-created post of Director of Labour, the scope of which was not defined, nor did it matter, since Mokgoatsane was merely the nominal head of the department and did not go to the office after the plenary meeting.

Mokgakala was maintained by the UNHCR at the Clock Tower Hotel in Dar-es-Salaam: while still a member of the Central Committee, he advised a number of recruits to follow his example by declaring themselves refugees, a step that necessitated such persons first making representations to the Tanzanian authorities. Mokgoatsane, on the other hand, had been joined by his family whom he accommodated at the Central Committee's residence in Kijitonyama. While being

152 *The Crisis in the PAC: 1978–83*

accommodated and maintained by the PAC, he and his family were simultaneously maintained by the UNHCR.

Although it was recognised that the Administrative Committee could take disciplinary action against both these members of the Central Committee, the matter was shelved.

The meeting concluded with a warning by Edwin Makoti that the Central Committee should ensure that nothing was done which would provoke the Tanzanian government again.

Twentieth Anniversary of the PAC — Leballo Humiliated

On 8 April 1979 a meeting was organised in Dar-es-Salaam to mark the twentieth anniversary of the PAC. At the meeting were representatives of other national liberation movements, including ZANU-PF, the ruling party, Chama Cha Mapinduzi (CCM), the OAU Liberation Committee and the diplomatic corps. Among the speakers were the present writer and P.K. Leballo; Moses Dhlamini, former Chief Representative to Tanzania, was the master of ceremonies. A demonstration was staged by PAC cadres (the majority of them untrained), who jeered, heckled, shouted and sang during the keynote address by Leballo. The cadres shouted: 'For twenty years you have been wrecking this organisation'. They sang a song in Zulu which, when literally translated means, 'Growing old in exile for the sake of money'. Obviously embarrassed, Leballo tried to explain to the assembled dignitaries that the cadres were protesting against the delay in their being sent for military training. The cadres stood up and, still singing and shouting, walked out of the hall. Outside there were physical clashes between the demonstrating cadres and Leballo loyalists, consisting in the main of the high command and militarily-trained cadres, led by Justice Nkonyane. Clearly, the organisation was divided into two hostile camps.

That same evening, the present writer went to the PAC residence in Ilala where most of the cadres who had staged the demonstration lived. He was en route to the airport to travel to Khartoum on a mission connected with a proposed 'June 16 Azania Institute' to be established by the PAC in the Sudan. An explanation was sought from the cadres for their actions at the meeting. Through a delegation they had appointed, the cadres explained to the writer and Edwin Makoti (then Secretary for Defence) that their protest was a demonstration of their lack of confidence in Leballo and that this did not apply to other members of the Central Committee. Both Edwin Makoti and this writer seriously cautioned the cadres against doing anything that might jeopardise the position of the PAC in Tanzania.

It is necessary to explain why the writer was able to maintain lines of communication with the cadres in Dar-es-Salaam. This writer was the youngest member of the Central Committee, and having risen through the ranks of the student movement in South Africa to the position of President of the militant South African Students' Organisation (SASO), was personally known to many of those who had fled the country in the mid-seventies. Others had heard of the writer. After the 1976 township uprisings, the writer met most of the recruits who joined the PAC. At that time, the writer represented the PAC in Australasia, returning to Southern Africa during summer vacations. During the writer's tenure as Director of Education and Manpower Development, based in Dar-es-Salaam, he built up a rapport with both the untrained cadres and many of the militarily-trained cadres. The writer always attempted to communicate to the Central Committee, the views and feelings, grievances and recommendations of the cadres; this, in turn, created much petty envy among colleagues who on many occasions accused the writer of inciting the cadres.

The day following the demonstration in Dar-es-Salaam, the writer telephoned David Sibeko in New York from Khartoum. Since the situation was explosive and quite conceivably could deteriorate, with disastrous consequences for the PAC, it was necessary to alert members of the Central Committee so that the situation could be arrested. Sibeko was to have returned the telephone call the following Wednesday, by which time he hoped to have communicated with Vus Make in Nigeria. He failed to return the call. When this writer telephoned Sibeko again on the Thursday, it was to learn that Leballo had telephoned Sibeko in the meanwhile. According to Sibeko, Leballo accused the present writer of having incited the cadres, an allegation based on the fact that most of the cadres who were involved in the demonstration against Leballo were from the transit centre at Pongwe, a project under the Department of Education and Manpower Development. Sibeko appeared to have believed Leballo, hence his failure to telephone this writer as promised or to offer an explanation. He agreed, however, that a meeting of the Central Committee should be convened urgently to attempt to arrest the situation. This writer cut short the mission to the Sudan, leaving the Tanzanian educationist, Yusuf Gosi, to continue with the feasibility study for the proposed Institute.

PAC Divided into Two Hostile Camps

By Sunday, 15 April 1979 the situation in Dar-es-Salaam had deteriorated drastically. Leballo had, in the preceding days, summoned reinforcements from among his loyalists at the camp in Ithumbi. En route to Dar-es-Salaam, three of the APLA cadres were killed and several others injured when the truck in which they were travelling overturned. The PAC office in Dar-es-Salaam was not informed of the accident or of the fatalities. Instead, Leballo travelled to Ithumbi for the funeral which was arranged without reference to, or the participation of

154   *The Crisis in the PAC: 1978–83*

the Chief Representaive and Central Committee members resident in Dar-es-Salaam. The Chief Representative and others only learned of the tragedy through the Tanzanian Special Defence Unit (SDU) and the media.

In Dar-es-Salaam itself, the situation was explosive. Several cadres were assaulted by Leballo's high command, led by Justice Nkonyane, and other Leballo loyalists. At the PAC residence in Upanga, a number of cadres accused of being 'anti-Leballo' were assaulted and driven out of the house. One of them had all his clothing cut up. An old man who had left South Africa in the early 1960s was threatened by Nkonyane. In a written report to this writer, he stated:

> Some of the members of the high command came to the house drunk at night and, without showing any respect for the members of the house, they would play music loudly and dance until the early hours of the morning ... As if their actions were not enough provocation, they went further making very provocative remarks, and threats against those comrades whom they considered and referred to as 'anti-timer' (Leballo) counter-revolutionary and reactionary. Remarks such as these: (1) 'This is just an introduction, what will follow is slaughtering'. (2) 'Some of these dogs must be killed'. (3) 'When these events [sic] were reported to the office, I was confronted by Justice (Nkonyane), who was always a leading figure ... and he referred to Comrades Bennie (Sondlo) and D.D. (Mantshontsho) as "dogs" together with others working in the office'. (4) As a result of these provocations, there have come about two distinct groups in the Upanga house and the hostility between the two groups is growing stronger by the day because of the provocations and insults from the high command group.[1]

One militarily-trained cadre was woken up at 11 p.m. one night by Leballo loyalists wielding knives and pangas. He fled to a nearby police station.[2]

Leballo was fully aware of these incidents since many of the victims reported them to him. While threatening disciplinary action against the perpetrators, he privately encouraged them and financed their drinking.

In the meanwhile the cadres who had demonstrated against Leballo appointed a committee to represent them. The committee visited various embassies in Dar-es-Salaam, the OAU Liberation Committee and a number of Tanzanian government officials. The consequence was that the reports and rumours of political instability and internal problems in the PAC soon circulated on the diplomatic cocktail circuit.

Leballo Forced to Step Down

It was against this background that the Central Committee, meeting in

Leballo Ousted 155

extraordinary session in Dar-es-Salaam on 30 April and 1 May 1979 resolved to remove Leballo from his position as Chairman of the Central Committee and leader of the PAC.

At the meeting, presided over by Leballo, this writer (in his capacity as Acting Administrative Secretary), presented an administrative report analysing the developments in the PAC since the plenary meeting held in January 1979. While all the other Central Committee members agreed that the PAC was in grave crisis once more, Leballo's response was that the administrative report was 'orchestrated and one-sided', consisting solely of 'attacks on the army and the Chairman'. He went on to accuse the Central Committee of disrupting the programme of APLA; he asserted that the Tanzanian authorities had frozen the activities of the PAC at the instigation of Central Committee members who alerted the authorities to the fact that the 40 APLA cadres expelled from the country had not left. Leballo and the high command, using lists of names of Basutoland Congress Party (BCP) members who had departed from Tanzania over the previous two years, tried to convince the Tanzanians that the 40 APLA cadres had been deployed on military missions since the time of their expulsion order. Leballo's preoccupation seemed to be to convince those Central Committee members who had not been in Tanzania continuously that he alone cared about the PAC, its military wing, and the execution of armed struggle. Everyone listened in amazement as he informed the meeting that as a result of his efforts, the APLA cadres at the military camp at Ithumbi were armed with anti-aircraft weapons and heat-seeking missiles. The Tanzanian authorities prohibited possession of arms of any sort by APLA cadres, let alone such conspicuous heavy weapons as anti-aircraft weapons and heat-seeking missiles.

Leballo's denials of having acted unilaterally and his blowing of his own trumpet were unconvincing. Make, Makoti, Ntloedibe, Radebe, Xoxelelo and this writer were adamant that the end of the road had been reached, that there was no way in which the Central Committee could continue to function under Leballo's leadership.

Sibeko was in regular contact with Leballo from the time of the demonstration at the twentieth anniversary of the PAC. At the meeting, he argued that the demonstration by the cadres against Leballo was a rejection of the entire leadership. Sibeko called for an investigation into the role of Central Committee members in the events at the twentieth anniversary meeting,to be followed by appropriate disciplinary measures. Leballo had accused this writer and Edwin Makoti of having instigated the demonstration, so it was clear who Sibeko had in mind. There was, however, no support for his proposal, after which he added his voice to the others calling upon Leballo to relinquish his position as Chairman of the Central Committee and leader of the PAC.

Rather than dismiss Leballo ignominiously, the Central Committee

156 *The Crisis in the PAC: 1978–83*

decided on a formula that enabled him to leave Dar-es-Salaam for London as soon as possible. A press release specified ill-health as the reason for his departure and that a three-person Presidential Council appointed to assume the duties of Chairman would consult with him from time to time.

The idea of a Presidential Council was proposed by Leballo who pointed out that after the banning of the PAC in 1960 and the imprisonment of its top leadership, when the organisation established headquarters in Lesotho, a Presidential Council was appointed to take care of its affairs. That precedent could be followed again. He then proposed that a document to this effect and a press release be drawn up by the three Central Committee members who, according to him, had not been involved in the 'incidents' of the previous weeks, namely Vus Make, David Sibeko and Elias Ntloedibe.

When the meeting (which was held in the room of Count Pietersen, then Chief Representative to the Nordic Countries, at the Agip Motel) adjourned on the afternoon of 30 April, there were two groups of PAC cadres waiting outside. Justice Nkonyane and other APLA cadres who were escorting Leballo, travelled in a land-rover and an ambulance. Across the road from the motel were dozens of other cadres, mainly untrained cadres from the transit centre, who were part of a 'security operation' mounted by D.D. Mantshontsho at the suggestion of David Sibeko. When, however, Sibeko saw the scale of the 'operation' mounted by Mantshontsho, he was horrified and bitterly criticised him.

On the morning of 1 May this writer met with Make, Sibeko and Ntloedibe at their request at the apartment in Sea-View, a suburb of Dar-es-Salaam, where they were living (and where Sibeko was shot two months later). They showed this writer the documents they were entrusted to prepare. They indicated that they had decided that the three of them should comprise the Presidential Council, a decision that they rationalised on the following grounds: (i) Make was Administrative Secretary and since he would be based at the PAC headquarters, he required the enhanced authority to make representations to the host government and also to assert discipline among the cadres; (ii) Sibeko had to be included in the Presidential Council because, as Director of Foreign Affairs, he was well-placed to explain and defend the decision to oust Leballo; (iii) Ntloedibe, as the Chief Representative to Botswana, was placed in a sensitive area and his contacts with the liberation movement in South Africa would be facilitated by his enhanced status. These explanations were made by David Sibeko who also suggested that since the present writer was the youngest member of the Central Committee it would be appropriate for the writer to propose the names. This writer opposed the suggestion on the ground that the nominations should be left to the meeting.

When the meeting resumed that same morning, Leballo requested the privilege to nominate the members of the Presidential Council as the final gesture of his leadership. The Central Committee acceded to his request and, predictably, he nominated Make, Sibeko and Ntloedibe. The positions held by the three members at the time of their nomination to the Presidential Council were as follows: Vusumzi L. Make, Administrative Secretary and Director of Pan-African Affairs; David M. Sibeko, Director of Foreign Affairs and Observer Representative to the UN; Elias L. Ntloedibe, Director of Publicity and Information and Chief Representative to Botswana.

The idea was that the chairmanship of the Presidential Council would be by rotation, beginning with Make. Sibeko proposed that Make attend the International Conference on Refugees in Africa, in Arusha, the following week so that he could apprise certain African delegations of the outcome of the Central Committee meeting. It was also decided that the PAC's representatives should be apprised of the decision. A press release was issued announcing the decision.

With hindsight, it is very clear that the manner in which the removal of Leballo was effected was a serious mistake. While the Central Committee members, particularly those who participated in the meeting on 30 April and 1 May 1979 were clear that the decision meant the removal of Leballo from the leadership and while many observers also suspected as much, Leballo's status was ambiguous. Theoretically, he was still the Chairman of the PAC; according to the statement of the decisions of the meeting (dated 1 May 1979): 'The Presidential Council will maintain contact with the Chairman of the Central Committee.'

Fear of negative international reaction as well as a fear of a violent response from the militarily-trained cadres loyal to Leballo (including the high command) prompted the Central Committee to devise the formula adopted at the meeting, but in actuality it failed to achieve both objectives.

The announcement of Leballo's temporary departure for 'health reasons' created a great deal of confusion among PAC members, particularly those in other countries, many of whom only heard or read about it in the media. Among the cadres in Tanzania who led the opposition to Leballo, there was a mixture of anger and disappointment at the failure of the Central Committee to expel and denounce Leballo. Cadres loyal to Leballo on the other hand were deeply suspicious.

Leballo meanwhile pretended to acquiesce in the decision and even appeared relieved; he pledged his full co-operation in the transition. The day after the meeting of the Central Committee, Sibeko left Dar-es-Salaam for New York.

High Command Briefed on Central Committee Decisions
In the afternoon of 2 May 1979 a meeting was held at Leballo's apartment in Keko between members of the Central Committee and members of the high command. The Central Committee members present were: P.K. Leballo, Vus Make, Elias Ntloedibe, Erret Radebe, Reggie

158 The Crisis in the PAC: 1978–83

Xoxelelo and this writer. The high command was represented by Justice Nkonyane, Dan Mtimkulu, Richard Zakwe, Glenville Williams, Ingram Mazibuko and Cydrick Masters. The purpose of the meeting was to inform the high command of the decisions taken at the extraordinary meeting of the Central Committee.

At the outset of the meeting, Leballo emphasised the need for secrecy until the decisions were officially announced. He argued that 'rumour-mongering and speculation' were dangerous: since the situation was already tense, passions could easily be aroused, with serious consequences for the organisation.

Vus Make, in his capacity as Administrative Secretary, was charged with the responsibility of providing the background to the extraordinary meeting and communicating to the high command the decisions reached by the Central Committee. Make began by recalling the Arusha consultative conference, the purpose of which was to 'preserve and consolidate the unity of the PAC'. More importantly, it aimed at establishing 'a structure which could deal in a decisive manner with the problems confronting the organisation'. That structure was the Military Commission, a sub-organ of the Central Committee which would liaise with the high command. The Military Commission, presided over by Leballo as Chairman of the Central Committee and comprising three other members of the Central Committee, namely, Edwin Makoti (then Secretary for Defence), Victor Mayekiso and Esrom Mokgakala, and the high command were responsible for the implementation of the PAC's programme of action. He stressed that at Arusha it was firmly established that the members of APLA were first and foremost members of the PAC. Rather than being a separate organisation, APLA was the military wing of the PAC.

In the period after the Arusha conference, Make continued, problems arose between APLA and the Central Committee. The Military Commission, charged with the task of defining structures to streamline the functioning of the military, did not succeed. As a result, there were strains within the organisation between the military and political leadership. Make pointed out that from about November 1978 there were disturbing developments, with mass movements of the militarily-trained cadres from the camp at Ithumbi into Dar-es-Salaam. In December 1978, Central Committee members were assaulted during the siege of their residence at Kijitonyama by the militarily-trained cadres.

At the plenary meeting of the Central Committee in January 1979, cognisance was taken of the positive developments. The presence of the PAC in South Africa was manifested as a result of the activities of APLA. In the course of work, Make stated, errors were made, not intentionally, because the high command virtually 'had to start from scratch'. At the plenary meeting, the contributions of APLA were recognised. Similarly, at the OAU Liberation Committee meeting in January 1979, there was a recognition of these positive developments and a call for increased material assistance to the national liberation movements, including the PAC.

On the debit side, however, Make continued, the tension in the organisation jeopardised the positive developments. At the OAU Liberation Committee meeting reference was made to the unruly behaviour of undisciplined PAC cadres. The PAC acknowledged that there had been poor communication between the cadres and the political leadership but rejected the idea of general indiscipline. The Ghanaian delegation called upon the PAC not to fritter away resources on solving its internal problems. Brigadier Hashim Mbita, Executive Secretary of the OAU Liberation Committee, urged the PAC to abandon the notion of 'thriving on crises'.

Continuing to trace developments in the organisation, Make reported what the Chairman, Leballo, had told the plenary meeting about the Tanzanian warning, and the setting up of a Commission of Inquiry. The Tanzanian authorities again saw in the appointment of the commission a delaying tactic, said Make. They made it clear that the Tanzanian government would not allow the PAC to be a law unto itself, to break the laws of Tanzania with impunity. The Central Committee, according to Make, assured the authorities of the intention to solve the problems.

Make pointed out that in the period after the January plenary meeting the situation deteriorated even further. There were reports of threats and counter-threats between two groups within the PAC, culminating in the events on 8 April 1969. It was very clear that the PAC was once more faced with a very serious situation. He then described the expulsion of the 40 cadres and Tanzanian annoyance with the PAC.

The Chairman had been frankly asked for his opinion of the state of the PAC. Make explained that Leballo 'agreed to accept *any* structures decided upon to save the PAC'. The Central Committee had stressed that the stage had been reached when not only the PAC but Leballo's 'own person was in danger', he said. The Central Committee had therefore requested Leballo to take a respite, to travel to another country where the Central Committee would remain in contact with him. A three-person Presidential Council would assume the duties of the Chairman. Make stated that the decision would be conveyed to the rank-and-file members of the organisation and implemented. He pledged his personal commitment to do everything possible to solve all these problems and called for 'unity and co-operation because the PAC' was 'in danger'.

After Make's presentation, Leballo invited comments from other Central Committee members. Elias Ntloedibe vouched for the completeness of the report. He recalled that in 1968 the PAC had faced a similar situation in Zambia. While the leaders and members of the organisation were preparing for a meeting, they were arrested.[3] Subsequently, they were deported to Tanzania. He emphasised that insofar as Tanzania was concerned, the end had also been reached.

160   *The Crisis in the PAC: 1978–83*

Reggie Xoxelelo expressed the view that it was a sad decision to request the Chairman of the organisation to take leave. He reassured the meeting that Leballo would return to resume his duties when he was able to do so. He concluded his remarks by stressing the unanimity of the decision that Leballo should relinquish his position in favour of the Presidential Council.

Erret Radebe (then Director of Finance) stated that it was imperative that all members of the PAC rally round the Presidential Council in order to execute the tasks 'of the Azanian revolution'. He added that 'consultation and co-operation' were essential to achieve this goal.

Reactions of the High Command and the Tanzanians

After the Central Committee members concluded their remarks, Justice Nkonyane addressed the meeting on behalf of the high command. Nkonyane stated that 'the army' had always called for 'unity and progress'. That position remained unchanged. Referring to the decision of the Central Committee to set up a Presidential Council to assume the duties of the Chairman, he stated that the members of the Presidential Council should be aware of the tasks ahead, and asked, rhetorically, 'but are they aware of it?' He continued unemotionally: 'We have lost nine comrades. *The army will use the (maximum) ruthlessness to crush anybody who obstructs unity and progress. There will be no compromise this time.*' (Emphasis added.)

Expressing the view of the high command, Nkonyane saw the departure of Leballo as a 'sad blow' to the PAC. He added, ominously, 'The army will now not stomach anything'. They had, he said, learned much from Leballo who was held in 'high esteem by the cadres'. Nkonyane pledged the support of the high command for the Presidential Council. He concluded by saying that after the Arusha consultative conference the high command had implemented the 'home-going programme', but that the main problem had been that the 'members of the Central Committee don't understand the army'.

Following the statement by Justice Nkonyane, Vus Make again intervened. He agreed that 'for various reasons we have not known each other very well', and welcomed the pledge of co-operation made by Nkonyane on behalf of the high command. Make added: 'Comrade Justice has unique experiences which will be invaluable in solving the problems.' He again pledged the co-operation of the Presidential Council.

P.K. Leballo then took the floor. He thanked all present, from the 'bottom of [his] heart for the pledges of unity'. He recalled the work done by Lembede, Sobukwe and Mothopeng. The decision of the Central Committee, he continued, had been taken at his suggestion and the Central Committee had indicated that there would be regular consultations with him. Leballo intimated (despite the secrecy to which all members of the Central Committee had pledged after the meeting) that he had reported to the members of the high command that he felt that at that stage he had no place in Tanzania. People 'not involved in the mess', could, he thought, 'clear it up'.

From a document containing minutes of a meeting at the camp, addressed by Justice Nkonyane, after the decision that Leballo should relinquish his position as Chairman, it is very clear that what Leballo intimated was a report to the high command was actually a discussion of continued co-operation between the high command and himself, co-operation which the high command hoped would be useful in their efforts to gain control of the PAC leadership. The document, titled 'Summary of APLA meeting — 10th May, 1979 — Ithumbi', speaks of the need for the 'army' to wage a struggle to change the 'status quo within the Party (PAC)', simultaneously with the implementation of a military programme aimed at executing the armed struggle. The 'inner-party struggle', which they regarded as essential, is a reference to the need to remove the Central Committee whose members they regarded as being united in their intention 'to destroy the army'. This aspect will be dealt with in greater detail later on, but has been introduced here to illustrate the duplicitous nature of Leballo who, while pledging his full co-operation to the Central Committee to ensure a smooth transition to the Presidential Council, had made promises to the high command, promises that were sufficiently encouraging to them to reinforce their resolve to remove (by whatever means) the Central Committee members. The document states: 'The re-establishment of co-operation with P.K. [Leballo] depends on whether he fulfils the promises which he made to the high command before his departure.'

Leballo expressed concern about conditions at the camp in Ithumbi where, in spite of the hardships, the militarily-trained cadres remained, 'except for a few defectors who engaged in the events at the twentieth anniversary [meeting]'. (Obviously, Leballo was bitter at the fact that one of the main organisers of the demonstration on 8 April 1979 was his former bodyguard, 'Bobo' Moerane, hence his reference to 'defectors'. Almost all those who demonstrated against Leballo were not militarily-trained.)

Finally, Leballo said: 'Without showing results on the ground, we are nothing. the army without the party is nothing; the party without the army is nothing. The army without the people is nothing.'

At that point the members of the high command departed, leaving the Central Committee members to confer. The purpose of that session was to receive reports on the consultations held by Central Committee members with Tanzanian government officials. David Sibeko and Vus Make had had discussions with the head of the Africa and Middle East section in the Ministry of Foreign Affairs, Mr. Mwasegafuka. According to Vus Make, Mr. Mwasegafuka's reaction to the report that Leballo had

162 *The Crisis in the PAC: 1978–83*

relinquished his position was that the position of the PAC continued to be very grave. He informed Make and Sibeko that the Tanzanian government had decided on one of two courses of action, namely, that if the PAC could not handle its affairs it should be ordered to leave Tanzania or, alternatively, that Tanzania would press for the de-recognition of the PAC as a national liberation movement by the OAU. The only debate centred around the timing of the action. According to Mr. Mwasegafuka, the Central Committee, by pressurising Leballo to relinquish his position, had saved the organisation. He went on to assure the PAC delegation of Tanzania's support if the organisation put its house in order.

Other delegations of the Central Committee had held discussions with officials in the Ministry of Home Affairs and the Prime Minister's office. The general reaction was that the Tanzanian authorities had reached the end of the road with the PAC, but that the ouster of Leballo had earned the organisation a reprieve.

Leballo, for his part, informed the meeting that he was advised by Mr. Kibasa from the Prime Minister's office to leave the country as soon as possible.

The Tanzanian government had thus gone full circle in its relations with the PAC and with P.K. Leballo in particular. As a result of his role as the main state witness in the 1968 Treason Trial of several Tanzanians charged with plotting the overthrow of the government of President Julius Nyerere, Leballo had gained the support and full backing of the state in exercising his control and asserting his leadership of the PAC. Many of his opponents had been detained by the Tanzanian authorities at his request, others had been declared prohibited immigrants and deported. Many PAC members were denied entry into Tanzania at the behest of Leballo. Now Leballo and the PAC had become an embarrassment to Tanzania, an influential OAU front-line state which could use its power and status against the organisation. The question of Leballo's support by the Tanzanian government is important in attempting to answer the question, which will be done later on, why he was able to survive at the helm of the PAC for the length of time that he did, given his ineffectual leadership and the crises for which he was held personally responsible.

The statement made by Justice Nkonyane at the meeting with the Central Committee is important, in that it reflects the thinking and attitudes prevailing within the high command towards the removal of Leballo from the leadership and their attitude towards the Central Committee in general and the Presidential Council in particular. These attitudes would determine the course of events within the PAC during the ensuing weeks. Nkonyane pledged the co-operation of 'the army' with the Presidential Council but warned that 'the army' would deal 'ruthlessly' with any person who 'obstructed the revolution'.

Nkonyane's warning was lost on Make who subsequently intimated

Leballo Ousted   163

after the meetings in Keko that he believed that the members of the high command were genuinely co-operative. This point requires further amplification because repeatedly in the following months Make, as well as Sibeko, demonstrated the same poor judgement. This was because they did not really know the cadres (both military and untrained) intimately, nor were they fully conversant with the developments at the PAC headquarters. Both of them had been based away from headquarters, Make in West Africa and Sibeko in New York. Even though Make was appointed Administrative Secretary in November 1978 (and confirmed in that position by the Central Committee at the January 1979 plenary meeting) he did not effectively take up the post until after the removal of Leballo in May, by which time he had the responsibility also of the Presidential Council's chairmanship. Whenever they visit the PAC's headquarters, they lived in hotels in Dar-es-Salaam. In April 1979 when they attended the Central Committee meeting, they lived in the apartment of a friend in Sea-View. Their contacts with the cadres were limited, communication superficial. Moreover, Sibeko in particular was susceptible to flattery and believed that he could buy the loyalty of cadres through gifts of items of clothing and other commodities purchased abroad. Even though the two of them were informed by other Central Committee members of the depth of feeling against them personally, manipulated in the main by Leballo who told the cadres exaggerated stories of 'high living abroad' and embezzlement of funds by Make and Sibeko, they made little effort to correct these mistaken impressions and in a sense fuelled the situation. For example, they often invited some of the cadres to their hotel rooms where they entertained them with liquor — normally expensive brands of Scotch purchased duty-free abroad. Yet, the cadres had been informed by Leballo that the reason why they could not be sent back to South Africa to fight was because 'Sibeko was hoarding money in New York' and that there were 'vultures squandering money'.

Leballo's apparent co-operation with the Central Committee in consenting to relinquish his position, masked a more devious scheme, namely that he would leave for London as soon as possible while the APLA cadres loyal to him, led by Justice Nkonyane and the high command, would cause as much disruption as possible, and agitate for his re-instatement. The first hint that all was not well came when Leballo, rather than surrender all his property to the Central Committee, surrendered it to the high command. The pistols which he was permitted to carry for his personal protection were handed over to Cydrick Masters, a member of the high command. In breach of the agreement with the Presidential Council, he handed over to Justice Nkonyane, a small Yugoslav-manufactured automobile; he later explained that Justice would merely use it to travel to the camp at Ithumbi to apprise the cadres there of the recent developments.

The decision to entrust to Justice Nkonyane and the high command

164   *The Crisis in the PAC: 1978–83*

the responsibility of apprising the APLA cadres at the camp of the developments, including the departure of Leballo, was a grave error. Firstly, the high command was hostile to the Central Committee, especially to the members of the Presidential Council appointed to assume the duties of the Chairman. The Central Committee had no control over the nature and content of the briefing given to the cadres by Nkonyane and the high command. Secondly, the Presidential Council lost the opportunity to assert its authority over the military wing of the organisation from the very outset of its tenure of leadership. The high command and the militarily-trained cadres were able to continue as before, without respect for or allegiance to the central authority in the organisation. More importantly, they would implement the plan agreed upon with Leballo of agitating for his re-instatement. More of this later.

Leballo Leaves Tanzania

Leballo departed for London the Sunday morning immediately following the Central Committee meeting. Among the few people who were at the airport in Dar-es-Salaam to see him off were Ntloedibe and this writer. He was in cheerful spirit as he boarded the British Airways flight at Dar-es-Salaam international airport.

In London, Leballo was accommodated by Ngila Muendane, PAC's Chief Representative to the United Kingdom, a fact which aggravated the confusion surrounding his exact status and future role in the organisation. The confusion was to be seen in the correspondence directed to the PAC's headquarters in Dar-es-Salaam.[4] Many PAC members who were previously bitterly opposed to Leballo suddenly changed, arguing that the removal of Leballo and the appointment of a Presidential Council were 'unconstitutional'. One of the persons who argued that the removal of 'Acting President Leballo' was unconstitutional was Dipheko Abel Chiloane, who had spent fifteen years on Robben Island and who had been posted to London early in 1979 as Assistant Representative. Ironically, he had been one of the victims of the massive police swoop in the early 1960s following Leballo's infamous press conference in Maseru when he indicated that he had an army of 150,000 men ready to attack the Whites in South Africa.

Michael Tsolo, the PAC representative in the Netherlands, as well as Modipe Mokgadi, PAC's representative in West Germany, had not been fully apprised of the decision and the circumstances leading to the removal of Leballo. When they telephoned Muendane in London, the latter informed them that Leballo had relinquished his position for 'health reasons' and that he had gone to Iraq. Later, when they heard the news of the murder of Sibeko, they again telephoned Muendane only to be informed by Muendane's wife that Leballo was in London at their home.[5] Consequently, Tsolo and Mokgadi travelled to London after

Leballo Ousted   165

Muendane and his wife had travelled to Botswana for Sibeko's funeral. They went there ostensibly to enquire from Leballo himself what had happened. Leballo was able to convince Tsolo in particular that he had been unfairly treated by the Central Committee and that the murder of Sibeko was the result of APLA's protest against the usurpation of his leadership. Thereafter, Tsolo became one of Leballo's strongest supporters, as will be seen later on.

High Command Defies New Leadership
Leballo's departure from Tanzania did not solve the problems of the organisation; instead, it began to drift into a state of disintegration. Leballo remained in regular telephonic communication with the high command while in London. The high command and Don Morwatsehle, PAC's assistant representative and protocol officer in Dar-es-Salaam, were living in Leballo's apartment in Keko where they had use of a telephone. Their telephonic communications with Leballo in London and the APLA cadres in the camp, through the representative in the nearby town of Mbeya, were not monitored.

The members of the Presidential Council had dispersed. Sibeko returned to New York, Ntloedibe to Botswana, while Make went to Arusha to attend the Conference on Refugees in Africa.

The high command implemented its programme of disruptive activities, at the PAC headquarters in Dar-es-Salaam as well as at the military camp at Ithumbi. In Dar-es-Salaam they continued their reign of terror against those cadres who had opposed Leballo. Simultaneously, a reign of terror was unleashed at the camp; cadres suspected to be loyal to the Central Committee were assaulted, tortured and threatened with death.

One great danger was that the high command was armed. Apart from the pistols surrendered to them by Leballo, they also had an unspecified quantity of arms and ammunition which were part of the consignment smuggled into the country by Leballo and Mayekiso in November 1978 and which had been the object of the disagreement between them.

Ingram Mazibuko, a member of the high command, was despatched to the camp to inform the APLA cadres that the high command had decided to liquidate all 'counter-revolutionaries' both at the camp and in the leadership.[6] During his visit to the camp in May to apprise the cadres of the decision to remove Leballo from the leadership, Justice Nkonyane had already prepared them psychologically for what the minutes of the APLA meeting of 10 May 1979 refer to as 'inner-party struggle' and changing the 'status quo within the party'. By this they clearly meant the seizure of control of the central organs of the PAC by the high command and the militarily-trained cadres. The document speaks of:

The problem of establishing a rear base still remains, but steps are to be

166 The Crisis in the PAC: 1978–83

taken at [sic] changing the status quo within the Party. However, due to the present situation of insecurity prevailing within the Party the steps to be taken to change the status quo can neither be revealed nor discussed. Instead the highest form of military discipline must prevail.

Meanwhile, in Dar-es-Salaam on Saturday, 2 June 1979 a number of APLA cadres, led by the high command, intercepted Reggie Xoxelelo, a member of the Central Committee who acted as the organisation's accountant, as he was leaving the National Bank of Commerce in Independence Avenue after transacting a withdrawal of money. They confiscated four thousand shillings (approximately US$500) in cash. When questioned by Make about this criminal act, Justice Nkonyane, without remorse, offered neither an explanation nor an apology. After consultations, the Central Committee decided to report the matter to the Prime Minister's office, to Colonel Matiko who was in charge of the Special Defence Unit (SDU), and to the Police Department. That same afternoon, Justice Nkonyane and Mzwandile Ngqojane ('Zwai Maglas') were arrested in the PAC office by officers of the Criminal Investigation Department.

That night armed police officers were posted at all the PAC residences in Dar-es-Salaam and environs because of the threat of violence by other members of the high command and the militarily-trained cadres who had come from the camp in large numbers.

The following day this writer departed for New York to attend the governing council of the UNDP, with a view to submitting the report of the feasibility study of the Institute the PAC planned to establish in the Sudan. At the same time, David Sibeko was to be fully briefed on all the developments since he was due to travel to Dar-es-Salaam to attend a meeting of the OAU Liberation Committee a few days later.

Upon arrival in New York, this writer apprised David Sibeko fully of the developments at the PAC's headquarters, with a warning of the gravity of the situation. Sibeko demonstrated his usual lack of familiarity with the situation caused by his distance from the scene. In fact, on the day of his departure from New York — Friday, 8 June 1979 — he rehearsed for this writer the speech he indicated he would make when meeting with the APLA cadres in Dar-es-Salaam. He also sought the comments of the writer on the draft text of a memorandum he had prepared requesting the assistance of the Tanzanian authorities in dealing with the problems caused by the members of the high command as the first step. The reactions of this writer were two-fold: firstly, that talking to the high command would be an exercise in futility because they believed that they had the support of 'the army', while the 'political leadership' had only the support of a handful of militarily-trained cadres and untrained cadres at the transit centre in the Bagamoyo district. The objective of the high command was the seizure of control of the organisation — the 'strategic leadership', as they termed it. With the removal of Leballo they saw this objective recede from grasp; all along they had maintained, privately, that their support for Leballo was tactical and temporary and that after they had secured the 'strategic leadership', they would abandon him also. Secondly, the Tanzanian authorities seemed reluctant to intervene because in the past the PAC leadership had used them to detain 'dissidents' and cadres critical of the leadership.[8]

Sibeko felt that the Presidential Council would be able to deal with the situation. That Friday night this writer parted with him before he made the British Airways flight to London after warning Sibeko to be careful in Dar-es-Salaam because the high command was dangerous. It would be the last time that this writer would see David Sibeko alive. Ironically, his wife, Elizabeth, was to have accompanied him to the John F. Kennedy International Airport and to have returned with this writer. Upon reaching their apartment at 875 West End Avenue, on the west side of New York City, she quarrelled with her husband and he left without her; she did not even come out of the bedroom to say good-night. That would be the last time that she, too, would see David Sibeko alive.

Notes

1. Statement dated 2 April 1979.
2. Statement given to the author April 1979.
3. On 17 July 1983 in Harare, Zimbabwe, Mr. Aaron Milner, the former Zambian Minister of Home Affairs, related a different version of the PAC's expulsion. He claimed that the PAC's military cadres held their leaders hostage in a house which had been mined, threatening to kill them. The leaders were rescued by the Zambian army. The incident, he said, was the final straw that decided the Zambian government to order the PAC to leave the country. According to Mr. Milner, while the PAC was in Zambia the organisation had endless internal problems.
4. For example, letter from Kenya Branch of PAC, May 1979.
5. Information given to the author by Tsolo in Rotterdam, The Netherlands, in April 1980 and corroborated by Mokgadi at the plenary meeting in April 1980. Muendane was present at the plenary meeting and did not challenge Mokgadi's version of the sequence of events.
6. Information provided by APLA cadres who were at the camp at that time and who were among those assaulted and tortured.
7. They were released a few days later for lack of evidence; they argued, successfully, that Reggie Xoxelelo had voluntarily surrendered the money to them upon request for their weekly allowance. Unknown to the Central Committee members at that time, Xoxelelo collaborated with the high command.
8. At the trial in March 1981 of six PAC cadres charged with the murder of David Sibeko, Winston Mwaipyana, an official from the Prime Minister's office, in reply to a question by defence counsel for one of the accused, affirmed that the government attitude towards pleas of indiscipline among cadres within the liberation movements, especially the PAC, was one of scepticism, as it was often a ploy for dealing with 'dissidents' — *Tanzania Daily News*, 20 March 1981.

9. The Assassination of David M. Sibeko

David Maphumzana Sibeko arrived in Dar-es-Salaam on Sunday, 10 June 1979 on the British Airways flight from London.[1] Vus Make, meanwhile, had gone to the Seychelles, to attend the celebrations marking the fourth anniversary of their revolution under the leadership of President Albert René. That was in itself indicative of Make's leadership; despite the fact that the situation within the PAC was explosive, he chose to travel instead of dealing with the problems confronting the organisation. He returned to Dar-es-Salaam that same evening.

The Central Committee's Plans

As was customary, various members of the Central Committee gathered in Sea-View at the apartment of a friend where Sibeko and Make were living. They socialised, drinking the duty-free Scotch brought by Sibeko and Make from their respective travels. Unknown to them, they were under surveillance by members of the high command. While socialising, they also discussed the tense situation in the organisation and attempted to formulate a strategy to defuse it before the OAU Liberation Committee meeting scheduled for 25 June 1979. The danger was that should there be signs of further trouble within the PAC, certain members of the OAU Liberation Committee (like Angola and Mozambique, who were hostile to the PAC) might demand the de-recognition of the PAC as a national liberation movement by the OAU. That would cut off its major source of support and would almost certainly be followed by its de-recognition by the UN, as well as the Movement of Non-Aligned Countries. Without such international support the PAC would almost certainly disappear, unless a country was prepared to host the organisation while it nursed itself to life again — if it ever would.

The strategy formulated was that Sibeko, Make and other Central Committee members would sound out officials in the Tanzanian Government and the Secretariat of the OAU Liberation Committe and assess the degree of co-operation which they could expect in dealing with the situation. They would seek the arrest of the members of the high command. Thereafter, they would proceed to the camp at Ithumbi to assert discipline and the authority of the leadership. Precise modalities for this were not defined.

The Central Committee, incuding Sibeko, were warned on the day of the shooting by one of the cadres, Ray Johnson, who had fled from the camp, that the APLA cadres who were loyal to Leballo had arms and ammunition which were hidden at the camp. According to Johnson, Sibeko thought that he was exaggerating the gravity of the situation.[2]

The High Command Plots

A decision had been taken at the camp to eliminate physically the PAC leaders, beginning with the members of the Presidential Council. To coincide with this, there would be 'internal operations', a euphemism for the torture and the physical elimination, if necessary, of those APLA cadres at the camp who were known to be or suspected of being loyal to the leadership.

The idea was that after the liquidation of the Central Committee members, the high command would present themselves to the OAU Liberation Committee as the new PAC leaders and demand the reinstatement of Leballo. Certain members of the high command propagated the false notion that the OAU Liberation Committee was 'fed up' with the 'corrupt PAC leadership' which had no plans or intention to wage armed struggle and was sympathetic to the APLA cadres. It was argued and hoped that in the event of their eliminating their leaders, they would have the support of the OAU Liberation Committee. One young cadre, Lazarus Khumbuza, even informed them that after he fled from South Africa following the 1976 Soweto uprisings, he had had discussions with FRELIMO militants in Mozambique. According to him, the FRELIMO militants confided in him that they had also been faced with the problem of 'corrupt leadership' during their struggle against Portuguese colonialism, conveying the impression that the FRELIMO militants accused their founder president, Dr. Eduardo Mondlane, of corruption and accepted responsibility for his assassination in 1969. Such a version of FRELIMO history was patently untrue; Dr. Mondlane was killed by a parcel bomb sent to him by the Portuguese Secret Police (PIDE). Whilst it is true that FRELIMO charged a number of counter-revolutionary forces such as L. Nkavandame with corruption, they were expelled from the movement, not 'liquidated'. This incident demonstrates the extent to which APLA cadres loyal to Leballo were prepared to lie, intimidate and manipulate others in order to achieve their aims.

One of the escapees from the camp was Thobile Gola (at the time of

170   *The Crisis in the PAC: 1978–83*

writing, Chief Representative to Tanzania and member of the Central Committee) who attempted to reach Dar-es-Salaam so as to alert the leadership to the murder plans. In order to avert detection by the cadres who were involved in the plot to eliminate the Central Committee members, he escaped through the surrounding forest. Enduring great hardship, including having to walk many miles, he ultimately reached Dar-es-Salaam but by then Sibeko had already been fatally shot.[3]

The Murder

The evening of 11 June 1979 Sibeko and Make attended a reception hosted by the Ambassador of Burundi to Tanzania, after which they returned alone to the apartment in Sea-View.[4] Late that same night, there was a knock on the door of the apartment, followed by a male voice speaking in Swahili. The person requested help and indicated that Make's car blocked the driveway. Sibeko attempted to open the door but failed, whereupon Make opened it.

They were confronted not by Tanzanians, but by three PAC cadres; two of them were armed with pistols, the third brandished a knife. One of them was Leballo's former bodyguard, Titus Soni (alias Joe Bembe), who was the leader of the operation. He informed Make and Sibeko that they had come to fetch the two of them to attend a meeting with the cadres of APLA. He went into the bedroom, presumably to see whether there was anybody else in the apartment: before doing so, he issued instructions to the other two to 'shoot' if either Make or Sibeko attempted 'to do anything'.

Sibeko asked why they needed to go to a meeting at gunpoint. The three cadres aggressively replied that they had not 'come to debate'; they then confiscated the wallets of the two men, as well as Sibeko's gold wrist-watch. One of them attempted to manhandle Sibeko, who was bulky, and in the ensuing scuffle shots were fired, one of which hit Sibeko in the head. Shots fired at Make were deflected by the refrigerator behind which he stood. He ran into a store-room and locked the door.

The assailants fled, making their get-away in a PAC land-rover parked outside. Three other APLA cadres waited in the vehicle.

The sound of gunshots and Make's subsequent shouts for help awoke the neighbours in the apartment building. They rushed into the apartment, by which time Sibeko was unconscious on the ground, bleeding profusely from a gunshot wound in the head. An ambulance was called and he was rushed to the hospital where he died fifteen hours later, without having regained consciousness.

The Investigation

The police arrived at the scene and began their investigations immediately. It was fortunate that Make escaped miraculously because he was able to identify at least one of the assailants, Leballo's former bodyguard. Together with the police, he went to the PAC residence at Upanga only to find that for once everybody was 'asleep', including Justice Nkonyane and other members of the high command. They obviously knew what was afoot.

Fortunately also, one of Make's neighbours in Sea-View had seen the white land-rover with a brown canvas tent parked outside the apartment building and later drive away. Make identified it as a PAC vehicle that was used at the camp. With this information, the police mounted road-blocks en route to the camp at Ithumbi. The six APLA cadres were apprehended at Iringa early the following morning, Iringa being a town in Southern Tanzania mid-way between Dar-es-Salaam and the camp. The six had driven through the night. Had they not been apprehended there, they might have succeeded in reaching the camp and never have been arrested. Make's survival was fortuitous for another reason also. It saved innocent people from possible arrest on suspicion of complicity in the murder. At that time, the PAC members led by T.M. Ntantala, who had been expelled at the consultative conference in Arusha the year before, were still in Tanzania attempting to form their Azanian People's Revolutionary Party (APRP). Ntantala conjectured to this writer during an informal discussion in July 1981 after the conviction and sentencing of the six PAC cadres charged with the murder of Sibeko, that he and others belonging to his group might have been suspected of the murder had the assailants not been apprehended after Make's miraculous escape.

It is unlikely, however, that the assailants intended to liquidate their victims in the apartment. There was the danger that the attention of the neighbours would be attracted — which it was — increasing the risks of apprehension. One scenario is that the victims were to be driven to the PAC camp at Ithumbi and murdered on the way. Their bodies could have been buried in the forests without being discovered, possibly for months, if not years. The six could then have returned safely to the camp and either remained there with alibis being provided by the terror squads operating there, or been despatched out of the country under the military programme of the high command.

Make's escape created various personal and political problems for him. It created suspicion that he was implicated in the murder of Sibeko. Many detractors of the PAC interpreted the murder as the result of a power-struggle within the triumvirate of the Presidential Council. During the funeral of Sibeko in Botswana, Make was accused by Elizabeth Sibeko and other members of the bereaved family of complicity in the murder; he was cross-examined by several members of the

172 The Crisis in the PAC: 1978–83

family and asked to explain how he escaped considering that he was much larger in bulk than Sibeko. Upon her return to the USA after her husband's funeral, Elizabeth Sibeko, who was extremely bitter, conveyed to various members of the diplomatic corps at the UN and among supporters of the PAC the view that Make's escape was not fortuitous but contrived. Ntloedibe, who was in Botswana at the time of the shooting, without any first-hand information about the incident, gave an interview to a South African journalist in Botswana in which he informed the journalist that the shooting occurred in the PAC office in Dar-es-Salaam and that Make escaped by defending himself with a chair which deflected the bullets. When ultimately Make gave the correct version of the shooting, the journalist (as well as others who had received the same version from Ntloedibe) was confused and questioned Make closely, apologising for the trouble and pointing out that he had been given a different version by Ntloedibe.[5]

Make was not implicated in the murder of Sibeko; he, along with the other members of the Central Committee, had been targeted for physical elimination by the high command. This has become very clear as a result of the disclosures made by APLA cadres who were at the camp at Ithumbi throughout the period from the time of the removal of Leballo as Chairman of the Central Committee through the assassination of Sibeko and subsequently. A number of these cadres were themselves earmarked for physical elimination, on suspicion of being loyal to the Central Committee and had to flee for their lives.

On 15 June 1981 six PAC cadres were sentenced to 15 years' imprisonment by the Tanzanian High Court after having been convicted on charges relating to the murder of Sibeko.[6]

Notes

1. The following account is drawn from interviews and discussions with people who were in Dar-es-Salaam at the time, including conversations with Vus Make and other Central Committee members. In addition, Make made a very lengthy statement to the OAU Liberation Committee meeting in Dar-es-Salaam on 25 June 1979 at which the author was present.

2. Information from Ray Johnson in Dar-es-Salaam in June 1979 after the fatal shooting.

3. Information from Thobile Gola in Dar-es-Salaam, June 1979, repeated during his testimony at the trial of the six PAC cadres charged with the murder of Sibeko in February 1981 in the Tanzanian High Court, Dar-es-Salaam.

4. Information from the two female members of the PAC who accompanied the two leaders to the reception. At their request, their identities have been withheld, although it must be emphasised that there was no impropriety on the part of Make or Sibeko or the two ladies.

5. Information provided by Make to the author in Monrovia in July 1979 after the funeral of Sibeko. A report by Sophie Thema in the *Post* (14 June 1979) also states that the shooting occurred in the PAC office in Dar-es-Salaam.

6. The six PAC cadres were: Titus Soni, Daniel Monakgotla, Gilbert Nhlapo, Abraham Tatu Rueben Mahlangu, James Hlongwane, Shindo (alias Studio) Mahlangu Deboist Cyril. In April 1984 the Tanzanian Appeal Court reduced their sentences to 10 years' imprisonment each.

10. The Consequences of the Assassination

In this chapter I assess the consequences of the assassination of David Sibeko for the PAC, the first known assassination of a prominent leader of the organisation. Following shortly after the removal of Leballo from the position of Chairman of the Central Committee, his murder served to underscore once more the continuing internal problems of the organisation. His murder was to have far-reaching consequences for the organisation, both internally and internationally, and create lasting problems. This was understandable, given the fact that he was probably the PAC's best-known spokesperson. During the time that he served as the PAC's Observer to the UN and as Director of Foreign Affairs, he made innumerable friends, political acquaintances and contacts, witness the messages of condolence received by the PAC as well as by the Sibeko family from Heads of State, the OAU, members of the diplomatic corps and national liberation movements.[1]

At the UN, the news of his assassination came as a stunning shock to the diplomatic corps, particularly the representatives of the African countries and the non-aligned countries. The memorial service for him, organised jointly by the PAC and the OAU at the Church Centre for the United Nations, was well-attended.

Sibeko was well-known in the USA, particularly in the Black community. Tributes to him came from the Congressional Black Caucus in Washington, DC, and from political activists and various liberation support organisations across the USA and Canada. While still the PAC's representative to the UK and Continental Europe in the late 1960s and early 1970s, Sibeko had travelled to the USA at the invitation of many liberation support organisations and had travelled extensively in North America during the following decade. He was articulate and energetic, and had become one of the best-known representatives of the national liberation movements from Southern Africa in North America.

The Consequences of the Assassination   175

On 1 July 1979 he was finally laid to rest in Gaborone, the capital of Botswana, after the government of that country acceded to the request of his family and the PAC for him to be buried close to his home country. That enabled his parents and relatives, as well as friends and political activists in South Africa to attend the funeral if granted passports by the South African regime.

Death in African society is a period of mourning and penitence, a period when the evil that the deceased has committed during his or her lifetime is forgotten — at least temporarily. Throughout the two-week period before the burial, true to African custom, friends, acquaintances and even strangers, as well as the relatives who had travelled from South Africa, like David's father, William Sibeko, visited the home of the Sibeko family in Gaborone to offer condolences to the widow, Elizabeth, and the four children, Bongani, Lindiwe, Temba and David Jr.

Elizabeth Sibeko and Family vs. Make and the PAC

Both before and after the funeral, however, various struggles were played out in Botswana, between the widow, Elizabeth Sibeko, and other relatives on the one hand, and Make as well as other PAC Central Committee members on the other. There were also incidents that were out of character with the occasion. Sadly, many of the struggles revolved around money which had been contributed both to the PAC and to the bereaved family to defray the costs of the burial. Elizabeth Sibeko insisted that all the financial contributions received by the PAC for the funeral belonged to her, by right of being the widow, and argued that the well-wishers and sympathisers who had made contributions to the PAC did so because they knew and loved David. Outsiders were rudely shocked at the nature of the struggles over the ownership and use of the money. That, however, was the germ of a future struggle between the widow of David Sibeko and the PAC during the next fifteen months, which caused the organisation much harm.

Make, a close personal friend of Sibeko during his lifetime, was accused by various other members of the Sibeko family of complicity in his murder. Make was cross-examined at length and in great detail, about the events leading up to the shooting. He was subjected to the humiliation, as well as the pain, of having to re-enact, for the benefit of the family and others, the drama of the entry of the three armed cadres and his own escape into the store-room which he was able to lock. He was condemned for having survived. That, too, would create serious problems for the PAC because Elizabeth Sibeko would not only inform many people and organisations that Make was implicated in the murder of Sibeko, but she would be able to pressure Make emotionally by constantly reminding him of his personal friendship

176 *The Crisis in the PAC: 1978–83*

with the deceased and of his presence with him that fateful night. Make was therefore not able to reprimand or take any disciplinary action against Elizabeth Sibeko, despite the great deal of harm which she caused the organisation during his tenure as Chairman of the Central Committee.

The problems which were caused and the harm which all this did to the PAC will be explained in greater detail later: the issue has been mentioned here because already at the funeral in Botswana it was clear to most people that Elizabeth Sibeko would create difficulties for the PAC.

The Harrying of Mzonke Xusa and Others

For almost a year prior to the murder of her husband, Elizabeth Sibeko had conducted an intensive and extensive campaign of personal vilification against Mzonke Xusa, a PAC member who had been sent to New York in 1977 at the request of David Sibeko to assist at the PAC Observer Mission to the UN. Subsequently, Xusa was employed by the UN Radio Service in the anti-apartheid programme. She alleged that he was a 'drunkard', a 'disgrace to the PAC', and used every possible method of persuading the Central Committee to recall him to Dar-es-Salaam as a disciplinary measure. The impression that she successfully conveyed to many PAC members in the USA and Tanzania, as well as to outsiders, was that Mzonke Xusa was an alcoholic. Yet, in a 1978 report submitted to the Central Committee, David Sibeko had taken a much more balanced view of the matter:

> Comrade Mzonke Xusa continues to do a good job with the UN radio and TV programme. Occasionally he also comes into the office to help. Mostly, Mzonke, when not at the UN, takes up a number of speaking engagements around the country. However, the Comrade does seem to have a personal problem and I have difficulty getting through to him. I have all along urged him to take initiatives to go and complete his studies, he agrees but does nothing concrete about it, e.g. filling in application forms that Comrade Elizabeth Sibeko recently brought for him from Dar-es-Salaam. Previously there was an idea that he should try to get into school in Canada. Difficult as it may be, I do not think Mzonke exerted himself sufficiently. When I see him again I will attempt to get to the bottom of his problem so that we can see how to resolve it.[2]

Despite this commendation by David Sibeko of Mzonke Xusa's work with the UN, Elizabeth Sibeko, after David's death, persuaded Make to write a letter to Mr. Erik Walters, the Chief of the Radio Services (Radio and Visual Services Division) in the Department of Public Information at the UN: in the letter dated 11 October 1979, Make wrote:

> Our attention has been drawn to [Xusa's] behaviour which is not in keeping with members of the PAC in his work and in his social behaviour. The PAC feels that his behaviour has brought our organisation into disrepute and hereby wishes to discharge any further responsibility for him. In this regard we would urge that he be relieved from his position as an appointee of PAC recommended to the UN.
>
> We would therefore urge that we be given the opportunity to recommend a replacement for Mr. Xusa in keeping with the spirit of the original appointment.

To his credit, Walters refused to accede to the request: in a letter to Make, dated 31 October 1979, Walters wrote:

> I am deeply distressed to learn that you feel that Mr. Xusa has brought the Pan-Africanist Congress of Azania into disrepute and that your organisation wishes to discharge any further responsibility for him. I am at the disposal of your office in New York to discuss this matter further.
>
> On the other hand, I wish to assure you that Mr. Xusa's professional work has been fully up to our standards. Had this not been the case, we would not continue to employ him.
>
> I must also add that, when we lose the services of a senior broadcaster, it is our policy, based entirely on professional considerations, to move the junior broadcaster on that particular language team into the senior position and to employ a new broadcaster at the junior level . . .

This writer, as PAC Observer at the UN, refused to discuss the matter with Walters since the whole issue was clearly a personal vendetta in which the Central Committee (or, more accurately, Make) was simply being used. In the politics of exile, lies, smears, rumours and gossip are common, but what is disturbing is that the leaders of a liberation movement would be prepared to make a very serious decision regarding the professional career and affecting the future of an individual, purely on the basis of gossip and hearsay. The case of Xusa was all the more disturbing because exactly one year earlier, as we have seen, David Sibeko had written a report to the Central Committee in which he commended Xusa's performance.

Nevertheless, Elizabeth Sibeko even pursued this campaign after the death of her husband. Just before the burial, she despatched a cable to the PAC Observer Mission to the UN, addressed to this writer, stating that Mzonke Xusa was not welcome at the memorial service for David in New York. This writer had already left New York when the cable arrived but was later shown the cable. The writer was also informed by the persons who were at the office at the time, that they were so embarrassed that they were inclined not to act on

178 *The Crisis in the PAC: 1978–83*

the instructions contained in the cable. Molefe 'Ike' Mafole, then a student of business administration at Morgan State University in Baltimore (now the PAC's Chief Representative to the USA and the Caribbean) was also at the office at the time; he volunteered to telephone Mzonke Xusa to inform him of the cable and its contents.[3]

Mzonke Xusa, however, was not the only person to be treated in this fashion by Elizabeth Sibeko. Another young female member of the PAC, Nomakwezi Ganya, who was studying in West Germany (and subsequently in Switzerland) despatched a cable to the PAC representative in Botswana, expressing shock at the death of Sibeko and offering her condolences. Elizabeth Sibeko sent the cable back with a note to the effect that her condolences were not welcome.[4]

At the funeral itself, Mxolisi 'Ace' Mgxashe, a PAC member who was expelled at the consultative conference in Arusha in 1978, was asked to leave the church at the insistence of Elizabeth Sibeko.

Such behaviour during the very period of mourning was to be a harbinger of later actions and attitudes which caused the organistion serious embarrassment and harm.

David Sibeko: Protegé of Leballo or Victim?

One of the ironies of Sibeko's murder is that responsibility for the circumstances that led to his death lies, at least in part, with the man to whom he paid unswerving loyalty throughout the many crises which he faced, the man he revered as 'Mookameli', meaning 'President'. That man is Leballo. Throughout Leballo's struggles against his colleagues in the old National Executive Committee and later against the Ntantala faction, Sibeko supported him faithfully and strongly. When Leballo engineered the arrests of PAC members in Swaziland in April 1978 on false charges of supporting a Swazi faction engaged in treasonable activities, Sibeko had accompanied him on the mission.

In January, when Leballo was faced with the possibility of a vote of no-confidence from the Central Committee and representatives, meeting in plenary, Sibeko rescued him by proposing the appointment of a Commission of Inquiry. In April 1979, when it was absolutely clear that the continued leadership of the PAC by Leballo would result in the derecognition of the organisation, Sibeko supported the decision that resulted in the removal of Leballo from the leadership. Sibeko, however, also attempted to implicate other Central Committee members as instigators of the actions by the cadres against Leballo at the twentieth anniversary commemorative meeting in Dar-es-Salaam, actions which sparked the chain of events already described.

Even the US Embassy in Dar-es-Salaam identified Sibeko as being 'strongly pro-Leballo' in a cable to the State Department in May 1979:

The Consequences of the Assassination 179

> Reporting in other channels has indicated increasing dissatisfaction within the PAC in recent months with Leballo's leadership. Anti-Leballo dissidents have held demonstrations and on one occasion briefly occupied PAC headquarters in Dar. Concerned with the factional infighting in the PAC, TANGOV [The Tanzanian Government] has threatened to de-recognize PAC as a legitimate liberation movement unless unity was restored. Three-man Presidential Council appears to be effort to balance pro- and anti-Leballo factions. Make is strongly anti-Leballo, Sibeko is strongly pro-Leballo, while orientation of Ntloedibe is not clear.[5]

Leballo used Sibeko. He also incited the APLA cadres against him. Several of the accusations against Sibeko by Leballo have already been referred to; he informed the militarily-trained cadres that they could not be infiltrated back into South Africa to wage armed struggle because Sibeko was 'hoarding money in New York'. To the young cadres who joined the PAC after the 1976 Soweto uprisings, that was extremely inflammatory.

After the death of Mangaliso Robert Sobukwe, there was speculation in the South African media as to his probable successor. Most analysts ruled out Leballo in view of his unpopularity among the majority of PAC members and his widely-recognised lack of intellectual ability. The Johannesburg *Star* suggested that the most likely candidate was David Sibeko who was widely-known internationally and well-respected in various circles. That was probably Sibeko's undoing, because thereafter Leballo identified him as a potential contender for the leadership. The impression that Sibeko himself conveyed was that he was interested in the position of President.

At the Arusha consultative conference in June–July 1978, Leballo was extremely bitter that he had not been appointed President of the PAC. During the informal consultations which took place at the conference, he frequently stated that he had not been Acting President for nothing; since Sobukwe (for whom he was deputising) had died, Leballo saw no reason why he should not be confirmed as President of the PAC. The consensus at Arusha was that it was untimely to elect or appoint a President so soon after the death of Sobukwe, since that might be interpreted by the people in South Africa as a power struggle among the PAC members in exile even before expiry of the customary one year of mourning. Sibeko supported this view.

Sibeko, however, was not without ambition; at the consultative conference, he hinted to this writer on at least one occasion that 'some people' suggested that he should be appointed 'Deputy-Chairman'. He dismissed it jokingly, saying, 'they want Leballo to kill me'.

After the Arusha conference, there was a noticeable coolness, almost hostility, on the part of Leballo towards Sibeko. Leballo cultivated a close relationship with Victor Mayekiso as has already been explained,

180   *The Crisis in the PAC: 1978–83*

and strengthened his control over the high command to the exclusion of the Military Commission. On the one hand, Leballo incited the militarily-trained cadres against Sibeko and Make, and on the other hand (when it served his interests) he incited Mayekiso and other Central Committee members against them. Leballo's guile and deviousness, as well as his divisive and manipulative nature, will be examined in greater detail later on.

Sibeko and Leballo were able to maintain the alliance for as long as they did because they shared many common characteristics: they were both egocentrics, with both deporting themselves as head of state and foreign minister, respectively, of an independent country, rather than individuals still engaged in struggle. Both of them surrounded themselves with sycophants: many of the individuals who were appointed as representatives by the Central Committee on the recommendation of Sibeko were appointed not because of any demonstrated ability but because of their personal friendship with or allegiance to Sibeko, a fact which caused a great deal of resentment among many members of the PAC.

Sibeko was intolerant of educated individuals, often dismissing them as 'bourgeois academics' or 'bourgeois intellectuals', in the same vein as Leballo. But this could perhaps be explained by the fact that he was a man of humble origins and modest education; he was, however, self-taught and, it needs to be added, extremely capable.

Sibeko's close identification with Leballo earned him the enmity and wrath of many a PAC member, particularly those scattered in all parts of the globe as a result of Leballo's ruthless use of the state machinery of host governments in certain African countries against the members of the organisation.

Regardless of Sibeko's personal weaknesses and foibles, he served the PAC very ably and was a worthy ambassador for the national liberation struggle. His demise was a great and tragic loss to the PAC as well as the national liberation struggle to which he had made an outstanding contribution.

Sibeko's Assassination Widely Publicised

The murder of David Sibeko received much publicity in the press in South Africa, particularly the Black-run *Post*[6] and *The Voice*. The family and relatives of the slain leader were still in the Johannesburg area in South Africa; he originally lived there and worked in the advertisement department of *Drum*, a popular Black magazine. He had friends and acquaintances who still worked in the media. One of them was Percy Qoboza, former editor of *Post*, who had met Sibeko only a few weeks earlier in New York. He paid tribute to Sibeko in a column.[7]

The Voice commented that Sibeko's death again 'spotlights the painful dissension which has built up over the years among Black South African leaders in exile'.[8] Despite the disunity abroad, Blacks in South Africa were uniformly saddened by the murder of a fellow countryman who was perceived to be committed to the struggle for national liberation.

The White press also gave coverage to the assassination. The *Sunday Times* reported that former US Ambassador to the UN Andrew Young had visited Mrs. Sibeko and that Young had had extensive personal contact with Sibeko through Young's guardianship of the Sobukwe children.[9]

APLA Unleashes Reign of Terror

The PAC in Tanzania was seriously split, with the majority of the militarily-trained cadres at the camp in Ithumbi supporting the high command and those arrested in connection with the murder of Sibeko.[10] In addition, these cadres claimed to pay allegiance to Leballo as their leader.

The Central Committee could rely on the support of only a few militarily-trained cadres who had been victimised for their suspected loyalty to the Central Committee. Other cadres living at the transit centre in Bagamoyo also supported the Central Committee in varying degrees. In Dar-es-Salaam, there were also a number of untrained cadres loyal to the leadership.

Tanzanian authorities tightened security both at the camp in Ithumbi and in Dar-es-Salaam. The PAC office and residences in and around Dar-es-Salaam were guarded by armed police and the militia. At the camp in Ithumbi the size of the Special Defence Unit (SDU) was increased.

In addition to the increased security provided by the Tanzanian authorities, the cadres who supported the leadership maintained a high degree of vigilance in and around Dar-es-Salaam. These cadres apprehended a number of members of the high command who had gone into hiding. They also apprehended and turned over to the Tanzanian authorities a number of militarily-trained cadres who had left the camp. From documents which were subsequently discovered at the camp in mid-1980, also from subsequent evidence provided by cadres who were at the camp during that period but who did not support all the actions of the APLA cadres there, the supporters of the high command resolved to complete the task that had been begun with the assassination of Sibeko. To this end, a number of 'hit squads' (comprising two to three militarily-trained cadres each) were to be despatched to Dar-es-Salaam regularly in an attempt to eliminate the remaining Central Committee members. Simultaneously, with the despatch of the 'hit squads' to Dar-es-Salaam, there would be 'internal operations', a

182   *The Crisis in the PAC: 1978–83*

euphemism for torture of APLA cadres suspected of being loyal to the leadership.

In reality, the Central Committee had no access to the camp and could not provide protection for those APLA cadres who did not support the programme of physical elimination of PAC members. Consequently, a reign of terror prevailed at the camp, with violence and brutality being perpetrated against those suspected of loyalty to the Central Committee. One cadre killed and buried in a shallow grave at the camp was Cohen Ntuli, brother of the well-known sculptor and poet, Pitika Ntuli. Ironically, Cohen was one of the commanders of the APLA cadres during the raid on the residence in Kijitonyama in December 1978 when Central Committee members were taken hostage and assaulted. According to an APLA cadre who was a close personal friend of Cohen (and who was also involved in the raid on Kijitonyama), he was killed because he disagreed with the programme of physical elimination and the tactics of terror employed by the Leballo loyalists at the camp. Fearing for his own life, this cadre fled to the camp of the Special Defence Unit where he was given sanctuary and ultimately to Dar-es-Salaam where he reported to the Central Committee.[11]

Apart from the division of the organisation into two camps, there was also a general lack of leadership and direction. The disintegration of the organisation seemed a very real possibility. It would be several months after the assassination of Sibeko before the Central Committee would meet in plenary to review the situation. In the meanwhile the Central Committee members dispersed on various missions rather than immediately tackle the problems which had thrown the organisation into crisis.

Morale within the PAC was at a very low ebb. The prestige of the organisation internationally was at rock bottom.

PAC's International Standing Falls

It has to be pointed out that at the time of the assassination of Sibeko, the image of the PAC was already badly tarnished, its credibility increasingly questioned. Sibeko himself, in frustration, reported to the Central Committee on 16 September 1978:

> There is an urgent need for us to polish up our image after the slanderous reporting on our conference and the CPUSA's intensive drive to project the ANC. They had an extra bonus when the major TV station in this country [the USA], CBS, did an hour-long programme on South Africa in which 'Mkhonto cadres were featured training in Angola, Oliver Tambo and Thabo Mbeki were interviewed and a youth involved in the Gough Street adventure was made a 'star' of the film. It was unbelievable how the usually hostile CBS was bending over backwards to project ANC as posing a FRELIMO-size threat to apartheid in South Africa. The Boer police and ministers involved concurred. If I have said it once I have said it a

The Consequences of the Assassination 183

thousand times — we cannot match such propaganda [even if it may be] in the worst taste from a revolutionary point of view *with promises of action that never seem to materialise. Fund-raising is almost impossible under these pressures. Also there is the simple question of credibility with trusted contacts* ... (Emphasis added.)[12]

From the report, it was already clear to Sibeko in 1978 that international solidarity work, that is, attempting to raise support for the PAC, was being affected not only by the seeming endemic instability within the organisation, but more importantly, by the apparent inability to do what it claimed it wanted to do, namely, wage an armed struggle for liberation in South Africa or even establish an effective *military* presence on the ground there. Explanations, even to trusted and sympathetic supporters, about the political preparations, the 'politicisation and mobilisation of the masses', on which the PAC has placed much premium and which it has explained are essential pre-requisites for a sustained armed struggle for liberation, rang hollow in the light of the sustained mass resistance and political action by the oppressed people in South Africa in the period after the 1976 Soweto uprising.

Critical though the PAC might be of the incident in Gough Street, Johannesburg, which Sibeko refers to as the 'Gough Street adventure', it did have the effect of bolstering the international propaganda campaign of the ANC. The incident took place in June 1977. Three Black youths who were involved in the 1976 Soweto uprising and who had left the country thereafter for military training under the aegis of the ANC, were infiltrated back into the country. During a lunch hour when there were many Blacks and Whites around, they attacked a group of Whites at a business place in a major street of Johannesburg. Two Whites were killed. Two of the Black youths involved in the attack were apprehended, while one of them escaped. One of those apprehended was brutally assaulted, suffered brain damage in the process so that he was unfit to stand trial; the other, Solomon Mahlangu, was convicted of several charges, including murder (even though it was established in court that he did not fire the fatal shots) and executed on 6 April 1979.

The Gough Street incident boosted the ANC considerably, serving notice that the organisation was embarking upon a programme of infiltration of trained freedom-fighters into South Africa and that the ANC was 'serious about armed struggle', and had actually fired shots inside the country. The ANC launched an international campaign to save the life of Solomon Mahlangu, with a number of heads of state and government around the world, the UN Special Committee Against Apartheid and other international organisations calling upon the South African regime to show clemency. While the ANC was involved in these activities, the PAC was torn apart by internal strife, including factional violence in Tanzania.

Sibeko's reference to the 'Gough Street adventure', also exposes the

184 *The Crisis in the PAC: 1978–83*

PAC's lack of principle. Sibeko and other PAC leaders criticised the Gough Street incident as military adventurism, yet they tried to emulate it in 1978, for propaganda and fund-raising purposes. A former bodyguard of Leballo, 'Bobo' Moerane, who was involved in various acts of indiscipline in Tanzania, including smashing the automobile belonging to President Nyerere's personal physician, was despatched out of the country on a 'suicide mission'. He was given a substantial amount of cash in foreign currency and instructed to go into the country, via Botswana. His mission was to fire at point blank range into the first crowd of Whites he came across. He was given PAC pamphlets, prepared in New York, to leave at the scene. The authors of this 'suicide mission' were Leballo and Sibeko; the writer suspects that Make was also aware of the plan. The mission, if successful, was to be used as proof that the PAC had embarked upon 'armed struggle in Azania', during fund-raising campaigns. The cadre was dissuaded by his comrades in Botswana from undertaking the mission.[13]

Sibeko's report reflects the frustrations of PAC representatives who not only had to defend the PAC and its internal problems, but also try to convince even its supporters that it was engaged in armed struggle for liberation without any evidence of such involvement. Representatives are subjected to additional pressures as a result of the endless demands from the PAC headquarters for financial support. Sibeko listed a number of ways in which he would attempt to raise funds, including the establishment of support committees in various parts of the USA but warned: 'It has to be recognised that these are essentially students who will be carrying out solidarity work, so there cannot be much expectation funds-wise'.

Because both the ANC and PAC are recognised by the OAU as national liberation movements, and because they both state as their objectives the achievement of freedom and justice for the oppressed people of South Africa, principally through the armed struggle, they find themselves in competition for financial, material, political and diplomatic support. Inescapably, comparisons are made between the two organisations.

The ANC has had internal problems. In fact, it is true that all the national liberation movements in Southern Africa have had internal problems. In 1975 the ANC expelled eight of its leaders following a dispute which centred around the role of Whites in the organisation and its alliance with the South African Communist Party (SACP); the charges levelled against the ANC leadership by the expelled eight echoed those levelled by the Africanists who formed the PAC in 1959.[14] Similarly, within the Zimbabwean national liberation movements there were expulsions, splits and even violence.[15]

What has distinguished the PAC from all the other national liberation movements in Southern Africa, however, is that its internal problems have been constant and have taken place while the organisation

The Consequences of the Assassination   185

has not been involved in any military activity in South Africa. If the internal problems of ZANU-PF (the example regularly quoted by PAC spokespersons) were to be examined as a national liberation movement which also had serious and debilitating internal problems, it would be seen that the problems in that organisation were most intense during the years that its freedom-fighters were most successful in their military campaigns inside Zimbabwe.[16]

The PAC has failed to devise a system of solving its internal problems. Each crisis within the PAC has been accompanied by a great deal of bloodletting; each time the organisation has experienced internal problems, a great deal of attention has been attracted, in turn provoking negative comments from observers, scholars, analysts and commentators. The assassination of Sibeko was one of those crises for the PAC, attracting a great deal of negative media publicity and provoking fresh debate about the worthiness of continued support for the organisation.

OAU Threatens De-recognition

One of the immediate consequences of the assassination of Sibeko was a threat of de-recognition of the PAC as a legitimate liberation movement by the OAU. The OAU Liberation Committee met in Dar-es-Salaam a few days after the assassination of Sibeko. Although the PAC was not the first national liberation movement in Southern Africa to experience an assassination, detractors of the organisation cited the killing of Sibeko as evidence of its endemic instability, thus questioning the wisdom of continuing to support the organisation. Delegates to the meeting naturally expected an explanation. An attempt was made to meet the delegates privately so as to apprise them of the background to and circumstances surrounding the assassination of Sibeko. Most of the delegates so briefed showed understanding and sympathy for the organisation. Vusumzi L. Make, then chairman of the Presidential Council, as leader of the PAC delegation made a lengthy statement in which he provided exhaustive details about the internal problems of the organisation.[17] He described the breakdown in discipline within the organisation, the central role of P.K. Leballo in the problems and the events which led to removal of the latter as chairman of the Central Committee. When describing Sibeko's last hours, including the shooting, Make broke down. Edwin Makoti, then Secretary for Defence, continued with the presentation.

But Make made a fundamental error during his presentation. He quoted verbatim from an internal document of the PAC, namely the administrative report presented by this writer, which had formed the basis of the action against Leballo in April–May at the Central Committee meeting. Detractors of the PAC later quoted Make to illustrate serious problems within the organisation. Make's complete statement

186 *The Crisis in the PAC: 1978–83*

became a document of the OAU. Together with other documents from the meeting of the OAU Liberation Committee, it was presented to the OAU Council of Ministers in Monrovia, Liberia, several weeks later.

The PAC delegation to the OAU Council of Ministers and Summit of Heads of State in Monrovia comprised Vusumzi Make, Edwin Makoti and this writer. It was agreed during consultations among the Central Committee members in Dar-es-Salaam that Make and Makoti should travel to Gaborone, Botswana, to attend the funeral of Sibeko, while this writer should return to New York after the meeting of the OAU Liberation Committee to represent the Central Committee at a memorial service for Sibeko. Thereafter the three would meet in Monrovia.

For the greater part of the OAU Council of Ministers, this writer was alone. After Sibeko's funeral in Gaborone, Make and Makoti were stranded following the suspension of flights between Botswana and Zambia after the arrest in Zambia of an Air Botswana pilot on suspicion of spying for the Smith/Muzorewa regime.

At the Council of Ministers, during the discussion of the report of the Liberation Committee, the Angolan Foreign Minister, Mr. Paulo Jorge, called upon the OAU to 'take a stand' and give exclusive recognition and support to the ANC. He referred to the PAC as being in a state of 'disintegration'; to substantiate his assertion, he quoted from Make's statement to the Liberation Committee meeting in Dar-es-Salaam. He was supported by a number of other delegations, notably those of Algeria and Benin.

The call for the de-recognition of the PAC failed for several reasons. Firstly, the lobbying by the PAC delegation at the Liberation Committee meeting in Dar-es-Salaam generated a certain amount of sympathy for the organisation. In Monrovia, this writer again apprised a number of delegations of the problems that the organisation had had, pointing out that Sibeko's assassination was not the first such dastardly act and arguing that rather than call for the de-recognition of the PAC, the Council should examine ways and means of assisting the national liberation movements to obviate any further assassinations. One foreign minister who was very helpful and supportive was the late Cecil Dennis, the highly-respected Foreign Minister of Liberia. Since he was the chairman of the Council of Ministers, Dennis' support was crucial; he could, if necessary, prevail upon his colleagues from Angola, Algeria and Benin not to press the issue of de-recognition of the PAC.

The second reason why the call for the de-recognition of the PAC failed was Africa's pre-occupation with the situation in Zimbabwe. According to many of the delegates to whom this writer spoke, the general feeling was that the question of Zimbabwe should be treated as a priority; at a more appropriate time, the question of the recognition of the ANC and PAC could be examined by the OAU.

In a statement during the plenary meeting, this writer analysed current political developments in South Africa and the role of the PAC in those developments. Two political trials involving PAC members provided evidence that the PAC still existed inside the country and had a role to play in the national liberation struggle. The first was that of the Bethal 18 mentioned above; the second that of three youths who had joined the PAC after the 1976 Soweto uprisings and who were infiltrated into the country in 1978 after having undergone military training abroad. The Council of Ministers took note of the two PAC trials and, in the resolutions on South Africa, condemned the convictions and sentences passed upon the Bethal defendants.

By the time that Make and Makoti arrived in Monrovia, the PAC had survived a bid for its de-recognition.

PAC Isolated at Non-Aligned Summit

But the organisation was not yet out of the woods. Its stock was low. This was demonstrated at the Council of Ministers and Summit of Heads of State and Government of the Movement of Non-Aligned Countries, held in Havana, Cuba, in September 1979. The PAC delegation to the Havana meeting comprised: Ngila Muendane (Chief Representative to the UK and the European Continent), Leasoana 'Sam' Makhanda (who was assisting at the PAC Observer Mission to the UN) and this writer.

The conference was very well organised and the host country, Cuba, demonstrated great hospitality and cordiality to all the delegations. The PAC delegation certainly could not complain about the hospitality shown by the Cubans who, traditionally, supported the ANC. Of all the national liberation movements, however, the PAC was clearly the 'poor cousin'. The other national liberation movements were all represented by their leaders who were treated like heads of state. Significantly, they could all report on the progress in their liberation struggles.

The ANC, although an observer in the Movement of Non-Aligned Countries, was similarly in a favourable position in Havana. Its representative to Cuba, Alex La Guma (the well-known South African writer), had full diplomatic status. A large delegation was led personally by Oliver Tambo, the President, and included representatives from their Department of Publicity and Information to give full coverage in their publications to the Havana Summit and the ANC's participation. Tambo was invited at the opening of the Summit of Heads of State and Government to make a statement on behalf of the national liberation movements from Southern Africa, in reply to the opening address by President Fidel Castro.

The PAC was on the defensive. An attempt was made to meet as many of the delegations as possible so as to explain to them the reasons for the internal problems in the organisation and the efforts made by the leadership to solve the problems. On the whole, the opportunity afforded

188   *The Crisis in the PAC: 1978–83*

by the Summit to meet other delegations was fully utilised but the internal problems which had wracked the PAC were an acute embarrassment. The PAC was embarrassed even further during the address by the Mozambican President, Samora Machel, who declared the unequivocal support of his country and Party, FRELIMO, for the ANC. When President Samora Machel speaks, it carries considerable weight. As a result of his declared support for the ANC (without even mention of the PAC), many delegations sought an explanation from the PAC delegation as to why revolutionary Mozambique did not support the PAC. In other words, the impression conveyed was that the lack of support by Mozambique somehow raised questions about the credentials of the PAC as a genuine revolutionary liberatory organisation.

Ngila Muendane later remarked that to be a PAC representative at the Havana Summit was to be 'like something that the cat brought in from outside'.

UN Wary

At the UN there was an opportunity to meet many delegations, especially from those countries which have supported the national liberation struggles in Southern Africa, to explain to them the circumstances surrounding the assassination of the PAC's former representative to the world body, David Sibeko. Although almost all the delegations listened attentively and expressed sympathy for the PAC on the loss of its able representative, they reflected a general attitude underlying it all that suggested they expected something of that nature. The PAC's internal problems were common knowledge, even though most casual observers were not aware of the extent and intensity of the turmoil and strife within the organisation. To many, particularly the detractors of the PAC, the assassination of Sibeko seemed to confirm what they had said all along about the persistent internal problems of the organisation. They felt it vindicated their attitude of hostility towards the PAC.

In mid-August 1979 further problems were created for the PAC by the return to New York of Elizabeth Sibeko from Botswana. She was very bitter, and blamed everybody for the assassination of her husband, including Vus Make; neither did she hesitate to inform outsiders and supporters of PAC of her opinion. Immediately upon her return to New York, she returned to the PAC Observer Mission to the UN and was frequently to be seen in the UN headquarters. Her presence served as a constant reminder of the debilitating internal problems and conflicts within the PAC — problems that had culminated in the assassination of David Sibeko, her husband.

For a considerable period thereafter, various PAC spokespersons would have to answer the question, 'How did Vus Make escape?'

Notes

1. Among the Heads of State who sent messages of condolence were President William Tolbert, Jr. of Liberia, President Gaafar Nimeiri of the Sudan, President Khama of Botswana. The Executive Secretary of the OAU Liberation Committee, Brigadier Hashim Mbita, the Unesco projects co-ordinator in Dar-es-Salaam, Mr. Awad Idris, as well as various other members of the diplomatic corps in Dar-es-Salaam. ZANU-PF, ZAPU, SWAPO, the PLO and the ANC also sent messages of condolence.

2. Report dated 16 September 1978. The author has known Xusa for several years from the time that they were members of SASO. When the author first visited the USA in May 1978 and was given all the gory details by Elizabeth Sibeko about Xusa's degeneracy, he was shocked and wondered when the change had taken place. After living with him at the Sibeko residence, the author concluded that frustrations he suffered were largely a product of his living conditions and the manner in which he was treated by the Sibeko family, and his inability to communicate his frustrations and annoyance. The author communicated this to the Central Committee members in Dar-es-Salaam in September 1978 and opposed the disciplinary action against him proposed by Elizabeth Sibeko. The author argued that the Central Committee should also hear the other side of the story, or at least investigate before making an independent decision about Mzonke.

3. The two persons who were left by this writer at the PAC office in New York at that time were Clement Hlongwane and Leasoana 'Sam' Makhanda.

4. Information from Nomakwezi Ganya in Harare, Zimbabwe on 14 July 1981 during a discussion.

5. The file on Sibeko kept by the Department of State was secured by a PAC supporter and given to the author in January 1980. The file contains a copy of the cable.

6. See *Post*, 14 June 1979.

7. See *Post*, 19 June 1979.

8. *The Voice*, 17 June 1979.

9. *Sunday Times*, 17 June 1979.

10. Initially 19 persons were detained by the Tanzanian authorities in connection with the murder of Sibeko, but ultimately six were charged with the murder. The members of the high command, including Justice Nkonyane, were initially detained.

11. This cadre, known to the author as 'Killer' (Sayiso) was still in Dar-es-Salaam when the author last visited there in December 1981.

12. Report in author's files.

13. This incident occurred shortly before the consultative conference in June–July 1978. Moerane was one of the major actors in the factional clashes between the Leballo and Ntantala groups in 1977–1978. The author met Moerane in Botswana in November 1978, by which time he had abandoned his 'suicide mission'. He was subsequently deported from that country together with other PAC members and returned to Dar-es-Salaam in December 1978. After falling out with Leballo, Moerane became one of the leaders of the April 1979 demonstrations against Leballo. Moerane often boasted to PAC cadres about

190   *The Crisis in the PAC: 1978–83*

the 'easy cash' he secured for the 'suicide mission', cash he used to purchase shoes, clothes, etc.

14. African National Congress of South Africa (African Nationalists). *Statement on the Expulsion from the ANC (SA) of* . . . Issued by the expelled eight members (London, 27 December 1975).

15. See for example, Sithole 1979, which is written by someone partial to one of the factions but is nevertheless a good account of the problems which plagued the Zimbabwean liberation organisations.

16. For an account of the national liberation struggle by a journalistic team sympathetic to ZANU-PF, see: Martin and Johnson 1980.

17. Make did not attend the entire session of the ALC which met from 25 to 28 June 1979. He and Edwin Makoti left Dar-es-Salaam on Wednesday, 27 June for Botswana to attend Sibeko's funeral. The delegation to the session was then led by this writer who made a general political statement on behalf of the PAC.

11. The Emergence of Vusumzi Make as PAC Chairman

It was against this background of crisis that the PAC Central Committee and representatives met in Dar-es-Salaam in October 1979. On the one hand, the morale of the general membership of the organisation was very low. The organisation was divided into two hostile camps. The cadres of APLA had unleashed a reign of terror through their despatch of 'hit squads' to Dar-es-Salaam to eliminate physically the remaining members of the Central Committee and through their assaults upon and torture of cadres at the camp suspected of being loyal to the Central Committee. A number of cadres escaped from the camp; each one presented a grim picture of the situation at the camp, expressing fears even that there were likely to be murders there also. There was an atmosphere of helplessness, especially since the Central Committee, apart from its members being dispersed, had no control over the situation and was unable to provide any protection for those APLA cadres at the camp who were opposed to the activities of those loyal to Leballo and the high command, led by Justice Nkonyane. The members of the high command at that stage had been detained by the Tanzanian authorities in connection with the murder of Sibeko.

On the other hand, there was a crisis of confidence among the supporters of the PAC. The assassination of Sibeko followed less than a year after the consultative conference which resulted in the expulsion of almost seventy members of the organisation. The assassination of Sibeko had the effect of raising further doubts in the international community about the wisdom of continued support for the PAC.

Make and Ntloedibe Stir up Trouble in Lesotho

Make and Ntloedibe, as members of the Presidential Council, visited Lesotho in September 1979 for discussions with the government and the ruling Basotho National Party (BNP), led by the Prime Minister, Chief Leabua Jonathan. Their visit exacerbated existing divisions among the PAC members resident in Lesotho. Rather than work through the de

192 The Crisis in the PAC: 1978-83

facto representative, Napthallie Sidzamba, they spent most of their time with Gabriel Sandamela and Elliot Mfaxa, who were not regarded by Sidzamba and others as PAC members in good standing. The actions of Make and Ntloedibe were seen by Sidzamba and others as undermining the work they had done during the time that Sandamela and Mfaxa had not been actively involved in the affairs of the PAC. Moreover, because Sandamela had originally come from the Transvaal region in South Africa, whence Make and Ntloedibe had also come, this was seen as 'regionalism' and 'home-boyism'.

Make and Ntloedibe were also accused of opportunistically drawing the PAC into an alliance with the ruling party which, in the view of many PAC members in Lesotho, lacked popular support in the country. An alignment with the ruling party could jeopardise the long-term interests of the PAC.

While in Lesotho, the delegation of the Presidential Council promised Chief Jonathan that they would make available to his government the lists of names and photographs of all the cadres of the opposition Basutoland Congress Party (BCP) who had received military training abroad (including OAU member states) under the aegis of the PAC. (Of course, they were careful to blame P.K. Leballo for the past sins of the PAC.)[1]

At the plenary meeting in October 1979, there were four delegates from Lesotho, representing two opposing groups. The four were Napthallie Sidzamba and Douglas Suntele, Gabriel Sandamela and Elliot Mfaxa. The participation of Mfaxa and Sandamela at the meeting was wrong; the decisions taken at the Arusha consultative conference and re-affirmed subsequently, stipulated that the representatives would participate on a par with members of the Central Committee at plenary meetings. The two of them were not representatives in Lesotho, a fact known to the Central Committee. Sidzamba functioned as the de facto representative in Lesotho; the contact which the organisation had with its members in that country was through Sidzamba who also maintained close contact with David Sibeko in New York.

The actions of Make and Ntloedibe during their visit to Lesotho were strongly condemned by Sidzamba, Suntele and others, who prepared a memorandum for submission to the plenary meeting in October. They were, however, dissuaded by Make and Ntloedibe, during private discussions, from tabling the memorandum at the meeting since it was likely to be 'divisive' as it was also very critical of Sandamela and Mfaxa.

Rather than deal with the problems in Lesotho in a principled and honest manner, the Central Committee chose instead to shelve them. As a result the divisions among the PAC members in that country were rigidified. The factional violence among PAC members in Lesotho in 1982, as will be discussed later, can be traced back to Make and Ntloedibe's visit. During the October 1979 plenary meeting an intensive smear campaign against Sidzamba was launched, during the private and informal discussions among the participants at the meeting. He was accused of 'arrogance' and of running the affairs of the PAC in Lesotho 'like a dictator'. Sandamela and Mfaxa were privately encouraged by the Make faction to challenge the leadership of Sidzamba when they returned to Lesotho after the October plenary meeting.

Make on Background to the Crisis in the PAC

In his opening address to the plenary meeting on 3 October 1979 Make, in his capacity as chairman of the Presidential Council, pointed out that the PAC was in 'grave crisis', and that it was the first meeting since the death of David Sibeko. He addressed a special message of welcome to Elizabeth Sibeko and to the delegates from Lesotho.

Make then traced the developments within the organisation since the Arusha consultative conference, held in 1978. He stated that the organisation had 'emerged with a new programme of action and a new direction'. In addition, certain 'principles were laid down', he said, namely, accountability and collective leadership. Structures were laid down, he said, to reinforce the principles of accountability, and the innovation of plenary had been introduced in which representatives would participate fully as members of the Central Committee.

Make continued:

> After Arusha the home-going programme was implemented and under the aegis of the military commission, plans were drawn up for the implementation of the programme. Gradually, Leballo isolated the military commission and ultimately decisions were taken outside the Central Committee by APLA. APLA was built into a separate organ. The authority of the Central Committee was eroded by the Chairman.

He went on to outline the deterioration in the state of the PAC, culminating in the raid on the Central Committee's residence in Kijitonyama in December 1978. 'Leballo engineered much of the indiscipline and was part of the mass movements (of militarily-trained cadres from the camp at Ithumbi to Dar-es-Salaam). Cadres were congregating in Dar-es-Salaam.'

Make then provided the background to the Central Committee meeting of 30 April and 1 May 1979 at which Leballo was forced to relinquish the chairmanship of the PAC and then went on to explain why the device was used that he should depart for London, ostensibly for 'health reasons'.

According to Make, 'The PAC is still the greatest challenge to the racist regime', hence the 'concerted conspiracy from within and without' South Africa to destroy the organisation.

194 *The Crisis in the PAC: 1978–83*

In his address, Make did not provide any in-depth analysis of the situation in South Africa and the tasks facing the PAC. This was significant in view of the fact that the assassination of Sibeko received fairly wide coverage in the press in South Africa; moreover, the assassination occurred at the time of the Bethal 18 trial and the trial of the three former Soweto students.[2] For all practical purposes, the imprisonment of Mothopeng and others meant the collapse of any organised PAC presence in South Africa. For this reason, it was strange that Make's address did not offer any analysis of the organisation's response to political developments in the country. Yet, he fantasised that the organisation constituted the greatest threat to the South African regime.

Leballo Denounced and Expelled

During the discussion that followed Make's opening address, there was unanimity among the members present that Leballo should be expelled from the PAC. Muendane called for Leballo's expulsion and all the other speakers supported the proposal. Makoti stated that there was 'no longer any need to shield Leballo from exposure'. Sidzamba expressed satisfaction with the explanations offered by Make; he said that it was 'clear that Leballo was aware of the full implications of the "gentlemen's agreements". We must look into Leballo's criminal conduct and activities'. Another member present, however, proposed a more extreme measure, namely the physical elimination of Leballo, but there was no support for his proposal.

It was agreed that a document should be drawn up outlining the reasons for the expulsion of Leballo, but that strict confidentiality should be maintained until the conclusion of the meeting when the expulsion would be announced.

During the ensuing discussion, it was obvious that while there was a general awareness of the malaise within the PAC, there was also a realisation that Leballo could not be solely blamed for the problems plaguing the organisation. For example, Enoch Zulu (alias John Mvelase), who had been a member of a pre-Arusha Central Committee and had just been re-instated after two years' imprisonment in Swaziland, warned that the removal of Leballo should not herald the appointment of 'another P.K.'. Modipe Phillip Mokgadi, the PAC's representative to West Germany, on the other hand, stated that, 'We must analyse and identify the causes of the present crisis so as to avoid the same mistakes in future'. He attributed the problems to what he termed the 'style of work of Leballo', without offering any detailed analysis or explanation of that 'style of work'.

Muendane observed that a lack of 'ideological and political training brings about personal glory. The basic documents (of the PAC) should

The Emergence of Vusumzi Make as PAC Chairman 195

be given to the cadres and they should also be given instruction'. He attempted to analyse what he saw as core problems in the organisation. The organisation lacked a 'common code of conduct'. He felt that 'authority can only be exercised through this code'. Another problem which he identified was a lack of communication between the leadership and the cadres; he pointed out that 'when cadres went to military training there was no communication'.

Following all the interventions, Sandamela observed that 'both the internal and external organs are in very bad shape'. He sought clarification on the 'internal situation' of the PAC, that is, the state of the PAC in South Africa, if it existed at all.

PAC's Problems Deeper than Leballo's Idiosyncrasies

It will be seen from the above that there was vague awareness and even an admission that the problems in the PAC were much more profound than merely the shenanigans of Leballo over the years. But the Central Committee was unable to analyse the root causes of the problems facing the organisation, problems that were traceable to its history and its development abroad as a national liberation movement. The basic documents of the PAC, which Muendane suggested should be given to the cadres, were drawn up in South Africa in 1959, when the PAC operated overtly and legally as a political organisation. Whether or not the basic documents of the PAC would have proved efficacious even in the circumstances for which they were intended would remain forever unknown, because the organisation was banned within twelve months of its formation.

When the PAC established an external wing, it was not ascertained whether or not the constitution and basic documents adopted in 1959 were still operative. Whether they were suitable for the new circumstances in which the organisation found itself was another question. For example, the constitution and basic documents make no provision for a military wing, which is understandable given the fact that the PAC was initially an overtly legal political organisation. Abroad, the PAC established a military wing. Yet, the question of the applicability of the constitution to the military wing was not clearly defined. This was part of the reason for the perennial conflict between the 'political' and the 'military' leadership, between the Central Committee, on the one hand, and the high command, on the other. It has already been explained that the military leaders who were expelled at Arusha in June–July 1978 argued that the PAC was a *political party*, membership of which was highly selective; they equated the PAC with the Communist Party of the People's Republic of China, where following the decimation of the Communist Party by Chiang Kai-Shek in 1927, the Communist Party created an army of its own which it kept under firm control of the Party.

196   *The Crisis in the PAC: 1978–83*

This argument was erroneous since the PAC was clearly not a political party, let alone a Communist Party; it was basically a mass movement, a united front of patriotic forces which had contradictions with the White supremacist regime.

At its formation in 1959, the PAC was committed to orthodox African Nationalism and stated as its ultimate political objective, the creation of an 'Africanist Socialist Democracy'. At its formation, too, the organisation found itself accommodating racists, tribalists, anti-communists, nationalists and others who expressed a vague commitment to socialist ideas. Because of the short time of its overt legal existence, the organisation could not iron out all the weaknesses in its theoretical and ideological formulations. The organisation was not able to define clearly the relationship between *class* and *race*, a problem which has proven to be one of the most intractable in the writings on South Africa, even from the liberation movements. In more recent years several attempts have been made to address the issue.[3]

In its more recent history as a national liberation movement, the PAC has had within its ranks individuals and groups who have professed to be Marxists, and others who have prided themselves on their ability to recite Mao Tse-Tung's *Little Red Book*, while others still have not developed beyond the level of tribalism and nationalism.

In the 1970s the Central Committee attempted to address the question of the ideology of the PAC and adopted as documents for internal use, *The New Road to Revolution* and the *Freedom-Fighters Field Manual*. But these were unashamedly plagiarisms of the various writings of Mao Tse-Tung, particularly his thesis on 'People's War'. While the National Liberation Movement has to study and learn from the revolutionary experiences of others, such experiences cannot be transposed willy-nilly into the South African situation, in totally different social, political and economic conditions.

This points to the need for a clearly-defined ideology within the PAC. As one analyst has pointed out:

> A clear ideology gives a movement a definite and systematic way of thinking, of analysing events, and interpreting with a high degree of consistency, the world in which they operate. It also provides a guide to the many decisions that have to be taken and gives a cutting edge to decision-making.[4]

The ideological certainty of the PAIGC under the leadership of the gifted revolutionary, Amilcar Cabral, contributed largely to the political cohesion and unity of that liberation movement during the struggle against Portuguese colonialism. Another writer has observed that there has been no successful revolution which has not been grounded in ideology:

No revolution ever occurred without ideology. It is one thing for a citizen to think he knows *why* a revolution is needed; it is quite another to know *how* to go about making a revolution and to know *what* to put in place of the institutions that revolutionary violence destroys . . . Revolutionary ideology supplies the answers to the questions why, how and what — that is to say, it offers a critique of present conditions, a strategy for the use of political violence in order to change those conditions, and a vision of an improved society.[5] (Emphasis in original.)

The political commissar of APLA, Mzwandile Gumbi, was heard to remark in 1978 that 'Politics is boring'. He obviously did not understand the nature of the liberation struggle in which he was involved and the relationship between the political and military aspects of the struggle, yet he was technically responsible for the co-ordination of political education in the PAC's military wing.

These were a few of the aspects of the deep-rooted problems to which the leadership should have addressed themselves, so that the problems could have been defined with far greater accuracy at the plenary meeting. It would also have enabled them to address the questions, what is to be done? And, more importantly, how is it to be done?

The October 1979 Plenary

A number of decisions were taken at the October plenary meeting, perhaps the most important ones being:

(i) the expulsion of P.K. Leballo from the PAC;

(ii) the dissolution of the high command (led by Justice Nkonyane) and the expulsion of all its members from the PAC;

(iii) the dissolution of the administration at the PAC military camp at Ithumbi;

(iv) the dissolution of the Presidential Council and the appointment of Vus Make as Chairman of the Central Committee and leader of the PAC;

(v) the appointment of D.D. Mantshontsho as Administrative Secretary;

(vi) the appointment of this writer as Director of Foreign Affairs and Observer Representative of the PAC to the UN;

(vii) the confirmation of the expulsion from the Central Committee of the following members who had been appointed at the Arusha consultative conference: Mogale 'Jimmy' Mokgoatsane, Victor Mayekiso, Esrom Mokgakala, Deliwe Gertrude Mathutha and Reggie Xoxelélo;

(viii) the establishment of a task force to rebuild the PAC's military wing, APLA. A section of the militarily-trained cadres who had

198　*The Crisis in the PAC: 1978–83*

remained loyal to the Central Committee presented for its consideration at the plenary meeting a detailed document setting out proposals for the rebuilding of APLA. The document reads in part:

> We also feel that since the PAC has no army, the Secretary for Defence should select a few men and under his direction immediately embark upon reconstruction of the army. All avenues should be explored to ensure that the army meets the basic military and ideological requirements.[6]

(ix) the re-introduction of political education, responsibility for which would be under a committee comprising the Director of Education and Manpower Development (convenor), the Secretary for Defence and the Director of Publicity and Information, later to be joined by the political commissar.

Various other decisions of an administrative nature were also taken, including the overhauling of the Department of Finance and the implementation of financial controls, the appointment of a welfare officer, the preparation of reports for circulation among the members of the organisation, to name a few. Most of the decisions taken at the plenary meeting were never implemented, a pattern which would be discernible at every subsequent meeting.

Make's Appointment as Chairman Problematical

At the October plenary this writer opposed the appointment of Make as Chairman of the Central Committee and leader of the PAC because of the circumstances surrounding the murder of David Sibeko and Make's miraculous escape. Questions had been raised about Make's escape, with speculation of a power struggle among the three members of the Presidential Council and even of Make's possible involvement in a 'murder plot'. Sibeko's widow, Elizabeth, who was also a member of the Central Committee, had fanned the speculation by openly accusing Make of murdering her husband and suggesting to members of the diplomatic corps at the UN — as well as to PAC supporters — that Make's fortuitous escape was contrived.[7] During the meeting, however, she did not repeat any of the accusations, despite emphatic assertions before her departure from New York that she would confront Make.

When this writer raised the matter, Make cried. He responded that he was aware of the 'dreams' the late David Sibeko had for the PAC so he felt that he owed it to his colleague and friend to accept the burden of leadership. Makoti, then Secretary for Defence, stood up, walked up to Make and, shaking him by the hand, said, 'Vus, we have made our choice'. With those words, Make was appointed Chairman of the Central Committee and leader of the PAC.

There was no discussion at the meeting, or informally outside the meeting, of alternative candidates. Nor was there any discussion at the meeting of the suitability of Make as Chairman of the PAC. Informally, outside, however, there was the usual back-biting. Some persons expressed doubts about Make's appointment. Ntloedibe suggested to some persons that this writer sought the PAC chairmanship, because he opposed the appointment of Make and was also strongly critical of Ntloedibe. The latter reportedly said: 'That SASO boy wants power.'

The assumption of the chairmanship by Make would not solve the PAC's problems. Firstly, Make had a reputation for fiscal irresponsibility.[8]

Now, in the politics of exile, accusations of embezzlement of funds are common and must be treated with a great deal of circumspection, since such allegations are almost inevitably used during personal conflict or power struggles in national liberation movements to discredit individuals. It is as common as the charges of being a spy, or 'CIA agent', or 'agent of imperialism'. For this reason, in the absence of concrete evidence and clear proof, care has to be exercised by any person who is confronted with such allegations about other persons who are involved in the liberation struggle. Having said that, however, the fact that allegations of fiscal irresponsibility were made against Make by so many persons who have known or worked with him, many of them without malice, meant that it would be very difficult to try to 'sell him to the international community' as the new PAC leader. Liberation movements receive substantial contributions from the general public internationally in support of the cause; allegations of personal corruption at the level of leadership, therefore, have the effect of causing wariness among such supporters.

Secondly, Make was suspected by many PAC members (as well as other organisations) of having advised the late President Tolbert of Liberia to invite the former South African Prime Minister, B.J. Vorster, to make his secret visit to Monrovia. Make at that time was resident in Monrovia where he was a lecturer in International Relations at the university and also served as Political Adviser on Southern Africa to the President. Although Make has denied any role in the controversial visit by Vorster, the fact that his name was mentioned by South African exiles and by Liberian opponents of Tolbert, as being associated with its arrangement, attracted a certain opprobrium. Detractors of the PAC spread the allegation as substantiation of the smears levelled against the organisation that it was 'reactionary', or 'collaborationist'. There is no evidence that Make

200 *The Crisis in the PAC: 1978–83*

played any role in Vorster's visit to Liberia, nor are there any photographs depicting him shaking hands with Vorster, but this demonstrates the manner in which in the politics of exile, rumour and speculation are often elevated to the level of 'fact'.

Leballo Continues to Claim Leadership of PAC

Although Make was appointed Chairman in October 1979, the question of leadership would create problems for the organisation for a long time afterwards. P.K. Leballo, after leaving London, went to Nigeria where he joined 'Zwai Maglas', who had left Dar-es-Salaam two days before the assassination of Sibeko for Lagos and who continued to masquerade as the PAC representative even though he had been recalled to Dar-es-Salaam in June 1979. Leballo held himself out as the 'Chairman and Leader of the PAC'.

On 17 September 1979 Leballo despatched a cable to the PAC Administrative Secretary in Dar-es-Salaam; the text of the cable reads as follows:

> You have no authority whatsoever to convene Central Committee meeting plenary session nor any CC (Central Committee) without my consent and authority.
>
> Potlako Leballo Chairman PAC[9]

That cable had been preceded by another one which was much longer and more frantic in tone. The text reads as follows:

> My physicians have pronounced me fit and well stop I have now resumed my duties as PAC chairman as I never resigned nor relinquished my Party chairmanship stop Presidential Council is now dissolved stop No central committee meeting without quorum stop You have no authority to appoint transfer or dismiss PAC representatives in New York, Norway Lagos nor anywhere stop You violated clause 2(c) of central committee decisions of April 30th and May 1st stop You also sabotaged home-going programme and conspired to usurp Party leadership hence tragic bloodshed for which you and your cronies must be held responsible.
>
> Potlako Leballo Chairman PAC.[10]

Following his expulsion at the October plenary meeting, Leballo held a press conference in Lagos at which he announced the expulsion of six Central Committee members from the PAC, namely Vus Make, Elias Ntloedibe, Erret Radebe, Edwin Makoti, D.D.

The Emergence of Vusumzi Make as PAC Chairman 201

Mantshontsho and this writer.[11] The Nigerian News Agency carried the following report of Leballo's press conference on 22 November 1979:

> Addressing a news conference in Lagos yesterday, Mr. Leballo said that the men were expelled for various anti-Party activities, including conspiracy and a plot to overthrow the constitutional Party leader and usurp his post.
>
> He noted that the death of David Sibeko the former central committee member, was a result of subversion carried out by the expelled members.
>
> The PAC leader said that the movement could not embark on an intensive arms [sic] struggle against apartheid South Africa because most of the sister independent countries were too militarily weak [sic] to support the struggle.
>
> He then called on the Organisation of African Unity (OAU) to give the movement full support for a total confrontation against the racist enemy.
>
> Mr. Leballo said that Azania was the ancient and classical name for the area commonly known as South Africa, and that this was the name officially adopted by his movement.[12]

At a meeting of the OAU Liberation Committee Standing Committees (On Policy, Information and Defence), held in Dar-es-Salaam from 17 to 21 December 1979, Vus Make and this writer met with the Nigerian delegation, in particular with Colonel Baku who at that time was attached to the Cabinet Office and had special responsibility for liaison with the national liberation movements. They discussed with the Nigerians the question of Leballo's presence in Lagos and the harm his activities were causing the PAC. The Nigerians gave the assurance that Leballo's presence in Lagos was not an indication of official support for his stance or his activities but simply 'African hospitality'. The delegation also informed Make and this writer that (i) the press conference held by Leballo at which he announced the 'expulsion of six members of the Central Committee', had not been officially sanctioned, and (ii) Leballo had subsequently been told by the Nigerian authorities to refrain from making press statements since the question of his residence in Nigeria was still subject to official approval. It was also agreed that a PAC delegation would visit Lagos in mid-January 1980 to introduce the Chief Representative-designate, Count Pietersen, as well as to discuss further with the Nigerian authorities the question of Leballo's activities.

The visit to Nigeria did not materialise although Count Pietersen, who had been appointed Chief Representative, had shipped all his household effects to Nigeria in anticipation of taking up his post. He had also closed the PAC office in Oslo, Norway. For a while, the

202 *The Crisis in the PAC: 1978–83*

organisation had no office in either country. These were some of the problems faced by the newly-appointed Chairman of the Central Committee.

Notes

1. During the OAU Summit in Freetown, Sierra Leone, in July 1980, Lesotho's then Foreign Minister, Mr. Charles D. Molapho, in the presence of the author, reminded Make of the promise that he and Ntloedibe had made to Chief Leabua Jonathan. Make replied that the Central Committee was still sorting through documents discovered at Leballo's apartment in Keko outside Dar-es-Salaam.

2. *Post*, 14 June 1979. The three APLA cadres — Norman Vusi Thusi (20), Columbus Mazibuko (25) and Prince Mzimkulu Dube (20) — were sentenced to five years' imprisonment each for having left the country and undergone military training abroad 'to endanger the maintenance of law and order'.

3. See, for example, Turok 1974; No Sizwe 1979; Magubane 1979. A number of South African exiles have attempted to present an interpretation of South African history which is a refreshing departure from the liberal interpretation which seeks to explain the present system of White domination in terms of the visceral of the Afrikaners. Among such writers are Wolpe, Legassick, O'Meara, First, Mhlongo and Bunsee.

4. Shamuyarira 1975, introduction, p. viii.

5. Johnson 1973, p. 104.

6. The document criticised the Central Committee for its handling of the situation in the PAC from the time that Leballo was ousted to the time that Sibeko was murdered.

7. In mid-September 1979 a senior Swaziland official informed the author in the presence of Elizabeth Sibeko at the UN that Make and Ntloedibe were denied entry into Swaziland on their return from Lesotho because the Swaziland Government believed that Make was implicated in the assassination of Sibeko. According to the official, Make would have to 'build up trust'. A Swazi diplomat concurred with the Minister. The author communicated this to Make during a telephone conversation soon thereafter and also pointed out the difficulties which the allegations encouraged by Elizabeth Sibeko would cause the PAC.

8. See Maya Angelou (Make's former wife) in her book *Heart of a Woman* (1981). This book is autobiographical. The author alludes to the financial problems which she and Make experienced both in New York and in Cairo in the early 1960s when Make represented the PAC, and the reader is given an impression of fiscal irresponsibility on Make's part, especially during their sojourn in Cairo.

9. The cable was received in Dar-es-Salaam on 17 September 1979.

10. The cable was received in Dar-es-Salaam on 10 September 1979.

11. The 'expulsions' were widely reported in the Nigerian press. See the *New Nigerian*, 9 and 23 November 1979.

12. Copy of report in author's file.

12. Vusumzi Make at the Helm: the Crisis Deepens

The circumstances under which Vusumzi Make was appointed to the chairmanship of the PAC Central Committee have been described. At the plenary meeting of the Central Committee in October 1979 there was a vague awareness and a half-hearted recognition by the PAC leaders that the problems of the organisation would not be solved merely by the removal of Leballo. There was, however, an inability to define clearly the problem as being political and ideological, and were that what was required was a genuine restructuring of the organisation in all its aspects — administrative, political and military — and a clear statement on the ideology of the PAC. Because the root causes of the problems confronting the organisation were neither diagnosed nor addressed, the problems persisted during Make's tenure as Chairman of the Central Committee and leader of the PAC.

Make's Leadership Ineffective

Make's tenure was disastrous and was characterised by a deepening of the crisis in the PAC. On the one hand, the organisation's internal problems escalated, and on the other hand, although de-recognition by the OAU was averted, the diplomatic isolation of the PAC continued.

Certainly, for some or most of the problems confronting the PAC during his tenure as Chairman, Make has to be blamed, but others were entirely beyond his control. Upon his assumption of the chairmanship, Make enjoyed the goodwill and support of the Central Committee as well as the loyal cadres who had consistently supported the leadership. In addition, many PAC members scattered in different countries, showed renewed interest in the affairs of the organisation and there was a keen response to the decision taken in October 1979 to encourage the return of the many PAC members who had been disenchanted during the Leballo regime. Joe Mkwanazi, Joe Moabi and others who were deported from Swaziland at the instigation of Leballo and Sibeko (and

204   *The Crisis in the PAC: 1978–83*

who had been granted asylum in England), took the initiative to return to active involvement in the organisation. Many others, however, refused because they identified Make with the Leballo regime.

A number of diplomatic missions to various countries were undertaken immediately after the October 1979 plenary meeting. Their purpose was: to explain the decisions taken at the plenary meeting; to explain the developing political situation in Southern Africa in general and South Africa in particular; to explain the policy and programme of the PAC for the unfolding struggle and its preparations for the intensification of the armed struggle in South Africa; and to request diplomatic, financial and material support.

The progress made in the PAC's external relations were offset by the maladministration at the external headquarters, which manifested itself in: lack of consultation among Central Committee members on important issues; lack of co-ordination not only between the PAC headquarters (which constitutes the political centre) and the other centres, but also between various departments and even Central Committee members at the PAC headquarters; failure to implement decisions of the Central Committee; and fiscal irresponsibility.

Make could have remedied the situation if he had been prepared to provide the much-needed leadership and direction by remaining at external headquarters to ensure that decisions of the Central Committee were implemented. Instead, he travelled for long periods in Africa and Europe, often on unnecessary missions or to unimportant conferences to which others could have been sent.

Make's response to criticisms was increasingly to surround himself with sycophants, au Leballo! He recommended a number of individuals for appointment to the Central Committee as part of a strategy of buttressing his faction of loyalists.

The 'Cadre Forces' Movement'

Frustration among the military and untrained cadres and dissatisfaction with the direction of the organisation under Make's leadership, resulted in the re-emergence of the 'cadre forces' movement', a core of cadres forming a pressure group to make demands upon the leadership. In April 1979 the cadres had organised themselves into a similar pressure group to demand the expulsion of Leballo. In August 1980, they drew up a comprehensive memorandum containing a critique of the leadership as a collective, as well as recommendations and suggestions. A minimum demand before they would even discuss the memorandum with the leadership was the immediate dismissal from the Central Committee of Elias Ntloedibe and D.D. Mantshontsho. The cadres were able to press their demand because of their numerical strength and their awareness that the leadership feared any further crises or signs of turmoil within the PAC that might provoke demands within the OAU for the de-recognition of the organisation. The cadres also received secret

Vusumzi Make at the Helm: the Crisis Deepens 205

encouragement from certain quarters within the Tanzanian government; these quarters were hostile to the PAC because of what was perceived as Make's erosion of the Government's goodwill through his penchant for frequent travel rather than attending to the problems of the organisation. Tanzanian officials were also exasperated by an interview Make gave the BBC in London in which he disclosed, in reply to a question, that the Tanzanian army fatally shot four APLA cadres at the camp in Ithumbi in March 1980. The cadres visited various government offices as well as embassies in Dar-es-Salaam in an effort to secure Tanzanian and other support for their actions. The leaders of the 'cadre forces' movement' confided to this writer later that when they discussed their plans with a senior Tanzanian official in the Ministry of Foreign Affairs, his response was a question as to why Make's name was excluded from the list of names of Central Committee members whose immediate dismissal they demanded.[1]

This writer informed the Central Committee of this development and of the fact that the 'cadre forces' movement' was confident because of the support and private encouragement they received from certain Tanzanian officials. He also openly blamed the Central Committee for the resurfacing of the turmoil in the PAC because it failed to provide revolutionary role models for the cadres. Despite being warned of the frustrations among the cadres, Make did not change his ways, nor did he censure those Central Committee members of whose performance the cadres were most critical. Because this writer was not part of Make's faction, his counsel was ignored. Instead, he was increasingly perceived by Make and his inner circle as a 'threat' to their positions and they saw the 'cadre forces' movement' as his work instigating the cadres to oust them. His assurances to Make and the other Central Committee colleagues that he had no leadership ambitions and, if necessary, could resign his leadership position, did not satisfy them. Increasingly, the Make faction resorted to plots, scheming and manoeuvring against Makoti (who was also perceived by the Make faction as a threat to their position) and this writer.

While conveying to the Central Committee the views and feelings of the cadres, this writer also warned the 'cadre forces' movement' against being manipulated, that if Tanzanian officials were critical of Make and his leadership, they should address Make personally rather than encourage rebellion within the ranks of the organisation. Such rebellion would destabilise the PAC and provide a pretext for the organisation's detractors who called for its de-recognition as a genuine national liberation movement.

The 'cadre forces' movement' was not homogeneous. While there were many cadres who were genuinely concerned about the state of the PAC, who sincerely tried to effect a radical restructuring of the organisation, there were many opportunists among them who merely

206 *The Crisis in the PAC: 1978–83*

strove after leadership positions for themselves. They exploited the genuine grievances of the cadres for their personal interests. This writer cautioned the leaders of the 'cadre forces' movement' against this danger also.

Black Resistance in South Africa Escalates

While these problems plagued the PAC, Black resistance in South Africa continued to escalate, with strikes by Black workers and the boycott of schools by Black students protesting against the inferior system of education provided for Blacks under the system of apartheid. Black resistance became pervasive and generalised; the repression of the regime, rather than cowing Blacks into submission, had the opposite effect of increasing the resistance. The ANC, by responding to those political developments in South Africa and by its identification with the resistance, through its guerrilla campaigns, experienced a resurgence in South Africa and enhanced its international prestige. It was thus able to cushion off the impact of two potentially embarrassing events: (i) the November 1979 meeting in London with Chief Gatsha Buthelezi and his Inkatha Central Committee, who are regarded by politically sophisticated Blacks, including many ANC members in South Africa and abroad, as being collaborators and (ii) the Craig Williamson spy scandal, a few months later.

There was a realisation within the ranks of the PAC that the only way in which the organisation could be salvaged was for its military wing, APLA, to wage armed struggle in South Africa. In a report submitted to the Central Committee in January 1980, this writer in his capacity as Director of Foreign Affairs, warned:

> It is essential that we put our house in order and streamline our machinery so as to intensify the armed struggle on the ground because ultimately the armed struggle is the determining factor. Liaison with the internal wing of the PAC and with the internally-based mass organisations is imperative. We must build a truly *mass* organisation both in [South Africa] and outside, by which I mean that active mass participation in the struggle must be maximised.

For this reason, the plenary meeting of the Central Committee in April 1980 appointed Enoch Zulu (alias John Mvelase), a Central Committee member with considerable military experience, to the position of Director of Operations. After being provided with considerably more than the time and money requested by the Defence Department, however, the PAC's military wing would be no nearer to registering a presence in South Africa by the time that Make, too, was forced to relinquish his position as Chairman of the Central Committee in February 1981 than when he assumed the position.

Diplomatic Missions

Representatives and leaders of the national liberation movements in Southern Africa (as with representatives and leaders of national liberation movements everywhere) devote a great deal of time to diplomatic work which is aimed at raising support for the cause. This requires frequent travel to different countries in Africa and other parts of the world, but successful representation also requires constant reading and studying, to keep abreast of developments not only in the territories under foreign or minority domination, but throughout the world. Very often, international, regional and national events are very closely inter-related. In the case of the situation in South Africa this is particularly the case in view of the extensive imperialist interests involved and the international concern over the system of apartheid. The UN General Assembly has declared the system of apartheid not only a crime against the conscience of humanity, but also a threat to international peace and security.

In 1979, following the accession of P.W. Botha to the premiership, the South African regime embarked upon a massive propaganda campaign. Not only did he engage in much rhetoric about 'reforms' in South Africa, to the extent of questioning the continued need for the Mixed Marriages Act and the Immorality Act and warning the White populace that they would either have to 'adapt or die', but he also propagated the idea of a 'Constellation of Southern African States'. What was envisaged was the creation of an alliance of 'anti-Marxist states' in Southern Africa, comprising South Africa, the Bantustans which it has declared 'independent', and any independent African states willing to enter into such an alliance. The aim was that in return for certain economic benefits, those independent African states willing to enter into the alliance with Pretoria, would refrain from criticism of apartheid and would deny support to the ANC and PAC.

Given this background, the leaders and representatives of the national liberation movements had to apprise governments and non-governmental organisations which support them of these developments, and request diplomatic and political support to counter the schemes embarked upon by the South African regime. In the case of the PAC, the diplomatic missions had the additional objective of explaining the reasons for the expulsion of Leballo and of the steps taken to solve the internal problems of the organisation so that it would be able to play a more effective and prominent role in the national liberation struggle in South Africa.

In the period immediately after the October 1979 plenary meeting, PAC delegations visited a number of countries in Africa, namely, the People's Revolutionary Republic of Guinea, Sierra Leone, The Gambia, Senegal, Liberia and Egypt. They secured promises of support and assistance. The visits also helped ward off the threat of de-recognition. In February 1980 a delegation also visited Iraq.

Threat of De-recognition of PAC Still Lingers

Make and this writer returned to Dar-es-Salaam from their missions on 18 December 1979 in time for the OAU Standing Committees on Administration and Finance and Policy, Information and Defence. The report of the Standing Committee on Policy, Information and Defence was negative. It referred to the 'continuing crisis in PAC'. Leballo had written to the OAU Liberation Committee informing the Secretariat that he was still the Chairman of the PAC. The PAC delegation, led by this writer, challenged the accuracy of the report since the OAU Liberation Committee had recognised the expulsion of Leballo and recognised the leadership which was in effective control of the political centre. The effect of the report, however, was to put the PAC on the defensive.

Immediately after the meeting of the OAU Standing Committees, this writer travelled to a Southern African country, to meet a number of political activists from South Africa who had requested such a meeting. They provided detailed information about the political developments in the Black community, notably the increasing militancy among Black workers and students. This information was provided in order to explore the possibilities of future co-operation with the PAC and possible support for the activities of a number of the mass organisations which were involved in various activities inside the country. They hoped to return in March 1980 by which time the writer should have concrete proposals. This was a very important development for the PAC in that it offered the opportunity for the organisation to establish clandestine working relationships with the Black resistance inside the country. Great care would have to be exercised so as not to jeopardise the safety and security of persons still in South Africa. Reports were submitted to the Central Committee on the contacts established by this writer but the organisation was not able to respond to the political developments in the country, as will be shown. The question was repeatedly asked of the organisation's leadership and representatives: 'What role is the PAC playing in the mass resistance led by Black workers and students in South Africa?'

This question was asked by a number of delegates, both privately and during the open sessions, at the meeting of the OAU Liberation Committee which was held in Dar-es-Salaam from 21 to 25 January 1980. In a statement analysing the political developments in Southern Africa in general and South Africa in particular, this writer explained that the PAC placed a premium on the mobilisation and politicisation of the masses, in order that they might participate fully in the liberation struggle and to ensure that the armed struggle once launched would be sustained.[2]

From the PAC point of view, that session of the OAU Liberation Committee was successful. Unlike the report of the Standing Committees, the report of the Liberation Committee contained no negative references to PAC 'problems' or 'crisis'. There was a recognition of the continued efforts of the leadership to solve the internal problems of the organisation, but it was emphasised that the leadership would have to inspire the confidence of the followers and supporters of the PAC.

Since the Liberation Committee accepted the decision of the PAC's October 1979 plenary meeting to expel Leballo from the organisation as a recognition of the autonomy of the organisation, the expulsion was not an issue at all. OAU recognition of the new leadership was a major breakthrough for the PAC Central Committee. It meant that Leballo would no longer be received in Africa as the leader of the PAC, although the decision would not prevent him from continuing to claim to be 'the constitutional leader'.

Delegates to OAU Council of Ministers Lobbied against De-Recognition

After taking part in the delegation to Iraq, this writer proceeded to Addis Ababa, Ethiopia, to attend the 34th ordinary session of the OAU Council of Ministers, from 6 to 16 February 1980, while the remaining members of the delegation returned to Dar-es-Salaam. Meetings of the OAU provide a rare opportunity for the liberation movements in that all the independent African countries are represented at such gatherings. Representatives of the national liberation movements are thus able to meet and lobby delegations, including foreign ministers (during the Council of Ministers) and heads of state (during the Summit of Heads of State and Government). It also enables the liberation movements' representatives to follow up on earlier diplomatic missions undertaken or to enter into negotiations for aid on a bilateral basis with different countries. The important work is done outside the formal sessions. Since the PAC did not have abundant financial resources to pay the travel costs of its representatives to undertake numerous missions and trips to different countries, such meetings of the OAU were always exploited to the maximum to do diplomatic work.

Through the missions to various countries and the lobbying at the Council of Ministers, the campaign to have the PAC de-recognised by the OAU (which would be followed by de-recognition by the UN) was countered, so that the threat receded. The fact that the threat of de-recognition had receded, however, did not mean that the PAC could be complacent. It would continue to be under very close scrutiny, so that not only would the organisation have to put its house in order but would have to be seen to have done so.

In addition to the missions mentioned above, PAC delegations also participated in a number of international conferences in various countries at the invitation of UN agencies, the UN Special Committee Against Apartheid, and various non-governmental and anti-apartheid organisations. Such conferences provide similar opportunities to canvass

210   *The Crisis in the PAC: 1978–83*

support for the national liberation movement, but the success of such efforts depends also on the calibre of the representation of the PAC. Since the PAC has faced considerable hostility from a number of countries as well as organisations which support only the ANC (and campaign in favour of exclusive recognition of and support for the ANC), PAC representatives have had to work very hard at such international conferences to try to inform delegations about the policies and programmes of the organisation. In many instances, negative attitudes towards the PAC have been built up without any knowledge of the organisation. In the rivalry and competition between the ANC and PAC for influence and support, it is not uncommon for the organisations to spread falsehoods about each other. As a result, representatives of different organisations often absorb the antagonisms and prejudices of the rival movements and propagate them further. In this way, liberation support organisations, for instance, are drawn into the problems of the two liberation movements, thus aggravating the existing divisions and hostilities.

Shortage of Competent Personnel in PAC

In a report to the Central Committee of the PAC in January 1980, this writer stated:

> One of the problems encountered during discussions with many of our friends is that there has been a noticeable wariness, almost as though they are cautious about staking too much too early on the decisions we have taken. Ultimately, we will have to demonstrate by action on the ground.

The diplomatic missions undertaken and contacts made by the leadership and representatives of the PAC were extremely important, but there were a number of inherent problems.

Shortage of Manpower: The PAC has had and continues to have a serious shortage of manpower, a problem that has arisen in part from the fractionalisation of the organisation over the years. Many able and competent persons have either been expelled from the organisation during the innumerable power struggles and quarrels, or have been disillusioned by the seemingly interminable internal dissension and strife. Highly qualified individuals who are either members of the PAC, or who paid allegiance to the organisation at one stage, are scattered throughout the world. Among them are medical practitioners, scientists, lawyers and academics. Many of them pursued academic training only after having completed their military training. During the era of Leballo, the strong current of anti-intellectualism resulted in the talents of many of the PAC's most able people being wasted.

One of the problems is that the PAC has attracted into its ranks an

Vusumzi Make at the Helm: the Crisis Deepens 211

abundance of mediocre individuals whose attitude towards the organisation is that it exists to serve their personal interests. A criticism levelled against the PAC by the ANC was that it was formed by people who could not gain any leadership positions in the ANC. It is very difficult to avoid drawing the conclusion that many of the activists within the PAC would have been unacceptable to any other organisation. The problem of mediocrity is a problem faced by any mass or populist movement, as opposed to the more intellectual/leftist elite of an ANC or an MPLA. Given its populist/mass appeal or orientation, a PAC is likely to attract people with a keen sense of *grievance* but a less sophisticated or informed sense of public good, of ideological commitment, of *conscious civic obligation*. The task of leadership in educating and forming a more enlightened membership then becomes crucial.

Another way of viewing the problem of mediocrity in the PAC is that a *Sobukwe* can elevate the level of discourse and perception within a populist movement by virtue of being *of* the masses but also a *role model* with which they can identify. In the absence of such leadership, the less elevated notion of self-interest may dominate.

Because of the skills required in diplomatic work for successful negotiations, an inordinate amount of responsibilities devolve upon far too few individuals. Apart from diplomatic and negotiating skills, the political clarity and ability to perceive and articulate issues, the ability to communicate clearly in both the written and the spoken word, are just some of the requisite skills.

The PAC, unfortunately, does not have an abundance of people of high calibre so that to ensure the success of the organisation's efforts in the arena of international politics and diplomacy, a few selected individuals undertake most of the work. The criticisms levelled at Make for spending far too much time away from the PAC's external headquarters, personally leading all the PAC delegations on missions, has to be weighed against this reality. Whatever criticisms can be made of Make's leadership, it has to be recognised that he does have diplomatic skills; he is also intelligent and articulate.

The same observations could be made of the PAC Observer Mission to the UN. On the one hand, the observer status which the PAC enjoys at the UN provides an opportunity for the organisation to meet and to lobby representatives from more than 150 countries. On the other hand, it has meant that the organisation is exposed to scrutiny by the international community. Apart from the East–West rivalry and the Sino–Soviet rivalry which have played themselves out at the UN and which have also affected the fortunes of the PAC in the world body, the organisation has also been the subject of negative comments by journalists, academics and diplomats.

The PAC's response should have been to ensure a very high level of sophisticated representation at the UN. Dissemination of accurate information about political developments in South Africa to all

212　*The Crisis in the PAC: 1978–83*

delegations is one important function. Another is providing constant information about the PAC and its role in the national liberation struggle in South Africa. During the years that the PAC was represented at the UN by David Sibeko and his wife, Elizabeth, they were the only two persons at the Observer Mission on a regular basis. In 1977 they were joined by Mzonke Xusa, but he was subsequently nominated by the PAC for the anti-apartheid programme launched by the UN Radio Service. Technically, from then on he became a UN employee, and could not undertake official responsibilities on behalf of the PAC.

In late 1978, at the request of David Sibeko, Clement Mlongwane was sent to assist. But Mlongwane was ineffective both as an administrator and as a political representative. Indeed, his statements had to be prepared for him to read whenever he had to represent the PAC. In 1979 and 1980, a number of other individuals were assigned to assist at the PAC Observer Mission to the UN. Their competence and ability were also extremely poor, for which they compensated by 'dysfunctional behaviour'.[3]

Similarly the other major PAC office, in London, was often staffed by only one person, Ngila Muendane, although in 1980 Joe Moabi was appointed as his assistant.

The pool of people from which the PAC could draw for diplomatic work was and remains small. In this regard, other national liberation movements in Africa have been more fortunate. National liberation movements like FRELIMO in Mozambique, MPLA in Angola, the PAIGC in Guinea-Bissau and ZANU-PF in Zimbabwe were engaged in the armed struggle, which was their principal pre-occupation. Diplomatic work was secondary and was reinforced by their involvement and successes in the armed struggle. This was particularly the case with ZANU-PF. Those liberation movements like the ANC and ZAPU which placed a premium on the diplomatic struggle, have had a far larger number of competent people than the PAC to represent them internationally as well as to do diplomatic work on their behalf.

A solution would have been for the PAC to train personnel for diplomatic work, but it did not. When eventually a Department of Education and Manpower Development was established in 1977, the aim was less to train a cadre to meet the manpower requirements of the organisation than to utilise the assistance which was offered by the UN specialised agencies. Thus the appointment of an education officer and an assistant (namely, Mogale Jimmy Mokgoatsane and Erret Radebe), was formalised in order to secure from Unesco two stipends amounting to approximately US$750 each month specifically for the education department personnel, as well as office furniture and equipment. Unesco purchased office furniture, including desks and steel cabinets, and equipment like typewriters and a

Vusumzi Make at the Helm: the Crisis Deepens 213

photostat copying machine. These were not used exclusively by the education department, but rather by the organisation as a whole.

In similar vein, the view of Leballo and others around him was that the transit centre in Pongwe could be used to raise funds which could then be channelled into other activities, particularly of a military nature, since UN agencies, a number of governments (like those of the Nordic Countries, for instance), and many non-governmental organisations were quite prepared to provide humanitarian assistance to the national liberation movements in Southern Africa, but not to sponsor military programmes.

Lack of Appreciation of Diplomatic Work: The necessity for and value of diplomatic work and external relations were not always understood or appreciated by many PAC members, including many of those in the leadership. To people forced to endure the conditions of hardship and deprivation in a military camp in the bush in Ithumbi, or a transit centre at Pongwe where the dreaded tse-tse fly and mosquito abound, the constant travel often appears glamorous. Frustrations breed envy and petty jealousy. In addition, such feelings are often exploited by ambitious individuals or unscrupulous leaders, particularly during power struggles. In the PAC it has not been uncommon for the representatives of the organisation abroad, or those of its officials who engage in frequent diplomatic work or travel to be denounced as 'bourgeois', without an understanding of the concept by those who engage in such denunciations.

Other national liberation movements like the PAIGC in Guinea-Bissau, FRELIMO in Mozambique and ZANU-PF in Zimbabwe, were able to deal with this problem (and other attitudinal problems) through the political education organised for their combatants and recruits so that they were able to understand fully all the dynamics involved in their national liberation struggles.[4]

Lack of Appreciation of Financial Realities: A related problem was the expectation that each time a PAC delegation travelled anywhere it should return with suitcases full of bank notes, preferably American dollars to be exchanged on the black market. An examination of the diplomatic missions undertaken during the period October through December 1979, would show that not a cent was realised. Positive results came from visits to two countries, namely Guinea and Sierra Leone, which provided various forms of assistance to the PAC. Some countries pledged financial and material support but none was forthcoming, even after follow-up missions. In certain instances, this was due to economic difficulties; in other instances it was due to a lack of confidence in the PAC in the light of the recurring internal problems, so that while promising aid, some countries adopted an attitude of wait and see. Yet, from the point of view of the PAC the

214   *The Crisis in the PAC: 1978–83*

missions were successful; they helped stave off negative OAU action.

Of all the diplomatic missions undertaken in 1980 only two realised any financial aid — the mission to Iraq in January 1980 and a mission to the People's Republic of China in October 1980. The Arab Ba'ath Socialist Party provided an amount of US$100,000 to the PAC in April 1980 and also agreed to the establishment of an office there. The delegation to the People's Republic of China in October 1980 was given a sum of US$20,000 in cash.

Two PAC delegations visited Lagos in April and October 1980. Leballo had left Lagos by then. On both occasions, negotiations were initiated for financial and material assistance, as well as the reopening of the PAC office in Lagos. The fruits of these efforts, however, were only realised in 1981 when Theophilus Bidi was appointed Chief Representative to Nigeria and re-established a PAC presence there. In November 1981 the Government of Nigeria gave the PAC an amount of US$250,000 which was depleted by March 1982. Another PAC delegation visited Belgrade in September 1980 — the first ever by the PAC — as a result of which the Socialist Alliance Party of Yugoslavia extended support to the PAC. They agreed to provide training in various technical fields for PAC cadres. In addition, they agreed to print PAC publications. Negotiations were made for PAC delegations to visit Guyana, Mexico and Gabon. However, the visits did not materialise even after specific dates had been set for the visits. A PAC delegation visited Swaziland and Zambia in July 1980. Representations were made to the two governments for a normalisation of relations following the banning of the PAC in Zambia in 1968 and the arrests and deportation of PAC members in Swaziland in 1978. The representations did not produce the desired results.

In view of the problems facing the PAC and the campaign of diplomatic isolation to which the organisation was subjected, the diplomatic efforts described above were significant and important in countering the campaign and also in raising political and financial support.

Criticisms were made by the political cadres of the diplomatic work undertaken by the leadership of the organisation. In many instances the criticisms were uninformed. For instance, one criticism was that the diplomatic thrust of the PAC seemed to be geared towards the West. The truth of the matter was that the efforts of the Central Committee were directed principally towards the African countries; the only diplomatic work done in Western countries, apart from contact with liberation support organisations, comprised representations to those governments which provided humanitarian assistance to the PAC, e.g. The Netherlands Government. In some instances, the criticisms were legitimate; for example, the cadres

Vusumzi Make at the Helm: the Crisis Deepens 215

questioned Make's frequent and long absences from the external headquarters.

Other criticisms were purely mischievous. For example, the Director of Operations, Enoch Zulu (alias John Mvelase), frequently engaged in vituperous attacks upon what he termed 'Central Committee members gallivanting all over the world, yet we don't see the money they bring in'. Of course, such attacks were made to the cadres in the absence of the Central Committee members in question.

Cadres at the external headquarters increasingly regarded themselves as the 'real PAC' and, together with some members of the Central Committee, were critical of the representatives of the organisation abroad, and of those Central Committee members on whose shoulders the bulk of the diplomatic work fell. This has to be understood in the light of the ongoing power struggle between the 'political' and the 'military' and between those based at external headquarters and those based or forced to work abroad. The assumption or accusation was that the latter 'lived comfortably' or 'enjoyed the glamour and bright lights' of the Western capitals in particular. Cadres at the PAC headquarters had by the end of 1981 coined a new phrase, 'external force', to refer to any PAC member from abroad who returned to headquarters for consultations or any reason other than to remain permanently. The subsequent history of the struggle between the 'interior' and the 'exterior' for primacy in this case is instructive.[5] It demonstrates the expectations which militants often have of the performance of their political leaders, without in many cases understanding or appreciating the limitations and constraints under which such leaders operate. In the case of the PAC, the representatives of the organisation abroad (whether in New York or London) regularly received telephone calls or cables from the external headquarters literally requesting the transfer of thousands of dollars to different centres where PAC members lived, particularly in Africa. There was almost an assumption or belief that such representatives upon production of such cables from the PAC headquarters at any commercial bank in New York or London would be given thousands of dollars immediately. Failure of the representatives to despatch the requested sums of money were then interpreted as personal failure of such representatives. This attitude was demonstrated by the PAC's former Director of Finance, Lawrence Temba Mgweba, who habitually telephoned this writer in New York with the characteristic request, 'Send us money. We have no money here in Dar-es-Salaam', or 'Can you send the people in Lesotho ten thousand dollars right away?' It was simply beyond the comprehension of Lawrence Temba Mgweba that a PAC office in New York would not have ten thousand dollars to despatch at the mere drop of a hat! At a PAC Central Committee meeting in July 1981, Mgweba explained that

216   *The Crisis in the PAC: 1978–83*

the USA was a vast country and that the PAC representative to the UN should be able to collect a 'lot of funds in America'. His understanding of the reality of the situation in the USA was his description of the National Council of Churches at Riverside Drive in New York as being the 'headquarters of the CIA', even after a report to the effect that the National Council of Churches provides humanitarian assistance to South African refugees, including PAC members like the Sibekos and Makhandas.

In exactly the same manner, the Director of Operations plaintively informed a meeting of the US Chapter of the PAC in March 1982 that the New York and London offices of the PAC had failed to despatch funds to Dar-es-Salaam for 'operations'. What the Director of Operations, as well as the Director of Finance, chose to ignore is the fact that without evidence of the PAC's involvement in the struggle for liberation in South Africa the organisation will not receive financial assistance. That was a reality faced by the representatives of the organisation, as Sibeko reported in September 1978, but which was ignored by the external headquarters where the most convenient and politically expedient thing for people like Mgweba and Zulu to do was to blame the representatives.

The failure of the PAC to register a military presence in South Africa throughout Make's tenure as Chairman of the Central Committee, but before as well, seriously eroded international support for the organisation.

Central Committee Lacks Control over APLA

A second major problem facing the Central Committee during the regime of Vus Make was that the leadership had no effective control over APLA, the organisation's military wing. The organisation's military programme and the activities of APLA were immobilised as a result of the internal problems which had bedevilled the movement since 1978.

At the camp in Ithumbi there were militarily-trained cadres, less than 200 in number, the majority of whom refused to recognise the leadership and authority of the Central Committee. Among them were 40 cadres who had been declared prohibited immigrants and who were ordered out of the country by the Tanzanian authorities. These cadres claimed allegiance to Leballo and to the expelled members of the high command, led by Justice Nkonyane.

As a result of the failure or inability of the Central Committee to remove the cadres from Tanzania the activities of the PAC were frozen; the government prohibited the entry into the country of any new recruits pending the removal of the expellees from the country. In effect, this meant that any new recruits joining the PAC in either Lesotho or Botswana were not permitted into Tanzania. This caused serious bottlenecks, since the PAC did not have any country which was prepared to accept the 40 cadres who were declared prohibited immigrants; at the same time the organisation did not have a country or countries offering facilities for military training for large numbers at any given time. The only country which still accepted PAC cadres for military training was Guinea, but there were limits on the numbers which could be sent there at any one time.

The Central Committee had no access to the camp at Ithumbi where, according to the numerous reports received from cadres who fled the reign of terror unleashed by Leballo loyalists, the arms and ammunition smuggled into the country by Leballo and Mayekiso in November 1978 were still hidden.

The attitude of the OAU Liberation Committee was that the PAC could not claim to have solved its internal problems as long as the 'dissident' cadres remained in control of the camp at Ithumbi.

After numerous representations to the Tanzanian authorities by the Central Committee, the Tanzanian army went to the camp at Ithumbi on 11 March 1980 to disarm the 'dissident' cadres and to remove the 40 who had been declared prohibited immigrants. Four cadres were fatally wounded and several others injured after those who had been ordered to leave the camp refused to obey the orders of the Tanzanian army commander. Ultimately 46 cadres were separated and removed to another camp at Mgawawo near Iringa, pending their removal from Tanzania by the PAC. Eight sub-machine guns, eight empty pistol magazines, 16 charged magazines and 476 rounds of ammunition were also unearthed in a poultry pen.[6]

Even after the removal of the 46 cadres from Ithumbi, the Central Committee was unable to establish control and authority over the APLA cadres who remained at the camp. This situation of stalemate continued until the second half of 1981 after the assumption of the chairmanship by Nyati Pokela.

Leballo's Claims Continue

A third problem during the Make regime was the continued claim to the leadership by Leballo and the activities of his supporters.

Leballo remained in Nigeria for more than a year, during which time he travelled to various parts of Africa, claiming to be the 'constitutionally elected leader of the PAC'. He regularly issued press releases, despatched memoranda and communiques to various parts of the world, condemning what he termed the 'Make-clique', claiming his removal as leader of the PAC was engineered by President Julius

218 *The Crisis in the PAC: 1978–83*

Nyerere of Tanzania because he (Leballo) was a revolutionary, while President Nyere favoured 'detente' with the South African regime.[7] Leballo also successfully established lines of communication with the 'dissident' APLA cadres at the camp in Ithumbi. He promised them financial assistance and assured them that he had the support of several progressive African governments and that he would return 'shortly' to resume his duties as PAC Chairman. Although such assurances were false, they served to reinforce the resolve of the 'dissident' APLA cadres in their rejection of the authority of the Central Committee.

Leballo was assisted in his efforts by Nyakane Mike Tsolo (formerly the PAC representative in The Netherlands), Michael Wilson, a White South African expatriate and Stephen Burgess, an American who formerly lectured at the Institute of Social Studies in The Hague together with Wilson, after which he moved to Zambia where he taught at the University of Zambia in Lusaka. Tsolo distributed widely a statement purporting to explain the situation in the PAC and expressed his full support for Leballo. The statement was subsequently circulated at the UN where it was used by detractors of the PAC to support their contention that the organisation was faction-ridden and/or in a state of disintegration.

Tsolo's stance was clearly incompatible with his continued representation of the PAC without Leballo. Tsolo was relieved of his responsibilities as a representative by the Central Committee following a decision of the plenary meeting in April 1980.[8]

Tsolo wrote another letter to the newspaper of the Canadian Marxist–Leninist Party in which he claimed that the Make regime was 'reformist', that David Sibeko was a victim of a struggle between 'revolutionaries' and 'reformists', and that he was assassinated by the 'reformists' because he was a 'revolutionary'. Among his allegations was that the Tanzanian authorities had detained 500 PAC revolutionaries.[9]

Michael Wilson, in a letter to the New York *Guardian* claimed that there was a two-line struggle in the PAC between 'revolutionaries' and 'capitulationists' who were bent on negotiating with the South African regime.[10] This writer visited Montreal, Canada, from 28 to 30 November 1980 to participate in an International Conference on the Role of the Soviet Union in the Third World, held at McGill University, at the invitation of the Committee to Support People of the Third World (CAPT). While in Montreal, the writer took the opportunity to see the publishers of *In Struggle*, which had carried slanderous letters and articles written to Tsolo and Wilson. They admitted that they had published the letters and articles without checking the accuracy of the contents. The November 1980 issue of *International Forum*, also published by the same group, carried a scurrilous article by Wilson which was essentially the same article that he had published in two Indian Marxist–Leninist journals, *Mass Line* and *Frontier*. In the

Vusumzi Make at the Helm: the Crisis Deepens 219

articles, Wilson made out a case for support for the 'revolutionary leadership' of P.K. Leballo as opposed to what he termed the 'capitulationists'. Wilson and Burgess continued with their letter-writing in support of Leballo even after the assumption of the chairmanship by Nyati Pokela.[11]

Politics sometimes produces surprising alliances! In March 1979 this writer and the former PAC Director of Finance, Erret Radebe, visited The Netherlands for a series of meetings. We stayed with Tsolo, at his home, and during discussion there it became apparent that Tsolo was upset by the fact that David Sibeko, PAC's former Director of Foreign Affairs, not only regularly communicated with Wilson, but also assigned him certain responsibilities, such as making representations for humanitarian assistance to the government of The Netherlands. Tsolo felt that his position, as PAC's Representative in The Netherlands, thus became somewhat anomalous. He had written to the Director of Foreign Affairs in January 1979 (with a copy to the Administrative Secretary) asking for clarification of his status, but had received no reply. Obviously, under the circumstances, Tsolo's attitude towards Wilson was one of resentment, yet later he and Wilson co-operated closely in promoting Leballo's cause!

Wilson and Burgess had, however, been encouraged to concern themselves with the internal affairs of the PAC by Sibeko and Make: they had asked them to write articles for publication in PAC journals, and to prepare papers for presentation by the PAC. In late 1978, for example, Sibeko and Make had asked Wilson and Burgess to prepare a paper on 'The Development Strategy of the PAC' for Make to present to a conference of the African Association of Political Scientists in Maputo, in 1979. They did prepare the paper, but for some reason Make did not attend the conference. The extent of the involvement of Wilson and Burgess in the PAC's affairs can, however, be gauged from the following letter from Michael Wilson to David Sibeko, dated 12 January 1979:

Dear Dave:

This letter will hopefully catch you in Dar [Dar-es-Salaam] for the CC [Central Committee] meeting. Mike Tsolo phoned yesterday to ask for help towards an airticket, but I'm afraid its prohibitively expensive for the Azania Komitee.

Some points:

1. I do hope that PAC will take up directly contact with the *Ayatullah Khomaini* [sic] and other leaders of the Iranian opposition. They have done a great service to Azania by cutting off oil supplies — and, in the future, may well also be prepared to give financial support to PAC. Or has this (as is often the case!) already been done?

2. *Pope John Paul II*. Still think it's worth while for PAC to ask for an interview . . . It would, i.a. put PAC on the map in countries like Italy and Ireland . . .

3. *Ireland* . . . One major suggestion is to approach the Irish government officially for a donation to the humanitarian projects of PAC, e.g. schooling. I was unofficially advised that this would be sympathetically treated.

Best wishes for 1979.

Michael Wilson.

It would appear that Wilson and Burgess, by the process of flattering individuals such as Sibeko, were seeking to exert influence on the PAC. To take a minor example: in correspondence, Sibeko, Make, Ntloedibe and Leballo were always addressed as 'Dr.' by Wilson and Burgess — a distinction to which none of them was entitled — and which none of them refuted. Also, in their paper 'The Development Strategy of the PAC', Leballo, Sibeko and Make were especially singled out for praise.

Wilson and Burgess were fully aware of the destructive role played by Leballo in the PAC over the years, including his role in inciting the APLA cadres against individual Central Committee members. Nevertheless, long after the expulsion of Leballo from the leadership, they continued to refer to him as the leader of PAC. That Leballo had been ousted from the leadership can be seen as a disappointment to Wilson and Burgess in that it eliminated one potentially receptive channel which could have facilitated their influence on the PAC.

Wilson and Burgess are examples of the phenomenon of expatriates assuming roles in national liberation movements and becoming more revolutionary than the revolutionaries. Liberation movements are vulnerable to this kind of misplaced enthusiasm and motivation, and must, therefore, be alert to the existence and the history of such phenomenon.

The effect of Leballo's actions, coupled with the activities of Tsolo, Wilson and Burgess, was that they constantly exposed the PAC to charges of 'internal' or 'leadership problems'. In July 1980, Leballo, accompanied by two of his supporters, attempted to attend the OAU Council of Ministers and Summit of Heads of State in Freetown, Sierra Leone. Leballo and his followers were detained at an airport hotel; subsequently, they were deported from Sierra Leone. Needless to say, the incident was extremely embarrassing to the PAC. Several delegations had seen Leballo; others were present when the first two members of the official PAC delegation arrived at Freetown International Airport to be informed that the PAC delegation had already registered.

Several representations were made to the Nigerian authorities requesting that Leballo's activities be restrained but it was only in August 1980 that the PAC was informed through the Nigerian Acting High Commissioner to Tanzania that President Shehu Shagari had decided to recognise the leadership of Vus Make.[13] After leaving Nigeria, Leballo went to Zimbabwe where he remained for some time. The government of the newly-independent Zimbabwe was clearly placed in a very embarrassing and invidious predicament. ZANU-PF, led by Prime Minister Robert Mugabe, had had a close relationship with the PAC, from the time that ZANU was formed.

When Angola and Mozambique achieved their independence in the mid-seventies, the ANC was able to exploit its long association and political alliance with the MPLA and FRELIMO. The ANC was invited to open offices in both countries, thus establishing an effective political presence in two key front-line states. This had important consequences for the ANC, both in its work in South Africa and internationally, making capital out of its recognition by two countries whose governments have revolutionary credentials.

The PAC, by contrast, was unable to capitalise on the election victory of ZANU-PF in Zimbabwe. That country's geographic proximity to and economic dependence on South Africa, meant that for the foreseeable future Prime Minister Mugabe would not be able to offer the ANC, PAC, and SWAPO any support other than moral and diplomatic. Quite apart from that reality, the weakness of the PAC, torn as it was by internal strife, was acutely embarrassing to the government of Prime Minister Mugabe.[14] The invidious position in which the Zimbabwean government was placed could be seen in the fact that at one stage three delegations presented themselves in the capital, Harare — one led by Vus Make, another led by T.M. Ntantala and yet another led by P.K. Leballo — all claiming to be PAC.

The Problems Caused by Elizabeth Sibeko

Elizabeth Sibeko was, at this time, both a Central Committee member and the PAC representative to the USA and the Caribbean. From the time of her return to New York, in August 1979, after the funeral of her husband, until February 1981, when the Central Committee eventually decided to take disciplinary action against her. Following the theft of a blank cheque and the sum of US$5,000 from the PAC Observer Mission to the UN's bank account in November 1980, Elizabeth Sibeko created many difficulties for the PAC at the UN and in the USA.

The PAC's Reluctance to Act Against Elizabeth Sibeko

Even when in possession of clear proofs of her disruptive activities, the Central Committee failed to act upon it for a number of reasons:

1) She was a widow; quite understandably the Central Committee felt the PAC's image would be tarnished if disciplinary action were to be taken against her, particularly as her husband had been a leader of the organisation and the first to be assassinated.

2) Vus Make had been a friend of the late David Sibeko, had been with him when the assassination took place and, while in Botswana for
the funeral, had been accused by various members of the family of complicity in the murder. These facts rendered him vulnerable to emotional pressure from Elizabeth Sibeko.

3) Many individuals owed their positions in the organization to appointments made by the late David Sibeko and were, therefore, reluctant to take any action against his widow. Privately, however, they acknowledged the adverse effects her activities were having on the PAC, and several were very critical of her behaviour and attitude after Sibeko's funeral: she had accused Make of complicity in her husband's assassination, and had demanded for herself all financial contributions made to the PAC to defray funeral expenses.

Elizabeth Sibeko Challenged at Central Committee

At a meeting of the Central Committee on 25 September 1980 a detailed confidential memorandum was presented to the meeting outlining the actions of Elizabeth Sibeko (who was present at the meeting) and the consequences for the organisation. The following is a verbatim excerpt from that memorandum:

> The basic problem at the [PAC Observer] Mission [to the UN] stems from the fact that immediately after her return from Botswana, Comrade Elizabeth Sibeko resumed her duties at the office, which, with hindsight, was wrong because she was then returning to surroundings which were a constant reminder to her of the fact that Comrade David [Sibeko] was no longer going to be in those surroundings doing the things to which she had grown accustomed to seeing him do. This has made the process of re-adjustment extremely difficult for her . . .
>
> There have been numerous complaints from various persons, particularly those who telephone the office, of rudeness and impoliteness

Vusumzi Make at the Helm: the Crisis Deepens   223

from Comrade Elizabeth. I do not think that this is any vendetta against her by anti-PAC elements, because the complaints have also come from people who do not know her at all. For example, in November [1979] the projects officer of CORSO telephoned me in New York to request me to write a letter of protest to the New Zealand government after the decision of the latter to terminate their tax-deductibility status on donations received. The government cited as one of the reasons for the decision that
CORSO had supported a terrorist organisation', reference to the grant of
$48,000 made to PAC in 1977. When [the projects officer] called I was at the UN; she called back later and was told by Comrade Elizabeth Sibeko that I was still at the UN. No message was taken, nor was I informed of the telephone calls until several weeks later when I received a letter from CORSO together with press clippings, and enquired of the telephone call, that Comrade Elizabeth recalled that 'someone from New Zealand had called'.

The memorandum continued with a careful itemisation of Elizabeth Sibeko's actions and the difficulties these caused for the PAC and the smooth functioning of the PAC Observer Mission to the UN. For example, she rejected any criticism of her late husband to the extent of trying to put him above any other PAC leader; she acted independently, engaging the PAC without consultation with other colleagues; she used her husband's death to raise money, but not for the PAC, and insisted on the New York office paying her domestic bills. Such consideration had never been extended to any other PAC widow.

Elizabeth Sibeko's Response to the PAC's Challenge

In response to this detailed analysis and political case against her, Elizabeth Sibeko accused the author of the memorandum of persecuting her because she was a woman. She maintained that he was arrogant, that he had 'failed', and that the ANC observer at the UN was 'running rings around [him]'. She then submitted him to bitter personal attack during the course of which she indicated that the source of the rumours she was retailing was a PAC member who, upon completion of his studies had come to New York to assist at the PAC Observer Mission to the UN.

She went on to accuse the author of the memorandum of preparing documents about her 'like the CIA' and of having rallied the PAC Observer Mission's personnel against her, and additionally, of having incited the cadres in Dar-es-Salaam, which explained the memorandum they had drawn up criticising the leadership as a collective.

224 *The Crisis in the PAC: 1978–83*

The author, who, before this outburst by Elizabeth Sibeko, had presented the Central Committee with a report detailing the activities of the Department of Foreign Affairs and the PAC Observer Mission to the UN and which the Central Committee had accepted, offered to suspend himself from his position as Director of Foreign Affairs and Observer at the UN while the Central Committee conducted an independent investigation of his performance in both capacities. If such an independent inquiry established that he had 'failed in the performance of his duties' or that the report he had submitted was incorrect or not factual, he would resign. This offer was rejected by the Central Committee.

The Central Committee, however, neither reprimanded nor took any action against Elizabeth Sibeko. On the contrary, Make and a number of others argued that the problems at the PAC Observer Mission to the UN were personal and not political. Consequently the Central Committee urged the two Central Committee members based in New York to return and 'work together'. The Central Committee ignored reports submitted by personnel at the PAC Observer Mission, and reports by ordinary PAC members from Dar-es-Salaam, who had visited the New York office while in the USAA attending conferences, as well as a critical report submitted by the Administrative Secretary, D. D. Mantshontsho, who had spent some time at the PAC Observer Mission in May 1980, and instead, chose to compromise.

Such compromising cost the PAC dearly in the following months.

Elizabeth Sibeko and Leasoana Makhanda

Elizabeth Sibeko was now joined by Leasoana Sam Makhanda who, in September 1980, had writen a lengthy report to the Central Committee criticising her actions and attitude.

For an understanding of who Makhanda is, and the reasons for his subsequent behaviour and actions, it is necessary to provide some background information about him.

In the early 1960s Makhanda was expelled from the organsiation during a power struggle. The African-American Institute offered him a scholarship to study in the USA, where he had remained. His return to active involvement in the PAC in the mid-1970s, and eventual reinstatement as a member were facilitated by David Sibeko, and subsequently he became a Sibeko loyalist.

After the 1978 consultative conference, which he attended as a delegate of the North America chapter of the PAC, he was elected to the chapter's executive committee. These elections were, however, subsequently nullified by David Sibeko on the grounds that the PAC

Vusumzi Make at the Helm: the Crisis Deepens   225

chapter in North America could not be autonomous, but should be under his control as PAC's Observer at the UN and Director of Foreign Affairs. At a meeting of selected PAC members, organised by Sibeko in the USA, fresh elections for a more amenable executive committee were held. Makhanda emerged as the new Chairman of the Sibeko-approved PAC chapter with the result that PAC members in the USA were split into two factions, with Makhanda in the pro-Sibeko faction.

In June 1979, when Sibeko was assassinated, Makhanda, who lived in Pittsburgh, Pennsylvania, moved to New York, where he assisted at the PAC Observer Mission. But, as the author discovered, his reasons for this move were primarily personal and financial. In April and May 1980, after attending a UN conference in Nairobi, Makhanda undertook an extended visit to Tanzania and Botswana. In June 1980, this writer, in his capacity as PAC's Observer at the UN and Director of Foreign Affairs, summoned Makhanda back to the USA to attend to his personal matters, and in July 1980 discussed the matter with him in Tanzania, adivisng him to return urgently to New York. When he returned to the USA, in August 1980, Makhanda was advised to attend to his personal circumstances before returning to assist at the Observer Mission.

The Stolen Cheque

In November 1980, Leasoana Sam Makhanda and Elizabeth Sibeko took a blank cheque from the PAC Observer Mission and used it to withdraw $5,000 from the bank account, an action which had the effect of seriously disrupting the office administration. Indeed, in order to ensure the running of the office, this writer had to secure a loan of $10,000 from Mzonke Xusa. Still, the Central Committee was powerless, or more precisely, refused to act, even though it was the second time in two weeks that Elizabeth had withdrawn funds from the Observer Mission's bank account without approval. (The previous week she had withdrawn $500.)

The unauthorized withdrawal of the funds from the Observer Mission's bank account was then reported to the New York Metropolitan Police after consultations among Gora Ebrahim (who was in New York at the invitation of this writer to address the UN General Assembly), Molefe Ike Mafole, Clement Hlongwane and the writer. Ebrahim and Mafole were particularly emphatic in urging police intervention. In the presence of the others, this writer first telephoned Makhanda at the Sibeko residence to warn him that unless the money was returned to the office, the matter would be reported to the police. His only response was to say 'go ahead'.

226 The Crisis in the PAC: 1978–83

The matter was reported to the police, not as an act of vengeance, but for several important reasons. Firstly, the Central Committee refused to act against one of its members despite the gravity of the action and despite the fact that, in a telephone conversation with two Central Committee members in Dar-es-Salaam (namely Joe Mkwanazi and Count Pietersen), Elizabeth Sibeko admitted that she had withdrawn the funds from the Observer Mission's bank account. Secondly, the PAC Observer Mission was subsidised by the UN; if the information had leaked out that a PAC Central Committee member had misappropriated $5,000, the repercussions for the PAC (and all other national liberation movements in Southern Africa) would have been serious. Several Western countries were opposed to UN funding for the national liberation movements. They would have been able to point to the misappropriation of $5,000 by a PAC leader to justify their opposition. Thirdly, had the matter not been reported to the police, then the head of the PAC Observer Mission would have been implicated in the malfeasance, for he bore full responsibility for all income and expenditure.

Reporting the matter was, therefore, simply meeting an obligation. Although Gora Ebrahim was present when the theft was discovered and was part of the decision to report it to the police, he later conveyed the impression to PAC members in Tanzania that the decision had been a unilateral one and that it had been politically unwise.

Elizabeth Sibeko immediately informed several liberation support organisations, among others, the Patrice Lumumba Coalition and the now-defunct Southern Africa Support Committee that she was being 'persecuted', and being 'hounded by the FBI'. Both charges were untrue: the FBI was not involved in the investigation which was a local matter for the New York Metropolitan Police 17th precinct. She also telephoned Vus Make threatening to 'defend' herself (by which it was generally understood that she would expose others) in the event of a prosecution. Consequently, Make wrote a letter to the New York Metropolitan Police (delivered by Elizabeth Sibeko personally), informing them that she was entitled to the money and that the organisation would not press charges of theft against her.

Although Make rationalised the decision on the ground that the involvement of the police would have serious consequences for the PAC, the real reason for his actions was the fear that in the event of Elizabeth Sibeko being prosecuted for theft of PAC funds (with Leasoana Makhanda as an accessory), then other names of PAC Central Committee members who had also misused funds of the organisation would be exposed. There has been a failure of Central Committee members to engage in honest criticism among themselves, as well as to impose disciplinary measures when they became necessary, owing to an anxiety that individual indiscretions might be

Vusumzi Make at the Helm: the Crisis Deepens 227

exposed. As a consequence, the perpetuation of this attitude at the level of leadership in turn breeds indiscipline among the rank-and-file. How can leaders who do not criticise one another, or discipline one another in the event of patent wrongdoing, assert discipline or authority in the organisation?

Later Elizabeth Sibeko and Leasoana Makhanda were joined by Clement Hlongwane, who had also a few weeks earlier submitted to the Central Committee a report in which he complained about and criticised the actions and attitudes of Elizabeth Sibeko. The question which can be asked is how could two individuals, within the space of only a few weeks, change from a position of condemnation and criticism of Elizabeth to one of connivance and collaboration? The answer to this question is to be found in the personal problems of the two individuals and their inability to cope with them. Makhanda, in particular, was totally unable to take meaningful decisions to solve his personal and domestic problems which affected the work of the organisation, even after he was instructed to return from Africa in June–July 1980. Instead, these problems were compounded by an automobile accident in September 1980.[14]

Makhanda regularly visited the UN headquarters where he sat drinking in the delegates' lounge. As a result, the internal affairs and problems of the PAC were common knowledge in the corridors of the UN. Despite this, Makhanda was still taken seriously by certain Central Committee members belonging to Make's faction at the PAC headquarters in Dar-es-Salaam to whom he despatched regular reports about the 'failure' of the organisation's Observer at the UN.

In October 1981, Nyati Pokela visited the USA and the UN, where he saw Makhanda. Pokela observed to the Administrative Secretary, Joe Mkwanazi, and this writer that Makhanda had a long history of disruptive and dissident activities dating back to 1963. Pokela said that in that year he visited Botswana (then Bechuanaland) for the first time, after learning of problems among PAC members there. When he arrived in Botswana, the name of Makhanda was among the first mentioned.

In exactly the same way, Clement Hlongwane found himself so overwhelmed by his personal problems that he decided to leave the PAC Observer Mission. Apart from, or probably because of, his personal problems, he made no progress in his studies to which he returned in the fall of 1980 after much prodding from the author and a number of other persons.

Makhanda, as well as Hlongwane, made representations for financial assistance to a number of non-governmental organisations with which they had come into contact during their association with the PAC Observer Mission to the UN. Ultimately, Hlongwane was threatened by the European–American Bank with legal action for

228   *The Crisis in the PAC: 1978–83*

failing to repay a sum of $1,800 which had been erroneously credited to his bank account and which he had used.[15]

Individuals with personal problems pose serious security problems for a national liberation movement, in that in their search for sympathy, very often they demonstrate carelessness and a lack of concern for security. They are thus vulnerable to pressure or suggestion from agents provocateurs, or even tempted by what appear to be attractive offers of 'financial support for the cause', or even 'easy access to sources of arms'. It was, therefore, not very surprising when, at the height of Makhanda's personal problems, he found himself being befriended by someone whom he identified as being a 'CIA agent', but whom he was cultivating as a possible source of 'arms and ammunition'. Without regard for security, Makhanda took the person to the apartment he shared with the PAC Observer at the UN. Apart from demonstrating a lack of security-consciousness, this was also very imprudent. One of the slanders spread by detractors of the PAC is that there is 'evidence of CIA involvement' in the formation of the PAC.[16] Any person associated with a national liberation movement who receives unsolicited offers of 'financial assistance', or 'arms and ammunition', from complete strangers should be very circumspect. With his judgement clouded or distorted by his personal problems, Makhanda was incapable of such prudence. Yet, he remains within the liberation movement and has access to records and other documents of the organisation.

If the cases of Elizabeth Sibeko, Leasoana Makhanda and Clement Hlongwane have been dealt with in detail here, it is to demonstrate not only the problems which their personal problems and activities posed for the PAC, but also the psychological problems and impediments of exile. Unfortunately, not much research has been done in this field — and the tendency within the liberation movements has been to avoid even mention of such problems, as though they would thereby disappear. As Marcum points out:

> If an exiled political leader is going to organise a serious challenge to something as formidable as white rule in Southern Africa, he and his followers cannot afford to allow exile psychology — even though it represents a normal response to an abnormal condition — to cloud perception, distort purpose or misdirect action.[17]

He goes on to make a constructive suggestion which might be useful to the liberation movements in dealing with the pathology represented by the behaviour of the likes of Makhanda:

> Systematic efforts by political leaders to confront and understand,

Vusumzi Make at the Helm: the Crisis Deepens 229

rather than to deny the existence of, the particular problems of exile might improve their capacity to build and maintain effective movements . . . Beyond this, the leaders of such movements might be well advised to invest personnel and material resources in methodical analyses of refugee-exile behaviour as it relates to their own specific goals and circumstances.[18]

The Central Committee ultimately decided in February 1981 to relieve Elizabeth Sibeko of all responsibilities as a representative and to dismiss her from the Central Committee. This followed the report of her illegal withdrawal of the sum of $5,000 from the PAC Observer Mission's bank account, and the evidence that she had not been 'starved' and 'persecuted' as she had alleged in an attempt to justify her criminal action. The former Director of Finance, Erret Radebe, reported to the Central Committee that Elizabeth Sibeko personally admitted to him in October 1980 that she had dissuaded the National Council of Churches from supporting the PAC. Radebe also reported that Clement Hlongwane had explained to him, and also shown him the bank records, that weekly deposits were made by the PAC Observer Mission into a special bank account established for the Sibeko family. Hlongwane personally made the deposits into the 'Sibeko grocery account', Radebe reported. Her supporters in the Central Committee could not save her from ignominious dismissal. The harm which she did to the PAC during the fifteen preceding months, however, was incalculable.

Makhanda and Hlongwane were not subjected to any disciplinary action; instead they were re-instated as functionaries at the PAC Observer Mission to the UN. In August 1983, Makhanda was promoted by the Central Committee to the position of deputy Observer at the UN.

Maladministration

A fifth problem during Make's regime was the continuing maladministration at the PAC headquarters in Dar-es-Salaam. A senior PAC member, in a letter to the author, complained:

> I am still disappointed with the way things are done even after P.K. [Leballo] departed. Is it ignorance, inefficiency or suspicion? More organisation and co-ordination has [sic] to be done to make PAC what it once was before feuding began to sap its leadership.

In a report to the Central Committee in September 1980 this writer, in his capacity as Director of Foreign Affairs, stated:

230 *The Crisis in the PAC: 1978–83*

While admittedly, some progress has been made in our external relations, there have continued to be organisational problems and weaknesses which have been the subject of discussion at every plenary meeting since January 1979. A review of the decisions taken and recommendations made will show that very many of the problems afflicting the organisation have been the subject of much discussion and many resolutions in the past. These include:

(i)   Lack of co-ordination;
(ii)   Lack of consultation;
(iii) Lack of financial controls;
(iv) Lack of definition of responsibilities;
(v)   Accountability of leadership, that is, the need for communication with the members;
(vi) Lack of publicity and information.

Recommendations have been made for the solution of some of these problems but it seems that the chasm between resolution and implementation is too great or too difficult to breach.

The report analysed in great detail all the problems itemised. They make a catalogue of sad reading and reflect an organisation that is weak and ineffectual. On the one hand, there was no proper communication and co-ordination among the various Central Committee members and between the PAC headquarters and various offices. As a result, the left hand simply did not know what the right hand was doing. Central Committee members, as well as representatives, failed to submit reports as was required under various decisions taken by the Central Committee. In this way, not only was it impossible for the organisation to assess its own progress, but it also meant that negotiations which were initiated both with governments and non-governmental organisations for financial and material aid could not be followed up.

In April 1980 the then Director of Publicity and Information, Elias Ntloedibe, was given a three-month period in which to resuscitate the Department of Publicity and Information. He failed to abide by the decision nor did the department produce any literature or publicity materials thereafter; yet, the Central Committee did nothing about it. PAC representatives as well as its delegates to international conferences complained regularly and bitterly about the embarrassment of having to distribute publications which were often more than two years old. In contrast, the ANC had a well-organised and smooth-functioning publicity department which ensured the production and distribution of ANC materials and publications like its journal, *Sechaba* and *ANC Weekly Newsbriefs*, regularly. Such publications were available at every international conference as well as at the UN, various bookstores and

Vusumzi Make at the Helm: the Crisis Deepens 231

university libraries. PAC offices, on the other hand, regularly received letters from subscribers to its journals, *Azania News* and *The Africanist*, complaining that they had not received the publications for more than two years. The only two PAC publications which were available were *Azania Today* and *Azania Contact*, published by the PAC Observer Mission to the UN and the PAC office in London, respectively.

In his report, the Director of Foreign Affairs asked:

> How do we evaluate progress if we operate in this manner? More importantly, when we look at the state of [the PAC] can we honestly say that [it] is a match for the Pretoria regime and its imperialist sponsors, with their well-organised machinery and apparatus? Some may argue that I am too formalistic, or perhaps, legalistic. But I maintain that revolution is a science; its execution demands meticulous ORGANISATION.

The report continued, pointing out that the credibility of the PAC leadership had been drawn into question:

> When faced with indiscipline among the cadres, as at present, when cadres are demanding the dismissal of certain members of the Central Committee, a question which we must ask ourselves is whether the leadership . . . inspires confidence among the membership generally and among supporters of the liberation struggle? One of the recurring questions among many of the delegates we have met is whether the PAC leadership is capable of doing what it claims it wants to do? In other words, the credibility of the organisation and its leadership have been drawn into question, and we are being asked whether we are capable of executing and sustaining a war of national liberation? This is a fundamental question to which we have to address ourselves.

From this, it will be seen that within the Central Committee this writer identified problems, offered recommendations and suggestions, criticised ineptitude among the leaders. At each meeting, the writer presented detailed *written reports*, something that was not done by other Central Committee members or representatives, but these were simply shelved or allowed to gather dust in the overcrowded filing cabinet at the PAC headquarters. The same mistakes identified and criticised were repeated, the same problems were perpetuated.

Factionalism and Cliquism

Make was unable to respond to the criticisms as well as recommenda-

232 *The Crisis in the PAC: 1978–83*

tions and suggestions made by several of his colleagues in the interests of the organisation. Instead, he gathered around him a group of sycophants. Make's inner circle comprised Elias Ntloedibe (then Director of Publicity and Information and Representative to Botswana), D.D. Mantshontsho (then Administrative Secretary), Erret Radebe (then Director of Finance). Later they were joined by Ngila Mike Muendane (Chief Representative to the UK and later Director of Labour and Social Affairs), Count Pietersen (Chief Representative to the Nordic Countries and later Director of Education and Manpower Development) and Ahmed Gora Ebrahim (Representative to Zimbabwe and subsequently Director of Publicity and Information). The appointments of the latter three Central Committee members, in April 1980 (Ngila Muendane and Count Pietersen) and February 1981 (Ahmed Gora Ebrahim) were part of Make's strategy of buttressing his faction of supporters within the Central Committee.

Privately, many of those within Make's inner circle were critical of his leadership, particularly his frequent travels and his fiscal irresponsibility. Erret Radebe, in particular, regularly complained about Make's wastage of funds. Yet, none of them criticised or repeated in meetings of the Central Committee the charges they levelled against him privately. Erret Radebe, right up until the time of his resignation as Director of Finance, refused to make a full disclosure to the Central Committee about the disbursement of funds and Make's inability to account for amounts of funds which had been given to him to hand over to other representatives. In June 1980, for instance, Make was given the sum of US$1,000 in cash for Fezile Nhlapo, the representative in Cairo, but only surrendered $300 without explaining that it was from the Director of Finance. Later, when Nhlapo went to Dar-es-Salaam en route to Cairo, in response to his enquiries of the Director of Finance as to why he had not been supported financially even when he had made repeated requests to the external headquarters, did he learn from Erret Radebe that Make had been given the sum of US$1,000.[19] At the end of 1980, at a time of financial crisis at PAC's headquarters, Make similarly took an amount of US$6,000 to Botswana with the intention of purchasing a motor vehicle for his personal use as Chairman of the Central Committee. Radebe complained privately, but was not prepared to raise it in a Central Committee meeting; Enoch Zulu, Director of 'Operations', who was not one of Make's inner circle, raised the matter at a Central Committee meeting in January 1981, severely criticising Make. Make then disclosed that he had instructed the PAC representative in Botswana to cancel the transaction and make the funds available to Zulu. When, however, the latter was given the money, it had been reduced to US$3,000.[20]

Make shielded Ntloedibe even when the Central Committee was

Vusumzi Make at the Helm: the Crisis Deepens 233

unanimous in its demand that he should return to the headquarters in Dar-es-Salaam to provide leadership in the Department of Publicity and Information, of which he was head. At a Central Committee meeting from 15 to 18 April 1980, Make recommended that Ntloedibe be given a period of three months in which to revive and strengthen the department. The decision was not implemented. Ntloedibe remained in Botswana, even though Make himself expressed disquiet about Ntloedibe's activities in that country, adding that officials in government as well as private citizens were unhappy with the PAC's representative. Ntloedibe incurred numerous debts and was caught up in his own web of lies. Still, Make did nothing. He did not even censure Ntloedibe.

Similarly, there were numerous complaints from the personnel in the office in Dar-es-Salaam about the attitude of Mantshontsho, the then Administrative Secretary. He was unable to deal with the ordinary members; he adopted a bullying and threatening attitude towards them unnecessarily. When the PAC members in Dar-es-Salaam requested a general meeting to discuss the problems, Mantshontsho threatened them with a 'major shake-up'. The untrained cadres at the transit centre in Pongwe wrote a letter to Make as Chairman of the Central Committee, complaining about Mantshontsho. Make did nothing.

Make was unable to censure Ntloedibe or Mantshontsho because they were part of his inner circle.

In exactly the same way, Make undertook visits to Europe and diplomatic missions to Africa without consulting the Director of Foreign Affairs, or reporting to him. He did, however, co-ordinate many of his diplomatic efforts with Ngila Muendane, based in London, and with others who constituted his inner circle. On one occasion, Make and Muendane visited West Germany without even informing the PAC representative in that country, Modipe Phillip Mokgadi. What emerged during Make's tenure as Chairman of the Central Committee was a pattern of parallel foreign relations, one conducted and co-ordinated by Make and his supporters in the Central Committee and another conducted by the Director of Foreign Affairs. Thus the Director of Foreign Affairs stated in a report to the Central Committee in September, 1980:

> In May [1980], Comrade Gora Ebrahim undertook a tour of Europe. The first time that I was made aware of the tour was when Comrade Gora was in London already and I happened to telephone Comrade Muendane in connection with some other matter. When the tour was planned and what its purpose was were not disclosed to me until it was actually due to begin. To date I have not received any substantive report on the mission ... Comrade Mokgadi sent me a photostat copy of a letter which he has received from Comrade Muendane informing him of a tour [of Europe] by the

234   *The Crisis in the PAC: 1978–83*

Chairman [Vus Make] and requesting Comrade Mokgadi to arrange appointments with solidarity groups in West Germany. Perhaps after this communication he will not complain [about Muendane's lack of consultation]. But this has been the first time that I have learned of the proposed tour of Europe by the Chairman, yet numerous telephone calls have passed between the Chairman and I, and between Comrade Muendane and I. Perhaps tours by the Chairman do not require consultation with the Director of Foreign Affairs.

Make's sycophants distorted his perception of reality. And reality was that considerable dissatisfaction was brewing among the cadres who were becoming increasingly critical of his leadership, and restive.

Notes

1. This was confided to the author in September 1980 by three members of the 'presentation committee' nominated by the rank-and-file members to represent them in their discussions with the Central Committee.

2. The full text of the statement was reproduced in *Azania Today*, Vol. 1, No. 2 (PAC Observer Mission to the UN), March/April 1980, p. 10.

3. Marcum in Potholm and Dale (eds.) 1972, p. 263.

4. See Burchett 1978, for interviews conducted with FRELIMO leaders and combatants after liberation for an appreciation of the value of political education both during and after the armed liberation struggle.

5. Horne 1979, esp. pp. 129, 143–5.

6. Disclosed by Wilfred Kaigula, co-ordinating officer in the Prime Minister's office, in evidence during the trial of six PAC members charged with the murder of David Sibeko. See *Tanzania Daily News*, 28 March 1981.

7. Copies of letters, cables and memoranda issued by Leballo in author's files.

8. On Saturday, 12 April 1980 the writer met Tsolo at his home in Rotterdam in order to give him a return air-ticket to travel to Dar-es-Salaam with the author to attend the plenary meeting of the Central Committee. He refused. During the discussion with the author, Tsolo re-affirmed his total support for Leballo whom he described as the only 'revolutionary' in the PAC and the only leader who could lead the organisation in armed struggle in South Africa.

9. *In Struggle*, 26 August 1980.

10. *The Guardian* (New York), August 1980.

11. See, e.g., letter to editor of *Zambia Daily Times*, 3 March 1981; copy of postcard sent by Wilson to Azania Komitee in Holland given to the author by Azania Komitee.

12. Letter dated 5 August 1980.

13. The author was told as much by the Deputy Prime Minister, Mr. Simon Muzenda, in October 1980. ZANU-PF played a crucial role in encouraging unity between the PAC under Make and the group led by Ntantala, the latter having formed themselves into the Azanian People's Revolutionary Party (APRP) after their expulsion from the PAC.

Vusumzi Make at the Helm: the Crisis Deepens 235

14. Copies of citations in author's files.

15. Copy of letter from bank to Hlongwane sent to author as PAC Observer at the UN.

16. 'The ANC Struggle Against South African Agents', in *African Agenda*, Chicago–Illinois, June–July 1976. In this article, the author states bluntly that the PAC received financial support from the CIA and compares it with UNITA.

17. Marcum in Potholm and Dale (eds.) 1972, p. 273.

18. Ibid.

19. Confirmed by Fezile Nhlapo to the author in Francistown, Botswana, 30 December 1981.

20. Informed by Zulu in Botswana on 28 December 1981, in response to an enquiry by the author.

13. Vusumzi Make at the Helm: the Crisis Continues

Re-emergence of the 'Cadre Forces' Movement'

In July 1980 a series of meetings was held by the general membership of the PAC resident in Dar-es-Salaam, at which criticisms were levelled at the Central Committee for what was perceived as a general lack of direction and seriousness. The members resident in Dar-es-Salaam co-ordinated their efforts with the members of the organisation living at the transit centre in Pongwe. The majority of the members living in Dar-es-Salaam and at the transit centre were not militarily-trained; they were waiting either to undergo military training or for scholarships and placement at educational institutions. Such untrained cadres were supported by a very small group of militarily-trained cadres who had fled from the military camp in Ithumbi during the reign of terror unleashed by the APLA forces loyal to Leballo and the disbanded high command. For purposes of clarity, references made to the 'Dar-es-Salaam cadres' in this section, as opposed to the 'military cadres', include the untrained cadres in Dar-es-Salaam and environs, those at the transit centre in Pongwe, and the few militarily-trained cadres who supported them in their political struggle against the Central Committee.

Disenchantment and disillusionment among PAC members during the Make regime climaxed with the preparation by the Dar-es-Salaam cadres of a memorandum in which they assessed the state of the organisation, made criticisms of the leadership collectively and individually and also made a number of recommendations and suggestions which, according to them, were aimed at strengthening the PAC.

Leasoana Sam Makhanda, who was in Dar-es-Salaam at the time, participated in the meetings at which the members' grievances were discussed and documented. In August 1980 en route to the USA where he was summoned to attend to his personal problems, he spent several days in London with the PAC's Chief Representative, Ngila Muendane, whom he informed of the 'Cadre Forces' Movement', as well as of their intentions. From London, he telephoned Make in Dar-es-Salaam to alert him to the growing agitation, although he also conveyed the impression to Make and others that he had influence over the Dar-es-

Salaam cadres. In his words, he 'controlled the cadres'. He returned to New York where he reported to the author the developments in Dar-es-Salaam, including the existence of the 'memorandum'. Twice on Sunday, 2 September 1980 Makhanda attempted to telephone Dar-es-Salaam from Wilmington, Delaware, where he was visiting a friend who is a keen analyst of the national liberation movements and of the 'South African exile syndrome'. Twice this writer refused to permit the telephone calls to be billed to the PAC Observer Mission and to the apartment on Roosevelt Island, shared by Makhanda and the writer. Makhanda's aim in making the telephone calls to Dar-es-Salaam, was to fulfil a promise he had made to Make during their telephone conversation from London, namely that he would persuade Moseou Magalefa, one of the authors of the memorandum, to abandon the demand for the dismissal of Mantshontsho and Ntloedibe. Makhanda's reward for his efforts was to be an appointment as PAC Chief Representative to the Nordic Countries, a position which had become vacant following the appointment of Count Pietersen to the position of Director of Education and Manpower Development in April 1980.

The 'Cadre Forces' Movement' Memorandum

Before discussing the memorandum, the Dar-es-Salaam cadres demanded the immediate dismissal from the Central Committee of the Administrative Secretary, D.D. Mantshontsho, and the Director of Publicity and Information, Elias Ntloedibe.[1] The lengthy document contains criticisms of the Central Committee members and of the state of the PAC, with equally detailed recommendations and suggestions. The harshest criticisms, however, were reserved for Mantshontsho and Ntloedibe. Referring to Mantshontsho, the cadres stated in the memorandum:

> 5. *Mantshontsho as Administrative Secretary:* No one, unless he be a liberal of the first order can claim that he does not see the damage done by this man in his capacity as Administrative Secretary. Apart from the fact that it has become abundantly clear that he does not have a working relationship with anyone in Dar-es-Salaam, Mantshontsho continues to be a rack in the administrative machinery of the PAC because:
>
> (1) In the office he is the self-appointed and the 'know-all' authority. He constantly interferes in the work of almost all the Departments. For instance, his refusal . . . or failure to submit a job description for all functionaries of the [PAC] in the office has led to a crisis situation in the office. The confusion between the office of the Administrative Secretary and the office of the Chief Representative is a direct result of this situation which in some cases he creates purposely to hide his inability to administer the affairs of the organisation . . .
>
> 6. He has failed to supply the general membership with up-to-date reports and dossiers of [PAC] missions abroad as was ordered by the

238   *The Crisis in the PAC: 1978–83*

Plenary Decision No. 14 of 6th October, 1979.
7. He refuses or fails to supply the PAC with up-to-date membership lists of the organisation.
8. There is evidence in all the departments that this man consciously sabotages some of the departments by either using his position to frustrate the activities of those departments, e.g. (i) his constant hoarding of documents referred to the Education and Manpower Development Department, (ii) his tendency to make public statements against the [PAC] policy without consultation with (sic) the Publicity and Information Department. The recent Radio Broadcast on the 'Constellation of Southern African States' was a clear indication of his ignorance of the PAC's policy of non-collaboration. All this stunts the progress of these departments.

They concluded their charges against Mantshontsho with the demand that he should not be considered for any other position of responsibility in the PAC until he had acquired 'the necessary knowledge and education for such responsibility'.

The charges against Ntloedibe (who doubled at that time as Chief Representative to Botswana and Director of Publicity and Information) were even more damning:

This comrade, i.e. E.L. Ntloedibe, has a long history of opportunism. His outlook is based on where his interests as a person are best served. He was with Leballo in all his machinations as early as when the [PAC] was still legally operating [sic] He was with Leballo in his whole sell-out history. Ntloedibe is making a career out of the revolution. He is a liar known by almost everybody inside and outside the PAC, who is concerned with our [organisation] or who just happens to know him. Ntloedibe never operates on principle. He is a drunkard. He is a gambler. He is a political prostitute, he has [no] ideological conviction — he has once declared publicly that 'ideology is not a refinery'. Ntloedibe is a great embezzler of PAC funds. This man is an embarrassment and a liability in the [PAC]. As long as he remains in the leadership, PAC will soon be known as a bunch of liars, drunkards, gamblers, political prostitutes, ideologically bankrupt opportunists and an international mafia group. What deviation from what Comrade President Mangaliso Sobukwe taught us! His is a blasphemous role in our Movement and an insult to our people.

Behind Ntloedibe is a trail of failures and inefficiencies that make a mockery of our revolutionary commitment.

When Leballo was defied in 1979 on 6th April at Lumumba Hall, Ntloedibe was not there as usual when we marked the 20th anniversary of the birth of PAC. When he later came to Dar-es-Salaam, he was denouncing us as anarchists and non-[PAC] members who did not [respect?] the PAC anniversary and the PAC Chairman. Within a very short space of time Ntloedibe realised that Leballo's sell-out mission had rendered him a political right-off [sic], it was Ntloedible again who vociferously, true to his opportunist tendencies, condemned Leballo. This was opportunism at its best.

Having thus passed judgement upon Ntloedibe, the Dar-es-Salaam cadres then went on to analyse his performance during his tenure as Director of Publicity and Information and concluded that

> We have now come to a stage where we assert with all justification that 'up to here and no more', it is either that Ntloedibe resigns now or we face the ghastly consequences we contemplate. This is our stand.

Why the Memorandum?

The actions of the Dar-es-Salaam cadres were provoked by the failure of the Central Committee to assert discipline upon its own members. Discontent had long been simmering; complaints against Mantshontsho had been made regularly, verbally and in writing, to the Central Committee generally and to Make personally. The Central Committee was unable to act. In exactly the same way, the views expressed about Ntloedibe by the Dar-es-Salaam cadres in their memorandum were views commonly expressed by Central Committee members — *privately*. At the plenary meeting of the Central Committee in October 1979 one executive member criticised Ntloedibe's penchant for lying and exaggeration and warned, moreover, that his continued position in the PAC leadership, cast serious doubts upon the integrity of the entire leadership. Everybody else remained absolutely silent! Ntloedibe then made a spirited defence of his role in the leadership, in the process repeating one of the very same lies to which the executive member had made reference less than ten minutes earlier, namely, his claim that he had recently gone into South Africa clandestinely for two weeks, during which time he was able to see his father whom he had not seen for 20 years; in January 1979 he delayed in returning to Dar-es-Salaam because, he claimed, he had received sad news of the death of his father. People who knew Ntloedibe claimed then (January 1979) that that was probably his late father's twenty-fifth death!

Throughout the period after the consultative conference, held in June–July 1978, there were many instances of poor performance by members of the Central Committee, or even dereliction of duty and gross indiscipline on the part of Central Committee members — all of which went largely uncensured. The Dar-es-Salaam cadres as well as the military cadres at the camp in Ithumbi, were aware of this. In many cases, Central Committee members gossiped about their own colleagues to the ordinary members in the hope of currying favour with them. Deliberations of the Central Committee were, more often than not, divulged to the ordinary members despite pledges of confidentiality and secrecy until the conclusion of the deliberations. In the circles of the liberation movement, this tendency is termed 'empire building'.

240 *The Crisis in the PAC: 1978-83*

In the circumstances, it was extremely difficult for the Central Committee to attempt to assert authority or exert discipline within the organisation. On the one hand, the cadres were aware of the paralysing effect of 'liberalism' within the Central Committee, 'liberalism' taken to mean the tendency to refrain from criticism of individual or collective actions even where such actions are patently wrong, either out of fear of offending individual sensitivities or out of fear of one's personal indiscretions being similarly exposed. 'Liberalism' and mutual political blackmail were rife in the Central Committee, which explains the ability of individuals like Ntloedibe and Mantshontsho to have survived politically in positions of responsibility or leadership for the length of time which they did.

In the absence of a channel for the presentation of grievances by the cadres, or a forum where they could make constructive criticisms and suggestions, they were forced to organise themselves into a pressure group. But what made their efforts successful was the relative weakness, not only of the Central Committee vis-a-vis the cadres in terms of numbers, but the weak position of the PAC in Tanzania and within the OAU. Any further crisis would certainly have resulted in the de-recognition of the PAC by the OAU, and subsequent to that, expulsion from Tanzania — either of which would have been calamitous. The Central Committee was aware of this, hence a situation developed where the 'tail wagged the dog'.

Central Committee's Reaction
The Central Committee was forced at its meeting in September 1980 to yield to the demands of the Dar-es-Salaam cadres for the dismissal of Ntloedibe and Mantshontsho. Three Central Committee members supported the dismissal of the two; these were Enoch Zulu (Director of Operations), Edwin Makoti (Secretary for Defence) and this writer. This writer argued that the actions of the Dar-es-Salaam cadres were an indictment against the Central Committee which had failed to provide revolutionary leadership and direction to the PAC at a critical time. Moreover, the leaders of the organisation could not expect slavish obedience from the ordinary members in the face of obvious incompetence, corruption and indiscipline among the leaders. The members of the organisation who organised themselves into a pressure group were in close proximity to the Central Committee members based in Dar-es-Salaam; the major actors in the 'Cadre Forces' Movement' were PAC members who were functionaries in the Dar-es-Salaam office, often effectively running the affairs of the organisation in the absence of the leaders. They therefore had an informed knowledge of the competence, or lack of it, of their leaders. It was a political responsibility of the members, in the absence of action by the leaders against their own colleagues, to adopt appropriate measures to correct the situation in the organisation.

Vusumzi Make at the Helm: the Crisis Continues 241

It was very clear that the Dar-es-Salaam cadres realised their power and would make further demands upon the leadership, which, in the circumstances, the latter could not resist. But even after the humiliation of having decisions forced upon them, the Central Committee was not able to provide the firm and decisive leadership that was required. Instead, there was a steady slide into anarchy until Make himself faced a situation where the Dar-es-Salaam cadres had no confidence in him as Chairman of the PAC and held him personally responsible for the problems the organisation experienced. A few months later, the PAC would once more be in crisis, but before dealing with that crisis and the outcome, it is necessary to mention several points.

Firstly, at the September 1980 meeting of the Central Committee, a number of other recommendations and suggestions made by the cadres were accepted by the leadership. This gave the appearance of the Central Committee having been coerced by the Dar-es-Salaam cadres. That in turn, boded ill for the future.

Secondly, one of the decisions taken by the Central Committee was the appointment (upon Make's recommendation) of Joe Mkwanazi as Director of Labour and Social Affairs in the Central Committee. The decision was not based on merit concerning the duties of that particular post. Instead, it was pointed out that he still had contacts in South Africa from the time that he was the PAC representative in Swaziland. Since the welfare of the PAC members was an area that had been neglected, he would, it was argued, be able to use the contacts he had in order to obtain accurate information about the families and dependents of PAC members experiencing hardship in South Africa and neighbouring countries. After 20 years in exile, the PAC had no idea of the numbers, whereabouts and plight of the families and dependents of those who were killed in Sharpeville in 1960, for instance. Nor did the exiled organisation have any records of the names of its political prisoners, or those of its former members who were living under restriction in South Africa. In their memorandum the Dar-es-Salaam cadres pointed out that this was an area in which the PAC had failed, a situation that had to be rectified.

The main motivation for the appointment of Mkwanazi to the Central Committee was the belief expressed during the meeting that he would be able to play a crucial role in the reunification of the PAC, a task he had already undertaken in April 1980 when he visited Dar-es-Salaam for the first time since his deportation from Swaziland. He had not only had discussions with disaffected PAC members in Europe but during his stay in Dar-es-Salaam he also had discussions with Ntantala and those expelled at the Arusha consultative conference. His message was that in the wake of the ouster of Leballo, conditions in the PAC were favourable for the return to the fold of all those who had either been expelled or suspended or who had been disenchanted during the Leballo era. (In 1978, in transit in Lusaka after leaving Swaziland,

242   *The Crisis in the PAC: 1978–83*

Mkwanazi told PAC members living in Zambia who had gone to see him at the airport while waiting for his flight to London, that there was need for a new political party. He said that 'the people at home are demanding it'.)

It was hoped that he would be able to convince the APLA cadres at the military camp in Ithumbi to accept the political leadership of the Central Committee. This hope was grounded in the assumption that since most of the APLA cadres at the military camp had passed through Swaziland (while Mkwanazi and others were there) en route to Tanzania, he still had considerable influence over them. Several trips to the military at Ithumbi, however, confronted him with the fact that many months had passed and that many significant developments intervened between his arrest in Swaziland in April 1978 and his return to Tanzania in April 1980. Attitudes had hardened. The APLA cadres at the military camp were adamant in their rejection of the authority of the Central Committee. Mkwanazi's appeals to the APLA cadres whom he had known from Swaziland to 'trust [him]' because he is 'an honest man' were, he himself later admitted, greeted with scorn.

Thirdly, despite the decision of the Central Committee to yield to the demands for the dismissal of Ntloedibe and Mantshontsho, the two deposed were still permitted to cause further problems as a result of the protection afforded them by Make. Mantshontsho travelled to New York in October 1980, ostensibly after consultations among Central Committee members based in Dar-es-Salaam. The idea was that he would remain in New York pending negotiations for the establishment of an office in Guyana, to which the Guyanese Government had already agreed in principle. Despite the advice of this writer that he should not leave Dar-es-Salaam for New York since there were already problems there caused by Elizabeth Sibeko and her followers, particularly Makhanda, Mantshontsho arrived there with Erret Radebe, who came to address a meeting at the UN on the occasion of the International Day of Solidarity with South African Political Prisoners.

After this writer in his capacity as the PAC Observer at the UN and Director of Foreign Affairs, refused to accept responsibility for Mantshontsho during his sojourn in the USA, and also refused to assign him any tasks at the PAC Observer Mission to the UN, pending clarification from the PAC headquarters in Dar-es-Salaam as to his mission, he joined the Sibeko/Makhanda coalition. Together with Makhanda (who by that time was also living at the Sibeko residence), he went to the UN headquarters regularly and sat in the delegates' lounge searching for consolation. The two discussed the internal problems of the PAC with whoever was prepared to listen or to engage them in conversation.

During his stay in New York, Mantshontsho regularly telephoned the PAC external headquarters in Dar-es-Salaam, to report on what was then generally termed, 'the New York situation', by which they meant complaints against the PAC Observer at the UN.[2] One may logically

Vusumzi Make at the Helm: the Crisis Continues 243

assume that such international phone calls are monitored by various intelligence services and that the South African Government had a good running account of the PAC's fortunes. Elizabeth Sibeko, Makhanda and Mantshontsho maintained regular telephonic contact with Central Committee members belonging to the Make faction in a co-ordinated campaign against this writer; in the process, however, they disrupted the progress of the PAC and brought the organisation into disrepute. They also provided detractors of the PAC with adequate evidence of the turmoil within the organisation. The Make faction accused this writer of instigating the 'Cadre Forces' Movement' and, accordingly, began an intensive campaign aimed at removing the writer from the position of Director of Foreign Affairs and Observer at the UN. Mantshontsho subsequently departed from New York for London where he currently resides.

Elias Ntloedibe, on the other hand, after his dismissal from the Central Committee in September 1980, was assigned a mission to Geneva to attend the Board meeting of the UNHCR, on the recommendation of Make. According to a report from a very reliable source, at a reception in Geneva Ntloedibe created a very embarrassing scene when he went into tirade against a female staff member of the WCC and attacked her for the decision of the WCC Programme to Combat Racism not to make a financial grant to the PAC that year. According to the report, many of those present left the reception when the incident took place. Needless to say, it did not win the PAC any respect or friends.[3]

Ntloedibe then returned to Botswana where he continued to function as though nothing had happened. The Botswana Government was not informed of his dismissal from the Central Committee and as representative, with the result that he continued to make representations on behalf of the PAC to the Botswana authorities, friendly governments represented in Botswana, UN agencies and non-governmental organisations. Make visited Botswana several times after the dismissal of Ntloedibe; he was aware of Ntloedibe's activities, yet did nothing to rectify the situation, or to censure him. Make was later severely criticised for this by Enoch Zulu (Director of Operations); he accused Make of 'protecting Ntloedibe'.

Six months later, in April 1981, Ntloedibe wrote to a PAC supporter in the USA, requesting financial assistance for the maintenance of 'hundreds of refugees' who he claimed were in his custody in Botswana. Ntloedibe wrote:

> A lot of things have happened since our last contact in 1978. The worst tragedy of course as you know was the assassination of Brother David Sibeko our beloved colleague and outstanding fighter. We lost a real brother. I personally narrowly escaped the same attempt by racist agents. I am now here in the front line, still with PAC but doing more strenuous work . . .

244 *The Crisis in the PAC: 1978–83*

> We have just had another flood of students into Botswana here and after six months, I will arrange for their transportation to Tanzania. We need help desperately and we are engaging the enemy vigorously. Please extend our appeal to our Brothers and Sisters there and educate them on the struggle [sic] we are facing. Racist South Africa is the last bastion of white domination and oppression and with their friends now in Government in the States, it is even worse. Please pardon my silence, I shall contact you more regularly. We now have about two hundred and fifty (250) youths and we need help.
>
> In case you make some contribution the Bank Account is *MOKALAKE* NO. 3503453, Botsalano Branch Barclays Bank, Gaborone, Botswana, Africa. Give that number to all our Brothers and Sisters who may feel persuaded to assist.[4]

Ntloedibe's letter merits comment. Firstly, the Central Committee was unaware of any assassination attempt from which Ntloedibe escaped as he alleged in his letter. Secondly, there were not 250 students for whom Ntloedibe ever had to provide in Botswana, especially not in 1981 when the PAC's recruiting had virtually been immobilised. Most of the people leaving South Africa in the wake of the workers' and students' struggles in 1980 joined the ANC. Even at the height of the exodus of young people from South Africa after the Soweto uprising of 1976, the number of people who joined the PAC at any one time did not reach 250. Thirdly, PAC freedom-fighters were not 'engaging the racists vigorously' in 1981, nor at any time before or after then. Fourthly, 'MOKALAKE' is the name that Ntloedibe uses and is the name by which he is known to many of his colleagues in the PAC; it seems strange therefore that he should direct appeals for assistance for the '250 youths' to a bank account in his name.

The PAC Chairman, Nyati Pokela, and other Central Committee members are aware of the letter written by Ntloedibe; the PAC supporter to whom it was addressed visited the PAC headquarters in Tanzania shortly after she received it. She showed the letter to Pokela and the Administrative Secretary, Joe Mkwanazi. This writer also discussed it with Pokela and Mkwanazi and warned them of the gravity of the matter, since the Central Committee was not aware of the number of individuals and organisations to whom Ntloedibe addressed similar appeals. The matter was never debated nor discussed by the Central Committee; nor was any disciplinary action taken against Ntloedibe. After a brief period of isolation, Ntloedibe was once more given assignments by the Central Committee in early 1982; he represented the PAC at a number of international conferences in 1982 and 1983.

PAC's Inability to Respond to Political Developments in South Africa

The deepening crisis within the PAC coincided with escalating Black resistance in South Africa in 1980 when Black workers and students were able successfully to organise sustained strikes. While the PAC was unable to respond to the political developments inside the country and was not identified by independent observers and analysts (as well as individuals and organisations active in South Africa), as being part of the resistance, the ANC, as a result of its military activities such as the Silverton bank siege involving three of its freedom-fighters, the attacks on police stations and the attack on the SASOL oil-from-coal plant in June 1980, was to enhance its prestige in South Africa and internationally. The relationship between these events in South Africa and international efforts of the national liberation movements, was analysed by this writer in his capacity as PAC's Director of Foreign Affairs in a report submitted to the Central Committee in September 1980.

Two months earlier, in August 1980, this writer had despatched a memo to the Central Committee, expressing concern that the PAC was not identified as part of the growing Black resistance. The concerns were based on the fact that organisations and activists in South Africa, with whom this writer maintained close contact, complained about the lack of an active PAC presence or involvement in the resistance. Among them were former PAC members, as well as sympathisers of the organisation.

Not only was the externally-based PAC not involved in the resistance which was characterised by increasing organisation and militancy among Black workers and students, but even when an opportunity was provided for the organisation to identify positively with the political developments in the country, by providing financial assistance for the maintenance of families and dependents, it was not able to do so. In the memo, dated 6 August 1980, this writer reported:

> We received numerous requests for financial assistance merely for travel and for such things as publicity . . . I communicated this to the External Headquarters, in particular to the Administrative Secretary, and . . . the Director of Finance . . . I again repeated the information together with a request for funds so that we could respond positively. The New York office [at that time] was in dire financial straits; it was my understanding that the External Headquarters at that time had received financial assistance from Iraq and had also received the quarterly allocation from the OAU Liberation Committee.
>
> We thus lost a golden opportunity to respond positively during a time of need in [South Africa].

Because of repressive laws and the severe penalties for promoting the

246 *The Crisis in the PAC: 1978–83*

objectives of an unlawful organisation, which the PAC is in South Africa, it is both extremely difficult and dangerous for a liberation movement to channel financial assistance directly to individuals and organisations still operating legally in the country. It is, however, not impossible. The PAC offices in London and New York were able to appeal to sympathetic organisations for such assistance which was then made available to organisations in South Africa without endangering their security.

The truth of the matter is that the PAC was not involved in the political struggles in South Africa in 1980 and was unable to respond to the political developments in the country because of the devastating effects of the arrests and subsequent imprisonment of its leading activists in the 'PAC Bethal 18' trial, the arrests and subsequent deportation from Swaziland of Mkwanazi and other PAC members, and the debilitating internecine strife at PAC headquarters in Tanzania from 1977 onwards.

Rather than come to grips with the painful reality, the PAC engaged in massive self-deception, propagating the fiction of a non-existent 'underground'. Wishful thinking is no substitute for scientific analysis, and those directing the affairs of a national liberation movement, which states as one of its objectives, the waging of armed struggle, have to free themselves from 'emotional bias and wishful thinking'.[5] A careful analysis of the state of the PAC's fortunes in South Africa in the wake of the 'Bethal 18' trial, might have resulted in the organisation making serious efforts to re-establish effective links with existing organisations, trade unions, cultural organisations and individual sympathisers of the PAC in South Africa. But the Central Committee was unable to do so. The PAC representative in Lesotho, and others in that country, worked under difficult and dangerous conditions to perform this political function, but communications between Lesotho and Tanzania where the PAC has its headquarters, were tenuous until recently when direct flights between Maseru and Maputo and Maseru and Gaborone were established. Marcum points out:

> If a 'communications gap' is not to isolate exiles from what is being thought and done by their countrymen at home and vice versa, one of the principal functions of exile political structures must be to develop and maintain underground links with supporters inside the home country. This means not only that they must acquire the technical means to transmit information from outside . . . but also they must be psychologically prepared to receive, evaluate, and utilise information, however depressing, concerning changing conditions, including shifting popular grievances.[6]

Precisely such a 'communications gap' existed between the PAC external headquarters and the people in the home country. It was for this reason that the evidence of the resurgence of the ANC was repeatedly dismissed as 'liberal propaganda'. Opinion polls which showed that the ANC was favoured by most urban Blacks in South Africa were constantly faulted, yet various PAC spokespersons and ideologues did not fail to refer to a poll conducted in 1963 which revealed that the PAC commanded majority popular support.[7]

The Central Committee realised in April 1980, however, that the PAC could no longer continue merely theorising about armed struggle and guerrilla warfare. The consensus at that meeting was that the only way in which the organisation could be saved was for its military wing to register a military presence on the ground in South Africa. For this reason, Enoch Zulu (alias John Mvelase) was appointed Director of Operations. The Department of Defence stated during the Central Committee meeting in April 1980 that if provided with an amount of US$50,000 and given six months, APLA would show results; but $67,000 and ten months later, not a single freedom-fighter had been infiltrated into the country, not a single shot had been fired.[8]

There was an awareness among many PAC members that it was imperative for APLA to register a military presence in South Africa. One PAC member wrote to the author:

> I also want to agree with you and with the other comrades who are having the same views [sic] as yours about the pressing need to register a visible military presence on the ground in Azania. I was just informing comrades here that, the process of rebuilding unity within our own ranks; the one of re-establishment of party authority and organisational discipline in all [PAC] centres; the resultant restoration of the image of the [PAC] at home and abroad, will not be achieved to our satisfaction as serious revolutionaries, if it is not strengthened and deepened by the intensification of concrete revolutionary work inside Azania itself.[9]

Non-Governmental Organisations Withdraw Support

The internal problems of the PAC, coupled with its inability to play any meaningful role in political developments in South Africa, had the effect of eroding even further its support by non-governmental organisations in a number of countries.

Azania Komitee — Holland: The Azania Komitee in The Netherlands did not organise a Sharpeville Commemorative Meeting in March 1980 for the first time in many years. In a letter to Ngila Muendane, the PAC's Chief Representative to the UK, the Azania Komitee cited as one of the reasons, the leadership dispute in the PAC and their reluctance to involve themselves in the internal problems of the organisation.[10] The

248 *The Crisis in the PAC: 1978–83*

decision of the Azania Komitee was ominous because the formation of the Komitee had been motivated by the sectarianism of several anti-apartheid organisations in The Netherlands which supported the ANC to the exclusion of the PAC.

Emmaus Bjorka — Sweden: Emmaus Bjorka, a non-governmental organisation in Sweden, was more forthcoming in stating its reasons for terminating support to the PAC. In a letter to the PAC's Chief Representative in Dar-es-Salaam, Emmaus Bjorka cited unsatisfactory explanations given by the PAC for the disappearance of almost two tons of clothing sent by the group to the PAC but destined for anti-Mobutu Congolese living as refugees in Tanzania. The clothes were part of a consignment of twelve tons shipped to the PAC. PAC members living in Dar-es-Salaam ransacked the warehouse where the clothes were stored and stole even the bales that were earmarked for the Congolese refugees. Angry and certainly very bitter, the Congolese complained to the Executive Secretary of the OAU Liberation Committee as well as to Emmaus Bjorka.

The second reason given by Emmaus Bjorka for terminating its support to the PAC, was the participation by the latter in an International Conference on Kampuchea in Stockholm in 1979. In a letter to the PAC, Emmaus Bjorka stated:

> You have followed the Chinese bourgeois leadership on the Vietnam–Kampuchea question. You took active part in the reactionary so-called Kampuchea Conference in Stockholm and you are still supporting one of the biggest criminals in the world, Pol Pot.
>
> In other words, concerning the international questions you have joined the reactionary right-wings which are blowing over the world. This fact will make you more and more isolated from the progressive forces of the world.

The main reason for the withdrawal of support, however, was what Emmaus Bjorka termed 'the political instability within [the PAC]'. This was spelt out very clearly:

> As long as PAC has a system of ultra-democracy instead of democratic centralism we don't think you are able to take care of any support in a proper way. With the petty-bourgeois system of PAC today we don't think you are qualified to win, to lead or to serve the masses in your country. So to be frank, we think it is useless to support you [in] such conditions [sic] . . . In 1968 PAC cadres were able to write a correct analysis of your struggle. However, since then, as far as we understand, just anarchy and corruption has [sic] ruled your organisation. In spite of our support to the PAC since 10 years [sic] it has never been a true comradely relationship between our organisations. Your representatives, which [sic] have visited

us, have never in a comradely and intimate way informed us about the problems in your organisation such as representatives from other organisations have done.[11]

World Council of Churches: In the second half of 1980, the World Council of Churches (WCC) announced financial grants for humanitarian purposes to the ANC and SWAPO under the Programme to Combat Racism (PCR). The exclusion of the PAC was surprising, since the organisation had been represented (by Gora Ebrahim) at two consultative meetings organised by the WCC in Nairobi and Amsterdam where the question of humanitarian assistance to the national liberation movements recognised by the OAU was discussed. Although no reasons were given for the exclusion of the PAC from the grants for 1980, it soon became clear that apart from Ebrahim's ineptitude in his representations at the two meetings, a programme officer of the PCR with a long history of hostility towards the PAC convinced the body that the PAC's internal problems were so acute as to render the organisation unworthy of support. This writer, in his capacity as PAC's Director of Foreign Affairs, warned the Central Committee that because the WCC has achieved international credibility and respect for its position in supporting national liberation movements in Southern Africa, the exclusion of the PAC from support would have far-reaching consequences. It was thus necessary for the PAC to have the decision reversed. This writer wrote letters to a number of credible organisations throughout the world drawing their attention to the exclusion of the PAC from the grants for 1980; documentary proof was furnished showing the history of hostility of a particular programme officer of the PCR towards the PAC, from the time of his association with the American Committee on Africa. This writer lodged an official complaint with the Moderator of the WCC Commission of which the PCR is a unit. The PAC's Representative in Canada, Dan Mdluli, in co-ordination with this writer, had a meeting with the Moderator, Archbishop Scott of Canada. This writer made representations to and had discussions with the Moderator of the PCR. Several organisations expressed their concern to the WCC at the exclusion of the PAC from financial assistance in 1980. This writer also visited Harare in July 1981 while the PCR was meeting to consider applications for financial assistance. As a result of all the lobbying, the decision was reversed in 1981 and the PAC was given a grant of $45,000 by the WCC for 'publicity and information'.

By the time that the PAC Central Committee met in Dar-es-Salaam in January, the organisation was in crisis once more. There was general dissatisfaction with Make's leadership; many PAC members resident in Dar-es-Salaam stated openly that unless the Central Committee meeting resulted in meaningful changes, the 'Cadre Forces'

250 *The Crisis in the PAC: 1978–83*

Movement' would take matters into its own hands, an action that might jeopardise the continued existence of the PAC in Tanzania.

The commencement of the meeting was delayed because Make, the Chairman, was somewhere in West Africa. After attending a 'dialogue' between African and American leaders in Freetown, Sierra Leone, at the invitation of the African–American Institute, he was to proceed to Khartoum where he and Moseou Magalefa, a functionary in the PAC's Education Department, were scheduled to meet government officials to finalise the question of the June 16 Azania Institute. Make failed to put in an appearance in Khartoum, without any explanation or message being despatched. Magalefa abandoned the mission and returned to Dar-es-Salaam, an action which triggered off rumours and speculation among the Dar-es-Salaam cadres about Make's intentions.

When Make ultimately returned to Dar-es-Salaam, he explained to the Central Committee that his extended stay in West Africa was due to problems with flight connections. The mood within the organisation towards Make was one of hostility — he was held personally responsible for the crisis facing the PAC.

Notes

1. Memorandum dated 14 August 1980 submitted on behalf of 'Cadreship of PAC', by Sipho Majolo, Mpazama Yonana, Moseou Magalefa, Edmund Jiyane, Thobile Gola and Abel Dube. The six cadres constituted what they called the 'presentation committee' which served to liaise with the Central Committee.

2. At the Central Committee meeting in Dar-es-Salaam in January 1981 Makoti (then Secretary for Defence) charged that Mantshontsho telephoned the PAC headquarters regularly and had clearly taken sides in the problems in New York. Neither Make nor anyone else denied this.

3. At the Central Committee meeting in January 1981 Ngila Muendane, PAC's Chief Representative to the UK at that time, confirmed that he had also been informed about the incident at the reception. According to him, however, his informant was happy at the public embarrassment caused the WCC employee. In the words of Muendane, 'These people have to be told'. Muendane, of course, was defending Make who was questioned by this writer about the assignment given to Ntloedibe in the wake of the cadres' memorandum and for the failure to consult with the Director of Foreign Affairs before nominating him. Muendane was one of Make's most loyal supporters in the Central Committee.

4. Letter dated 7 April 1981 written by Ntloedibe, who styled himself 'Chief Representative and Member of the Central Committee', to Nylene Foxworth, an Afro-American poet.

5. Marcum in Potholm and Dale (eds.) 1972, p. 273.

6. Ibid., p. 274.

7. The poll regularly quoted by the PAC spokespersons was conducted by Brett 1963.

8. The figure of $67,000 has been computed from the figures obtained from the records of the former Director of Finance, Erret Radebe, in Dar-es-Salaam in February 1981.

9. Letter dated 4 November 1981 from Glen Mpukane, former Secretary of the PAC Unity Committee, to the author.

10. Letter dated 13 January 1980 to Ngila Muendane. Initially, the Azania Komitee was influenced by Nyakane Mike Tsolo who supported Leballo. He worked with the Azania Komitee for a long time; he convinced them initially to withhold support from the PAC under Make's leadership. They subsequently changed their position and supported the PAC, as an organisation, rather than any fraction of it.

11. Letter dated 10 December 1980 from Emmaus Bjorka.

14. John Nyati Pokela: Saviour of the PAC?

Central Committee Meeting, January–February 1981

The Central Committee meeting commenced in January 1981 in Dar-es-Salaam under the chairmanship of Vus Make and concluded in February with the appointment of John Nyati Pokela as Chairman of the Central Committee and leader of the PAC. A number of issues confronted the Central Committee: the crisis in the PAC, which has already been described in great detail in the previous section; the disruptive activities of Elizabeth Sibeko and her minions; the resignation of Erret Radebe as Director of Finance in the Central Committee; the problems in Lesotho between two opposing PAC factions; and the Azanian People's Revolutionary Party (APRP) and the possible re-instatement of T.M. Ntantala and other former PAC members who were expelled at the consultative conference held in Arusha in June–July 1978.

The meeting was opened by the Chairman, Vus Make, who analysed the problems confronting the PAC. He tendered his apologies for his late arrival in Dar-es-Salaam following his mission to West Africa. In his address, Make pointed out that the PAC was 'in crisis, once more', a crisis that was political, military and financial. He drew attention to the memorandum drawn up by the 'Cadre Forces' Movement' the previous September and to the demands they had made for the immediate dismissal of two Central Committee members, D.D. Mantshontsho and Elias Ntloedibe. It was obvious, said Make, that there were 'two centres of power', one consisting of the Dar-es-Salaam cadres and the other of the leadership. The Central Committee was held in contempt by the Dar-es-Salaam cadres; he wondered how the Central Committee could function in the circumstances.

Enoch Zulu (alias John Mvelase), the Director of Operations, responded to Make's opening address by pointing out that the morale of the cadres was very low and that they blamed Make personally for the crisis the organisation faced. According to Zulu, the cadres blamed Make for having 'failed to unite the PAC'. He had failed, too, to ensure that decisions of the Central Committee were implemented; he had failed to assert the political leadership of the Central Committee over APLA and he continued 'to protect Ntloedibe' even though he was fully aware of

Ntloedibe's activities in Botswana where he continued to masquerade as the representative, thus posing serious difficulties for the appointed representative, Pat Kohlo, and 'security problems' for the Department of Defence. Zulu indicated that he would not like to see Make 'personally humiliated by the cadres', which was inevitable if he were to continue in the chairmanship of the PAC.

Make's response was that if it were felt that his leadership was an obstacle to the progress of the PAC and to the achievement of its objectives, then he was prepared to step down. He denied that he had protected Ntloedibe and he also stated that he was prepared to 'defend [his] record' as Chairman of the organisation. A dangerous precedent had been established, he pointed out, by the cadres in their demands for the dismissal of certain members of the Central Committee without being prepared even to discuss the memorandum in which they had levelled serious allegations and charges against the said members. Make continued by stating that he had received information that Pokela, a veteran of the liberation struggle and a founder member of the PAC, had escaped from South Africa and was in Lesotho; if the Central Committee agreed, then the question of his own future role in the organisation could be deferred until Pokela's intentions were clarified.

Without defending Make, who was obviously not up to the assignment, an element of organisational scapegoating was evident in the charges levelled against him by the Dar-es-Salaam cadres. It would have taken an almost superhuman effort to pull the PAC together. Rather than honestly address the problems confronting the organisation, there was a tendency to blame all the failures on someone else, most easily 'the errant leader'. Nonetheless, one has to make the highest demands on the top leadership, which must set standards of behaviour, articulate goals, implement policies and ensure *regular* legitimate procedures within a liberation movement. So, perhaps outstanding qualities *are* essential. This, in turn, relates back to the absence of discussion at the time of Make's appointment. If the Central Committee members and representatives present at the meeting in October 1979 at which Make was appointed leader of the PAC had *honestly* and in a principled manner discussed the matter then he would perhaps have been found lacking in the leadership qualities required for the position. Reservations were expressed by most people about Make's suitability for the position of PAC Chairman, but such reservations were expressed outside the meeting. Fifteen months later, Make faced the possibility — or *probability*, in the view of Enoch Zulu — of 'personal humiliation' at the hands of the Dar-es-Salaam cadres. In the PAC the same mistake was repeated time and time again, of appointing individuals to positions, even top leadership, without any consideration of the merits of such positions or the suitability or qualifications of the candidates. In certain instances, such individuals were reduced to objects of ridicule. There were no clearly-defined criteria to apply in the selection of

254   *The Crisis in the PAC: 1978–83*

candidates for appointment to leadership positions. Factionalism and cliquism prevented any subsequent objective evaluation of the performance of individuals once appointed to leadership positions. This is related also to the lack of ideological struggle at the level of leadership within the PAC.

Because of various commitments of a number of Central Committee members, the Central Committee meeting was adjourned. It would thus be appropriate to discuss all the issues with which the Central Committee was confronted during the meeting, rather than deal with the issues discussed during the various sessions of the meeting in January and February 1981.

Enter John Nyati Pokela

John Nyati Pokela, a man of medium height, slender physique and earnest demeanour, was born in the Herschel District of the Transkei, of 'peasant stock', as he describes himself.[1] After matriculating in 1946, he left the Transkei to commence studies for a BA degree and Teacher's Diploma at Fort Hare University in the Eastern Cape. At Fort Hare, which was the centre of political activity for the Black intelligentsia at that time, he met Mangaliso Robert Sobukwe with whom he struck up a friendship that would be maintained for many years. While a student at Fort Hare, Pokela was attracted to the ideas of African Nationalism, propagated by Anton Muziwakhe Lembede (who died in 1947) and Ashby Peter (A.P.) Mda. He joined the Congress Youth League (CYL) of the ANC and was a delegate, with Sobukwe, to the national conference of the ANC in 1949 at which the historic *Programme of Action* was adopted. According to Pokela:

> In fact, that is the crucial stage in the struggle in that country. For the first time the African people [adopted a] Programme of Action which embraced the principle of self-determination for the African people in that part of the Continent. Secondly, they accepted the ideology of African Nationalism as a liberatory force . . . It is this which gave us a start.[2]

Throughout the 1950s he was active in the Africanist Movement within the ANC and was a member of the Cape-based Bureau of African Nationalism.[3] '[Those of us] who accepted African Nationalism came to be known as Africanists because we felt that we [had to] start from African Nationalism [which] at its highest is Africanism.'[4]

At that time there were a number of individuals within the ANC, like Pokela, whose ideological outlook can be categorised as 'orthodox nationalism'.[5] They were critical of the role being played within the ANC by Indians and Communists and feared that this might dilute African Nationalism and blunt the militancy of the African masses. The

John Nyati Pokela: Saviour of the PAC? 255

Bureau of African Nationalism saw itself as the watchdog of African Nationalism, as Gerhardt explains.[6] While teaching at Standerton, in the Transvaal, he remained active in the Africanist Movement. Sobukwe was also teaching in Standerton at that time. Together, they were frequent contributors to the bulletin published by the Bureau.

Pokela was a founder member of the PAC, although he was not elected to the leadership and did not gain national prominence. At the PAC's inaugural conference in Orlando in April 1959 Pokela, together with Phillip Kgosana (who subsequently served as Cape Regional Secretary of the PAC) served on the Resolutions Committee of the organisation.[7] After the banning of the ANC and the PAC by the South African regime following the Sharpeville Massacre in March 1960 Pokela was initially involved in the co-ordination of POQO activities, after which he fled the country to Lesotho. In 1962 he was appointed to the Presidential Council which was established to direct the affairs of the PAC after Leballo and others were released from prison upon completion of their sentences for their role in the Campaign Against the Pass Laws in March 1960.

On 20 August 1966 he was lured across the unmarked border between the then Basutoland (now Lesotho) and South Africa, by an agent of the Pretoria regime. He was arrested by the South African Security Police and detained for approximately eight months. He was convicted the following year on charges of sabotage, attempted murder of policemen and furthering the aims of a banned organisation. He was sentenced to two terms of imprisonment, 13 years and 7 years, the latter term running concurrently. He spent 13 years on Robben Island.

He is credited with having unified the various factions existing among PAC political prisoners on Robben Island; as a result of his leadership role, he was placed in solitary confinement and deprived of the meagre privileges allowed political prisoners by the South African regime.

Upon his release from prison in June 1980 Pokela spent seven months in South Africa before fleeing once more to Lesotho on 7 January 1981. Pokela explains:

> I spent about seven months inside the country just to assess the situation and on January 7, I escaped . . . While I was on Robben Island, the majority of members of the PAC felt that I had to [leave the country]. [Upon my release from prison], committed members of the PAC also felt that I should [leave]. I also received a message that the external wing of the PAC wanted me out so I could not stay long.[8]

After spending approximately one month in Lesotho, Pokela flew to Dar-es-Salaam, Tanzania, where he arrived on 12 February 1981. Upon arrival in Dar-es-Salaam, he was invited to participate in the Central Committee meeting then in progress. At that meeting, by unanimous

256 *The Crisis in the PAC: 1978–83*

decision of the Central Committee, Pokela was appointed Chairman of the Central Committee and Leader of the PAC. Make surrendered the chairmanship gracefully; he offered Pokela his full co-operation and expressed the view that Pokela's experience, especially the leadership he had exercised during his incarceration on Robben island, would be a positive factor in solving the problems of the PAC.

Pokela, for his part, in accepting the responsibility of the chairmanship, indicated that he had been mandated by his colleagues on Robben Island and the PAC members still in South Africa, to come abroad to help in uniting the members of the PAC in exile as well as orienting them 'homewards'. It was hoped that because he had not been involved in the debilitating internecine strife and power struggles of the past few years, he would be acceptable to as many of the PAC factions as possible, thus serving as a rallying figure.

Prior to the decision to appoint Pokela to the chairmanship, Ngila Muendane, a Make loyalist in the Central Committee, sounded out the opinion of at least one Central Committee member on Pokela's possible appointment as Secretary for Defence.[9] The Central Committee member responded with a stony silence. At a subsequent session of the meeting, Muendane strongly criticised the performance of the then Secretary for Defence, Edwin Makoti.

There was no discussion or debate at the meeting about Pokela's suitability for the position of PAC Chairman. Had the long period of incarceration on Robben Island had a deleterious effect upon him? Did he possess the political and ideological clarity to articulate issues clearly? Could an individual who had been out of political circulation for 13 years, who was new to exile politics, and who was joining the exiled organisation at a time of deep crisis, be expected to salvage the organisation? These questions were neither asked nor addressed. The Central Committee as well as the PAC members generally were desperate in January 1981 to find a substitute for Make; it is no exaggeration to say that the mood then was, 'anybody but Make for Chairman!'.

But there was no discussion or debate about the suitability of most of the other individuals appointed to top leadership positions at the January–February 1981 Central Committee meeting. These included Ngila Mike Muendane, who was appointed Director of Labour and Social Affairs; Joe Mkwanazi, appointed to the key position of Administrative Secretary; Ahmed Gora Ebrahim, appointed Director of Publicity and Information. The only appointment that provoked much discussion and debate was that of Temba Lawrence Mgweba as Director of Finance. Make and Muendane questioned the wisdom of the appointment and Mgweba's suitability for the position; Muendane referred to Mgweba's failure as Representative to Cairo during the 1960s and his erratic behaviour in despatching impertinent cables to African leaders requesting financial aid for the PAC.

What to Do with Make?

With the assumption of the chairmanship by Pokela, the Central Committee had to decide where to place Make. Muendane proposed that Make be appointed Deputy Chairman and Director of Foreign Affairs, arguing that Make was well-known and had diplomatic skills, and that the Director of Foreign Affairs be switched to the position of Director of Finance, arguing that the Director of Foreign Affairs, who had drafted a document containing recommendations for the restructuring of the Department of Finance, had a sound knowledge of financial management.

One of the criticisms levelled against Make by both the Dar-es-Salaam cadres and Central Committee members, however, was his incessant travelling. As a result of his absences from the PAC headquarters, there was a lack of leadership and direction in the organisation. One consequence was the failure to implement decisions of the Central Committee. Another was the increasing restiveness among the cadres. Central Committee members were appalled at the idea of Make being nominated for the position of Director of Foreign Affairs, a position that necessitates much travel. Consequently, Muendane's proposal received no support: Make was simply appointed Deputy Chairman.

Plotting, Intrigues and Power Struggles

Muendane's proposal that the Director of Foreign Affairs be appointed Director of Finance was also reflective of a struggle within the Central Committee being led by the Make faction against the then Secretary for Defence and the Director of Foreign Affairs, who at that time served also as Observer Representative to the UN. At the Central Committee meeting in September 1980 Vus Make, as Chairman of the PAC, was given responsibility for drawing up job analyses and job descriptions for each department in the Central Committee, to be presented to the Administrative Committee within one month. He failed to do so.

At the same meeting, Elizabeth Sibeko made a number of unsubstantiated charges against the Director of Foreign Affairs, charges of 'arrogance' and of 'failure' as the PAC's Observer at the UN. She also accused the Director of Foreign Affairs of inciting the Dar-es-Salaam cadres against other Central Committee members. Make and others who were in Tanzania when the 'Cadre Forces' Movement' presented the memorandum of cadres' grievances did not censure or correct her, even though they were fully aware that the Director of Foreign Affairs had been based in New York. Make, in particular, was informed by Makhanda about the Dar-es-Salaam cadres' memorandum. Thereafter, the Make faction led an intense campaign against the Director of Foreign Affairs. It was strengthened by the appointment in February 1981 of Ahmed Gora Ebrahim to the Central Committee.

258 *The Crisis in the PAC: 1978–83*

At the Central Committee meeting in January–February 1981, Make finally presented the guidelines that he should have presented two months earlier. They contained a provision stating: 'It is desirable that all heads of departments be based in Dar-es-Salaam'. At that time the Director of Foreign Affairs was the only departmental head based away from PAC headquarters. There was general agreement with the spirit of the proposal but some doubt about the *motive*, especially when Make and one of his loyalists, Count Pietersen (then Director of Education and Manpower Development), argued that agreement on the spirit of the proposal constituted a decision of the Central Committee. The argument was rejected by the other Central Committee members. Enoch Zulu, the Director of Operations, stated bluntly that he was not going to be used by Elizabeth Sibeko and Leasoana Sam Makhanda who had conducted an intensive and extensive smear campaign against the Director of Foreign Affairs. Makhanda had even gone to the extent of telling a number of people in the USA that the Director of Foreign Affairs was going to be removed as the PAC Observer Representative to the UN and replaced by Ahmed Gora Ebrahim.

Elizabeth Sibeko failed to attend the Central Committee meeting in January–February 1981. Instead, she sent Makhanda to Dar-es-Salaam, armed with a lengthy report about 'the New York situation' and the Director of Foreign Affairs. He did not, however, present it to the Central Committee but instead showed it to a number of persons privately in Dar-es-Salaam, including the Director of Operations, Enoch Zulu, and Raymond Johnson, a senior APLA cadre, and Edgar Motau, a political cadre who had come to Dar-es-Salaam in early 1979 but who had been known to Makhanda since the early 1960s when the two of them had been involved in dissident activities as a result of which they had been forced to leave Tanzania under orders of the PAC leadership. Makhanda did not remain in Dar-es-Salaam in January 1981 but left for Botswana about two days after arrival in order to attend to his private affairs.

Given the weight of evidence against Elizabeth Sibeko, the Central Committee decided unanimously to dismiss her from the Central Committee and to relieve her of all responsibilities as a representative. Enoch Zulu, the Director of Operations, was adamant in demanding her dismissal. He pointed out that her disruptive activities against the PAC Observer Mission to the UN were aimed at undermining the efforts of the Director of Foreign Affairs whose performance might then be unfavourably compared with that of her deceased husband. By requesting the National Council of Churches and other liberation support organisations not to support the PAC, however, she was no longer fighting the Director of Foreign Affairs but the PAC, he stated. According to Zulu, when he questioned Makhanda about his disruptive activities with Elizabeth Sibeko, his response was to show him a voluminous, slanderous report about the Director of Foreign Affairs. He reported also that Makhanda had already informed people that Gora Ebrahim

John Nyati Pokela: Saviour of the PAC? 259

was going to replace the Director of Foreign Affairs as the PAC Observer Representative to the UN. Zulu continued that he was not going to serve the personal interests of Elizabeth Sibeko. It is arguable that had the Central Committee, under the leadership of Vus Make, summoned the courage to take disciplinary action against Elizabeth Sibeko one year earlier, the PAC might have been saved the embarrassment and problems which ensued as a result of her activities. But Elizabeth Sibeko was not alone; her disruptive activities, with the support of Makhanda and Hlongwane in New York, were co-ordinated with and condoned by, the Make faction in the Central Committee. After the conclusion of the Central Committee meeting and after the departure of the Director of Foreign Affairs for New York, Make arranged for Makhanda to present his 'report' to a meeting of the Administrative Committee, an action that was highly irregular; Makhanda was an ordinary member of the PAC who was implicated in a criminal act in New York and in other disruptive activities of which the Central Committee was aware, yet he was presented to a meeting of the Administrative Committee to report about a Central Committee member in the absence of such member. Make's expressions of 'concern about the situation in New York', following Makhanda's report to the Administrative Committee, were not shared by most other Central Committee members.

The Central Committee decided in January–February 1981 also that a delegation would be sent to the USA to inform Elizabeth Sibeko of her dismissal. The delegation would also explain to a number of significant liberation support organisations the background to the decision. The idea was that the despatch of such a high-level delegation would convey the grave light in which Elizabeth Sibeko's disruptive activities were viewed and would also dispel any idea that she was being 'persecuted' by the Director of Foreign Affairs. As it turned out, however, the nature of the delegation's composition and the secret ambitions of its members, led to a different result. It furthered the campaign against the Director of Foreign Affairs and the personal interests of individuals who subsequently plotted and engaged in intrigues in order to secure appointments to the positions of Observer Representative to the UN and Representative to the USA. Ever since the UN General Assembly decision in 1979 to provide financial assistance to the ANC and PAC to maintain offices in New York, the position of Observer at the UN has been considered a 'plum post' to be sought because the Observer does not have the problem of raising funds from sympathetic organisations and individuals for maintenance of the office, rents, and personal maintenance. In the PAC, the position of Observer Representative to the UN has become an escapist post for some whose revolutionary commitment is slight. It has given rise to the phenomenon of the 'delegates lounge exile'. It has nurtured a host of 'hangers-on' who believe that as PAC members they are entitled to personal shares of the UN financial aid;

260 *The Crisis in the PAC: 1978–83*

each day, they flocked to the PAC Observer Mission, not to assist in any assignments or tasks, but to hustle for 'money for tokens' to travel on the subway system or buses, 'money for lunch' and a host of other things ranging from dry-cleaning to accommodation. PAC members in New York, rather than contribute financially to the PAC, exploited all avenues of sponging off the organisation through the Observer Mission to the UN. Some desired the post for the wrong reason, namely personal self-interest.

The delegation comprised two Central Committee members, Count Pietersen and Ahmed Gora Ebrahim. (In 1978 David Sibeko had taken certain initiatives to facilitate Ebrahim's return to active involvement in the PAC; Ebrahim had earlier been expelled from the PAC by Leballo. It was, however, only in 1980 that this was effected. He was invited to the Central Committee's plenary meeting in April 1980. In the second half of 1980, he was appointed PAC Representative to Zimbabwe, a decision based on family and personal considerations as explained by Make when he made the recommendation. Ebrahim, who had worked in Iraq as a journalist, could take up employment in Zimbabwe and there he could be joined by his family.)

Both Ebrahim and Pietersen were part of the Make faction, although after the assumption of the leadership by Pokela, Ebrahim immediately transferred loyalties to Pokela, working his way into what one journalist has described as Pokela's 'inner circle'.[10]

Even after his appointment as Director of Publicity and Information, Ebrahim, rather than apply himself to his responsibilities as a member of the Central Committee and a representative, schemed and manoeuvred in order to be appointed to the position of either Director of Foreign Affairs or Observer Representative to the UN. This effort intensified after his visit to the USA in March 1981 to address a Sharpeville Commemorative Meeting at the UN, and with Count Pietersen to inform Elizabeth Sibeko of her dismissal.

Plots and intrigues, power struggles, scheming and manoeuvring by individuals and cliques are endemic to the PAC. They intensified shortly after the assumption of the chairmanship by Pokela, since a number of individuals and cliques exploited the fact that Pokela was new to the politics of the PAC of the past decade. As a result, he was manipulated and misled.

Plight of PAC Exiles in Lesotho

Reference has already been made to the visit to Lesotho by a delegation of the former Presidential Council in September 1979 comprising Vus Make and Elias Ntloedibe, which had aggravated the existing divisions among PAC members resident in that country; the de facto representative, Naphthallie Sidzamba, and others were bitter that the delegation seemed bent on co-opting into the leadership two persons whom they regarded as having been politically inactive during the previous decade.

John Nyati Pokela: Saviour of the PAC? 261

In January 1981, prior to the Central Committee meeting, Ngila Muendane attended a conference in Lesotho organised by the Economic Commission for Africa (ECA). His visit provoked intense anger and bitterness among PAC members in Lesotho. In a letter addressed to the Administrative Secretary, Sidzamba complained about Muendane's actions during his visit to Lesotho:

> We want to express our dissatisfaction with the manner in which Comrade Mwendane [sic] handled [PAC] affairs here . . .
> 1. Although the main purpose of his coming here was to attend the ECA conference, we expected him to report to the [PAC representative] on arrival. We had to search for him until we found him on Sunday afternoon when we learned from [him] that he had arrived on Friday evening. We feel that this was improper.
> 2. He did give the committee of the local Branch a report on the position of the [PAC] internationally, but he did not allow himself time to consult with us on [PAC] matters in this region.
> 3. He reluctantly released the funds which he initially attempted [to hand over] to one *Gabie Mphakalasi* who is known to have been [inactive in the PAC] since 1963.
> 4. The amount of 1,500 pounds (sterling) is too meagre to cope with the [PAC] work on the home front. However, it will certainly assist to alleviate [sic] the outstanding demands, the main one being to feed the cadres.
> 5. We expected him to bring us [PAC] literature but to our disappointment there was nothing [relevant] to the [PAC] in the European magazines which he brought with him.
> 6. He was at variance with the local branch on several matters. In some instances there was a flare of emotions and consequently unpleasant words were [exchanged] between him and comrades here.
> 7. He attempted to rebuke the local branch for refusing to work with Gabie Mphakalasi. There was strong disagreement with him on that.
> 8. He claimed that he had a mandate from the Central Committee and when we asked him to tell us of the date of the Central Committee meeting, he did not furnish the information.
> 9. He also attempted to reverse the decision which was taken by Comrade Mantshontsho [the former Administrative Secretary] and the branch here last year on the question of the regularisation of membership by inactive members. Again we disagreed bitterly with him.
> *Conclusion*:
> (a) Henceforth, we shall not tolerate comrades who visit here from the external mission when they consciously foment divisions among us.
> (b) It is our declared policy here to work, inter alia, to maintain and promote fraternal relations among the branches of [the PAC].
> (c) It is also our resolve to abide strictly with [sic] the Constitution and properly taken [sic] decisions of [the PAC].[11]

262 *The Crisis in the PAC: 1978–83*

Muendane did not respond to the cogent case brought by Sidzamba, but at the Central Committee meeting, offered his own version of what transpired in Lesotho as well as his own observations of the problems. In doing so, he engaged in a personal attack on Sidzamba to whom he attributed the problems. He also called upon the Central Committee to demand of Sidzamba a financial report, even though Sidzamba had voluntarily submitted a financial statement to the Administrative Secretary, copied to the Director of Foreign Affairs.

The matter was deferred upon recommendation of the Director of Foreign Affairs that a delegation of the Central Committee, led by the Director personally, visit Lesotho not only to observe the situation but, more importantly, to present to the PAC members resident there, guidelines to regulate the relationship between the Representative and the branch. In view of the sensitive political situation in Lesotho, there was need for the PAC to handle the question of its representation in that country as well as its relations with the government very delicately. The PAC, during Leballo's regime, had a political alliance with the opposition BCP; a number of BCP members received military training in Libya under the aegis of the PAC.

The Central Committee's decision for a delegation to visit Lesotho was not implemented. The problems in that country between the two opposing groups deteriorated. Later, Sidzamba and fourteen other PAC members were detained by the Lesotho authorities briefly, following a visit to that country by a Central Committee delegation. More of that later.

Reinstatement of Members Expelled at Arusha in 1978
While the Central Committee meeting was in progress in January–February 1981 there were negotiations between certain Central Committee members and the PAC members expelled at the second consultative conference in Arusha in June–July 1978. The negotiations were aimed at ensuring the return of the 70-odd members to the PAC. Initially, the negotiations were conducted in secrecy between three Central Committee members (namely, Joe Mkwanazi, then Director of Labour and Social Affairs, Enoch Zulu, the Director of Operations, and this writer in his capacity as Director of Foreign Affairs) and the leaders of the expelled members. The secrecy was necessitated by the suspicion and mistrust that existed between the two sides. Some Central Committee members were opposed to the reinstatement of the expelled group who had since formed themselves into the Azanian People's Revolutionary Party (APRP) for fear that they would demand as condition for their return to the PAC, their reinstatement in their former leadership positions. There was also resentment concerning their return on the part of a number of Dar-es-Salaam cadres who recalled that they had been 'victimised' by the expelled group while Ntantala and others were in the leadership. They, too, feared that Ntantala and the other

former leaders might seek the leadership of the PAC if reinstated.

During the negotiations, the APRP members made it clear that their return to the PAC fold was unconditional and that they would not be challenging the Central Committee, nor did they expect to be reinstated in their former positions. These assurances paved the way for a formal meeting between delegations representing the two sides. At the meeting, it was agreed that the APRP would be dissolved; all those members expelled at the 1978 consultative conference would be reinstated, and everything possible would be done to ensure their physical integration into the PAC and all its organs.

The reinstatement in the PAC of the former APRP members was widely welcomed. However, deep suspicions remained and the reinstated members were not completely reintegrated into the organs of the PAC. There continued to be two distinct groups, with one believing that its members constituted the 'loyal forces' who had remained in the organisation through the crises of 1978 and 1979, and referring to the reinstated members as 'the Ntantala group'.

Erret Radebe Resigns as Director of Finance

At its January–February 1981 meeting, the Central Committee also had to address the resignation of the Director of Finance, Erret Radebe. He tendered his resignation, he explained, because he was aware that he was among the next four Central Committee members whose resignations would be demanded by the Dar-es-Salaam cadres. The 'Cadre Forces' Movement' had adopted the strategy of tackling the Central Committee, by attacking the weakest first, so as to divide the leadership. They were aware that certain Committee members were critical of the performances of individuals like Ntloedibe, Mantshontsho, Elizabeth Sibeko, Ngila Muendane, Count Pietersen, and Erret Radebe, but such Central Committee members were unable to secure the dismissals of these individuals because of the prevailing factionalism. Radebe was aware that his dismissal on the grounds of incompetence would be demanded by the Dar-es-Salaam cadres. Having failed to dissuade him from resigning, the Central Committee accepted his resignation.

The resignation of Erret Radebe created two major problems for the Central Committee. Firstly, he was unable to produce any financial report, so the Central Committee had no idea of the organisation's financial status. The PAC's financial affairs were in a shambles. To say this is not to imply any impropriety or personal corruption on Radebe's part. The chaotic state of the PAC's financial affairs was merely reflective of the inefficiency within the organisation, its loose structure, the lack of definition of responsibilities and controls.

The second problem caused by Radebe's resignation was the choice of a successor. Ultimately, Lawrence Temba Mgweba was appointed to the position, simply because he was employed at that time by the National Insurance Company in Dar-es-Salaam as an accountant and

264 *The Crisis in the PAC: 1978–83*

was the only person with the expertise in financial management, or rather, the book-keeping and accountancy aspects of it. Ngila Muendane and Vus Make voiced strong opposition to the appointment of Mgweba, not least because of his lack of political finesse which had caused the PAC embarrassment in the past.

Mgweba's appointment did not solve the problems of the Department of Finance. Apart from being extremely parsimonious — at times ridiculously so, as when he refused to provide subsistence allowances for the PAC delegates to a meeting of UN agencies in Dar-es-Salaam — he did not introduce any innovations in the department, either in terms of financial management or fund-raising for the activities of the organisation. Worse still, within six months of his appointment, he demonstrated the same crudity of which Sibeko had complained in his report six years earlier. In June 1981 he attended a meeting in Arusha, Tanzania, of the OAU Liberation Committee even though he was not a nominated PAC delegate; to avoid embarrassment to the organisation, he was permitted by the delegation to attend the sessions. He made a number of private approaches to various delegations attending the meeting, requesting financial aid, apparently believing that the delegations to such meetings carry dollars in their briefcases for donation to the PAC (or any other liberation movement) upon request. He repeated the same behaviour two weeks later at the OAU Council of Ministers and Summit of Heads of State in Nairobi. Mgweba was eventually relieved of his responsibilities as Director of Finance by the PAC Central Committee in August 1983 although he was retained in the Central Committee.

Other Appointments

A number of other appointments were also made at the January–February 1981 meeting. Joe Mkwanazi was moved from the Department of Labour and Social Affairs to the position of Administrative Secretary; Ngila Muendane was appointed Director of Labour and Social Affairs in succession to Mkwanazi. Ahmed Gora Ebrahim was appointed to the position of Director of Publicity and Information, a position which had been vacant since the dismissal of Elias Ntloedibe the previous September. In addition, it was decided that the Department of Defence would nominate someone to be despatched to Nigeria as the Representative. The latter decision was necessitated by the fact that Molefe Ike Mafole who had been appointed to the position of Chief Representative to Nigeria several months earlier had not been able to take up his post as a result of difficulties in securing a travel document. At the Central Committee meeting in January–February 1981 his appointment was rescinded following a report made by Erret Radebe about Mafole's attitude and 'arrogance', exhibited during a visit to New York by Radebe in October 1980. Radebe's recommendation was reinforced by a memorandum which Mafole submitted to the Central

John Nyati Pokela: Saviour of the PAC? 265

Committee shortly before the meeting in which he vehemently denounced the leadership. The emotive and intemperate language in the document raised questions as to whether Mafole was the appropriate person to represent the PAC in such an important country when he harboured such views about the leaders of the organisation. Ultimately, it was decided that he should be recalled to Dar-es-Salaam for 're-orientation', a decision he found insulting.

Shortly after Mafole's return to Dar-es-Salaam in May 1981, however, the same persons (essentially the Make faction) who had raised questions about his suitability to serve as a representative in Nigeria would nominate him in July to be Representative to the UN. This followed the introduction by the Administrative Secretary, Joe Mkwanazi, to a Central Committee meeting, of a report by Mafole on 'the New York situation'. In the report, he criticised the situation at the PAC Observer Mission to the UN as a 'one-man show'. The nomination of Mafole surprised even Pokela who questioned whether Mafole was the suitable candidate for the position. The nomination was then dropped.

The Central Committee meeting concluded in February with a new Chairman having been appointed and with the Central Committee having been enlarged beyond the number provided for in the documents on the restructuring of the PAC adopted at the consultative conference in Arusha in June–July 1978. The Central Committee in February 1981 comprised the following members:

1. John Nyati Pokela, Chairman;
2. Vusumzi L. Make, Deputy Chairman;
3. Joseph R. Mkwanazi, Administrative Secretary;
4. Edwin L. Makoti, Secretary for Defence;
5. Lawrence T. Mgweba, Director of Finance;
6. Henry E. Isaacs, Director of Foreign Affairs and Observer Representative to the UN;
7. Ahmed Gora Ebrahim, Director of Publicity and Information and Chief Representative to Zimbabwe;
8. Count Pietersen, Director of Education and Manpower Development;
9. Ngila Mike Muendane, Director of Labour and Social Affairs and Chief Representative to the UK and the Continent;
10. Enoch Zulu (John Mvelase), Director of Operations;
11. Benedict Sondlo, Administrative Assistant;
12. Thobile Gola, Chief Representative to Tanzania;
13. Vus Nomadolo, Chief Representative to Guinea (Conakry);
14. Patrick Kohlo, Chief Representative to Botswana;
15. Morgan Nogaga Gxexwa, Member of Central Committee.

A few months later, Theophilus Bidi was appointed Chief Representative to Nigeria and appointed to the Central Committee as the sixteenth member.

Reactions to Pokela's Appointment

Pokela's assumption of the chairmanship of the PAC was welcomed by many PAC members and well-wishers of the organisation. Pokela lacks the energy of Leballo, the intellectual and diplomatic ability of Make, but compensates for this by his sincerity and honesty. But sincerity and honesty alone are not sufficient to lead an organisation, especially a national liberation movement. The fact that he came abroad after having been incarcerated on Robben Island for 13 years and came into the PAC in exile at a time when it was in deep crisis, meant that he would be subjected to pressures from factions and individuals within the organisation jockeying for positions and influence. As a consequence he faced enormous difficulties.

Soon after Pokela assumed the chairmanship, the 'Cadre Forces' Movement' expressed a lack of confidence in four Central Committee members and demanded their dismissal. The four members — Vus Make, Edwin Makoti, Count Pietersen and Ngila Muendane — were accused of promoting 'factionalism, cliquism and splittism'. Pokela responded by insisting that the four members were entitled to a fair hearing; he appointed a Commission of Inquiry made up of Mfanayasekaya Pearce Gqobose (chairman), David Dube, Hamilton Keke and a fourth person known to this writer only as 'Bamba', to investigate the charges.

Pokela also announced that there would be a return to the PAC constitution. But, as has already been observed, the PAC constitution was written at a time when the organisation operated overtly and legally in South Africa. Obviously, therefore, the constitution of the organisation was not ideally suited to the conditions in which it was now forced to operate. Later, a call was made to the members to make recommendations and suggestions regarding the revamping of the PAC constitution to make it accord with present-day realities and the objectives of the organisation.

In April 1981 a Unity Committee was appointed to advise the Central Committee on all questions relating to the reunification of the PAC and also on the question of unity with other national liberation movements and patriotic organisations in South Africa.[12] By June 1983, however, the Unity Committee had accomplished nothing and its secretary resigned from the PAC with a strong denunciation of the organisation.

Pokela personally emphasised repeatedly the need for unity in the national liberation struggle. Unfortunately, no specific principles were defined for such unity; instead, there seemed to be an assumption that unity could be built around an individual. This ignored the bitter personal enmities that exist among the older PAC members, particularly those who left their home country in the early 1960s; it ignored also the hostilities between the two national liberation movements, the ANC and PAC, and the manner in which such hostilities are fanned by the continuing competition between them for support and influence internationally. As a result, although under Pokela a certain amount of stability in the PAC ensued, genuine and effective unity eluded the leadership and the prospects for unity with the ANC are as remote as ever.[13]

Although a number of the members who were expelled at the consultative conference in Arusha in 1978 were appointed to positions of responsibility after their reinstatement, their complete integration into the body of the PAC was impeded by the suspicions of certain Central Committee members as well as those cadres who regarded themselves as the 'loyal forces'.[14] The latter suspected that the APRP had not really been dissolved, or at least its former members had not really abandoned the idea of establishing themselves as the 'vanguard group or party', and that the former APRP members were merely biding their time before challenging for the 'strategic leadership'. By the end of 1981 the Dar-es-Salaam cadres spoke about the APRP plotting 'a coup'. A document purportedly written by members of the dissolved APRP to this effect was reportedly intercepted by members of the APLA Task Force which was charged with the responsibility of re-organising the PAC's military wing.[15] Despite assertions to the contrary, by the end of 1982 unity within the PAC was still not achieved. In Tanzania, apart from the different factions and cliques within each group, there were still two distinct groups, with one paying allegiance to the leadership of Pokela and referring to the other as the 'Ntantala group'. A small core, principally of militarily-trained cadres at the military camp in Ithumbi as well as among the 46 who were removed to the camp at Mgagao pending their removal from Tanzania, still claimed allegiance to the deposed Leballo.

The End of Leballo?

Even after Pokela assumed the chairmanship, Leballo continued to claim the leadership of the PAC. He remained in Zimbabwe until April 1981 when, shortly before a visit to that country by Pokela, he was ordered by the government to leave the country. Thereafter, while reportedly living on a government pension in Libya, Leballo continued periodically to mail out pamphlets in which he made wild and fanciful claims, inter alia, that a significant section of APLA was still loyal to him, and that his supporters had on a number of occasions escaped from captivity and attacked Pokela in his office.[16] In another pamphlet, he was the self-styled 'Chancellor' of a 'university' he had established somewhere in Britain. Latest reports indicate that he is in The Netherlands.

One commentator has written of Leballo:

In seeking material on the PAC in 1962, the author interviewed the then head of the organisation, Potlako Leballo. Rarely, if ever, in twenty years' experience with African nationalism in all of the countries south of the Sahara, had one been asked to swallow such preposterous dreams and such sweeping lies as Leballo insisted upon. The absolute certainty with which he said, 'I will see you in Pretoria in 1963 because I will let you into our country . . .' was characteristic of the sense of unwarranted optimism and megalomania which eventually contributed to a rejection of him as PAC head by many of his followers.[17]

Although this assessment was made by an academic who can be described as hostile to the cause of African liberation, it is an assessment which is shared by many, both in the liberation movement and outside. In the 1968 Tanzanian Treason Trial in which Leballo was the main state witness, the presiding judge, Chief Justice Telford Georges, made a scathing attack on Leballo's propensity for lies and exaggeration. Matthew Nkoana, Leballo's former colleague, wrote:

No folly has been too great, no deceit too mean, no lie too shameful, no gambol [sic] too low in Leballo's ruthless pursuit of money, personal power and the glory that goes with it.[18]

At the height of the power struggle between Leballo and Ntantala in 1978, the latter stated:

[Leballo] will unjustifiably call [his Central Committee colleagues] all sorts of ugly political names, fabricate hair-raising tales about them, falsely accuse them of everything and anything that takes his fancy. But worse [sic] of all, he will get so carried away by his own imagination that he will blurt out [PAC] confidences and strategic or tactical secrets of a most sensitive nature.[19]

This writer can certainly testify to Leballo's propensity for exaggeration from his own experience.

Nkoana and Ntantala have documented the crises and problems which plagued the PAC during Leballo's regime. Nkoana has been particularly scathing in his criticisms of the maladministration, factionalism, embezzlement of funds on the one hand, and more serious 'errors of judgement' on the other.[20] The recurring crises and internal problems had seriously weakened the PAC, its image and prestige were tarnished, its influence in South Africa and internationally diminished.[21]

Given the inefficacy of Leballo's leadership and his unpopularity within the PAC, how was he able to survive at the helm of the organisation for the length of time that he did? Four reasons can be isolated:

(i) The legitimacy of his leadership and his role as founder of PAC: Leballo was active in the Africanist Movement within the ANC, a pressure group committed to orthodox African Nationalism.[22] Together

John Nyati Pokela: Saviour of the PAC? 269

with Sobukwe, Leballo was one of the principal architects of the formation of the PAC. Abroad, Leballo appealed to the loyalty of PAC members by invoking the legitimacy of his position as founder of the organisation and a leader who was 'elected by the people at home'. Those who opposed him were simply expelled under dubious emergency powers he claimed were available to the head of the organisation under clause 14(b) of the PAC constitution. A litany of expulsions and suspensions characterises the history of the PAC in exile as a result of the use by Leballo and his various supporters at different times of the emergency powers under clause 14(b).[23]

(ii) The support of the Tanzanian Government following Leballo's evidence for the State in the 1968 Treason Trial. The role played by Leballo in the 1968 Treason Trial involving a number of Tanzanian nationals charged with plotting a coup d'etat against President Julius Nyerere earned him (Leballo) the support of the Tanzanian authorities. One of Leballo's former colleagues in the National Executive Committee explained that the Tanzanian Government frustrated all actions against Leballo. The National Executive Committee condemned Leballo's role as a state witness in the Treason Trial, arguing that it was unwarranted interference in the internal affairs of a sovereign African state. In November, 1968 Leballo's colleagues decided to expel him from the PAC. The Tanzanians responded by declaring all of Leballo's adversaries prohibited immigrants. One explanation for the Tanzanian action is that the Government did not want as a state witness in the Treason Trial, an individual who had been discredited within his own organisation.[24]

(iii) His ability to play off different factions and individuals against each other: Leballo's critics within the liberation movement, particularly those who have been victimised by him, tend to attribute all the problems within the PAC to him as an individual. Whilst it may be true that in large measure Leballo was responsible for the disarray that afflicted the PAC during his tenure as head of the organisation, it is equally true that there were always others around him. He could always count on the support of the like of David Sibeko, Elias Ntloedibe and others whose loyalty to Leballo as an individual was unflinching as long as they were rewarded with top leadership positions. All Leballo's henchmen learned a bitter lesson that they were all dispensable once they had outlived their political usefulness.

Leballo was a past master at playing off different individuals and factions against each other. Writing in 1978, Ntantala stated:

> After unnecessarily provoking differences between himself and his leading colleagues... Leballo will invariably go to the rank and file members (nowadays this includes the very young new recruits since Soweto June 16, 1976) to junior [PAC] officials such as representatives in the office and even to total outsiders of any rank — e.g. members of the BCP [that is, the

Basutoland Congress Party] and villify his central committee colleagues behind their backs, and to the worst possible extent.[25]

One reason why the Ntantala faction received little sympathy from many PAC members in 1978 was because they had also at various times collaborated with Leballo, or acquiesced in his victimisation of others in the past. The tendency developed within the PAC, particularly at the leadership level, to point out Leballo's weaknesses only during power struggles or when individual cliques were either victimised or threatened with victimisation. It is more accurate to say that those who have been in positions of leadership with Leballo have been guilty, by omission or commission, for the problems that have plagued the PAC over the years.[26]

(iv) His appeal to the young recruits who joined the PAC after Soweto. A fourth reason why Leballo was able to survive one of the most serious challenges to his leadership in 1977 to 1978 was his appeal to the young recruits who joined the PAC after the Soweto uprisings of 1976. The majority of the recruits were people after Leballo's own heart — undisciplined, impressed by demagoguery and demanding of *action*. They spurned political education and ideological training, citing such education as the reason for the older generation's 20-year sojourn in exile. Their conception of the liberation struggle was that they should merely be provided with arms and ammunition, given elementary training in their use and sent back 'home to fight'.[27]

They were impressed by Leballo's demagoguery, by his exaggerated tales of his war-time exploits and his denigration of intellectualism. At the end of 1976 and early 1977 political education was conducted by a number of senior PAC members in Dar-es-Salaam, with a view to providing not only an historical and ideological perspective for the new recruits, but also orientation. Leballo banned the political education classes. In their stead, he organised a daily ritual called 'parliament', which was basically a mass meeting where he harangued the recruits. Gradually, he succeeded in building a personal following amongst them and used them against his colleagues in the Central Committee.[28]

Leballo's influence upon many of the young people was undoubtedly immense. Many of the young recruits would not have hesitated to kill if so instructed by Leballo. For several years they were brainwashed by Leballo into believing that he was the only revolutionary in the PAC and that all his colleagues in the Central Committee were in the struggle to 'enjoy high living and good times'. Leballo often boasted to them: 'Without me, you are stuck in the mud'. The high command interpreted the removal of Leballo as part of a 'conspiracy' by the Central Committee 'to destroy the army', and 'the Azanian revolution'. By some strange Leballoist logic, therefore, by killing the Central Committee members they would be 'saving the Azanian revolution'.

John Nyati Pokela: Saviour of the PAC? 271

Today, the six APLA cadres convicted of the murder of David Sibeko are serving their prison sentences. Justice Nkonyane and the other members of the high command he led are living in a refugee settlement at Tabora in Tanzania, under the care of the UNHCR. The 40-odd APLA cadres who were involved in the siege of the Central Committee on 26 December 1978 have been joined by six others; after being detained at a camp in Mgagao in Tanzania pending deportation, they were subsequently removed to the same refugee settlement in Tabora. They, too, believed that they were 'rectifying the situation', because they had been told by Leballo that there were 'vultures [in the Central Committee] squandering money'. Cohen Ntuli lies buried in a shallow grave somewhere in the woods of Chunya (Ithumbi), a victim of senseless brutality in the name of the 'Azanian revolution'. In a sense, they are all victims of the struggles-within-the-struggle. Leballo, chief architect of many of the struggles-within-the-struggle is reportedly in The Netherlands after having been expelled ignominiously from a number of African countries — Guinea, Sierra Leone, Nigeria, Zimbabwe, Libya — a taste of the treatment to which an untold number of South Africans were subjected as a result of his actions.

Pokela Takes Over but Problems Persist

Even after the removal of Leballo and Pokela's accession to the chairmanship, the problems which have plagued the PAC are still discernible. The performance of the politico-military functions of the organisation has shown little appreciable improvement. Tandon, in his analysis of problems faced by national liberation movements in Southern Africa, cites the following: 'Insufficient organisation, insufficient arms, and inadequate logistics are some of the main deficiencies of the present liberation movements in Africa.'[29] Tandon was writing in 1972, before the accession to power of national liberation movements in Guinea-Bissau, Angola, Mozambique and Zimbabwe. Ten years later, the PAC continued to exhibit the same deficiencies analysed by Tandon. At the present time, however, we restrict our examination to the problem of insufficient organisation. This is not to deny the problems caused by the lack of a sufficient quantity of arms, or the problems caused by the lack of bases or sanctuary in a country or countries contiguous to South Africa, all of which affect the 'return capability'[30] of the PAC. It may, however, be argued that it is the objective of a liberation movement to develop skill and capability to capture arms from the enemy so as to minimise dependency on external sources for arms and ammunition necessary for the conduct of the war of liberation. The contention of this writer, however, is that even if the PAC did not have the problems of the lack of rear bases and supply lines provided by countries contiguous to South Africa, or of 'insufficient' arms and ammunition,

272 The Crisis in the PAC: 1978–83

it would still not be able to use such assistance to the best advantage because of the poor organisation that the movement exhibits. This is a point that requires amplification.

Marcum points out that:

> The 'return' capability of exiled liberation movements will also depend upon their capacity for resolute, disciplined action to improve levels of political and politico-military performance. *Self-reliant movements which have developed well-ordered structures and procedures and have defined, clarified differentiated leadership roles and responsibilities have a comparative advantage.* In the words of Eqbal Ahmad, the guerrilla must concentrate on 'out-administering' and isolating the enemy. He must be concerned with administrative structures and with meeting his obligations to the local populace.[31] (Emphasis added.)

He supports his argument by citing the example of the success of the PAIGC. Admittedly, the 'objective' and 'subjective' factors in Guinea-Bissau and South Africa are not similar; the argument here is that a national liberation movement, in order to achieve its objectives, must establish the necessary organisational structures and procedures through which to pursue those objectives. Thus far, the PAC has not succeeded in doing so. This point can be illustrated by examining the performance of the PAC in three functions which have been analysed by Marcum — the political, military and social services functions.[32]

Political Functions:

Administration: Chaos reigns supreme at the PAC external headquarters in Dar-es-Salaam, the organisation's political centre. Despite repeated discussions, criticisms and decisions of the Central Committee, there has been a failure to establish even a modicum of administrative infrastructure and function. For instance, a liberation support organisation in Belgium wrote to the PAC Observer Mission to the UN in January 1981 requesting details of the PAC bank account in Dar-es-Salaam so as to transfer a sum of money which had been collected for the PAC transit centre in Tanzania.[33] The spokesperson of the Belgian organisation indicated that he had written to the PAC headquarters in Dar-es-Salaam requesting the information so that the funds could be transferred, but had received no reply. Similar problems were faced by the Workers' Communist League in New Zealand,[34] and an aid agency in Australia.[35]

In October 1981 this writer, at that time PAC's Observer at the UN, received a letter from the PAC's Assistant Representative in Dar-es-Salaam with a request that he should distribute a number of automobile stickers to the PAC's Assistant Representatives in the USA. The stickers had in fact been produced by the PAC Observer Mission to the UN and

John Nyati Pokela: Saviour of the PAC? 273

had been sent to Dar-es-Salaam in September 1981 with Maphiri Masekela, a functionary in the PAC's Education Department. After the stickers had been returned to Dar-es-Salaam by this writer with a note to the effect that they had in fact originated in the New York office, the Assistant Representative in Dar-es-Salaam replied:

> The information about the red stickers! You have to be in Dar [-Es-Salaam] to know how things are run out here; these stickers had to find their way back to their original source before people could know that you sent them, otherwise there was complete silence.[36]

Although these are random samples, they reflect a general pattern namely, the inability of the PAC external headquarters to respond even to routine correspondence even as a mere formality or out of common courtesy to its own supporters. This has had the effect of discouraging even keen supporters of the liberation struggle in Southern Africa from supporting the PAC. Organisational inefficiency does not inspire confidence. If a liberation movement is unable to acknowledge receipt of a letter from its own supporters, how can such supporters be confident that the movement has the capacity to challenge successfully an enemy as formidable as the South African regime?

PAC members also complained about the lack of communication with the external headquarters. A PAC member wrote angrily:

> I want to emphasise that to salvage the PAC now, there must be genuine reconciliation among all who want to fight the enemy under the PAC flag or for some reason were forced to leave. There is simply no one who can go it alone. The enemy is mighty. To achieve unity there must be a sense of statesmanship and sincerity. We need everybody, even those whose point of view we do not appreciate. Otherwise the exit of P.K. [Leballo] means nothing. People want to see that there is a change. And, indeed, unless this is done the Dar [-es-Salaam] leadership of PAC shall be judged very harshly by History for having betrayed Sobukwe, Mothopeng and thousands of PACITES who have made untold sacrifices. For a long time the PAC has been run as a private property ... No wonder people will not even send ordinary cuttings from newspapers when requested. They have no sense of belonging. They are not treated as belonging except when a crisis breaks up and each faction wants to win votes. Time is running out. PAC must clean its house fast if it should restore confidence and credibility in itself ... Without communication and information from leaders there is very little the members and supporters can do.[37]

There has been a failure to appreciate or understand the effects that internal problems and crises in the PAC have had, not only on the image of the organisation, but more importantly, in demoralising both its members and its supporters. When in mid-January 1982 a founder-

274 *The Crisis in the PAC: 1978–83*

member of the PAC wrote to Pokela cautioning him against the implementation of Central Committee decisions regarding abrupt changes of personnel which might arouse speculation of a further crisis in the PAC, his constructive letter was not even accorded the courtesy of a reply.[38] The changes were made in a manner that resulted in precisely the kind of adverse publicity the member had forecast.

Publicity and Information: National liberation movements operate in a world where the media have a powerful effect in shaping views and opinions, not only of those who make decisions about the liberation struggles and those who support the objectives of such struggles, but also those of the oppressed masses themselves. In the battle for the hearts and minds, propaganda and information are crucial. The PAC has failed dismally in the area of publicity and information.

Although the PAC has a Department of Publicity and Information, the performance of that department has been erratic. At the Arusha consultative conference, Elias Ntloedibe was appointed Director of Publicity and Information; during the first six months of his appointment, he succeeded in producing the official organs of the PAC, namely *Azania News* and *The Africanist*. For the remainder of his term, there were regular complaints about the lack of publications, until he was eventually dismissed from the Central Committee in September 1980 under pressure from the 'Cadre Forces' Movement'. In the period between the dismissal of Ntloedibe in September 1980 and January 1981 Edwin Makoti was appointed head of a committee that was set up to reorganise the Department of Publicity and Information. Recommendations made by the personnel of the Department were made available to the Central Committee at its meeting in January–February 1981.

At that meeting, the Central Committee appointed as Director of Publicity and Information, Ahmed Gora Ebrahim, who was to combine this post with that of representative in Zimbabwe. During his tenure as head of the Department of Publicity and Information, Ebrahim failed to produce a single issue of the PAC journals, *Azania News* and *The Africanist*. He failed, too, at crucial times to issue press releases stating the position of the PAC on various political developments in South Africa, for example, the strikes by Black workers, the 'independence of the Ciskei Bantustan', and other issues on which the organisation should have pronounced itself. Although he participated in an International Seminar in East Berlin in August 1981 on 'The Role of the Mass Media in the Struggle Against Apartheid', he failed to prepare a substantive paper setting forth the PAC position on the subject and the programme of the PAC in the area of publicity and information to counter the propaganda of the South African regime and a part of its general programme of politicisation of the people in South Africa. This was a glaring omission in view of the disclosures of the expenditure by the South African regime of millions of dollars in an effort to sell its racial policies internationally. The 'Muldergate Scandal' involving the unauthorised use of state funds to set up a number of 'secret projects', including the establishment of an English-language newspaper in South Africa (*The Citizen*) and the attempts to purchase the *Washington Star* in the USA, led to an exposure of Pretoria's international propaganda effort, aimed partially at undermining the national liberation movements, as well as the dismissal of the Minister of Information, Dr. Connie Mulder, and the resignation in disgrace of B.J. Vorster as State President. Ebrahim did not even address the matter. The ANC, on the other hand, submitted a paper (quite apart from a general statement) entitled, 'South Africa's Propaganda War', which subsequently became part of the UN documents, together with the documents of the Seminar which was sponsored by the UN Special Committee Against Apartheid.

ANC publications are produced regularly and distributed internationally. It is no exaggeration to say that copies of the ANC journal, *Sechaba*, are available at numerous bookstores in various parts of the world, and also in university libraries throughout the world as well as at international conferences and seminars. Recently, the ANC has begun to publish a weekly digest of press reports from the South African newspapers. The ANC also produces a 'Solidarity Kit', containing information about South Africa and its apartheid policies, about the ANC and the liberation struggle; it also produces information packages, including photographs of their leaders imprisoned on Robben Island. ANC publications are also infiltrated into South Africa, where they are, of course, most needed. The South African media have been reporting for a number of years now, and almost with monotonous regularity, the discovery of ANC publications by the regime's security police. A number of individuals in South Africa have confirmed to this writer that there is an abundance of ANC literature in circulation in the country.[39]

The PAC does not have the resources to match the ANC, nor the extensive international contacts. But the PAC, if properly organised, could have established and maintained an information service which could have concentrated on the regular publication of accurate information and analyses of political developments in the liberation struggle.

Apart from publications, the ANC has radio broadcasting facilities in a number of African countries from which regular radio programmes are beamed at South Africa. The PAC, on the other hand, only has such facilities in Dar-es-Salaam from where the personnel of the Department of Publicity and Information broadcast, but there has been no feedback from people in South Africa as to the reception.

The ANC has recognised the visual impact of film and has also begun to use that medium. On 10 August 1983 the Zimbabwe Broadcasting Corporation TV screened an ANC documentary entitled, 'The Sun Will Rise', which highlights the ANC activities in South Africa and focuses upon

276 The Crisis in the PAC: 1978–83

recent political trials of its freedom-fighters sentenced to death or to long terms of imprisonment for high treason. The strength of the documentary lies in the interviews conducted with the families (in South Africa) of the ANC freedom-fighters who have been hanged (like the mother of Solomon Mahlangu who was hanged on 6 April 1979) or sentenced to long prison terms.

An ANC cultural group, the Amandla Cultural Group, performs in different countries in Africa and Europe, conveying the ANC message while raising funds for the organisation. In this way, too, the ANC is able to draw upon the various talents within the movement and also to appeal to a different audience in different parts of the world. Persons who might not attend a political rally might be persuaded to attend a cultural performance.

This writer, during his tenure in the PAC leadership, repeatedly emphasised the importance of and need for a viable and strong Department of Publicity and Information. The writer not only raised funds for the organisation's Publicity Department, but also produced a publication, *Azania Today*, and publicity materials such as automobile bumper stickers, PAC T-shirts and posters and buttons. The writer also prepared a film proposal, with a view to producing a documentary about the PAC. The film proposal was submitted to Unesco for consideration. A film crew, comprising Canadians who have been involved in liberation support work, was also assembled. The Central Committee paid lip service to the projects; rather than encourage or support such efforts, there was instead much petty envy and back-biting. These projects were abandoned when the writer resigned from the Central Committee.

In May 1981, following negotiations made by this writer with Unesco, the latter agreed to purchase a printing press for the PAC as well as train four of its students in research and writing. Ebrahim, who was the Director of Publicity and Information at that time, failed to follow through on the negotiations. It is, therefore, not as though opportunities do not exist for the situation to be remedied, but the problem exists in the lack of organisation within the PAC.

After the assumption of the Directorship in the Department of Publicity and Information by Edwin Makoti in December 1981 several issues of *Azania News* appeared in 1982. But that was merely another example of the proverbial new broom sweeping clean; the Department very quickly lapsed into its former state of non-productivity.

There have been two responses from the PAC to the massive publicity which the ANC has enjoyed in the media in South Africa and internationally in recent years. The first response has been the mechanical repetition of what Sobukwe said in 1960 in response to a question about support for the PAC among the oppressed people in South Africa. He said: 'No press has built us, no press can destroy us!' What Sobukwe said in 1960, however, was not meant to be a sterile response to camouflage non-performance.

The second response has been that the PAC is the victim of a massive conspiracy, by both the left and the right, to deny both the existence and the functioning of the PAC in South Africa and internationally. The argument is that the South African regime is prepared to promote the ANC by giving credit to that organisation for all political activity in the country, because of its 'moderate' outlook. Because it is a 'moderate' organisation, the argument goes, the ANC is not committed to the prosecution of a protracted armed struggle and the socialist transformation of South African society after the seizure of political power, but simply engages in 'military adventures' aimed at extracting concessions from the regime or alternatively, of pressurising the regime into convening a 'national convention' for the purpose of drawing up a new constitution for the country. The establishment media in South Africa and internationally, this argument goes, support the ANC precisely because of its 'moderate' outlook which does not threaten the status quo and the vested capitalist interests. On the other hand, the PAC, because of its 'radicalism', is a mortal enemy which has to be destroyed, 'by any means necessary'.

The second leg of this argument is that the PAC is despised by the Soviet Union and its allies because of its fierce political independence. By this argument, the ANC is favoured by the Soviet Union and its allies as well as Soviet-aligned organisations throughout the world because it is manipulable. This would cast the ANC in the mould of 'Communist tool', which, ironically, is the portrait that the South African regime as well as many Western governments, especially the USA, paints of *all* national liberation movements in Southern Africa.

Whilst it is true that the South African regime attempts to portray all Black resistance in South Africa as being centred in a single organisation, rather than being diffuse, this has to be seen in terms of its own security and political objectives. By portraying the ANC as the single most important 'Soviet-sponsored threat', it aims to rally the White populace behind the regime and at the same time to justify the massive defence expenditure. At the same time, the South African regime seeks to exploit the ANC's alliance with the South African Communist Party and its support by the Soviet Union in an attempt to corroborate its propaganda in the West that it is a bulwark against Communist expansion in Southern Africa. With the cold war rhetoric that is being refuelled, particularly in Washington, which views all situations, particularly that in Southern Africa, in terms of the global struggle between the superpowers, Pretoria's 'concerns' about 'Soviet expansionism' are greeted with sympathy. The Reagan Administration, for example, introduced, and South Africa quickly supported, the argument that any negotiated settlement of the Namibian question must be linked with the withdrawal of Cuban troops from Angola. In March 1982 the South African regime collaborated extensively with the US Senate Sub-Committee on Security and Terrorism, in the hearings held in

278   *The Crisis in the PAC: 1978–83*

Washington, D.C., aimed at showing the extent of 'Communist control' of the ANC and SWAPO.

Another response of the PAC to the extensive publicity given to the ANC is to draw an analogy with the situation in Zimbabwe where ZAPU, which had Soviet support, was portrayed by the Soviet Union, its allies, as well as by Soviet-aligned Communist parties in many parts of the world as the 'authentic' national liberation movement. ZANU was termed 'racist' and 'splittist' and denied political and material support. When, however, free and fair elections were held in Zimbabwe, following the Lancaster House Agreement, ZANU-PF, under the leadership of Robert Mugabe, won a majority of votes at the polls.

The implication of this argument is that if a similar exercise were to be conducted in South Africa soon, the PAC would emerge victorious. Of course, there is a world of difference between ZANU-PF and the PAC. The freedom-fighters of ZANU-PF established a visible military presence on the ground in Zimbabwe and established the primacy of that national liberation movement in the liberation struggle. At the same time, ZANU-PF was both *organised* and *serious*, a fact that was recognised even by the White minority regime of Ian Smith. It was a combination of the organisational infrastructure established by ZANU-PF inside the country, and the successful prosecution of the armed struggle which accounted for the success of ZANU-PF at the polls in March 1980.

Diplomatic Bungling: Another area in which the PAC has demonstrated ineptitude has been in its external relations and diplomatic efforts. In the previous chapter we examined the problems which the organisation experienced as a result of the lack of co-ordination and consultation among its various officers, which was exacerbated by the factionalism within the Central Committee as a result of which virtually two sets of foreign relations were conducted, one supervised by Make and the other by the Director of Foreign Affairs.

Upon the accession to power of Pokela, the problems were compounded as a result of the individuals around him offering advice largely in pursuit of their personal interests. There was no reference to previous negotiations or established relations: instead, the theme was, 'We are starting from scratch'. An excellent example was the attempt by the Central Committee to normalise relations with Zambia from which the PAC has been banned since 1968. For several years, the Central Committee explored the possibility of having the ban abrogated: to this end, representations were made to the Government and the ruling United National Independence Party (UNIP) at various levels. Much of the effort can be described as 'quiet diplomacy', because of the sensitivity of the matter. Ultimately, in July 1980 a PAC Central Committee delegation comprising the then Chairman, Vus Make, and Administrative Secretary, D.D. Mantshontsho, visited Lusaka for discussions with

John Nyati Pokela: Saviour of the PAC? 279

Government and UNIP officials. A report would be presented to President Kaunda, the PAC delegation was informed, after which the Zambian Government's decision would be conveyed to the PAC.

When Pokela was appointed to the chairmanship, he was advised to make representations to the Government and ruling party in Zambia for the ban on PAC to be lifted. This was done without reference to the negotiations that had been conducted over several years.[40] Not surprisingly, the response of the Zambian Government to Pokela's memorandum was negative; at the OAU Council of Ministers in Nairobi in June 1981 Zambia was one of the countries that warned the PAC that it was high time the organisation solved its 'internal problems' and 'got on with the job'.

During a visit to Iraq in June 1981 Pokela openly expressed support for Iraq in the conflict with Iran, whereas the position of the PAC as a national liberation movement had been and ought to have remained one of neutrality between two member states of the Movement of Non-Aligned Countries. Shortly after the outbreak of hostilities between the two countries, when the Iraqi Ambassador to Tanzania requested a statement of solidarity from the PAC (in return for which he indicated that the financial assistance which the PAC delegation to Baghdad in January that same year had requested would be released immediately), this writer in his capacity as Director of Foreign Affairs, advised the then Director of Finance, Erret Radebe, not to bind the PAC to a position which might harm the long-term interests of the organisation since sections of the opposition forces in Iran supported the national liberation struggle in South Africa and the PAC. Many sections of Iranian society, as well as the exiled opposition to the Ayatollah Khomeini, opposed the Iran–Iraqi war on the grounds that the war was not in the interests of the peoples of both countries.

The position of supporting Iraq was pure opportunism and was prompted by prospects of financial aid, which was why also Pokela was advised to undertake a mission to Iraq at that time and, as it turned out, jeopardised his full participation in the OAU Summit of Heads of State and Government in Nairobi.[41] Pokela is unknown in Africa and the Summit would have been an opportunity to meet the Heads of State and Government of the independent African countries. Due to a combination of circumstances, including being delayed at the Kenyan border with Tanzania for two days, Pokela was only at the Summit for two days; his presence did not have the impact that it could or should have had if he had been able to attend the Summit from the very outset. The Presidents of the ANC and SWAPO, Oliver Tambo and Sam Nujoma, were received with the Heads of State when they arrived in Nairobi; Pokela, on the other hand, slipped into Nairobi unnoticed, having been driven from the border with Tanzania by local taxi.

In March 1982 a tour of seven West African states by a PAC delegation, led by Pokela personally, had to be cancelled because, after the

280 The Crisis in the PAC: 1978–83

Director of Foreign Affairs had finalised the itinerary, it was learned that the PAC external headquarters in Dar-es-Salaam had simultaneously organised a visit to the Middle East for Pokela.

The latter is an illustration of the chaos at the PAC external headquarters with the right hand not knowing what the left hand does. It is also an indication of the manner in which the PAC, under the influence of individuals like the ambitious Gora Ebrahim, exploiting the naivete of Pokela and others, has pursued petro-dollars in the Middle East. Yet, a constant complaint in OAU circles is that Afro-Arab co-operation has not resulted in billions of petro-dollars and part of the wealth of the Arab oil-producing countries trickling down to the independent African countries or to the national liberation movements in Southern Africa. Three oil-producing countries that have good records in terms of assistance to independent African countries as well as national liberation movements are Algeria, Iraq and Libya.

The diplomatic blunders made by Pokela were due to his inexperience, which was exploited by careerists jockeying for positions and influence. Soon after he assumed the chairmanship Pokela imagined that the hostility of certain countries toward the PAC, and the international diplomatic isolation of the organisation, would disappear simply because he had taken over the helm, coming as he did only recently from Robben Island. During a tour of the USA in October 1981 in interviews with several journalists, he repeatedly said, 'The PAC is now back on the international scene', as though it had been absent until his arrival, until this writer pointed out to him that even during the worst crisis in 1979, the Central Committee maintained its diplomatic efforts, as a result of which the organisation was not de-recognised. It was, therefore incorrect to say that 'The PAC is now back on the international scene'. But that was what he had been led to believe by some of the elements by whom he was surrounded. Similarly, in a meeting in New York with the Zimbabwean Foreign Minister in October 1981, in reply to a question by the Foreign Minister about the state of the PAC's relations with Mozambique, Pokela replied that relations were 'not good', but he planned to go to Maputo to sort the matter out. With a chuckle, the Foreign Minister replied: 'Come, come, Mr. President, you are being modest. There are no relations with Mozambique and if you go there you will be locked up.' But Pokela believed, or was led to believe, that the attitude of Mozambique towards the PAC would be changed by a visit from him. His inexperience, coupled with his enthusiasm about 'orienting PAC members homeward', the difficulty of which he did not fully grasp, were exploited by the innumerable 'advisers' and 'confidantes' by whom he was surrounded during his first year abroad. It is for this reason that this writer has pointed out that Pokela faced enormous difficulties. Some of the mistakes he made during the first difficult months of his leadership have to be viewed in this light.

The PAC in Zimbabwe: Zimbabwe is one country in Southern Africa which has special significance for the PAC in view of the long-standing and fraternal relations that have existed between ZANU-PF and the PAC. The two liberation movements were not within the alliance of Soviet-supported organisations, hence were subjected to a campaign of diplomatic isolation by the Soviet Union and the Eastern Bloc generally, as well as by Soviet-aligned Communist parties and other organisations in numerous countries.

At independence in April 1980, however, ZANU-PF found the PAC in a state of disarray, or 'falling to pieces', in the words of a Zimbabwean friend of long-standing. While it was obvious from the outset that the Government of the newly-independent Zimbabwe, under the leadership of Prime Minister Mugabe, would not be in a position to offer the national liberation movements from South Africa and Namibia anything other than moral and diplomatic support, it was also very obvious that even if the Government had been in a position to do so, the PAC would not have been in a position to utilise such support. A parallel with this situation would have been the disarray within ZAPU in 1972 when the Mozambican liberation movement, FRELIMO, invited the freedom-fighters of that organisation to infiltrate into Zimbabwe through the operational front in the Tete Province of Mozambique, opened by the Mozambican freedom-fighters during their struggle against the Portuguese. ZAPU, however, was unable to accept the offer made by FRELIMO because of the serious internal problems which were being experienced by that organisation.[42] FRELIMO then made the offer to the freedom-fighters of ZANU-PF who were able to exploit the opportunity to the full. The logistic support provided by FRELIMO for the freedom-fighters of ZANU-PF both before and after the independence of Mozambique, was crucial to the success of the armed liberation struggle in Zimbabwe. It also created a firm alliance between FRELIMO and ZANU-PF, which was cemented by the independence of the two countries for which the two had waged protracted struggles. It was a lesson that was lost on the PAC.

The PAC appointed as its representative to Zimbabwe, Ahmed Gora Ebrahim, in the second half of 1980, even though the newly-independent country had not officially invited the national liberation movements to send representatives or open offices there. There were and still are numerous problems with which the Government and ZANU-PF have had to contend and it cannot jeopardise the independence of Zimbabwe by adopting a confrontationist attitude towards the South African regime by offering military facilities to the ANC and PAC.

During his term of office as a representative in Zimbabwe, Ebrahim was a failure. He made no impact at all. During visits to Zimbabwe by this writer in July 1981 and again in December 1981 as well as January and May 1982, it was very clear from the discussions with a wide range of people, both in and out of government, including ministers, civil

282 *The Crisis in the PAC: 1978–83*

servants and academics, that the PAC was unknown at the mass level in Zimbabwe. On the contrary, the ANC was well-known and received much publicity in the media. This was partially explained by an official of the Zimbabwe Broadcasting Corporation (ZBC) who pointed out to this writer that the ZBC regularly received press releases, statements and general information from the ANC. They received no information from the PAC.[43] During the time that he was in Zimbabwe as the PAC representative, Ebrahim had not given them statements or any materials which they could use. Consequently, the impression might be conveyed that the ZBC was partial to the ANC, whereas it is committed to supporting both the ANC and PAC. An experienced newspaper editor expressed the view to this writer that while the PAC had to be 'begged for information', his newspaper received literally reams of information from the ANC in the form of press releases, telex messages, general news updates and personal visits from ANC spokespersons.

The media in Zimbabwe are very supportive of and sympathetic to the national liberation movements in South Africa and Namibia. Extensive coverage is given to the activities of the ANC, PAC and SWAPO. Ebrahim failed, during his tenure as representative in Zimbabwe, to utilise the opportunities available to publicise the PAC, especially since he was not only the representative but subsequently also the Director of Publicity and Information.

In their choice of a representative to Zimbabwe, the ANC were astute. They appointed Joe Gqabi, a veteran of the liberation struggle who had received his military training in China, like many ZANU-PF freedom-fighters. In addition, he had not been involved in any of the enmity and hostility between sections of ZANU-PF and the ANC, as a result of the alliance between the ANC and ZAPU. (Gqabi had been incarcerated on Robben Island for ten years and had fled the country in the late 1970s after his acquittal on charges of treason in South Africa.) The tragic assassination of Gqabi, suspected to have been done by South African agents, in Zimbabwe in August 1981 also had the effect of boosting the ANC further in that country.

The activities of the PAC, on the other hand, have had the effect of causing acute embarrassment to ZANU-PF and the Government of Zimbabwe. In June 1981 Enoch Zulu (alias John Mvelase), the PAC Director of Operations, while on a visit to Zimbabwe, was arrested for illegally trying to import Zimbabwean currency which he could only have secured from Zimbabweans who had fled the country. He was convicted and declared a prohibited immigrant.

In December 1981 two APLA cadres were arrested in Zimbabwe in possession of a sizeable quantity of arms and ammunition which they had purchased from dissidents. The incident had serious implications for national security, not only in view of the quantity and the source, but also the unsophisticated manner in which the transaction was handled. A cable had been despatched to one of the cadres in Botswana instructing him to come to Zimbabwe 'to fetch eggs'. In view of the abundance of eggs in Botswana, it can logically be assumed that any person or persons seeing such a message would immediately be suspicious. The incident also illustrates the rather disturbing practice among PAC leaders and activists of conducting the organisation's affairs through the public communications systems, such as telephones and telegrams. Moreover, a diplomat in Harare was informed by Gora Ebrahim that the PAC was 'ready to purchase arms from ZIPRA forces in Bulawayo'.[44] It is difficult to fathom why a foreign diplomat was informed of such an intention. In view of the PAC's relations with the Government and ZANU-PF and especially being aware of the threats to national security faced by the government of Prime Minister Mugabe, it was very imprudent on the part of the PAC to have entered into the transaction in the first place and secondly, to have trumpeted such information on the diplomatic circuit. This writer raised these issues in a letter addressed to Pokela on 18 December 1981 after learning the full details of the incident and after being questioned by the foreign diplomat. Pokela did not provide any explanation; neither was the matter ever discussed by the Central Committee, nor was Gora Ebrahim censured.

The incident has been described here because it demonstrates the lengths to which Ebrahim was prepared to go in his quest for power and influence. He served as the PAC representative in Zimbabwe for more than a year; he was fully aware of the problems faced by the new government, particularly the security problems, evidenced by the sabotage by South African agents of an arms and ammunition depot outside Harare and the subsequent escape to South Africa by the two agents involved in the sabotage; the assassination of Joe Gqabi in August 1981 following an earlier attempt on his life in March 1981; the confessions by two former Central Intelligence Organisation (CIO) officers of their involvement in a South African spy ring in Zimbabwe; the repeated public statements by various Zimbabwean officials, including the Prime Minister, that the South African regime was training dissidents to carry out acts of sabotage in Zimbabwe to destabilise the country. Ebrahim and other PAC Central Committee members were aware of these problems. They were aware, too, of the diplomatic support provided by the Government of Prime Minister Mugabe to the PAC in the OAU and other forums, support which was crucial in countering the attempts to have the PAC de-recognised by the OAU. At the OAU Council of Ministers and Summit of Heads of State in Nairobi in June 1981, for instance, of all the front-line states, only Botswana and Zimbabwe supported the continued recognition of the PAC when other delegations lobbied during the informal discussions for its de-recognition. Yet, the PAC entered into and concluded transactions with persons involved in plans to overthrow the government of Zimbabwe. A matter of such magnitude was not even discussed by the PAC Central Committee nor were disciplinary measures taken against the individuals involved.

284   *The Crisis in the PAC: 1978–83*

The tendency on the part of the PAC is to take for granted its historical relations with ZANU-PF. But, as has already been pointed out, FRELIMO supported ZANU-PF even though FRELIMO had had a political alliance with ZAPU. The Mozambican government has argued that its support for ZANU-PF was principled; the freedom-fighters of Zimbabwe *earned* the support of FRELIMO *because they were involved in armed struggle*. They have urged the government of Zimbabwe and ZANU-PF to adopt the same principle vis-a-vis the ANC and PAC, that is, they should support the ANC because 'the ANC is fighting'. It is a convincing argument and cannot be dismissed; the only way in which the PAC can counter the argument is by being identified with the political and military struggles taking place in South Africa.[45]

Military Functions

It has already been explained that as a result of the internal problems experienced by the PAC between 1978 and 1981, the organisation's military programme was immobilised. In the period between December 1978 and December 1981 not a single PAC freedom-fighter was either infiltrated into South Africa or captured by the regime's security forces. A further problem was caused by the ban placed by the Tanzanian authorities in February 1979 on the entry into Tanzania of any new recruits; this had the effect of seriously hampering the PAC's recruitment efforts, since Tanzania is the only country where PAC freedom-fighters have sanctuary.

At the bush camp in Ithumbi, the militarily-trained cadres continued to reject the leadership and authority of the PAC Central Committee even after the accession to power of Pokela. On 8 March 1981 a delegation of three militarily-trained cadres from the camp travelled to Dar-es-Salaam to the PAC office. Their mission was to inform the Central Committee that the militarily-trained cadres at the camp no longer regarded themselves as PAC members; they continued, however, to occupy the camp in Ithumbi, which is a PAC facility.

As a result of the stalemate at the camp, a situation in which the Central Committee was powerless, there were negative reports from the Executive Secretary of the OAU Liberation Committee about the 'continued crisis in the PAC', at the meeting of the Liberation Committee in Arusha in June 1981. In addition, the Assistant Secretary-General of the OAU, Dr. Peter Onu, in his opening address to the meeting of the Liberation Committee, also made negative references to the 'internal problems' of the PAC. He went on to say that the only way in which the PAC could justify the support which it receives from Africa is by being seen to be 'doing something', by which he meant, fighting the enemy.

The militarily-trained cadres who were removed the previous year from the camp in Ithumbi to another camp at Mgagao pending deportation from Tanzania also rejected any rapprochement initiated by Pokela. They wrote letters to Pokela telling him that he was 'out of order', and that he merely echoed the Central Committee.[46] These letters were circulated to embassies in Dar-es-Salaam as well as to the Executive Secretary of the OAU Liberation Committee. From the latter they also requested agricultural implements, tobacco and financial assistance.

Clearly, as long as the situation at the camp in Ithumbi was not resolved, the PAC could not be taken seriously.

The APLA Task Force, charged with the responsibilities of re-organising the PAC's military wing, presented to the Central Committee in July 1981 proposals for the re-occupation of the camp at Ithumbi and the establishment of the political authority of the Central Committee. This entailed the Central Committee directing an operation in which the camp would be occupied by militarily-trained cadres loyal to the leadership, and a military headquarters and a leadership structure or camp administration established there.

The take-over was successful and was completed without any violence or loss of life. When challenged by the contingent of militarily-trained cadres who recognised the political authority of the Central Committee, the recalcitrant cadres at the camp succumbed. The majority of them chose to leave the camp and sought refugee status in Tanzania; a small number remained after indicating that they were prepared to accept the leadership of the Central Committee.

At the Central Committee meeting in July 1981 there was tremendous dissatisfaction with the performance of the Department of Defence. It was clear to the Central Committee that that department had neither a programme that it was implementing, nor a progress report to make. While it was clear that the problems of the past few years had greatly impeded the work of the Department of Defence, members felt that they were entitled to be taken into confidence by the military leadership. Grave dissatisfaction was expressed by a number of Central Committee members, particularly Make, Muendane and Mgweba about the lack of results on the ground. The former Secretary for Defence, Edwin Makoti, responded by saying that the Central Committee members failed to appreciate the problems that were experienced by the military wing and then proceeded to say that it is the 'leadership in the [home] country' which would decide 'when to shoot'.

It was very clear that the Department of Defence had nothing to report because it was doing nothing inside the country. Various military leaders in the PAC have always succeeded in camouflaging their non-performance by invoking 'reasons of security'. Matters relating to the department are alleged to be 'sensitive' and cannot be disclosed to the Central Committee, except in barest outline, simply to assure the Central Committee that 'the work is progressing', in the words of the Director of Operations, Enoch Zulu. Meanwhile, they failed to establish any contact with the resistance inside the country.

286 *The Crisis in the PAC: 1978–83*

Dissatisfaction with the performance of the Secretary for Defence climaxed in 1981, as a result of which he was replaced by a younger man whose experience includes being captured in November 1978 and detained for two years by the Transkei's security forces. There is as yet, no evidence that under his direction the PAC's military wing has been reactivated, or that the organisation has a military programme.

Social Services Functions

A national liberation movement also has to provide social services not only for the people who have fled their home country and have joined the movement, but also for the people still subject to political oppression and economic exploitation. These services include health care and medical services, training and skills development, most commonly in the form of educational and vocational training. In the home country, there is need to provide also for the families and dependents of political prisoners and detainees. In the case of the PAC, this aspect of the functions and responsibilities of the organisation was largely neglected; the first generation of exiles frequently relate the tales of the difficulties that they experienced after they left South Africa and arrived in the independent African states. Many of the problems were not of the organisation's making: firstly, there was the general inexperience of guerrilla warfare and the necessary support organisation and functions involved. Many of the early exiles thought that all that was required was to acquire certain basic military skills and then march back to fight. It was only after frustrating experiences that many resigned themselves to the fact that their sojourn outside of their home country would not be a short one. Secondly, there were the high expectations which many of the early exiles had: rightly, or wrongly, there was a belief that upon setting foot in the independent states of Africa, all doors would be open to them. In the words of a UN specialist, many South Africans 'left because they imagined, rightly or wrongly, that the rest of independent Africa was anxiously waiting to offer them whatever assistance they required'.[47] They discovered the realities in due course.

It was only in the 1970s that the PAC paid serious attention to the provision of social services for its members; then, too, it was prompted by the crisis the organisation faced after the Soweto uprising of 1976 when there was a sudden exodus of young people from South Africa, swelling the ranks of the national liberation movements. The PAC was organisationally ill-equipped to cope with the contingency, a fact that exacerbated the crisis that led to the physical clashes between the Leballo and Ntantala factions. The PAC residences in Dar-es-Salaam and environs were over-crowded; the new recruits were accommodated in the cheap hotels of Dar-es-Salaam for months, without any programmes while the leaders tried to secure facilities for military training in Africa and elsewhere. Illness (like the dreaded malaria), boredom, frustration and manipulation by the leaders of the two factions created an explosive situation.

In 1977 the Tanzanian Government made available to the PAC land at Pongwe in the Bagamoyo district to establish a transit centre. Since the settlement had been abandoned by missionaries, there were several buildings in various stages of dilapidation. With pledges of assistance from the UN specialised agencies, supplemented by financial aid from governments and non-governmental organisations, the PAC planned, or said it planned, to establish a centre where the people who had fled from the repression of apartheid would have sanctuary, where they would engage in various activities aimed at fostering self-reliance and at the same time, be provided with the opportunity to manage an organised community with the attendant social services, as well as develop care for the environment.

With promises of support from the government of Sudan, a number of other countries like the Scandinavian countries and The Netherlands, and Unesco, the PAC also announced plans to establish a 'June 16 Azania Institute' in Khartoum, which would be an academic institution and (later also) a military academy. After numerous delays, a feasibility study sponsored by Unesco was actually conducted for the PAC by an educational planner from the university of Dar-es-Salaam and this writer in April 1979 and the report submitted to the Central Committee, Unesco, the UNDP and the Sudanese Government.

Four years later, at its meeting in December 1981 the Central Committee decided formally to abandon the idea of establishing the 'June 16 Azania Institute', without the project ever having got off the ground. The abandonment of the project was necessitated by a lack of progress related to the internal problems of the PAC, and by political developments in Sudan. In the feasibility study, questions were raised about the problems which might be experienced by South Africans having to adjust in the completely different cultural, religious and geographic climate of Sudan. This concern was shared by several experts, including experts from Unesco. Initially, the Central Committee, especially under Make's leadership, was determined to proceed with the project because it 'was a political decision', and the Sudanese President was 'personally committed' to it.

Four years later, the UNDP invited several other UN specialised agencies, the Tanzanian Government, the OAU Liberation Committee and the national liberation movements from Namibia and South Africa to a meeting in Dar-es-Salaam from 7 to 11 December 1981, on the 'Evaluation and Programming of UNDP Assistance to the African National Liberation Movements Recognised by the OAU'. Prior to the meeting a team of UN experts visited the African front-line states to assess the progress that was made in the projects of the national liberation movements which received assistance from the UNDP and other UN agencies, and to assess their future needs in terms of their priorities.

It was clear both from the report of the team of experts and also from the discussions during the meeting that of all the national liberation

288 *The Crisis in the PAC: 1978–83*

movements in Southern Africa, the PAC had shown the least progress in the projects that were being supported by the UN agencies. However, the report of the team of experts who visited the transit centre at Pongwe prior to the meeting was charitable in its analysis of the causes of the problems experienced in the implementation of the project:

> This project is running into serious difficulties because of poor Agency backstopping (Habitat), lack of initial Inter-Agency planning (Habitat-FAO), complicated further by a change in the nature of the project site (from a transit camp to a permanent one) poor assessment of the resources endowment of site, bad access road where work cannot be pursued because of lack of equipment (additional truck, a tractor and a grader).[48]

Mfanayasekaya Pearce Gqobose, who in April 1981 was appointed co-ordinator of all PAC self-help projects, with immediate responsibility for the administration of the transit centre, was more honest in his analysis of the problems. In a report that he prepared in November 1981 he pointed out that apart from the UNDP and other UN agencies, the PAC had received financial aid and material assistance from a number of governments, notably, the Tanzanian Government, the Norwegian and Netherlands Governments, and non-governmental organisations in Tanzania, Switzerland, Australia, New Zealand and Canada. There was, however, little to show for all the support which the organisation had received, a fact that he attributed to the internal problems of the previous four years: 'Owing to internal difficulties within the PAC over the years, the developmental work in Bagamoyo has been a disappointment.'[49] Gqobose analysed in detail the causes of the failure:

> The question of work and self-reliance has become a problem. Our projects are supposed to be based on self-reliance but in practice this is not so. The donor agencies who were given this impression are disappointed by our poor performance. Several threats have come from them to the effect that funds donated to the PAC may be switched to other movements whose performance is said to be better than ours.
>
> Several reasons for [this] state of affairs can be [enumerated]:
> 1. Bagamoyo has always been a transit centre. This is not conducive to the proper development of the place. No planning can be [done] if the population of the centre is in transit. A settled community is necessary.
> 2. The majority of PAC members now in Tanzania come from urban areas. They are, therefore, not [accustomed] to rural life. It will take some time with patient handling before they [can] do satisfactory work in a place like Bagamoyo.
> 3. Members in Bagamoyo complain that they have no work kits [like] overalls and boots. There is also talk of incentives. It has been

John Nyati Pokela: Saviour of the PAC? 289

explained that these will be provided when available. In any case these items are scarce if not unavailable in Tanzania. Nevertheless, it has been pointed out to the members that in self-reliance, we have to start from nothing to get something. Instances have been quoted such as the experiences of the Tabora group and the Mgagao group.[50] Above all, members of the office staff in Dar-es-Salaam go to work in Bagamoyo every week-end. The reasons advanced for not working can be regarded as an excuse.

4. Lack of proper ideological orientation is the reason behind refusing to engage in manual labour. The PAC must, through political study, persuade its members to appreciate self-reliance both as a principle and method of struggle in a liberation war. Understandably, it will take a long time before this lesson is understood but the [PAC] must persevere [in] it.

The reasons enumerated by Gqobose are illuminating. Firstly, the perception among many PAC members that manual work is not 'for urbanised people' like themselves reflects more upon the quality of some of the people who were attracted to the PAC than upon South African exiles generally. Moreover, it illustrates the need for proper screening and selection by the liberation movement, rather than simply recruiting able-bodied persons. South Africa has a large base population from which the liberation movements can draw, so such selection is possible. Also perhaps, in screening, the liberation movement must be *realistic* but *exacting*; in that way, it would attract high calibre membership which in turn would pull in others of such calibre. In the absence of such screening, the movement discourages the entry of talented leadership, perpetuating a mediocrity of leadership. There is a need in the PAC to break the cycle, to get a *quantum leap* to improved leadership, then attract new and old talent of real quality.

The ANC, for instance, has within its ranks many young persons from the urban areas in South Africa. Yet, they engage in manual labour on the ANC projects that are also aimed at making the exiled community of that organisation self-sufficient in food production. There are also PAC members in Tanzania from the urban areas in South Africa and who are not averse to manual labour; the groups to which Gqobose refers in his report as the 'Tabora' and 'Mgagao' groups, have among them persons from the urban areas, yet after they had been settled in those two areas of Tanzania (the former a refugee settlement, the latter a military camp where those awaiting deportation were kept), they immediately engaged in agricultural production and poultry-farming.

Secondly, it is difficult to see how individuals who claim that they cannot engage in manual labour because they are from the urban areas in South Africa can endure the rigours of life of guerrilla fighters, especially if, as the PAC leaders state, the organisation's strategy is one

290   *The Crisis in the PAC: 1978–83*

of waging guerrilla warfare first in the countryside. If the success of guerrilla warfare lies in the extent to which the guerrilla forces are integrated into the local populace so as to politicise and mobilise them, it is difficult to see how persons who do not believe that they can, or should, engage in manual labour because they are 'urbanised', will function successfully as freedom-fighters in the rural areas.

These criticisms notwithstanding, Gqobose's report indicated that creditable work was under progress at the transit centre.

From the foregoing discussion it is obvious that the problems of the PAC were not solved by the removal, first of Leballo and then of Make, as head of the organisation. In exactly the same way, it cannot be expected that Pokela will single-handedly 'save' the PAC. The revitalisation of the PAC and raising the level of its performance in South Africa and internationally, militarily, politically and diplomatically, mobilising the enthusiasm of the broad masses of the people within and without the movement, depends on the combined efforts of the leadership and the members. No individual can save an organisation, let alone one which has revolutionary pretensions. To say this is not to denigrate Pokela, or to belittle the role that he has already played and the great contribution he has made within a short time in effecting a certain degree of stability within the PAC.

Recent Developments in the PAC

More recent developments within the PAC, however, do raise questions as to whether Pokela has the *capacity* to provide the firm, decisive, revolutionary leadership that the PAC requires at this stage in its history and in the history of the South African liberation struggle. Some of the worst features of 'Leballoism' have already resurfaced during the past two years of his chairmanship, namely, factionalism and cliquism, scheming and manoeuvring, plots and intrigues among his top aides and close confidantes. That explains some of the appointments of representatives as well as Central Committee members in December 1981 for example.

Central Committee Meeting, December 1981
The PAC Central Committee met in Dar-es-Salaam in December 1981 under the chairmanship of Pokela. An inordinate amount of time was spent discussing trivia and deliberating about matters that could have been handled administratively. At the end of the meeting, it was clear that the PAC was no better than it had been during Leballo's regime. The Central Committee failed to address the crucial problems and fundamental questions confronting the PAC and the South African liberation struggle; instead, individuals were jockeying and manoeuvring for positions.

No Objective Assessment of Performance: The Department of Defence failed to present a substantive report to the Central Committee on its activities, or lack of activities, nor were the Secretary for Defence and Director of Operations called upon to account for the funds provided for the 'operations' of the department. The Director of Operations, in particular, had personally received US$67,000 in ten months yet had nothing to show for it. There was general dissatisfaction with the Defence Department; several Central Committee members who had concrete proof of the Director of Operations' dereliction and corruption failed to raise the matter in the meeting, but expressed their disquiet privately outside the meeting.

Similarly, the Director of Finance, of whom there was much criticism outside the meeting, failed to present a financial statement to the Central Committee but reported on two grants received by the organisation: a grant of US$45,000 from the World Council of Churches for Publicity and Information, and US$250,000 from the Nigerian Government. Consequently, the Central Committee had no idea of the organisation's financial status, which was precisely the case in January–February 1981.

The Director of Publicity and Information, Gora Ebrahim, had failed to produce a single issue of the PAC journals, *Azania News* and *The Africanist* since his appointment in January–February 1981. He had failed also as representative in Zimbabwe, a fact he did not challenge when the Director of Foreign Affairs presented his report.

This writer, in his capacity as Director of Foreign Affairs, presented a written report, 49 typed pages in length, outlining the activities of the Department of Foreign Affairs, including the PAC Observer Mission to the UN. The report analysed the progress and achievements, as well as pinpointing weaknesses, setbacks and failures. The report was accepted without amendment, except a minor detail that Gora Ebrahim had in fact attended a state dinner during a visit to Zimbabwe by President Kenneth Kaunda of Zambia. The report contained criticisms of Ebrahim's performance as representative in Zimbabwe and recommended that he return to the PAC external headquarters to run the Department of Publicity and Information. The report contained detailed recommendations and suggestions not only for the Department of Foreign Affairs but also other departments. All the recommendations and suggestions were adopted.

Following the adoption of the Director of Foreign Affair's report, the Administrative Secretary, Joe Mkwanazi, tabled a report on a visit to the USA and Canada, by a delegation comprising Nyati Pokela, Mkwanazi, Hamilton Keke, Enoch Zulu and Junior Majova. During the visit, from 3 to 31 October 1981, the delegation visited New York, California, Washington, D.C., West Virginia, Toronto, Montreal and Ottawa. They met African Foreign Ministers, Ambassadors, the former UN Secretary-General, Dr. Kurt Waldheim, representatives of liberation support

292 The Crisis in the PAC: 1978–83

organisations, American and Canadian legislators and policy-makers, and were interviewed by the media. They also met PAC members in the USA and Canada. Mkwanazi reported that '[The PAC Observer Mission to the UN] is big, well-equipped, well-organised and well-run'. He also reported that the Director of Foreign Affairs/Observer at the UN 'maintains contact with Ambassadors of friendly countries that support the PAC and also with solidarity organisations'. He also reported that the Director of Foreign Affairs handled the office administration as well as the diplomatic work alone, and observed that 'it [was] too much for one person'. During the delegation's visit to the USA and Canada, they were not accompanied to all the centres by this writer; they were accompanied in certain centres by the PAC's assistant representative in the USA, Puledi Shoba, who was based in California, and by the PAC's representative to Canada, Dan Mdluli, based in Toronto.

The delegation's observations about the volume and quality of work accomplished by this writer at the PAC Observer Mission to the UN contrasted strongly with a negative report made by Gora Ebrahim only five months earlier, after a few days in New York in March 1981, discussed above.

Violation of Earlier Central Committee Decisions: On the final day of the Central Committee meeting, the Chairman simply announced, without prior consultation with the Director of Foreign Affairs, a number of appointments of representatives. He announced appointments of representatives to Zimbabwe, Iraq, Syria, the UK, USA and the Caribbean, and the UN. This writer protested, pointing out that this was a deviation from decisions made at Arusha in 1978 and later re-affirmed. The writer also pointed out that the Central Committee had adopted his report encompassing the work of the Department of Foreign Affairs which pointed out that Gora Ebrahim failed in two previous posts — as representative to Zimbabwe and as Director of Publicity and Information. Yet he was being appointed Observer Representative to the UN, which was in fact a promotion. Ebrahim who was present at the meeting said nothing.

This writer also opposed the appointment of Mafole to the position of Chief Representative to the USA and the Caribbean on the grounds of his incompetence. It was an objective assessment based on his performance at the PAC Observer Mission to the UN for almost twelve months. Ngila Muendane also opposed Mafole's appointment. On the contrary, Enoch Zulu, supported Mafole's appointment. Zulu said Mafole 'is an old [PAC] cadre and is disciplined'. Whether or not he was competent was immaterial. Six months before Mafole's appointment, he was regarded even by Pokela as being 'erratic'.

Decisions Made Outside the Central Committee Meeting: It was clear that the opposition of individuals like Muendane and this writer were ignored because the decisions had already been taken outside the Central Committee meeting and were simply brought to the Central Committee to be rubber-stamped, a fact that this writer emphasised at the meeting. The Central Committee decisions were foreshadowed in the Johannesburg *Star* (2 and 9 November 1981). A correspondent of the Argus Africa News Service, in a despatch from Harare, Zimbabwe, reported on a reshuffle in the PAC leadership, a reshuffle that would be effected at the Central Committee meeting in December 1981. When Muendane and this writer questioned the source of the reporter's information, information that was correct, as the decisions of the Central Committee meeting illustrated, Enoch Zulu hastily replied in defence of Gora Ebrahim, even though nobody in the meeting accused Ebrahim of the leak to the press. Zulu said that the newspaper report was designed to 'raise suspicions about Comrade Gora [Ebrahim] as he is the person based in Zimbabwe'. It would have been easy for the Central Committee, if it so wished, to investigate the leak because the newspaper report emanated from Harare. But the Central Committee did not. In May 1982 the correspondent of the Argus Africa News Service confirmed to this writer that Gora Ebrahim provided the information about the changes to be effected in the PAC Central Committee at a luncheon meeting he had with Ebrahim in Harare at the end of October 1981.

All Heads of Departments to be Based in Dar-es-Salaam: The Central Committee decided at its December 1981 meeting that all heads of departments should be based at the PAC external headquarters, a decision rationalised on the grounds that that would facilitate consultation and co-ordination. At that time there were three heads of departments based away from external headquarters, namely Ngila Muendane, the Director of Labour and Social Affairs, this writer as Director of Foreign Affairs, and Gora Ebrahim as Director of Publicity and Information. Despite the fact that the majority of the Central Committee members who headed departments were based in Dar-es-Salaam there was neither consultation nor co-ordination at the PAC external headquarters. Moreover, as both Muendane and this writer pointed out, there would be very few occasions when *all* heads of departments would be physically present in Dar-es-Salaam. The Central Committee members always travelled. The Director of Foreign Affairs, in particular, travelled incessantly. The reasons advanced by Pokela and Mkwanazi for the decision were spurious. The *real* reason for the decision was that the Pokela/Mkwanazi/Ebrahim faction was anxious to remove Muendane from his position as representative to the UK, not because of dissatisfaction with his performance, but because they believed that he was loyal to the former Chairman, Vus Make. They were concerned that since he had access to financial aid [for the PAC] from the International Defence and Aid Fund for Southern Africa (IDAF) and other sources, he would use such contacts to promote the interests of Make's faction.

294 *The Crisis in the PAC: 1978–83*

They were anxious to replace him with someone loyal to Pokela. At different times in 1981, Mkwanazi and Mgweba went behind Muendane's back to the IDAF and requested that organisation to transfer funds directly to the PAC external headquarters in Dar-es-Salaam rather than channel the financial aid through Muendane, the PAC's resident representative in the UK. This clumsy action harmed the PAC because it aroused speculation within IDAF circles about a struggle within the PAC for money.

Both Muendane and this writer supported and accepted the *principle* of the decision, but questioned and opposed the *motives*. The PAC's problems were more profound than the physical absence of two or three individuals from the organisation's headquarters. Moreover, the Pokela faction was determined to implement the decision without regard to an orderly transition. As far as they were concerned all heads of departments had to return to Dar-es-Salaam by the end of December 1981 — barely three weeks from the conclusion of the meeting. Yet the Central Committee was informed by this writer of certain projects which were in the process of implementation. The decisions and the implementation had not been thought through. It was only as a result of the writer insisting that he had to complete certain assignments he had already initiated, that the Central Committee decided that all heads of departments should relocate to Dar-es-Salaam by 1 March 1982.

Other Appointments Made in December 1981: The Central Committee made a number of important appointments at its meeting in December 1981.

Hamilton Keke was appointed to the Central Committee and appointed Chief Representative to the United Kingdom and the Continent, one of the key positions in the PAC's Department of Foreign Affairs. Keke had fled South Africa earlier that same year and had had no experience in diplomatic work. There was no discussion about his suitability for the post because, as has been indicated, the Pokela faction had already made the decisions outside the meeting and all debate and discussion at the meeting was purely procedural. As already noted, Hamilton Keke had been one of the defendants in the PAC 'Bethal 18 trial'. He had received a suspended sentence when all the other 16 defendants were sentenced to long terms of imprisonment.

Another important appointment was that of Sabelo Victor Gqweta as Secretary for Defence in the Central Committee. Gqweta had spent two years in detention in the Transkei from the time of his capture in November 1978 to the time of his flight from South Africa to Lesotho in 1980 after his release by the Transkeian security police. When he arrived in Tanzania, he was not interviewed by the Central Committee to determine whether his ordeal during detention had affected him

John Nyati Pokela: Saviour of the PAC? 295

adversely. Early in 1980, Sidzamba and other PAC members in Lesotho received a letter (written on newspaper), smuggled out of the Transkeian prison where Gqweta and other PAC members were detained. The letter had been written by one of the detainees. It stated that Gqweta had been tortured by the security police to the point of insanity. Sidzamba and the other PAC members in Lesotho were of the view that the letter was authentic; they despatched it to this writer in New York, after they had issued a press release drawing attention to the detention and torture of the PAC detainees in the Transkei. The Central Committee did not try to determine the veracity of the reports of torture, or whether the detainees had divulged any information under torture, information that might have incriminated PAC supporters in the Transkei or other parts of the country, or that might jeopardise future plans of the organisation. Instead, Gqweta was appointed to a crucial leadership position soon after joining the PAC external mission in Dar-es-Salaam.

The aim of these questions is not to cast aspersions, or to suggest that either Keke or Gqweta was suspect, but as a routine security measure, they should have first been debriefed before being given leadership responsibilities as they were given so soon after arrival in Tanzania. This is a further illustration of the absence of discussion at meetings of the Central Committee about the qualities or suitability of candidates nominated for top leadership positions. It is an illustration, also, of the failure of the PAC leadership to learn from the mistakes of the past, for example the case of Justice Nkonyane. The appointment of individuals to positions of leadership, even sensitive leadership positions, immediately or soon after arrival at the PAC external headquarters from 'the home front', is symptomatic of the casual attitude towards security within the PAC. Another instance of lack of security consciousness occurred in 1980 when Enoch Zulu, the Director of Operations, deployed an individual as a courier even after suspicions about the individual had been expressed by a number of persons. That person returned to South Africa in 1982; the PAC confirmed then that he was a security police agent because he exposed the efforts of the organisation, efforts of which he had learned through his association with Zulu.

The irony is that the PAC leaders and members rubbed their hands gleefully and chuckled in delight each time that the ANC was reported to have been infiltrated, as in the Craig Williamson spy scandal. But the PAC was equally vulnerable to infiltration. In 1979 and 1980, a number of ANC political prisoners (Muombaris, Jenkins and Lee) as well as freedom-fighters escaped from prison in South Africa after which they left the country. But, they were not immediately appointed to leadership positions.

Gqweta was appointed Secretary for Defence to replace Edwin

296 *The Crisis in the PAC: 1978–83*

Makoti whose performance in that position had drawn increasing criticism since 1978. However, Makoti was not told in an honest and comradely manner that he was removed because of his failure as Secretary for Defence; there was no principled discussion of his performance, performance that, in turn, had to be judged within the context of the situation within the PAC over the past few years, its overall political and military performance and diplomatic isolation. In that way, the Central Committee and the members of the organisation could avoid the danger of scapegoating, of blaming individuals and everybody else for the problems of the organisation.

Makoti was appointed Director of Publicity and Information, a position he held and in which he did not excel, in the pre-Arusha period. It was, in the circumstances, both unprincipled and unfair to appoint him to that position again, especially since the two previous Directors of Publicity and Information, namely Elias Ntloedibe and Gora Ebrahim, had failed dismally.

Guidelines for Each Department: The Central Committee decided in December 1981 that all heads of departments should draw up 'guidelines' for their departments, to be submitted to the Central Committee by the end of January 1982. Yet, in January–February 1981 the former Chairman, Vus Make, had presented to the Central Committee 'guidelines' for each department, 'guidelines' that were adopted by the Central Committee. At that meeting also the Central Committee adopted a detailed document presented by this writer containing proposals for the restructuring of the Finance Department. The Central Committee also adopted a document containing proposals for the revival and strengthening of the Department of Publicity and Information. A Task Force was appointed to restructure the PAC's military wing, APLA.

The Department of Education was restructured in 1978 when this writer held the position of Director of Education and Manpower Development. At the January 1979 plenary meeting, the Central Committee adopted the proposals presented by this writer for the Department, proposals that contained, inter alia, a policy and programme in the area of educational and vocational training, and guidelines for the functioning of the Department of Education and Manpower Development.

Similarly, soon after his appointment as Director of Foreign Affairs and Observer Representative to the UN, this writer prepared and presented to the Central Committee in April 1980 job analyses and job descriptions for the Observer Representative and functionaries at the Observer Mission. These were adopted by the Central Committee and were a functional definition of responsibilities. The Department of Foreign Affairs, of which this writer was head, also had clear 'guidelines'.

The point here is that at almost every Central Committee meeting since 1978, the Central Committee had adopted 'guidelines' and

John Nyati Pokela: Saviour of the PAC? 297

'blueprints', 'recommendations and suggestions', for the functioning of the various departments of the organisation. In addition, the Central Committee at each meeting had taken decisions of a purely administrative nature to govern various aspects of the work of the organisation. After each meeting, the Central Committee published catalogues of 'decisions and recommendations'. Clearly then, the problem was not one of a lack of 'guidelines'.

The confusion and contradictions reflected two things. Firstly, the general confusion at the PAC external headquarters and the administrative incompetence of the Central Committee members based there. No reference was made to previous decisions of the Central Committee, or to reports submitted by various individuals from time to time. Secondly, it demonstrated the manner in which Pokela was flattered by those around him who peddled the line that the PAC 'was starting from scratch'; in other words, they led him to believe that until his arrival, the PAC was dysfunctional. This was both untrue and ideologically unsound. The PAC had to learn from the totality of its experiences, both good and bad, successes and failures.

At the Central Committee meeting, which was also the last one attended by this writer, it was clear that the factionalism and cliquism which have plagued the PAC in the past are as strong as ever. This writer pointed this out; he also pointed out that if the Central Committee imagined that it could continue to tread the same old path, without honest debate and discussion, without criticism and self-criticism, the problems confronting the PAC would persist and deteriorate. Neither Pokela nor any other Central Committee member denied the charges made by this writer at the meeting, charges of disunity, plots and intrigues by individuals scheming for positions and influence, nor did they disagree with the observation made by this writer that Pokela would soon find himself in exactly the same positions as Leballo where he would be beholden to factions and cliques within the organisation and would not be able to provide the principled, revolutionary leadership the PAC requires.

The writer tendered his resignation at that Central Committee meeting but was dissuaded by the members present. In a subsequent private meeting with Pokela and Mkwanazi, he repeated the charges and observations he made during the Central Committee meeting. He left that meeting convinced that Pokela lacked the capacity to lead a revolutionary struggle but was still prepared to give him the principled support and co-operation he needed, support that demanded principled criticisms of the developments within the organisation. Subsequent developments within the PAC, however, necessitated a re-assessment of that position.

The appointments and the reshuffle within the Central Committee took place six months before a PAC consultative conference was to be held, at which all positions in the leadership of the organisation were to

298   *The Crisis in the PAC: 1978–83*

be elected. At that conference also, the PAC constitution and other basic documents were to be overhauled, to accord with the present-day realities in South Africa and the world and the revolutionary tasks of the liberation movement. It was rather optimistic, however, to expect persons who were appointed to positions (some of them after much scheming, plotting, manoeuvring and intrigue), to risk going into a conference where they might be unseated. Not surprisingly, the conference was 'postponed'.

The same arrogance towards the members of the organisation that characterised the Leballo era continue to be evidenced in that the views of the members regarding recent developments in the organisation have been ignored. In the USA, PAC members expressed their opposition to the appointment of Gora Ebrahim to the position of Observer Representative to the UN.[51] They stated as their reasons that they failed to see how the Central Committee could appoint him to the position — which was in reality a 'promotion' — when he had not accounted to a conference for his performance in his two previous posts as Representative to Zimbabwe and Director of Publicity and Information. A founder member of the PAC, Dr. Peter Molotsi who had been in the first National Executive Committee of the PAC, also wrote to Pokela suggesting that the decision to appoint Ebrahim to the UN post be shelved for at least twelve months because changes in personnel at a stage when the PAC attempted to present an image of reconstruction and revitalisation would once more arouse speculation about a crisis in the PAC.[52] Another PAC member based in England, Bennie Bunsee, who is the editor-in-chief of *Ikwezi*, 'a Marxist–Leninist journal on South African and Southern African Liberation', also wrote to the PAC's Unity Committee criticising Ebrahim's appointment and pointing out that not only had Ebrahim failed in his two previous posts but that the Central Committee was pandering to him because of the hope that he would be able to secure the PAC financial aid from the Arab countries.[53]

Factional Violence among PAC Members in Tanzania and Lesotho

At the end of April 1982 15 PAC members from the transit centre in Pongwe fled to Kenya after they had been assaulted by a faction of the militarily-trained cadres from the camp at Ithumbi.[54] The members who were assaulted were predominantly former Soweto students who were trained in civil aviation in Nigeria from 1977 to 1981. Because of the close contact Leballo maintained with those students prior to their return to Tanzania, they were suspected of being 'Leballo loyalists'. After fleeing to Nairobi, the 15 were accommodated and maintained by the Kenyan authorities, after which they were sent back to Tanzania. When they reached the border between Kenya and Tanzania, however, they were stranded in 'No Man's Land' after the PAC office in Dar-es-Salaam, when contacted by the Tanzanian authorities, refused to accept any responsibility for them. They were later taken into custody by the Special Defence Unit (SDU) of the Tanzanian People's Defence Forces. Unconfirmed reports at the time of writing indicated that the group of 15 were subsequently removed to a refugee settlement in Tabora.

Early in May 1982 there were physical clashes between two opposing groups of PAC members resident in Lesotho, as a result of which 15 members of the organisation, including Napthallie Sidzamba who had been the representative there for many years, were detained by the Lesotho authorities. The detentions received wide publicity in the South African and British media.[55] The problem, however, had its origins in attempts, through plotting and intrigue over many months by many members of the PAC, to have Sidzamba removed from the position of representative. They ultimately succeeded in April 1982 when the Central Committee decided to appoint Benedict Sondlo, the Administrative Assistant in Dar-es-Salaam, as representative to Lesotho, although he was ultimately not sent there. The decision provoked tension among the PAC members in Lesotho.[56] A delegation of the PAC Central Committee, comprising the Director of Finance, Lawrence Temba Mgweba, the Chief Representative to the UK, Hamilton Keke, and the Director of Education and Manpower Development, Elliot Mfaxa, visited Lesotho at the end of April 1982, inter alia, to apprise the Lesotho Government of Sidzamba's replacement as representative. Without first discussing the matter with Sidzamba, the PAC delegation went directly to the Lesotho authorities.

According to the PAC members who were detained by the Lesotho authorities, their detention followed representations made to the Lesotho Government by the PAC delegation of the Central Committee, to the effect that the representative, Sidzamba, and a number of other persons collaborated with the Lesotho Liberation Army (the military wing of the Basutoland Congress Party, led by Ntsu Mokhehle, which formerly had a political alliance with the PAC). According to these members, the Central Committee delegation intended to have Sidzamba and the others who supported him, deported from Lesotho.[57] If that be the case, and there is no reason to doubt Sidzamba and others, then there is a parallel with the situation in Swaziland in April 1978 when representations made to the Swaziland Government by P.K. Leballo and David Sibeko to the effect that the PAC representative, Joe Mkwanazi, and others were providing military training for a faction that was opposed to the Swazi monarchy, resulted in the detention and subsequent deportation of Mkwanazi and almost 50 PAC members from Swaziland. Just as the PAC members in Swaziland had maintained contact with the political resistance in South Africa and had established a recruitment network, so too had Sidzamba and his colleagues. The history of the PAC has been such that in all the power struggles and factional strife, the organisation has been harmed and the cause of liberation impeded.

300 *The Crisis in the PAC: 1978–83*

The Central Committee tried to explain the developments in Lesotho by insisting that they were the result of the refusal by Sidzamba to abide by the instructions of the Central Committee that he should take up a scholarship offered by Unesco to study curriculum development in France.[58] The explanation was not very convincing; in view of the history of the problems in Lesotho where Mfaxa and Sidzamba were ranged against each other in two opposing groups, and the efforts by certain individuals within the Central Committee to remove Sidzamba from his post in Lesotho, the explanation that was offered by Sidzamba and the other PAC members who were detained seems more credible, namely, that their detentions were engineered by the PAC Central Committee delegation which visited the region in May 1982. Physical violence between the two PAC factions in Lesotho flared up once more in October 1982 following the despatch by the Central Committee of a number of militarily-trained cadres from Dar-es-Salaam to Lesotho, with instructions to 'sort out' Sidzamba and other 'PAC dissidents', as they were called. In the fighting, in which, according to a Lesotho government official, shooting was involved, two persons were so seriously injured as to require hospitalisation.

In Tanzania, tension between the Pokela and Ntantala factions in 1983 resulted in physical harassment and intimidation of a number of persons accused of being an APRP fifth column within the PAC. A number of former APRP members resigned from the PAC; among them were Isaac 'Sakie' Mafatsche who had spent twelve years on Robben Island for PAC-related activities before he fled the country in 1975; Glen Mpukane, former secretary of the PAC Unity Committee and Bicca Maseko, one of the PAC activists formerly based in Swaziland. Their letters of resignation were a damning indictment of the PAC.

In July 1984 Benedict Sondlo, a Central Committee member, was killed by Pokela's former bodyguard who was also the organisation's Chief of Security. The PAC tried to portray the murder as a 'criminal assault' yet it was politically motivated, reflecting the ongoing struggle between the 'political' and 'military'.

Bunsee sees the problem in the PAC as being one of a lack of leadership; although he is critical of some of the developments of recent months, he is careful to distance Pokela from the more unfortunate aspects, arguing instead that they have been the result of 'chicanery, dishonesty and manouevring' of those around Pokela:

> The re-organisation and restructuring of the PAC [are] taking place under the leadership of Comrade Pokela who assumed the Chairmanship of the Movement as soon as he arrived here. He is the person [in] whom we have placed faith. He is undoubtedly not a corrupt person, and a leader who places the interests of the struggle and the revolution foremost. Whatever mistakes he might make might be those of judgement but not of corruption or ineptitude. He is, after all, [assuming] a formidable task in the

reorganisation of the PAC and the task of all [the members] is to help him in his job. It is his task to forge a worthy leadership and since his assumption of the Chairmanship of the PAC the Organisation has made positive strides. Greater confidence has been inspired in the Organisation . . . and the July Conference which is to elect a leadership of the movement is being organised. A CENTRAL PROBLEM OF THE PAC IS STILL THE QUESTION OF LEADERSHIP. And it appears to me that some of the things taking place in the leadership are unsavoury. This does not reflect upon Comrade Pokela or the better elements in the Central Committee. It is absolutely essential that we eliminate chicanery, dishonesty and cliquish manoeuvring in the Central Committee. [The PAC needs] a Central Committee which truly reflects the interests of the organisation and [of] the struggle. Dishonest, dubious and opportunist elements should have no place in the Organisation. [The PAC] is still far from having a harmonious and stable leadership that knows what it is doing and which acts in the highest interests of the struggle and the revolution.[59]

Far from being simply a problem of leadership, the problem of the PAC is a political and ideological one. The organisation cannot have a united leadership or a united membership until there is ideological and political cohesion within the organisation. A national liberation movement needs a leadership that is truly united, more importantly, *that knows how to lead*, to formulate policies on the basis of criticism and self-criticism, that reads, studies and investigates. As Mao-Tse-Tung explained in his address to *An Enlarged Central Work Conference* of the Chinese Communist Party in 1962:

> The question of right or wrong, correct or incorrect, in our work has to do with contradictions among the people. To resolve contradictions among the people . . . we can only use the method of discussion, reasoning, criticism and self-criticism . . . Criticism and self-criticism is a kind of method. It is method of resolving contradictions among the people and it is the only method. There is no other. But if we do not have a full democratic life and do not truly implement democratic centralism, then this method of criticism and self-criticism cannot be applied.[60]

Revolutionary organisations are built on the basis of correct policies, on the basis of revolutionary principles. As Lenin repeatedly emphasised, without revolutionary theory, there cannot be revolutionary practice. The South African liberation organisations are no exception. Their leaders are equally duty-bound to study revolutionary strategy and tactics, revolutionary theory, that is, the theory of Marx, Engels, Lenin, Stalin and Mao-Tse-Tung, as well as the revolutionary experiences of others, like the Algerians, the Russians, the Chinese, the Cubans, the

302 *The Crisis in the PAC: 1978–83*

Vietnamese and the Kampucheans, the Mozambicans, the Angolans, the people of Guinea-Bissau and Zimbabwe, as well as South African society. Or, to put it differently,

> It is no longer sufficient to be oppressed and determined to be free. There is now in existence a science of revolution for the oppressed masses of our epoch, and that is Marxism, as well as the enormous addition to Marxism of the concrete revolutionary experience of many peoples of the 20th century. All this knowledge must be studied as much in detail as possible by all those who take themselves seriously as revolutionaries ... Knowledge by itself will not save us, but we shall not be saved without knowledge.[61]

In the PAC at the present time there are two kinds of people. Firstly, there are those who seek power and know how to play the power game. They know how to curry favour, to say the right things at the right time as well as mouth the right slogans. They know how to make the relevant twists and turns that keep them in power and always to ensure that they curry favour with the right person or persons. At the present time, there are many such elements in the organisation, particularly at the level of leadership: individuals have been rewarded with positions in the leadership precisely because of their opportunism. Secondly, there are those who base themselves upon revolutionary principles, who wish to see the PAC organised on the basis of those principles from the bottom up. They have the interests of the struggle and of the organisation at heart. The difference between the two is the difference between opportunism and revolutionary politics; it is also the difference between bourgeois and proletarian ideology.

To expect the revitalisation of the PAC to be effected by a single individual is to expect too much, especially considering the *crisis* of credibility facing the organisation at this time, when the crucial question is the role of the PAC in the current mass struggles of workers, students and all sections of the politically oppressed and economically exploited majority of the South African population. For those hailing Pokela as the 'saviour' of the PAC, perhaps a word of caution is not inappropriate, that is, that in another context, the very person who only a few days earlier had been hailed as the 'saviour', in whose path coats of many colours had been strewn for him to walk upon, was on one Good Friday crucified — by the very same crowd!

Notes

1. Tape recorded interview of Pokela by Mimi Rosenberg, New York, 7 October 1981.
2. Ibid.
3. Gerhardt 1979, p. 135.

John Nyati Pokela: Saviour of the PAC? 303

4. Mimi Rosenburg. interview. 7 October 1981.

5. Gerhardt 1979. p. 13.

6. Ibid.. p. 135.

7. Information provided by Phillip Kgosana in a tape recorded interview with the author. New York. 8 May 1982.

8. Mimi Rosenberg. interview. 7 October 1981.

9. Information provided in February 1981 in Dar-es-Salaam to the author by Enoch Zulu. the Director of Operations. to whom the approach was made.

10. See 'Isaacs' resignation affects PAC'. *The Sowetan*. 16 April 1982.

11. Letter dated 11 January 1981 from N. Sidzamba to the PAC Administrative Secretary.

12. Memo dated 6 April 1981 from the Administrative Secretary. Joe Mkwanazi. lists the names of the Unity Committee members as: J.N. Pokela (Chairman). Glen Mpukane (Secretary). Mpazama Yonana (Assistant Secretary). Nogaga Morgan Gxexwa. Zabulon Mokoena. Edmund Jiyane. Mosoeu Magalefa. Moses Palweni. Moses Mhlahlane and Joe Mkwanazi.

13. The PAC. through various spokespersons in 1981 and early 1982. called for the creation of a united front with the ANC. at times even creating the impression that discussions were underway for the creation of such a united front. According to the Johannesburg *Star* (23 February 1982). however: 'Authoritative ANC sources in Lusaka have rejected the PAC claim as "nonsense". adding that the PAC was again flying kites and that it was not the ANC's job to "carry PAC people on its back to the battle front".'

14. Among the former APRP members appointed to various positions were: Glen Mpukane (Assistant Chief Representative to Tanzania). Nimrod Wezo Tshongoyi (Welfare Officer). Mfanayasekaya Pearce Gqobose (Administrator and co-ordinator for all PAC self-reliance projects). T.M. Ntantala (Chief Representative to Zimbabwe). Theophilus Bidi (Chief Representative to Nigeria and Member of the Central Committee). The Central Committee at a meeting in August 1983 appointed Gqobose to the Central Committee.

15. The interception of the document was first reported to the author in New York in October 1981 by an APLA cadre who claimed to have actually seen it. This was corroborated by another APLA cadre in Dar-es-Salaam in December 1981 in Dar-es-Salaam: he also assured the author that he had actually seen it and that after a photostat copy of the document was made it was passed on to the addressee. Pokela and other Central Committee members denied knowledge of such a document when questioned by Ngila Muendane during a session of the Central Committee on 6 December 1981. From Glen Mpukane's letter of resignation. dated 10 June 1983. however. it is clear that Pokela. Joe Mkwanazi and Enoch Zulu were aware of the document because these three Central Committee members discussed it with Glen Mpukane and other former APRP members.

16. Pamphlets mailed out by Leballo and/or his supporters were regularly received by the author.

17. Munger 1967. p. 109.

18. Nkoana 1969. p. 8. In a long letter dated 2 December 1966. Nkoana speaks of Leballo's 'megalomania'.

19. Ntantala 1978. p. 10. Document addressed to 'All Representatives and Members [of the PAC] abroad and at home'. dated 14 April 1978.

304 *The Crisis in the PAC: 1978–83*

20. Nkoana 1969, pp. 8–10; Gibson 1972, pp. 102–3.

21. Most serious academic writing on South Africa refers more often than not to the PAC in the past tense, or refers to its fractional nature. See, for example, Karis, Carter and Gerhardt, Vol. III 1977, p. 77: 'Within the splintered ranks of the PAC abroad, Potlako Leballo runs an office in Dar-es-Salaam and endures'. See also Saul and Gelb 1981, p. 140: 'A deeper understanding of the complexity of the South African revolution has also helped to further undermine the credibility of the PAC, seen initially by some Black Consciousness militants as a more natural historical point of reference than the ANC because of the racial question; moreover, the PAC, in disarray (despite occasional forays into the country), can provide no real answer on the military front'. It has to be pointed out that, although this work is a valuable analysis of the current political developments in South Africa and the attempts by the ruling class to perpetuate itself and its society, the authors are patently partial towards the ANC. Another South African academic who is associated with the ANC, Ben Magubane, is even more disparaging of the PAC: 'There is no doubt that the PAC's demise would have come sooner if the police at Sharpeville and Langa had acted with some caution, instead of unleashing their fury on the peaceful demonstrators. The Sharpeville massacre and the march of some 30,000 Africans from Langa to Cape Town made a historical landmark out of what would have passed as a quiet day, and created a legend for the PAC'. (Magubane 1979, p. 11).

22. See Gerhardt 1979, p. 138 for biographical details of Leballo and his role in the Africanist Movement.

23. The clause reads as follows: 'The President shall have emergency powers, which he may delegate, to suspend the entire constitution of the PAC so as to ensure that the Movement emerges intact through a crisis. At that time, he directs the Movement by decree, and is answerable for his actions to the National Conference.'

24. Telephone interview with Dr. Peter Molotsi, New York, 18 July 1982. According to Molotsi, the entire National Executive Committee was deported from Tanzania and Leballo was reinstated by the Tanzanian authorities. Molotsi and others were 'sacrificed on the altar of Tanzanian national interest', to quote Molotsi. As a result of the leadership dispute, the OAU Liberation Committee, meeting in Algiers in June 1968, suspended support to the PAC. The Executive Secretariat of the ALC suspended all PAC activities in Dar-es-Salaam; assistance was, however, given to the cadres of the organisation.

25. Ntantala 1978, p. 10.

26. Nkoana 1969, pp. 31–47, 64–65 is instructive on this point.

27. At the end of 1976 and beginning of 1977, the author met many of these new recruits in Tanzania. In all the discussions, they repeated that they simply wanted to return to South Africa to fight. They were extremely contemptuous of any person who left South Africa before 16 June 1976, the date on which, to their thinking, the liberation struggle began.

28. Ntantala, in his document referred to above, cites the various acts of violence, including stabbings, in Dar-es-Salaam, to which members of his faction were subjected.

29. Tandon in Potholm, C.P. and Dale, R. (eds), 1972 , p. 260.

30. I am borrowing a phrase used by Marcum in Potholm and Dale (eds) 1972, p. 274.

31. Ibid.

John Nyati Pokela: Saviour of the PAC? 305

32. Ibid., pp. 273–5.

33. Letter dated 30 January 1981 to PAC Observer Representative to the UN from Bogdan Van Doninck in Brussels.

34. Letter dated 19 March 1981 from Political Secretary of Workers' Communist League, to PAC Director of Foreign Affairs.

35. The author was informed on 5 April 1982 by the projects officer of a donor agency which has consistently provided financial aid for various PAC projects that twelve months after the sum of money (a little over US$10,000) had been transferred to the PAC external headquarters in Dar-es-Salaam there had been no acknowledgement of receipt and there was no way that the remaining two instalments of similar amounts would be transferred to the PAC.

36. Letter dated 4 November 1981 from Glen Mpukane, Secretary of PAC Unity Committee and Assistant Representative to Tanzania, to the PAC Observer Representative to the UN.

37. Letter dated 10 August 1979 from David Dube to E.L. Makoti.

38. Letter dated 18 January 1982 from Peter Molotsi to Pokela.

39. These sources are former PAC members and others who are PAC sympathisers with whom the author has been in contact.

40. Complaint by Vus Make to the Central Committee meeting, Dar-es-Salaam, 3 July 1981.

41. The interview in which Pokela expressed support for Iraq in the conflict with Iran was published in the magazine, *IRAQ*, September 1981. The PAC Central Committee, at its meeting in Tanzania in August 1983 reversed its position of support for Iraq and instead called upon the 'brotherly peoples of Iran and Iraq' to resolve their differences through diplomatic means.

42. Martin and Johnson 1980, p. 88.

43. Discussion by the author with the then Deputy Director-General of the ZBC, Tirivafi Kangai, in December 1981 at the ZBC in Harare. He repeated this to the author on 12 May 1982 in Harare.

44. During a visit to Zimbabwe in December 1981 the author was so informed by the Counsellor at the Yugoslav Embassy in Harare, Comrade Vujovic.

45. This information was disclosed to the author by several Zimbabwean officials whose identities cannot be disclosed. It is an argument, however, which the Mozambican Foreign Minister, Mr. Joachim Chissano, advanced at the OAU Liberation Committee meeting in Arusha, Tanzania in January 1981 when he pointed out to the meeting that even Ton Vosloo, editor of the Afrikaans-language newspaper, *Die Beeld*, recognised that the Pretoria regime would ultimately have to negotiate with the ANC.

46. Report by Administrative Secretary, Joe Mkwanazi, to the Central Committee in Dar-es-Salaam on 3 July 1981.

47. Quoted by Marcum in Potholm and Dale (eds) 1972, p. 271.

48. Draft report of the Evaluation and Programming Mission of UNDP Assistance to the African National Liberation Movements recognised by the OAU, SWAPO ... and ANC and PAC ... November 1981, p. 27. The report was prepared to serve as a 'tentative basis for discussion' at the Inter-Agency Meeting, held in Dar-es-Salaam from 8 to 11 December 1981.

49. Gqobose, M.P., 'Report on the Co-ordination of Self-Reliance Projects, from April to November 1981'.

50. The 'Tabora group' to which Gqobose refers in his report comprised

306 *The Crisis in the PAC: 1978–83*

the PAC members expelled at the consultative conference in Arusha in 1978. They were subsequently sent by the Tanzanian authorities to a refugee settlement at Tabora, where they immediately engaged in agricultural production and poultry-farming so that they were soon self-sufficient in food production. The 'Mgagao group' comprised the 46 militarily-trained cadres who were declared prohibited immigrants by the Tanzanian authorities in February 1979 following the siege of the residence of and assaults upon Central Committee members. They, too, achieved self-sufficiency in food production through agriculture at the camp in Mgagao in southern Tanzania.

51. The North American Branch of the PAC, through the executive, despatched a cable to the PAC Chairman, Pokela, at the end of January 1982 urging him to withdraw the appointment of Gora Ebrahim. In a letter dated 11 February 1982 PAC members in New York stated that it was not 'strategic' for the PAC to appoint one of its 'Indian' members to the UN since that might offend the sensitivities of the African group at the UN, as well as the Afro-American supporters of the PAC. The opposition of the PAC members was not heeded and the appointment was effected.

52. Letter dated 18 January 1982 addressed to J.N. Pokela by Peter Molotsi. Molotsi did not receive a reply to his communication.

53. Undated, unpublished document to the PAC Unity Committee by Bennie Bunsee as contribution to the debate on the updating of the PAC's basic documents.

54. Information provided by PAC members resident in Nairobi, Kenya, on 5 June 1982.

55. The *Rand Daily Mail*, 3 May 1982; *The Guardian* (London), 6 May 1982.

56. Unsigned cable to author from Lesotho received 3 May 1982 states: 'Sidzamba axed by Dar. Bennie Sondlo new man for region. Tension.'

57. Telephone interview with Nhlabathi Mbuli, one of the detainees, from Harare on 19 May 1982.

58. Letter to *Lesotho Weekly News*, 23 May 1982 by Elliot Mfaxa, PAC Director of Education and Manpower Development in the Central Committee.

59. Bunsee, B., supra, note 53.

60. Quoted in Schram (ed) 1974, p. 161.

61. Vilakazi 1978, pp. 85–6.

Part III:
The National Liberation Struggle: Problems and Prospects

15. The Resurgence of the ANC

In contrast with the decline of the PAC, its tarnished image and loss of influence in South Africa and internationally, the ANC has undergone a resurgence, particularly since the Soweto uprising of 1976. This was clearly revealed in a poll conducted at the end of August 1981 by the Johannesburg *Star*.[1] The poll was conducted among a random sample of 396 Africans in Johannesburg, Cape Town and Durban, 199 Coloureds in Cape Town and 101 Indians in Durban. The interviewers were drawn from the three racial groups; the interviewees were questioned by persons of their own racial group. The poll found that 40% of Africans would vote for the ANC in parliamentary elections based on universal manhood suffrage. Chief Gatsha Buthelezi's Inkatha tribal movement polled 21%, the Azanian People's Organisation (AZAPO) 11%, and the PAC 10%. The poll can be faulted on several grounds. Firstly, it tests only 0.0034% of the total Black population (Africans, Coloureds and Indians) whereas normally a national poll is conducted upon a random sample of 0.03% of any given population. Secondly, it distorts the population figures of the various racial groups whose views were canvassed. The sample includes 14.5% of Indians, whereas the Indian ethnic group constitutes only 2.8% of the total population. Similarly, the Coloureds, who constitute 9.8% of the total population, comprise some 28.5% of those whose views were canvassed; the Africans, who constitute almost 72% of the total population represented 56.8% of the views canvassed by the *Star*. The poll was conducted in three large urban centres, thus ignoring the mass of Africans who are confined to the rural areas. In addition, in the choice of urban centres, the poll excluded the centres in the Eastern Cape (Port Elizabeth, East London and King William's Town, for example) which have had a long history of Black political involvement and a high (some would argue the highest) level of political consciousness among the Black masses. It has to be borne in mind also that two of the organisations are banned in South Africa. Any person expressing any preference for the ANC and PAC in South Africa risks imprisonment. If such risks did not exist, then the expressed support for the two organisations might be even higher.

These criticisms notwithstanding, the poll does point to a growth in

310 *The National Liberation Struggle: Problems and Prospects*

influence of the ANC, which has been confirmed also by independent analysis.[2] Saul and Gelb attribute the resurgence of the ANC as the leading liberation force in South Africa to two factors: its military capacity and its legitimacy and links with the popular struggles of the past particularly the struggles of the 1950s.[3] We examine these aspects below.

ANC's Military Capacity

Saul and Gelb point out that the military capacity of the ANC is due to the preparations which the organisation made for this stage of the armed struggle and its connections with the Socialist countries which are a source of arms and also offer military training, as well as training in the use of explosives and in intelligence for ANC freedom-fighters.[4] As a result, the ANC's military wing, Umkhonto we Sizwe, has been able to carry out a number of military actions in the country, including the sabotage of strategic installations like the SASOL oil-from-coal plant, electricity supply stations and power plants, and attacks upon police stations (at Booysens, Soweto and Soekmekaar, to name a few) the military base at Voortrekkerhoogte, and attacks upon security police and other state collaborators.

They admit that these military actions do not pose a 'major military threat' to the White establishment; rather they offer hope to the 'mass of Africans'.[5] In this regard, the attacks by ANC guerrillas on various targets have succeeded in gaining for the organisation publicity and legitimacy, both domestically and internationally.[6]

There was an awareness within the ANC that in the decade after the Rivonia trial when the organised resistance was crushed by the South African regime, the exile organisation had concentrated too much on international solidarity work at the expense of political organisation in the country. Thus, Turok, writing in the early 1970s, stated:

> The view is now growing within the movement itself that solidarity work and international questions have absorbed the exile leadership to the point where internal work has been neglected.[7]

The growing repression in South Africa and the lack of friendly borders made difficult the establishment of contact with the emerging resistance led by students and intellectuals who belonged to the South African Students' Organisation (SASO), the Black People's Convention (BPC) and other cultural organisations which, collectively, came to be termed the Black Consciousness Movement (BCM). Following the strikes by Black workers in 1973–74 there emerged a fledgeling Black labour movement which grew in strength and organisation in the succeeding years. The response of the South African regime to the burgeoning mass resistance was to ban individual leaders, as occurred in March 1973 when eight Black student leaders and eight White student leaders were banned; the Black student leaders who were elected to replace those who were banned were themselves restricted. White trade union organisers who were active in Natal where the first major strikes took place in 1973 were likewise banned.

The establishment of links with the internal resistance was facilitated by the independence, first of Mozambique, then of Angola and subsequently by the exodus of thousands of youths after the Soweto uprisings. Prior to March 1984 when the Mozambican Government signed a non-aggression pact (the 'Nkomati Accord', named after the town on the border between the two countries where the ceremony was held) with the South African regime and undertook to prevent the ANC from launching military operations from Mozambican territory, it did not permit the organisation to establish military bases in the country, but permitted the organisation a political presence and granted sanctuary to persons fleeing from South Africa. After the independence of Angola, the ANC similarly established a mission in that country, also transferring part of its military personnel there from Zambia and Tanzania.

Early attempts in 1975 to establish a network within the country suffered setbacks with the arrests and trials of ANC activists and sympathisers.[8]

A combination of facilities in a country contiguous to South Africa and the infusion of new talent after Soweto created favourable conditions for a successful symbiosis between the internally-based resistance and the exile organisation, whence the increase in ANC activities since late 1976. The ANC had the organisational capacity to absorb the new membership after the Soweto uprisings. Recruits did not spend long periods of time at reception points in the countries of sanctuary; they could be transported with a minimum of delay for military training (or academic training) in a number of African countries where the ANC has facilities, or to the Socialist countries, including the Soviet Union. Upon the completion of their training, they could likewise be reinfiltrated without spending too long a time in military camps in Tanzania and other places. For this reason, within one year of the Soweto uprisings, the infiltration of trained freedom-fighters and equipment began in earnest. Although Mozambique did not permit military operations by ANC guerrillas from its territory, they succeeded in surreptitiously transporting freedom-fighters and materials from Mozambique, through Swaziland, into the country. As will be discussed later, the non-aggression pacts signed by these two countries with the South African regime and their crackdown against the ANC, slowed down the scale of infiltration and military operations by ANC freedom-fighters in 1984.

Phases in ANC Guerrilla Activities

Several phases are discernible in the guerrilla activities of the ANC

312 *The National Liberation Struggle: Problems and Prospects*

military wing, Umkhonto we Sizwe. Firstly, in the latter part of 1976 through 1979, military actions comprised the following: sabotage of railway lines; explosions of pamphlet bombs; assassinations and attempted assassinations of former guerrillas who had become state collaborators, either working as security police or as informers, or as state witnesses in political trials; armed contacts with members of the security forces, of which the chief of the security police Colonel Zietsman, reported in 1978 there were five, although there could have been more;[9] the establishment of arms caches.

During this period, the guerrillas were engaged in attempting to establish lines of communication and infiltration and in attempting to establish arms caches and cells inside the country.[10] Kane-Berman writes:

> The security police [stated] that since the beginning of [1977] they had been systematically cracking down on cells of a nation-wide ANC network that had been recruiting in the country. So far two separate networks had been uncovered and about 75 people detained.[11]

During the same period the police reported the discovery of arms caches in places as far away as Soweto, Kwa Thema (Springs), Graaff-Rienet, Mafeking, Durban, Northern Natal, Middleburg in the Eastern Transvaal and Natalspruit. In 1977 and 1978, no fewer than twelve such discoveries were reported.[12]

The period 1977 to 1978 also saw a number of clashes between guerrillas and security forces, normally on patrol in the border areas. The clashes followed the interception by the security forces of such guerrillas infiltrating.[13] In some instances, the guerrillas themselves attacked such patrols in order to divert attention away from the urban areas on the Reef where they were heading, to areas in Natal, including Durban.[14]

In 1978 several security policemen as well as former guerrillas who had turned state collaborators were assassinated. These included Stephen Mtshali, a former ANC guerrilla who was fatally shot by masked gunmen outside his home in Kwa Mashu, outside Durban. He had given evidence against the ANC in a trial under the Terrorism Act. In April, Abel Mthembu, former Transvaal vice-president of the ANC was shot dead at his home; he was formerly a member of the ANC military wing but had turned state witness in a number of political trials involving members of the ANC. Detective-sergeant Stephen 'Hlubi' Chapi, a senior Black detective who had gained notoriety for his role in the shooting of students during the Soweto uprisings, was fatally shot outside his home in Soweto in June. Less than one month later, Shekithemba Mayeza, a Black member of the Bureau of State Security (BOSS), was assassinated while seated in his van in Umlazi, outside Durban.

The assassinations of security policemen continued into 1981. In May

The Resurgence of the ANC   313

1981 a Black detective-sergeant, Zipheniah Makemi, was fatally wounded in an incident near Cottondale in the Eastern Transvaal when a guerrilla threw a hand grenade at him after he had gone to investigate reports about the presence of a 'terrorist'. In August 1981 two Transkeian security policemen were shot to death in Msombomvu township outside Butterworth. Two days later, five Blacks in a car were stopped at a road-block between Gala and Elliot. In an exchange of fire with the police at the road-block, two of the men were killed, one captured and the others escaped.

Hand grenades were thrown and shots fired into the homes of a number of persons who had either given evidence for the state in trials involving ANC members, or who were regarded as being collaborators with the regime. Among them was Freddie Motaung, a state witness in the trial of 12 ANC men under the Terrorism Act in the Pretoria Supreme Court. He had been taken out of his house by the police earlier, but his wife was injured in the hand-grenade attack which shattered the house. In April 1978, shots were fired into the home of Oscar Xaba, a member of the Community Council in Magabeni, Natal; another member of a community council in Cheterville, Natal, was shot in the arm. At the beginning of 1983, Bartholomew Hlapane, a former member of the SACP who had testified against ANC members in numerous political trials, was fatally shot at his home. The ANC denied responsibility for the killing which was clearly politically notivated.

The second phase in the guerrilla campaign involved attacks upon police stations in which a number of policemen, as well as civilians, were killed. These included Moroka police station (May 1979); Orlando police station (November 1979); Soekmekaar police station (January 1980); Booysens police station (April 1980); Sibasa (Venda) (November 1980) and Mabopane (Bophuthatswana) (September 1981). The Moroka, Orlando and Soekmekaar police stations are all located in Black townships, and in the attacks upon these targets, in which explosive devices, grenades and automatic weapons were used, Black policemen and civilians were killed and injured — which drew criticisms from the PAC, as well as several Black organisations and individuals in the country.[15] The attack on the Booysens police station, located in a White suburb of Johannesburg, might have been a counter to these criticisms; in that attack, the ANC guerrillas used RPG rocket launchers which caused extensive damage to the buidings but no loss of life. Attacks on police stations, in both the urban and rural areas, continued through 1981. The Fort Jackson police station in East London was extensively damaged during an attack by guerrillas in May 1981 and in September the Mabopane police station was attacked by four guerrillas armed with AK-47 assault rifles and hand grenades. Two Black policemen were killed in the attack. In October 1981 the Sibasa police station in the Venda Bantustan was destroyed during a rocket attack in which two Black policemen were killed.

314 *The National Liberation Struggle: Problems and Prospects*

The third phase, which began in 1980, involved selection of targets which were economically and strategically important. The most impressive armed action undertaken to date has been the sabotage by ANC freedom-fighters of two oil-from-coal plants of the South African Oil and Gas Corporation (SASOL) at Sasolburg and Secunda, 25 miles apart, on 1 June 1980. The attack resulted in the destruction of a vital economic target and damage estimated at approximately $7 million. The attack on the SASOL oil-from-coal plant was followed a few days later by the destruction of a factory in Cape Town, causing damage estimated at approximately $5 million; the factory produced rugby jerseys and socks for the South African Springbok rugby teams and the British Lions. It was generally believed that the attack was politically motivated.

In April 1981 an electricity sub-station in Lamontville, Durban, was destroyed in an explosion for which the ANC claimed responsibility.[16] It was reported to be the most serious case of sabotage since the attack on the SASOL plant the previous June, while the importance of the installation lies in the fact that it supplies power to the Prospelton-Mobeni complex, which is one of the largest industrial areas in Natal. In May, guerrillas cut the electricity supply lines near the town of Vrede in the Orange Free State, plunging the town into total darkness for several hours before the lines were repaired. That same month, a recruiting office of the South African Defence Force was severely damaged when a bomb exploded in the building housing the office.

In July 1981 within a week of a confident statement by the chief of South Africa's Defence Forces, General Constand Viljoen, that the ANC's sabotage actions were generally 'unprofessional', ANC guerrillas launched a well co-ordinated attack on three power stations in the Transvaal (at Arnot east of Middleburg in the Eastern Transvaal; at Camden, east of Ermelo; and at Rietvlei, near Pretoria), causing thousands of dollars of damages and disrupting supplies of electricity to Ermelo.

This was followed by explosions which blew up part of the showrooms and offices of two automobile companies in central Durban, a city that was repeatedly hit by various acts of sabotage throughout 1981. At that time, there was a dispute between labour and management at the two companies, McCarthy Leyland and McCarthy Sigma.

In August 1981 the military base at Voortrekkerhoogte was subjected to attacks by rockets fired from the Indian township of Laudium. In November, a house used to accommodate military personnel of the South African Defence Forces near the border with Swaziland was destroyed during a rocket and grenade attack carried out by ANC guerrillas.

Towards the end of 1981 the attacks on economically strategic installations in *various parts of the country* were accelerated. For example, in October damage was caused to the following installations during guerrilla attacks: an electricity sub-station at Evander in the Transvaal, a water purification plant at the Secunda plant of SASOL-3, and an electricity sub-station in Natal. In the industrial complex of Rosslyn, near

The Resurgence of the ANC 315

Pretoria, two transformers were damaged in four explosions in November. At the beginning of December an oil storage depot in Germiston was destroyed.

There is also evidence to suggest that the Koeberg nuclear power station near Cape Town was attacked by guerrillas in July 1982.[17] Initially, a spokesperson for the Electricity Supply Commission (ESCOM) claimed that the damage (estimated at several hundreds of thousands of dollars) was caused by a fire and denied that the damage was caused by sabotage carried out by ANC guerrillas, as the liberation movement had claimed. One week later, however, it was admitted that the fire at the nuclear facility was caused by a 'blast in the building housing the nerve centre of the complex'.[18] ANC freedom-fighters repeated their attack on the Koeberg nuclear power station in December 1982 shortly after the raid on Maseru, Lesotho, by South African military forces in which 30 South African refugees and ANC members as well as 12 Lesotho nationals were killed.

Public Resonance

A feature of this phase of the ANC's military actions has been the selection of other targets in order to 'create maximum public resonance'.[19] The attack on the Soekmekaar police station in January 1980 was carried out for 'armed propaganda purposes', in the words of one of the guerrillas who was later captured and put on trial, to demonstrate ANC support for the people in the area who were the victims of forced removals from their homes implemented by the South African regime. In October 1980 the railway line to Soweto was sabotaged, an action that coincided with the visit to Soweto of Dr. Piet Koornhof, the cabinet minister responsible for 'Co-operation and Development' who was given the dubious honour of the 'freedom of Soweto' by Black collaborators, notably David Thebehali, himself the target of an assassination attempt a few months later. In November 1981 the offices of the South African Indian Council in Durban were attacked, in protest against the elections which produced a poll of less than 10%. Attacks on police stations, offices of Bantu Administration Boards, buildings of Bantu Administrations and other symbols of oppression could likewise be described as demonstrative.

Several observations can be made about the ANC's military actions. Firstly, there was, up until May 1983, an assiduous avoidance of civilian targets. In those instances where there were civilian casualties or fatalities, such as the Goch Street shooting of June 1977 when guerrillas killed two Whites in a warehouse, and in the Silverton bank siege in January 1980, the guerrillas acted precipitously, believing that they had either been detected by the South African security forces or were trapped.[20]

The commitment to 'selective sabotage' — as in the case of the first campaigns by Umkhonto we Sizwe in the period 1961 to 1963 — appears to

316 *The National Liberation Struggle: Problems and Prospects*

have been aimed at gaining legitimacy for the ANC, domestically and internationally, particularly in liberal circles in the West, as a liberation movement rather than a 'terrorist organisation'. In November 1980, the ANC signed the Geneva Convention on the treatment of prisoners of war and called upon the South African regime to accord prisoner of war status to ANC combatants. This, of course, is not likely; the regime continues to regard all freedom-fighters as common criminals who are tried and sentenced according to the Criminal Code.

In August 1981, Oliver Tambo, the President of the ANC, announced that henceforth 'officials of apartheid' would be targeted by guerrillas of his movement and warned that there might be 'combat situations' in which innocent civilians would be killed or injured. That, however, has already happened. Black policemen have been killed; attempts have been made on the lives of Black collaborators and ethnic functionaries of apartheid-created institutions. Similarly, innocent civilians have already been killed in a number of incidents, including attacks on police stations and bomb explosions. Table 15.1 shows the number of persons killed during the period 1976 to 1981.[21]

Table 15.1

Casualties	*Number*
White soldiers or police	13
Other Whites	10
Black policemen or security policemen	17
State witnesses	1
Black guerrillas	8
Black bystanders	3
Total Killed	52

The number of persons injured during the same period appears in Table 15.2.

The number of fatalities and casualties has increased since 1981 as a result of a number of further sabotage actions. Early in 1983 a bomb explosion at the Bloemfontein railway station, an action attributed to the ANC by the South African regime but denied by the ANC, resulted in one fatality and some 76 injured. That was followed a few months later by the Pretoria car bomb attack which resulted in 18 fatalities and almost 200 injured. In May 1984, 7 people including 3 guerrillas were killed during a clash between security forces and ANC guerrillas following the sabotage of an oil storage depot in Durban. In July 1984, there were 5 fatalities and a number of casualties when another car bomb exploded in Durban. The implications of the Pretoria car bomb attack and the two actions in Durban in mid-1984 are discussed later.

Table 15.2

Casualties	Number
White soldiers or police	8
Other Whites	36
Black police	17
Black state witnesses	1
Black guerrillas	17
Black bystanders	34
Total Number of Persons Injured	113

A word of caution has to be expressed about the reliability of casualty figures as well as the extent of military actions by the national liberation movements in South Africa. Firstly, the authorities have attempted to exaggerate the danger by portraying Black resistance, led by the national liberation movements, as part of a communist-inspired conspiracy, a 'total onslaught' against the Christian, civilised, White-ruled South. This has been used to suppress human rights and individual freedoms as well as to curb press freedom. It has also been used to justify the massive defence budget. At the same time, the South African regime has tried to downplay the threat posed by the national liberation movements. This is necessary not only to reassure the White populace that the security situation is well under control, but more importantly, to reassure foreign investors whose confidence in the stability of the country is crucial to their continued economic involvement, since foreign investments continue to play an important role in the maintenance of the status quo. The contradictory postures of the South African regime could be seen in the reactions to the increase in guerrilla actions in 1980 and 1981. Following the sabotage of the SASOL oil-from-coal plant by ANC guerrillas in June 1980, the Minister of Minerals and Energy, Mr. de Klerk, in denying opposition allegations of indiscretion by SASOL during a debate in parliament, said: 'It is clear that we are faced with a sophisticated attack, which is evidenced by the fact that there were three separate attacks on three separate installations almost simultaneously.'[22] Yet, in July the following year, the Chief of the South African Defence Forces, General Constand Viljoen, dismissed the actions of the ANC guerrillas as 'generally unprofessional'. The Minister of Police, Mr. Louis le Grange, in turn, pointed out that the police had a very good record in capturing ANC guerrillas. Despite these confident boasts, however, there were regular complaints from the regime about what was regarded as excessive publicity being given to the growing guerrilla campaign, hence the attempts to suppress information about the activities of the liberation movements.[23]

Tom Lodge has described the escalating Black resistance, including the armed struggle, in the period between 1976 and 1981 as:

318 *The National Liberation Struggle: Problems and Prospects*

The most violent rebellion in South African history and all indications are that it will develop into a full-scale revolutionary war. A chronology of guerrilla activity made in 1981 records 112 attacks and explosions between October 1976 and May 1981. In March 1978 it was reported that one explosion a week had taken place since the previous November.[24]

This optimistic assessment, however, has to be tempered by pointing out that the liberation movements at this stage do not have the capacity to take on the military might of the South African Defence Forces. The line of defence in the cities is held by the police rather than by the much stronger Defence Forces who beef up security in the rural areas, forming a cordon sanitaire against infiltrating guerrillas. The police at this stage have a fairly good record in capturing guerrillas, as is evidenced by the large number of political trials involving freedom-fighters who have been involved in many of the ANC's military actions. Sabotage and armed actions will not of themselves achieve liberation for the people who are presently oppressed and economically exploited; the achievement of that objective will depend on the extent to which the liberation movements succeed in mobilising the mass of the population to participate in a multi-frontal struggle that involves not only military actions but also industrial and political strikes.

The political editor of the London *Economist*, after visiting South Africa, wrote in an eight-page survey:

> ANC bombing incidents have increased though the primitiveness of the devices and the organisation's inability to secure its agents' escape is regarded even by sympathetic observers as a sign of chronic inefficiency and susceptibility to informers. ANC training camps are a shambles, regularly vulnerable to South African hit squads.[25]

This view echoes that of the Chief of the South African Defence Forces, General Constand Viljoen. The attacks on the SASOL plant in June 1980 and the subsequent attacks upon power stations in 1981 — which are regarded as key installations and therefore tightly guarded — suggest the existence of a highly-organised intelligence network, the presence of highly-trained guerrillas operating in South Africa and a well-organised back-up system to provide for the guerrillas both before and after their missions. So that while some of the operations might be characterised as amateurish and the equipment used described as crude, the efforts of the guerrillas cannot be dismissed as lightly as the political editor of the *Economist* or General Viljoen attempt to do. ANC guerrillas have demonstrated the capability to mount a wide range of operations in widely-dispersed parts of the country. The knowledgeable journalist, Patrick Laurence, in a perceptive analysis of the ANC's military campaigns, has written:

The Resurgence of the ANC   319

Railway lines are blown up 1,000 miles apart, police stations attacked in densely populated urban areas, pylons are blown up in several different areas and — most important — co-ordinated attacks launched against strategic and well-guarded installations.

The well-timed, simultaneous attacks on power stations and SASOL plants reflect the growing expertise and sophistication in ANC guerrilla units. *Few observers would agree without qualification with General Viljoen's characterisation of ANC saboteurs as 'generally unprofessional'.*[26] (Emphasis added.)

Laurence adds that the military campaigns of the ANC guerrillas cannot be viewed in isolation but have to be viewed together with the organisation's attempt to win mass support, through 'armed propaganda'. He explains that the armed actions are succeeding in winning mass support for the ANC:

There is little doubt that the campaign has been successful. Surveys of Black opinion conducted by independent researchers point to a growing endorsement of revolutionary action and a corresponding rise in the appeal of ANC leaders, especially of Nelson Mandela.

The plumes of smoke which rose over power stations and petroleum plants after the ANC raids were a visible sign to the Black people that the ANC was a visible movement with direct relevance to South Africa, not a clique of exiled theorists.

The clearest evidence of how Black people see ANC guerrillas came at the funeral [in 1980] of the three ANC gunmen killed by a crack police unit after they had held Whites hostage in a Silverton bank. All three were given heroes' funerals in an uninhibited display of Black solidarity which shocked the White establishment. (Emphasis added.)

Pretoria Car-Bomb Attack — Phase Four?

On 19 May 1983 a car bomb exploded outside the headquarters of the South African Air Force in Pretoria, killing 18 and injuring almost 200 persons. The ANC claimed responsibility for the attack, the impact of which exceeded any of the previous acts of sabotage carried out by freedom-fighters of the liberation movement. The Pretoria car-bomb attack marks a deviation from the previous ANC strategy of avoiding, as far as possible, targets that might result in civilian casualties. In explaining this shift, the ANC President, Oliver Tambo, addressing a news conference in the Kenyan capital Nairobi, said that the car-bomb attack was in retaliation for the South African military raid into Lesotho the previous December in which 30 South African refugees and 12 Basotho were killed.

The Pretoria car-bomb attack raises certain questions. Was the attack

320   *The National Liberation Struggle: Problems and Prospects*

a sporadic action, or did it signal the start of a sustained military campaign by guerrillas of the liberation movement? Does the ANC have the capacity to sustain a prolonged military campaign? Is the country going to experience more car bomb attacks as in Northern Ireland or Lebanon?

The car bomb heralds the beginning of a new phase in the ANC's strategy and tactics. Civilian casualties are inevitable, not as a deliberate strategy, but in the process of attacking enemy personnel. This is a qualitative development from the 'armed propaganda attacks' of the past few years. ANC military strategists could not ignore the criticisms emanating from the Black community in South Africa that in the ANC's military operations in which there were casualties, as in the attacks upon police stations, the casualties were predominantly Black. Nor could they ignore the pressure from those militarily-trained cadres who have called for attacks upon enemy personnel even at the risk of civilian casualties. Raids by South African military forces into neighbouring countries, like Mozambique and Lesotho, which have resulted in scores of civilian deaths, have also served to reinforce the arguments of those within the ANC who have advocated confrontations with enemy military forces as opposed to attacks upon 'inanimate objects'. They were probably encouraged, too, by the positive response among Black South Africans to the bombing. One foreign correspondent pointed out in a despatch from South Africa that most Blacks appeared to applaud the attack.[27] Bantustan leaders, regarded by most politically-sophisticated Blacks as collaborators, condemned the attack.

A more difficult assessment to make at this stage is whether the ANC has the capacity to sustain a prolonged campaign of military operations that include combat with the South African armed forces. The organisation has sustained sporadic attacks ever since 1976. During the period between 1976 and 1983, there was a discernible growth and development from explosions of pamphlet bombs to sabotage of strategic and economic installations. During the same period the ANC has, according to estimates made by the CIA, successfully infiltrated over 1,000 guerrillas into the country.[28] That figure, coupled with the estimated 5,000 to 10,000 militarily-trained cadres the ANC has in reserve, gives the organisation a capacity or potential capacity to sustain its military activities for quite a while yet.

Much depends on other factors, inter alia, whether Black support in South Africa for the ANC would be translated into active participation in the armed struggle; and the commitment of the African front-line states to an intensification in armed struggle in South Africa. One lesson of the armed struggles for liberation in other parts of Africa, including Mozambique and Zimbabwe, is that as the struggle developed, there was a corresponding increase in the exodus of people leaving the country, either to escape the repression of the ruling class, or consciously leaving to join the liberation forces. As the conflict escalated, the liberation movements in Mozambique and Zimbabwe were able to generate cadres. Even in the case of the ANC, during the past few years, the organisation has been able to recruit persons inside the country for military training abroad. The organisation has also successfully recruited individuals to undertake various assignments on its behalf, ranging from research and information-gathering to caching arms. The PAC, on the other hand, which has been inactive, has recruited very few persons during the past seven years.

Stricter control over the movements of persons inside the country, increased border patrols and other measures may *contain* the number of guerrilla attacks, but will not eliminate them.

Similarly, the attacks will be sustained in spite of the African front-line states. Freedom-fighters will continue to operate surreptitiously across the borders of the neighbouring independent countries, even though the national liberation movements will not be permitted military facilities in these countries. FRELIMO freedom-fighters infiltrated into Mozambique through Malawi during the struggle against the Portuguese despite the hostility of the Banda regime to the liberation movement. South Africa, in 1983 and 1984, intensified military, diplomatic and economic pressures upon the African front-line states in an attempt to deter them from supporting the ANC, overtly or covertly. In September 1983 South Africa demanded the expulsion from Lesotho of almost 100 ANC and PAC exiles living in that country, on the grounds that they constituted a 'security threat' to the White minority regime. The extent to which the African front-line states succumb to such pressures will affect the capacity of the ANC to sustain a prolonged campaign of military activities, including combat with South African armed forces, because of the ANC's predominantly external location. In March 1984, Mozambique signed a non-aggression pact with South Africa under which the FRELIMO government undertook to prohibit guerrilla attacks by ANC freedom-fighters from Mozambican territory. This was a setback for the ANC in that the organisation's military programme since 1976 was facilitated by the existence of a friendly government in Mozambique, even though officially the organisation was not allowed to establish military bases there.

In the aftermath of the Nkomati Accord the ANC's military operations seemed to be a panic reaction rather than the result of a sober reappraisal of the implications of the pact. ANC statements condemning the Nkomati Accord were accompanied by a few bomb explosions within the country as though to create the impression that the organisation was not about to have the rug pulled from under its feet. It was only in May, June and July 1984 that there appeared to be a re-affirmation of the phase ushered in by the Pretoria car-bomb attack. In May 1984 ANC guerrillas clashed with South African police and armed forces after the guerrillas were caught blowing up an oil depot in Durban. The guerrillas were heavily outnumbered and outgunned but engaged the

322 *The National Liberation Struggle: Problems and Prospects*

police and troops in a battle lasting several hours. On 11 June 1984 South Africa's Commissioner of Police, Brigadier Johann Coetzee, announced that two freedom-fighers were killed in a confrontation with security forces near Welkom on Friday, 8 June 1984. Police seized quantities of explosives and limpet mines, he said. In July 1984 a car bomb exploded in Durban killing 5 people and injuring several others. These incidents are significant in that they took place after the signing of the Nkomati Accord between Mozambique and South Africa when many observers and analysts predicted that guerrilla attacks against South Africa by the ANC's military wing would cease.

The Pretoria car-bomb attack raised the spectre of similar attacks being repeated in future. Even if the ANC were to resort to the use of this weapon again, the organisation would demonstrate a concern to keep civilian casualties to a minimum. The Durban car bomb in July 1984 went off a few minutes after a military convoy had passed. Clearly, it was aimed at a military target rather than civilians even though civilians were ultimately killed when the bomb missed its intended target. Image, particularly in the liberal circles of the West, is important to ANC leaders who repeatedly emphasise that they are not 'terrorists'. A danger is that the South African security forces may plant car bombs in areas where Black civilian casualties would be great, in order to discredit the ANC among the Black masses. Or, alternatively, White extremist groups, determined to prevent any concessions to the Black majority, may resort to the same tactics. The Rhodesian security forces perpetrated numerous atrocities against Black civilians (as well as White liberals, like the clergy, suspected of being sympathetic to the cause of liberation) in an attempt to alienate the liberation forces from the masses and also erode the support of sympathisers in the White establishment. The armed struggle for liberation in South Africa has not reached the same level of development as it did in Zimbabwe and Algeria, but the lesson which can be drawn from the liberation struggles in the two countries is that greater civilian casualties can be expected as a result of outrages committed by the security forces of the ruling group and extremist groups determined to maintain their privileged status.

This examination of the armed actions launched by ANC freedom fighters has revealed a qualitative change since 1976 and indicates that guerrilla warfare, although still limited in its impact upon the White population, is growing in extent and sophistication. The South African Defence Minister, General Magnus Malan, complained in October 1983 that the Whites were still complacent and did not fully realise the extent of the 'total onslaught' against the regime; he reported that there had been 13 sabotage operations by freedom-fighters in 16 days. A few days later, ANC freedom-fighters blew up oil storage facilities at Warmbads in the Transvaal, in an operation the Minister of Law and Order, Mr. Louis le Grange, admitted was 'sophisticated'.[29] Damage caused in the ANC's armed actions thus far has been estimated at

The Resurgence of the ANC   323

millions of dollars and although it is clear that the armed actions that have been launched during the past eight years are not sufficient to bring about a sudden transfer of political power to the oppressed and exploited majority of the population, the important question to consider in assessing the efficacy of these armed actions is their effect upon the mass of the people. There can be no doubt that there has been an upsurge in mass support for the ANC.

Legitimacy of the ANC

The second important factor in understanding the resurgence of the ANC, is the fact that it is the oldest national political organisation in South Africa and has a legitimacy born of struggle.[30] The history of the organisation has become far more recognisable in the country in the past decade, for a number of reasons other than the armed actions of the guerrillas of Umkhonto we Sizwe. Firstly, some of the people who were on the scene in early struggles resurfaced, such as Oscar Mpetha, the 72-year-old trade unionist from the Western Cape who was convicted in 1983 on charges under the Terrorism Act for his role in organising the resistance of the Nyanga residents to rent increases and in organising a bus boycott in protest against increased bus fares. Mrs. Albertina Sisulu, wife of the imprisoned ANC leader, Walter Sisulu, and mother of the much-persecuted Zwelakhe Sisulu (banned President of the Media Workers' Association of South Africa) returned to the political arena during her brief period of freedom when, for the first time in 17 years, her restriction order was not renewed when it expired in July 1981. In 1983 she was detained soon after being elected to the leadership of the United Democratic Front (UDF), a coalition of some 400 organisations that increased in 1984 to 600 organisations with a membership of 2 million, formed to oppose the South African regime's constitutional proposals which grant limited parliamentary representation in a tricameral chamber to Coloureds and Indians but exclude the majority African population. The assassinations of attorney Griffiths Mxenge in November 1981 and Harrison Dube, a Lamontville community leader in March 1983 — both of them former ANC members and veterans of Robben Island — have also heightened the visibility of the ANC and highlighted the continuity of its involvement in the political struggle. Mxenge, for example, was the instructing counsel in many of the recent political trials. Harrison Dube was undoubtedly assassinated because of his leadership role in the struggle of the people of Lamontville against rent increases.

The Black-run media have also played a significant role during this period. *The Post*, prior to its banning in January 1981, initiated a campaign for the release of Nelson Mandela which was soon taken up internationally. After the victory of ZANU-PF in the Zimbabwean elections

324 *The National Liberation Struggle: Problems and Prospects*

which resulted in the accession to power of Prime Minister Robert Mugabe, the former editor of *The Post*, Percy Gqobosa, urged the South African regime to release Nelson Mandela and conduct a dialogue with the authentic leaders of the Black community with a view to a peaceful solution of the country's problems. The argument was that just as Bishop Muzorewa and other Black collaborators in Zimbabwe were disgraced during the elections when the Zimbabwean masses had the freedom to choose their own leaders, so too would the Black collaborators in South Africa be disgraced. Thereafter, *The Post* helped popularise the ANC Freedom Charter.

The Freedom Charter was debated and adopted by the general conference of the South African Council of Churches (SACC) in 1980; it was also debated by students at the Black University at Turfloop. Among the organisations which subscribe to the Freedom Charter are the Azanian Students' Organisation (AZASO), the Congress of South African Students (COSAS), and the Natal Indian Congress (NIC).

The resurgence of the ANC as a military and political force is reflected in the bitter ideological struggles taking place in the country between the organisations that subscribe to the principles of the Freedom Charter and the organisations that are committed to Black consciousness, the Azanian People's Organisation (AZAPO) and, before its split, the Media Workers' Association of South Africa (MWASA) being representative of the latter. One of the major differences between the two centres around the role of Whites in the liberation struggle, in itself reflective of the ideological struggles of the 1950s between the 'Charterists' and the 'Africanists'. The organisations that subscribe to the Freedom Charter stress the primacy of *class* over race; they argue that the cause of exploitation and oppression is to be sought in the capitalist mode of production in South Africa. They thus welcome the participation of White radicals, professional trade unionists and liberals in the liberation struggle. The organisations that subscribe to Black consciousness emphasise the primacy of the *race* question, encapsulated in the maxim adopted at the conference held in May 1981, that race is a determinant of class.[31] The Black Consciousness Movement remains opposed to co-operation with Whites, arguing that Whites, regardless of their ideological professions, remain 'part of the problem' and cannot be part of the solution.[32]

Coupled with the resurgence of the ANC as the leading liberation force in South Africa has been the 'defection' of leading protagonists of Black consciousness to the ANC, among them Barney Pityana, a founder member of SASO, and Thozamile Botha, former chairman of the Port Elizabeth Black Civic Organisation (PEBCO), so that coupled with the military capacity of the ANC is the fact that it is a political home in which many ideologues of the Black Consciousness Movement can feel comfortable. This has served also to undermine the PAC.[33]

This does not mean, however, that the ANC in exile has not had problems. The decision in 1969 (at the Morogoro conference) to admit

The Resurgence of the ANC   325

individuals from the other racial groups to full membership of the ANC resulted in a backlash that reached its zenith with the expulsion in 1975 of eight leading members, who hived off to form the 'ANC-African Nationalists'.

This was followed by the Okhela affair and the arrest in South Africa of the well-known poet, Breyten Breytenbach, who was sentenced in 1975 to nine years' imprisonment after his trial and conviction on charges under the Terrorism Act. Breytenbach was released in 1982, reportedly as a result of representations by the French Government. It would seem that Okhela was formed by a group of White South African exiles, with the encouragement and support of certain leading members of the ANC, in an effort to counter the influence and control of the South African Communist Party over the ANC.[34] The arrest of Breytenbach, and the return to South Africa of another leading figure, Barend Schuitema, who confessed to being a police informer, resulted in the demise of Okhela.

In January 1980 the South African spy scandal which ultimately resulted in the folding up of the International University Exchange Fund (IUEF) threatened to have far-reaching consequences for the ANC, since the spy, a captain in the security police, had been given letters of credence by officials of the ANC. Captain Craig Williamson, during the time that he worked for the IUEF, which not only provided scholarships for South African refugees but was also a major sponsor of the Black Consciousness Movement in South Africa, was also a lobbyist for the ANC. He gathered a wealth of information about the ANC's activities abroad and its contacts inside the country. The detention of the late Steve Biko in August 1977 has been attributed to information gathered by Williamson.[35] He was one of the first members of the security police to go to the scene of the siege of the hostages by ANC guerrillas in a Silverton bank in January 1980; he was the main state witness in the trial on charges under the Terrorism Act of Dr. Renfrew Christie in 1980. The latter, a research fellow at the University of Cape Town, was charged with having conspired with the former Director of the IUEF, Lars Gunnar-Erikson, and/or members of the ANC, to obtain information about South Africa's energy programme.[36] He was convicted and sentenced to a total of ten years' imprisonment.

The Craig Williamson scandal was followed by the suspension in that same year of Rob Petersen (the former editor of the SACTU journal, *Workers' Unity*), Martin Legassick (the eminent historian) and two others, as a result of their criticisms of the failure by the ANC and SACTU to engage in underground political work among the South African masses, particularly the workers, a failure which they saw as encouraging a dangerous attitude of 'militarism' among the liberation forces.[37]

It is testimony to the resilience of the revitalised ANC that these internal problems have not had as debilitating an effect on the organisation as the problems of the PAC have had on that organisation.

326 *The National Liberation Struggle: Problems and Prospects*

Notes

1. *The Times*, 24 September 1981.
2. Lodge 1982, p. 9.
3. Saul and Gelb 1981, p. 137.
4. Ibid.
5. Ibid.
6. See Paul van Slambrouck: 'Sabotage in South Africa: Guerilla raids are gaining legitimacy', in *Christian Science Monitor*, 17 December 1981.
7. Turok 1974, p. 52.
8. Hirson 1979, p. 199.
9. *Rand Daily Mail*, 17 April 1978, quoted in International Defence and Aid Fund For Southern Africa Research Paper, 'Developments in South Africa since the Uprising of 1976', (April 1981) London, p. 13.
10. Lodge 1982, p. 9.
10. Kane-Berman 1979, p. 223.
12. 'Twenty years of Armed Struggle in South Africa: 1961–1981' (16 December 1981), a chronology published by the UN Centre Against Apartheid, New York.
13. Kane-Berman 1979, p. 223.
14. Lodge 1982, p. 9.
15. The implication of the criticism is that the targets should be White persons in White areas. The PAC, of course, has coined a new phrase, namely that it has 'no quarrel with inanimate objects', but thus far has done nothing about the animate objects with which, presumably, it has a quarrel. Chief Gatsha Buthelezi's Inkatha adopted a resolution at its conference in 1981 criticising what it termed the 'destruction of property as a strategy for liberation'. See South African Institute of Race Relations, p. 27.
16. Statement issued by ANC office in Dar-es-Salaam, quoted in UN chronology.
17. *Cape Times*, 20 July 1982; *The Sowetan*, 25 July 1982.
18. *The Sowetan*, 25 July 1982.
19. Lodge 1982.
20. Ibid.
21. The calculations are based on the figures provided in the UN chronology, the IDAF research paper, press reports as well as ANC publications, *Sechaba* and *Weekly News Briefing*.
22. Quoted in UN chronology, p. x.
23. For example, the report of the *Steyn Commission of Inquiry into the Reporting of Security Matters* gave considerable space to the threat posed by banned organisations and devoted several pages to justifying the banning of *The Post* and *Sunday Post*. The Minister accused them of fomenting a revolutionary situation, of being infiltrated by the ANC, and of disseminating ANC propaganda. Further evidence of the regime's attempts to suppress news and information about guerrilla activities has been provided by US intelligence documents leaked to the press by TransAfrica, the Black American lobbying organisation. According to the intelligence documents, there were sabotage blasts in South Africa in January and February 1982 but they were not reported in the media because the media did not know; after concealing the news, the regime then carried out the repairs in similar secrecy. See *Rand Daily Mail*, 21 July 1982.

The Resurgence of the ANC 327

24. Lodge 1982, p. 7.

25. See 'Divide and Rule', in The Survival Ethic, *The Economist*, 18 September 1981.

26. *The Guardian* (London), 27 July 1981.

27. Joseph Lelyveld, *The New York Times*, 25 May 1983.

28. US intelligence documents leaked by TransAfrica provided the estimates. See *TransAfrica Forum*, April 1983.

29. *The Herald*, 12 October 1983.

30. Saul and Gelb 1981, p. 139.

31. See South African Institute of Race Relations 1982, p. 28 for report of conference held in May 1981 attended by 200 delegates. The purpose of the conference was to examine the 'ideology' of Black Consciousness. The conference was marked by acrimonious debate.

32. See Patrick Laurence, 'Black Consciousness Survives Biko', in *The Guardian* (London), 13 September 1981.

33. Ibid.

34. See Dreyer 1980 for details of Okhela, its formation and the role of Breytenbach.

35. South African Institute of Race Relations 1984, p. 80.

36. South African Institute of Race Relations, 1981 p. 251 for details of indictment and trial of Christie.

37. Saul and Gelb 1981, pp. 142-3.

16. Unity Within the National Liberation Movement

Unity Between the ANC and PAC?

At a symposium on 'terrorism' in August 1981, South Africa's chief of the security police, Brigadier Johann Coetzee, speculated on the possibility of a united front between the ANC and PAC, on the lines of the Patriotic Front between ZANU and ZAPU in Zimbabwe. Coetzee warned the White populace to brace themselves for an increase in 'terrorism' in both the urban and rural areas.[1] The prospects for unity between the two organisations, however, are remote. In 1978 the OAU appointed a seven-member ad hoc committee under the chairmanship of Zambia to try to effect a reconciliation between the ANC and PAC. Thus far there has been no progress. The Committee has not met since late 1978.

The ANC has set out its position on the question of unity in the liberation struggle in a document entitled, 'Strategy and Tactics', adopted in 1969 at the Morogoro Conference:

> Whatever instruments are created to give expression to the unity of the liberation drive, they must accommodate two fundamental propositions: firstly, they must not be ambiguous on the question of the primary role of the most oppressed African mass, and secondly, those belonging to the other oppressed groups and those few white revolutionaries who show themselves ready to make common cause with their aspirations, must be fully integrated on the basis of individual equality.[2]

In the formulation of these principles, the ANC was mindful of the charge levelled by its detractors that non-Africans played too prominent a role, hence the emphasis upon the leading role of the Africans. At the same time, it made clear the fact that there is a role in the liberation struggle for Coloureds, Indians and White radicals.

The ANC has argued that attempts to impose unity upon the two liberation organisations are not likely to succeed and that genuine unity can only be achieved on the field, in struggle inside the country.[3] More recently, in response to the ANC declaration of 1982 as the 'Year of Unity in Action', activists of the ANC again ruled out any formal unity

Unity Within the National Liberation Movement 329

with the PAC, or any other organisation. They argued instead that any organisational unity must flow from unity among the broad masses of the people in the country in active participation in the liberation struggle:

> 'Unity in action' . . . in practical terms means that we . . . must seek to broaden the areas of mobilisation, increase the numbers of people mobilised into revolutionary structures and increase and make more specific the campaigns around which we fight.[4]

In the absence of any discussion between the two organisations, and agreement not only on the propositions put forth but also, and, perhaps, more importantly, the implementation, it is difficult to conceive of such unity in action being achieved, particularly inside the country where the ANC and PAC are banned, where new organisations have emerged and are engaged in overt legal activity. Moreover, the tendency in recent years, as during the 1976 township revolt and again during the 1980 student-worker struggles, has been for the masses to respond (and even to organise) without regard to party political affiliations. Many activists who were united in action inside the country have been bitterly divided after leaving the country and joining the exiled organisations. In the absence of defined and agreed areas of co-operation between the two organisations, quite clearly the envisaged 'unity in action' seems elusive.

The PAC has expressed itself in favour of a united front with the ANC (and, in recent years, with the Black Consciousness Movement). The views of the PAC on the creation of a united front were enunciated by Potlako Leballo at the second consultative conference held in Arusha, Tanzania, in 1978:

> The formation of a progressive front is not aimed at setting up a single party, no matter how desirable this may be, but to achieve unified command. A united front of progressive forces is a voluntary coalition of parties and organisations that retain their organisational identity, political independence and ideological outlook but deliberately and sincerely work together to ensure, through joint efforts, the success of an accepted programme.

This formulation envisages a formal alliance between the ANC and PAC, which may also be expanded to include other progressive organisations. Each organisation would retain its autonomy but there would be co-operation in defined areas of operation. But this is exactly what the ANC rejects, arguing that unity at the top must be the culmination of unity in action at the base.

The PAC call for the creation of a united front with the ANC is, however, politicking aimed at demonstrating to the OAU member states

330   *The National Liberation Struggle: Problems and Prospects*

and supporters of the liberation struggle that while the PAC is prepared to discuss unity, the ANC is intransigent. PAC leaders and representatives reserve their venom for the ANC, whose leaders they dismiss as 'puppets' of the White radicals and communists in the organisation. Without a military programme for armed struggle, PAC leaders consistently attack the ANC leaders for adopting a military strategy 'drawn up by Whites', a strategy that avoids loss of White lives but dispenses with Black lives. In June 1983, two members of the PAC stated in their letters of resignation that they were tired of hearing from PAC leaders and representatives how they had 'trounced' or 'crushed' the 'Charterists' (a derogatory term for the ANC) without ever being informed of the progress which the PAC was making in the execution of armed struggle in South Africa.[5]

Apart from the political differences between the ANC and PAC, there are additional factors which make unity between the two organisations an unattainable objective at present. Firstly, there is the bitter personal enmity between the members, particularly the older exiles, arising out of the history of the ideological struggles which preceded and also succeeded the split in 1959 when the PAC was formed. Secondly, there is the bitter experience of the failure of the effort in the early 1960s to establish a South African United Front in exile, with mutual accusations for the failure of the Front. Thirdly, and perhaps more importantly, the competition between the ANC and PAC for support and influence internationally has widened the cleavage between them — so much so that the ANC refuses to share a platform with the PAC except at meetings of the OAU, the UN, the Movement of Non-Aligned Countries and selected forums which the ANC regards as being sufficiently important to compromise, as for instance, the frequent meetings of African and American leaders organised by the New York based African–American Institute.

Super-power Rivalry and Implications for Liberation Unity

If the history of the liberation struggles in other parts of the subcontinent provides any lessons for the South African National Liberation Movement it is that the intensification of the armed struggle will result in a corresponding increase in external intervention, particularly rivalry between the super-powers. The USSR and the Eastern Bloc countries are currently the principal source of material support for the ANC. Barring any change in fortunes for the ANC, this support can be expected to continue. The major Western powers, which are the principal sponsors of the Pretoria regime, can be expected to continue to frustrate efforts to impose mandatory economic sanctions and other punitive measures against the regime, while simultaneously pursuing diplomatic efforts aimed at a negotiated 'peaceful solution', as they have

Unity Within the National Liberation Movement 331

done on the question of Namibia, enabling South Africa to devise endless delaying tactics.

The motivation of Western, particularly United States, diplomatic efforts in Southern Africa, is the fear that protracted armed struggle will result in the accession to power of radical national liberation movements which would undermine, if not terminate, their economic and strategic interests in the sub-continent. At worst, the region would become part of the Soviet sphere of influence. This was a major concern of the USA in Angola after the Portuguese coup of April 1974. Similarly, Kissinger's shuttle diplomacy in Southern Africa in 1976 (after the ill-fated US-backed South African invasion of Angola in an attempt to prevent the accession to power of the MPLA, and overt and covert support for the FNLA and UNITA) was partially motivated by the desire to prevent the success of the National Liberation Movement, particularly ZANU-PF, in Zimbabwe, for fear that such an eventuality would have far-reaching consequences for US strategic and economic interests in the region. In other words, successful armed struggle would result 'in chaos' which would be 'exploited by the communists'.[6]

The Reagan Administration views the situation in Southern Africa in terms of global power politics: the Pretoria regime, regardless of its racial policies of apartheid, is a bulwark against the spread of Soviet influence in Southern Africa and is an ally worth courting. In a television interview in March 1981 with the former CBS anchorman, Walter Cronkite, President Reagan, in reply to a question about South Africa, said:

> Can we abandon a country that has stood beside us in every war we have ever fought? A country that, strategically, is essential to the free world in its production of minerals that we all must have?[7]

In pursuit of its policy of 'constructive engagement', the Reagan Administration has increased diplomatic contact with South Africa, arguing that 'quiet diplomacy', rather than public posturing, would be far more effective in dealing with Pretoria. In March 1981, several South African military officials, including the chief of military intelligence, visited the United States in violation of a long-standing ban on such visits. By the time the visit was publicised and the officials asked to leave the country, they had already had discussions with various Reagan Administration officials, including Mrs. Jean Kirkpatrick, the US Ambassador to the UN.

One of the first visitors to the White House when President Reagan returned after his hospitalisation following the attempt on his life in April 1981, was the South African Foreign Minister, Roelof 'Pik' Botha. The latter was toasted by former Secretary of State, General Alexander Haig, with the words: 'Let this be the beginning of mutual trust and confidence between the United States and South Africa — old friends . . . who are getting together again.'[8]

332　*The National Liberation Struggle: Problems and Prospects*

The Reagan Administration permitted the training of the South African coast guard in the United States; granted permission for the South African Government to increase the number of consulates in the United States; granted visas to the South African Springbok rugby team enabling them to play a number of matches in the USA following their demonstration-troubled tour of New Zealand in 1981. Attempts by the Reagan Administration in 1982 to relax the ban on exports to the South African police and military were opposed by the US House of Representatives. In May 1982, the House approved the Foreign Aid Bill which re-imposed restrictions on military aid to South Africa.

Although the Reagan Administration stopped short of according diplomatic recognition to the Bantustans, US embassy officials in South Africa are now permitted to visit these areas. Pretoria's plans to create a Presidential Council under which Coloureds and Asians — but not the majority African population — would be granted representation in a tri-cameral parliament, were likewise welcomed by the US Ambassador to South Africa as well as the Assistant Secretary of State for African Affairs, Dr. Chester Crocker, as a step in the right direction.[9] The Reagan Administration supported Pretoria's application for a loan from the IMF, despite the opposition of various lobbying groups and individual US Congressmen and the UN Special Committee Against Apartheid.

In contrast with the Carter Administration, the Reagan Administration has refused to criticise publicly excesses of South Africa's racial policies or condemn violations of human rights in that country. While the Reagan Administration has cosied up to Pretoria in this fashion, *verkramptes* like Senator Jeremiah Denton (Republican, Alabama) have attempted to demonstrate the extent of 'communist control' over the ANC and SWAPO. The US Senate Sub-Committee on Security and Terrorism conducted hearings in Washington, D.C., in March 1982 at the instigation of Senator Denton, to the delight of the South African Government. A number of defectors from the ANC and SWAPO were brought to testify to the 'fact' that the two national liberation movements are 'Communist controlled'.

If US actions in Angola are anything to go by, then, simultaneously with support for the South African Government, it can be expected to hedge its bets by seeking to support liberation forces opposed to those supported by the Soviet Union. In this regard, it is probable that the US would make overtures to the PAC. Although the PAC is weak and ineffectual, it nevertheless still enjoys recognition by the OAU and the UN as a national liberation movement. In 1965 an approach was made to the PAC by the State Department which was concerned about Soviet support for the ANC; a PAC official even travelled to Washington for discussions.[10] During the regime of Leballo and Sibeko a vigorous effort was made by the PAC to secure US recognition and support. The effort was pursued through the PAC offices in Dar-es-Salaam and New York.

Unity Within the National Liberation Movement   333

In Dar-es-Salaam close contact was maintained with Donald Weaver, a US embassy official who has been named as a CIA operative.[11] Weaver was transferred to Nairobi in 1979.

On 1 June 1979, the PAC received, through its New York office, a sum of $18,500 from the CIA. The funds were transferred by David Sibeko into his personal bank account. Sibeko was assassinated in Dar-es-Salaam less than two weeks later. The PAC Central Committee refused to heed repeated calls made by this writer for a thorough investigation into Sibeko's personal finances and the sources, especially since there were no records. The question posed by the writer as to how Sibeko was able to maintain a personal bank account with a balance of several thousand dollars when he had not been gainfully employed was not answered. Nor did the Central Committee bother to investigate an amount of $7,000 out of a total of $17,000 which had been given to Sibeko by the writer a few days before his death. The money, in travellers' cheques, was to have been converted to cash and taken to Dar-es-Salaam by Sibeko. When he arrived in Dar-es-Salaam two days before his death, however, he surrendered an amount of $10,000 in cash to the former Director of Finance, Erret Radebe. There was never any account for the outstanding $7,000, nor was there any trace of the funds in the PAC bank account in New York when a few months later this writer assumed the position of Observer Representative to the UN. This incident has been cited here as an example of the many irregularities in financial administration in the PAC, so that the sources of the organisation's funds and their disbursement remain highly questionable.

There is no evidence to support the charge made by detractors of the PAC that the organisation was created by the CIA in order to counter the ANC.[12] But running through the history of the PAC in exile is a streak of opportunism at the level of leadership which has by no means been exorcised. If some of the more recent actions of the PAC leadership are any yardstick, like their support for Iraq in the war against Iran, without having any idea of the historic ethnic rivalries and complex origins of that conflict, then *for promises of money the PAC leadership will probably respond favourably to US CIA overtures*.

To say this is not to suggest that the PAC as an organisation is a tool of reaction or imperialism, nor does it mean that all the members of the organisation would willingly play such a role. What it does mean, however, is that among the leaders there have always been individuals who, out of opportunism or pure corruption, would adopt unprincipled political positions (which have inevitably compromised the PAC), merely for financial gain or some immediate advantage. As a consequence, the PAC has found itself in league with the most reactionary and discredited movements in Africa, like COREMO, FNLA, UNITA and Muzorewa's UANC, and supported by the most corrupt and brutal dictatorships — Idi Amin, Mobutu Sese Seko, and the Shah of Iran.

334 *The National Liberation Struggle: Problems and Prospects*

PAC Opportunism Retraced

The pattern of the PAC's lack of principle in its external relations and actions can be traced.

The PAC in the Congo

In the early 1960s, the PAC had military training facilities in the Congo (now Zaire), made available to the organisation by the regime of Cyril Adoula, an adversary of Patrice Lumumba in whose assassination the CIA had been deeply involved. The facilities were secured for the PAC and several other nationalist movements by Holden Roberto, President of the FNLA. Although Roberto was recognised by the OAU as a genuine Angolan nationalist, he also received, annually, a personal retainer from the CIA.[13] The PAC's operations in the Congo collapsed as a result of ethno-regional conflict, with a group from the Transkei (the military leadership) clashing with a group (of urban background) from the Reef. In addition, the PAC recruits were unprepared for the hardships of guerrilla warfare and many deserted within a few days of arrival in the Congo.[14] Among the people who had been sent to the Congo by the PAC are two members of the Central Committee, Molefe Ike Mafole (Chief Representative to the USA and Caribbean) who subsequently remained in the Congo for 14 years, and Enoch Zulu (Director of Intelligence). Mafole and Zulu, however, had no part in the arrangements, or any of the negotiations, either with the Adoula regime or with the FNLA. They had merely been sent there. Mafole readily admitted later that the PAC base was 'monitored by the CIA'.

Nga Machema, or Ndi'bongo, one of the PAC members who had been sent to the Congo, ultimately became an officer in Roberto's army. In 1965, he was sent to the USA to study Police Science at Michigan State University. Michigan State University had received a sum of $25 million from the CIA to run a covert police training programme for the puppet regime of South Vietnam.[15] Nga Machema has been named as having had contacts with the CIA; James Hooker of the African Studies Centre at Michigan State, a CIA operative on campus, reportedly suffered a heart attack while typing a letter to him:

> At the time of his death in May 1976, Hooker was in close contact with a Black South African trained in police administration at Michigan State, whom two of Hooker's colleagues described as a security officer for Holden Roberto's FNLA in Angola. He used various names: to some he was Machema Machema, to others Nga Ndibongo. Hooker told one professor that Machema was 'between the CIA and the military'.
>
> When he died, Hooker possessed Machema/Ndibongo's field notes on Angola: the beginning of a letter in his typewriter read, 'Dear Nga'.[16]

Unity Within the National Liberation Movement 335

Following the defeat of the FNLA and UNITA by the MPLA in the Angolan civil war, Nga Machema returned to the Transkei where he is an instructor in the army of the Bantustan. Before returning to the Transkei he had contact with the PAC leadership.

The PAC maintained the same opportunistic position after the accession to power of Mobutu Sese Seko in the Congo. In 1966, PAC offices in Cairo and Algiers issued statements expressing support for freedom-fighters opposed to Mobutu's regime. In March 1967, however, Potlako Leballo, during a visit to Kinshasa, praised the 'wisdom' and 'far-sightedness' of Mobutu.[17] In November of that same year, the PAC again expressed support for anti-Mobutu guerrillas in its publications. Marcum describes this as 'externally-induced inconsistency'.[18] Opportunism is more apt.

Throughout the 1970s the PAC maintained contact and cultivated relations with Zairean refugees living in Tanzania and anti-Mobutu groups. At the beginning of 1982, however, the PAC leaders once more appealed to Mobutu to resist attempts to have the organisation de-recognised by the OAU. Nyati Pokela personally led the PAC delegation to the meeting of the OAU Liberation Committee, held in Kinshasa in January, so as to canvass the support of Mobutu against the de-recognition lobby led by such radical countries as Mozambique. Appealing to Mobutu's known anti-communism, the PAC alleged that the campaigns for its de-recognition by the OAU were 'Soviet manoeuvres'.

The PAC and the Angolan Liberation Struggle

It has already been explained that the PAC had established relations with Holden Roberto's FNLA in 1963, as a result of which the organisation secured politico-military facilities and financial assistance from the Adoula regime in the Congo. The PAC maintained the alliance with the FNLA even after the collapse of their joint military venture under which the PAC was to have provided instructors and volunteers for Roberto's army. After the formation of UNITA by Jonas Savimbi in 1966, the PAC established an alliance with that organisation. The PAC shared certain affinities with UNITA — both were critical of the role of White communists and radicals in their rival organisations, the ANC and MPLA, respectively. Both were given to mouthing Maoist slogans and rhetoric, denouncing their rivals and their rivals' sponsors as 'revisionists'.

The Angolan civil war exposed the contradictions within the PAC. The Central Committee, led by Leballo, sent a congratulatory cable to Dr. Agostinho Neto on 11 November 1975, the day the MPLA declared independence and proclaimed the People's Republic of Angola. At the same time, however, the Central Committee decided at a meeting in Dar-es-Salaam that T.M. Ntantala (then Deputy Chairperson) should prepare a position paper on the situation in Angola for consideration by the Central Committee at a subsequent meeting; but

336 *The National Liberation Struggle: Problems and Prospects*

the PAC was overtaken by events in Angola.

In the USA, David Sibeko in his capacity as the PAC Director of Foreign Affairs, shared platforms with representatives of the FNLA and UNITA and denounced the MPLA as a 'Soviet puppet' organisation. Various Black organisations in the USA supported the FNLA and UNITA because of the narrow nationalism espoused by the two groups. The Congress of Racial Equality (CORE), led by Roy Innis, was even prepared to recruit mercenaries from among Black American Vietnam veterans to fight against the MPLA.

The PAC sent a token force of about six (from its small pool of twenty-two) trained freedom-fighters to join UNITA in the war against the MPLA. Thus, in the Angolan civil war, the PAC found itself fighting alongside South African forces and mercenaries recruited in different parts of the world to assist the FNLA and UNITA against the MPLA. The PAC cadres were trapped with UNITA forces in southern Angola when the MPLA launched its counter-offensive against the South African invaders, mercenaries, FNLA and UNITA. In January 1976, a number of SWAPO cadres who arrived in Dar-es-Salaam from southern Angola brought a message to the PAC headquarters from the guerrillas who were trapped with UNITA forces. In 1978 at the consultative conference, the Leballo faction denied any role in the despatch of the six freedom-fighters to assist UNITA, blaming the Ntantala faction instead. Not all PAC members supported the FNLA and UNITA. The younger members of the PAC, this writer among them, supported the MPLA.

The hostility encountered by the PAC from the Governments of Angola and Mozambique is the result of the alliances fashioned and maintained with reactionary groups like FNLA, UNITA and COREMA. There are individuals within the present leadership of the PAC who still revere Savimbi, despite his collaboration with the South African regime.

The PAC and Biafra
Other instances of PAC opportunism can be cited, such as support for Biafra in the Nigerian civil war. This support was not out of any principled commitment to the Biafran cause, but merely to seek popularity or favour in Tanzania which supported Biafra.

The PAC and Idi Amin
The PAC maintained a close relationship with Ugandan dictator Idi Amin even when there was irrefutable evidence that Amin and his regime were ruthlessly butchering Ugandans. A huge, framed picture of the dictator adorned the wall facing the entrance to the PAC office in Dar-es-Salaam. Potlako Leballo, who maintained a close personal relationship with Amin until the late 1970s, was furious when he

discovered one day that the picture of 'the field-marshal', as he called him, had been removed. Six female cadres of the PAC who had been sent to Uganda for military training in 1977 gained notoriety in that country because of the high profile maintained by some of them. They were regularly in the company of Amin and his aides. They were ultimately rescued by the Tanzanians and Ugandan liberation forces after the overthrow of Amin in 1979.

While maintaining this relationship with the Amin regime, certain elements within the PAC cultivated relations with the Ugandan revolutionary forces living in Tanzania.

There have been persistent but unconfirmed reports that through Amin the PAC had access to financial and material support from the Israelis. Prior to the 1973 Arab–Israeli war when most African countries broke off diplomatic relations with Israel, it is alleged that contact was maintained by the PAC through the Israeli embassies in Dar-es-Salaam and Nairobi. The Israelis maintained economic interests in Uganda after 1973.[19] Credence to the allegations of a PAC–Israeli connection is given by the fact that even though Libya was a major ally of Amin's Uganda and also supported the PAC, the latter's relations with Libya were with the military leadership, not with the politicians. The Libyan Foreign Ministry at that time was hostile to the PAC, and to Leballo in particular, because of reports circulated by A-APSO about a visit to Israel by Leballo. Victor Mayekiso, the PAC representative in Libya, had to deal with the military leadership through whom all requests for financial and material support were channelled. Whether the PAC had dealings with the Israelis and whether Leballo really visited Israel will probably never be known, but if it turned out to be so, it would not be surprising.

The PAC and the Shah of Iran

Despite the fact that the Iranian regime of the late Shah provided 90% of the apartheid regime's oil needs, the PAC, through David Sibeko in New York, made contact with and appealed to the Iranians for financial assistance. At least once, in February 1978, Sibeko received an amount of $10,000 from the Shah's regime. Once more, the PAC was in company with such reactionary groups as Bishop Muzorewa's UANC in receiving financial assistance from the Shah.

It has to be pointed out, however, that the Shah, in response to criticisms from the OAU and progressive countries for supplying oil to the apartheid regime, made a financial contribution to the OAU Liberation Committee. When the Shah tried to make a financial grant to FRELIMO during the struggle against Portuguese colonialism, FRELIMO rejected the grant as a matter of principle.

While the PAC actively pursued and obtained financial support from the Shah, the organisation also maintained contacts with the forces opposed to the Shah's regime. In the USA, PAC representatives

338   *The National Liberation Struggle: Problems and Prospects*

participated regularly in activities (including demonstrations) organised by the Iranian students. As a result of this moral support for the struggle against the Shah, the PAC was invited to a conference in Teheran organised by the Iranian Union of Students after the overthrow of the Shah. The PAC was represented at the conference by Ngila Mike Muendane who met Abolhassan Bani-Sadr, then a presidential candidate. He also requested financial assistance for the PAC; although promises were made, no financial assistance was received from the new regime in Iran.

The PAC and ZANU-PF

A similar lack of principle was to be discerned in the PAC's relations with ZANU during the liberation struggle in Zimbabwe. While the PAC and ZANU were political allies, the PAC also welcomed the formation of a splinter group, FROLIZI, by Zimbabweans who claimed to be disillusioned with ZANU and ZAPU. FROLIZI was given use of the PAC office facilities in Dar-es-Salaam. Several years after FROLIZI was defunct, that organisation's rubber stamp was still in the PAC office.

While maintaining close relations with ZANU, elements in the PAC leadership opposed the exclusive recognition of the Patriotic Front by the OAU, seeing in such a decision the hand of the Soviet Union. Elias Ntloedibe, at that time the PAC's Administrative Secretary, wrote to David Sibeko in March 1977:

> We don't have the details yet, but the news from Lomé (Togo) seems to indicate that the Patriotic Front has failed to get the endorsement of the OAU Council of Ministers for its sole support or recognition. This is a setback for the Soviet Union and the 'Front-Line States'! It is the first time in the history of the OAU that the Council of Ministers [has rejected] the recommendation of the Liberation Committee. The credibility of the 'Front-Line States' is no doubt greatly affected — *hulle lang sterte is afqekap*. (Their long tails have been cut off).[20]

It was patently clear by March 1977 that the armed struggle in Zimbabwe was being led by the Patriotic Front, particularly ZANU, under the leadership of Robert Mugabe, yet the PAC leadership was opposed to the recognition of this fact by the OAU through granting the Front exclusive recognition and support. Probably, the opposition of the PAC leadership to such a decision was based on the fear that should the OAU adopt such a decision vis-a-vis the Zimbabwean National Liberation Movement, then it might adopt a similar position in respect of the South African Liberation Movement and grant recognition and support to the ANC exclusively.

After the decision of the OAU Heads of State at the Summit in Libreville, Gabon, in mid-1977 to grant exclusive recognition and support to the Patriotic Front, the PAC continued to collaborate with

Unity Within the National Liberation Movement 339

Muzorewa's UANC. In mid-1978 when a number of recruits affiliated to Muzorewa's group went to Libya for military training, they were transported to Dar-es-Salaam airport by the PAC. In Libya, the PAC's representative worked closely with the UANC representative; he declared to the PAC recruits undergoing training that '[Muzorewa] is going to take over that country'.[21]

The PAC and the Palestinians

In the 1970s, the PAC cultivated friendly relations with the Palestinian Liberation Movement. While Al-Fatah, the largest group within the PLO, supported the ANC, the PAC established relations with the PFLP, led by Dr. Georges Habash. More recently, the PAC has strengthened its relations with the PLO under Yasir Arafat, hoping thereby to gain access to petro-dollars from the Middle East. In March 1982, Nyati Pokela cancelled a tour of seven West African countries to travel instead to the Middle East with Gora Ebrahim, his top aide. At that time, the PAC office in Dar-es-Salaam informed the writer that the PLO leader was going to introduce Pokela to a number of Arab sheikhs. On the day that Pokela and his delegation left Dar-es-Salaam, however, Arafat arrived in the German Democratic Republic for discussions with Erich Honeker after which, it was reported, he would visit several other countries. The PAC delegation did not meet Arafat, nor has the organisation's dreams of sharing in the wealth of the Arab oil-producers materialised. While still the PAC Director of Foreign Affairs, this writer warned the leadership against placing too much hope on the Arab oil-producers; apart from Libya, Algeria and Iraq, these countries did not have a record of supporting African liberation movements. This writer warned, too, that there was growing dissension within the ranks of the PLO over Arafat's diplomatic campaign and his seeming quest for US recognition. These warnings were ignored. A few months later, however, the Israelis invaded Lebanon with the declared objective of driving the Palestinians out of that country. The Arab League could not even agree on a statement condemning the Israeli raid, let alone come to the aid of the Palestinians. The Palestinian withdrawal from Lebanon was followed several months later by a violent struggle within Arafat's Al Fatah Movement. A section of the leadership led by Colonel Abu Mussa staged a militant struggle against what they termed Arafat's moderate policies and his abandonment of the armed struggle against Israel. These developments within the Palestinian Liberation Movement affect the PAC directly, in that the organisation has sought to use its relations with Yasir Arafat to gain access to the Middle East. But, there was no analysis by the PAC leadership of the dynamics of Middle East politics prior to venturing into these troubled waters. One individual convinced the PAC leaders that a world of bounteous wealth awaited the organisation and they dived in, fully clad, only to emerge empty-handed.

Opportunism

The dealings with Zimbabwean dissidents, the expressions of support for Iraq in 1981, are further examples of the streak of opportunism at the level of leadership, that poses a very real danger of the PAC being manipulated by external forces to play a divisive and anti-revolutionary role in the South African liberation struggle.

An indication that the PAC has been perceived by Western intelligence agencies and Social Democrats as being a potential counter to the 'pro-Soviet ANC', was the attempt in the mid-1970s by Lars Gunnar-Erikson, Director of the International University Exchange Fund (IUEF) to promote the ANC (African Nationalists) and the PAC.[22] The Social Democratic Parties of Scandinavia and Western Europe, the major donors of the IUEF, were concerned about what they perceived to be Soviet influence in the ANC. In order to counter that, they assessed their options in terms of supporting opposing forces. Initially, the eight members of the ANC who, after their expulsion in 1975, formed the ANC (African Nationalists) together with the PAC, were considered as candidates. But the ANC (African Nationalists) were a non-starter; the group disintegrated. One of the leaders, Tennyson Makiwane, returned to the Transkei Bantustan where he joined Matanzima's 'Foreign Service' and was later assassinated.

The IUEF had at one time offered the PAC, through David Sibeko, office accommodation in Geneva, but the internecine strife within the PAC, coinciding as it did with the growing influence of the Black Consciousness Movement in the country, resulted in Erikson deciding to try to promote the BCM (which he regarded as more dynamic than the PAC) as a 'Third Force'. Through ANC lobbying and the influence of Captain Craig Williamson of the South African security police who had risen to the position of Deputy-Director, the IUEF, in July 1978, decided to grant exclusive recognition to the ANC. The decision infuriated David Sibeko who had regarded Erikson as 'the PAC's man', especially since the decision was taken only a few months after the IUEF (and Erikson personally), had been very co-operative at the time of Sobukwe's death, permitting use of their telex facilities and offering other assistance. Sibeko had also submitted to Erikson, a comprehensive list of the PAC's requirements for the maintenance of 'the hundreds of refugees' who were in Tanzania in the care of the organisation. So incensed was Sibeko that when he was in Geneva in August 1978 to attend the International Conference to mark the commencement of the Programme of the Decade to Combat Racism, he met with Erikson at his home to confront him about the decision of the IUEF to grant exclusive recognition to the ANC.[23]

The lack of political cohesion and lack of accountability have facilitated opportunism among the PAC leaders. This has permitted individuals in the organisation to enter into negotiations as well as maintain associations with dubious characters, without question from

Unity Within the National Liberation Movement 341

others, just as long as the associations bring financial rewards, or promises of such rewards, or some immediate advantage. This would explain the association in the early 1960s of Leballo with Hans Lombard, a White South African suspected by Matthew Nkoana and other leaders at that time of being a security police agent; it also explains the close association of Leballo and David Sibeko with Richard Gibson, despite the suspicions voiced about him not only by PAC members but also by activtists involved in anti-imperialist struggle.[24] Gibson was even a candidate for the board of trustees of the Research Centre proposed by Leballo and Sibeko in the late 1970s. It also explains the naive action of Hamilton Keke, a member of the PAC Central Committee and the organisation's chief representative in London, in handing over to a complete stranger, 40 PAC documents because, he explained during the trial of the individual on charges of theft, he wanted 'publicity for the PAC'. It transpired that the stranger, a Swedish journalist, was a South African agent, working directly on the instructions of Captain Craig Williamson.[25]

This loose-structuredness of the PAC and the lack of principled struggle within the organisation make it extremely vulnerable to infiltration and also to suggestion, so that it is not inconceivable that the organisation will play a counter-revolutionary role as the struggle intensifies and as the rivalry between the super-powers correspondingly increases. To counter this argument it may be pointed out that the PAC has adopted a very strong position in condemnation of super-power rivalry, condemning both US-led Western imperialism and 'Soviet social imperialism'. But so did Savimbi during the anti-colonial struggle in Angola. So strident was Savimbi in his criticisms of the Soviet role in Angola where it supported the MPLA, for example, that he was denounced in the Soviet media as a 'Maoist thug'. Savimbi collaborated with the Portuguese colonialists; subsequently, he collaborated with the South African regime, collaboration which continues today. UNITA also receives financial and material support from certain Western countries because it is regarded as an 'anti-communist force' in Angola.

Rather than attempt to deny the probability of the PAC playing an anti-revolutionary role in the South African liberation struggle, members of the organisation should consider ways and means to ensure that the organisation does not end up playing a role akin to that of UNITA because, as this analysis has attempted to demonstrate, that capacity exists in the opportunism which continues to plague the organisation and in the manner in which the PAC is perceived in certain quarters as being 'anti-communist'.

342   *The National Liberation Struggle: Problems and Prospects*

Unity with Other Patriotic Organisations

Since the Soweto uprising in 1976, a number of other organisations have established missions in exile, notably, the Black Consciousness Movement of Azania (BCM-A) and the South African Youth Revolutionary Council (SAYRCO). Thus far, neither has been accorded recognition by the OAU which has been wary, in view of the problems which plagued the Angolan Liberation Movement up to and including independence, of encouraging a multiplicity of organisations from a single country. Instead, the OAU has emphasised the need for unity among the forces of liberation although, as has already been explained, such unity has not yet been achieved.

Because the two organisations lack OAU recognition, they have experienced difficulties in making any impact internationally. In addition, the trials and tribulations of exile have also affected the BCM-A and SAYRCO, so that the turmoil that has afflicted the older movements has also surfaced within the two newer organisations.

Since 1977 SAYRCO has set up headquarters in Lagos, Nigeria, where their representatives enjoy diplomatic status, along with the representatives of the other liberation movements. Nigeria, frustrated with what appeared then to be the ineffectiveness of the ANC and PAC, had hoped to promote SAYRCO as the 'third force', but thus far, remains the only patron of the organisation although probably is not alone among OAU member states in seeking to promote another movement independent of the two older organisations.[26] While the courage of the students who faced the armed might of the South African regime in Soweto and other places cannot be denied, and while the older movements ought to recognise the role and potential of the students, it also has to be recognised that no successful revolution has ever been led by students. The realisation has begun to dawn upon many of those who left the country after the events of 1976, that the path to liberation does not lie in a hasty flight from the country, a short sojourn abroad, some basic military training and a quick return to 'fight'.

Unity between the ANC and BCM-A
There was a belief within the BCM during the early years of exile that the Movement could play a unifying role among the older organisations. Such a belief was grounded more in hope that in reality since the BCM adherents were ignorant of the contradictions between and within the ANC and PAC. In pursuit of the BCM goal of promoting unity among the patriotic forces in exile, a delegation comprising Nyameko Barney Pityana, Ben Khoapa and Jeff Dumo Baqwa (founder members of the BCM in South Africa), travelled to Lusaka, Zambia, in early 1979 for discussions with the ANC leaders. From all accounts, the BCM met with little success; the ANC leaders indicated that there was room in the ANC for individual members of the BCM, the implication being that the latter should disband.

Unity Within the National Liberation Movement   343

There have been no further discussions between the ANC and the BCM, although several prominent individuals from the BCM, like Barney Pityana, have joined the ANC.

Unity Between the PAC and BCM-A
Since the assumption of the chairmanship of the PAC by Pokela, the organisation has emphasised the need for unity with the BCM. Pokela claimed that during his imprisonment on Robben Island he had reached agreement with a number of the BCM leaders who were imprisoned there in the mid-1970s, to forge unity between the PAC and BCM. While the two organisations, sharing a common Africanist tradition and being 'embattled' as a result of the resurgence of the ANC domestically and internationally, see mutual advantages in such a united front, there are a number of problems militating against such unity. Firstly, within the BCM there are a number of individuals who are former members of the older movements and who for various reasons, including personal enmity, have opposed the creation of a united front. Secondly, the experiences of such attempts at unity in the mid-1970s were unsuccessful, not least because of the factionalism within the PAC and the personal ambitions of some of the individuals who had assumed the leadership of the BCM, particularly in Botswana. Since the individuals of the BCM who had fled South Africa in the early 1970s had had no mandate to represent the BCM abroad and since there was no exile structure, individuals who had been in positions of leadership in the country attempted to transpose that leadership in the new conditions of exile. As a result, there were bitter personal rivalries and factions among the BCM exiles resident in Botswana. This was exacerbated by the fact that the two opposing factions of the PAC, the Leballo and Ntantala factions, each attempted to forge alliances with different contenders for power within the BCM. Each of the factions ended up with different interpretations of the agreements that they believed they had concluded, so that the 'accords' fell apart, with a great deal of acrimony among the various parties. Victor Mayekiso, at that time the PAC's representative in Libya, wrote to David Sibeko in 1976:

> The student body (the BCM) has been most disappointing wherever we take them. Now our latest friends have told me in no uncertain terms that at most we have been infiltrated through this element and, at worst, they are just a group of adventurers who have no dedication to the cause but are just out seeking new experiences. In both cases, they cannot be trusted ... Now we have at all Party levels decided to freeze our relations with the student body . . . If X is there, tell him about the half-baked intellectualism of their boys, their anti-PAC, anti-China and pro-Soviet stance after reading a few books from Novesti on Lenin, and their general Trotskyite, anti-less educated, Unity Movement attitudes. Their position is Trotskyite vis-a-vis the Bolsheviks, but without Trotsky's intellectualism. Of course, a complete lack of seriousness of purpose and sadly, an apparent vein of anti-people's

344 · *The National Liberation Struggle: Problems and Prospects*

> war. They seek the smallest excuse to go back to where they came from because there is an inherent fear of finishing training because they will then be unmasked without excuses . . .[27]

Since many of the persons who had been involved in the early initiatives at unity or co-operation between the PAC and BCM are still politically active, it is clear that the achievement of unity between the two organisations will not be easy, although the circumstances today are different. The BCM has an exile organisational structure; the fact that most of the organisations which constituted the BCM in South Africa, like SASO and BPC, have been banned since October 1977 means there is not the fear or danger of jeopardising the security of individuals and organisations still active in the country by exiles purporting to represent them. That had been one of the constraints in the earlier years.

In October 1982, a BCM-A delegation, led by their chairman, Mazibudi Mangena, visited Dar-es-Salaam to discuss with the PAC leaders, the question of unity between the two organisations. They arrived in Dar-es-Salaam to find the PAC headquarters at sixes and sevens, without any preparations having been made either for the arrival of the delegation, or for the substantive discussions, even though the PAC representatives had been notified months earlier.[28] The BCM-A delegation was further disappointed when Pokela informed them the following day that he was travelling to the USA to address the UN, hence would not be available for the discussions. The BCM-A felt that unity among South African revolutionaries is paramount, so that the discussions should have taken precedence over a trip to the USA to address the UN.

When ultimately the discussions commenced, the PAC was represented by a low-level delegation which had not prepared a discussion paper. The Central Committee was represented by a hapless Nogaga Morgan Gxexwa, a member of the military, whose only contribution to the discussion was to ask the BCM-A's delegation that since they represented the BCM-A, where was the BCM-B?

In short, the meeting achieved nothing, but it afforded the BCM an opportunity to witness at first hand the disarray within the PAC.

We have examined the attitudes of the liberation organisations towards unity in the struggle, prospects for which are not good. The multiplicity of organisations poses a problem in that it creates opportunities for enemy infiltration and at the same time increases the chances for external manipulation once the armed struggle for liberation escalates in South Africa.

Notes

1. *The Guardian* (London), 23 August 1981.
2. Quoted by Slovo in Davidson, Slovo and Wilkinson 1976, p. 175.
3. Memorandum submitted by ANC delegation to a meeting of the OAU Liberation Committee in 1974, quoted by Slovo, ibid., p. 176.
4. See ANC Unit, Western Cape, 'Letter to the Editor', *Sechaba*, June 1982, p. 31.
5. Letters dated 10 June 1983, and 18 June 1983, by Glen Mpukane and Bicca Maseko, respectively.
6. This view was expressed in National Security Study Memorandum (NSSM) 39, which was the review of US policy towards Southern Africa ordered by then US Secretary of State, Dr. Henry Kissinger.
7. Quoted in Saul and Gelb 1981, p. 147.
8. Ibid.
9. South Africa/Namibia Update, March 1983, *Washington Post*, 4 December 1984.
10. This information was provided by a PAC member who had been requested by the US State Department to name a PAC representative with whom discussions could be held. He informed the PAC who sent one of its leaders to Washington for the meeting.
11. His name is listed in Ray, Schaap, Van Meter and Wolf (eds) 1979, among the CIA operatives in the various US embassies in Africa. As far as the author is aware, the list is reliable; the said official was based in Dar-es-Salaam before his transfer to Kenya. This was ascertained by the author.
12. This is a view put forth by Winter 1981, pp. 430–2. Winter claims that his informant was General Hendrik van den Berghe, the former head of South Africa's Bureau of State Security (BOSS).
13. For details of Roberto Holden's relations with the CIA, see Stockwell 1978.
14. Marcum 1978, pp. 116–8.
15. Marchetti and Marks 1974, 1980, p. 205.
16. Lawrence, K., 'Academics: An Overview', in Ray, Schaap, Van Meter and Wolf 1979, p. 84.
17. Marcum in Potholm and Dale (eds) 1972, footnote 53, p. 384.
18. Ibid.
19. Avirgan and Honey 1982.
20. Letter dated 2 March 1977.
21. Interview 24 July 1983, with PAC cadre Junior Majova who was in Libya at that time.
22. See the series of articles by Ken Owen entitled, 'War in the Shadows', in *The Sunday Times* (Johannesburg), 12, 19 and 26 October 1980.
23. Sibeko's report to the Central Committee dated 16 September 1978.
24. See Winter 1981, p. 432, for details of Gibson's suspicious activities.
25. The Swedish journalist, Bertil Olov Wedin, admitted during his trial in the Old Bailey, England, in April 1983 on charges of dishonestly handling stolen PAC documents, that he had received R 1,600 from the South African security police, paid into his Swiss bank account. He was acquitted on the charge because he argued successfully that the documents had been given to him by Keke.
26. For an account of Nigeria's role in the Southern African liberation struggle, see Olajide Aluko, 'Nigeria and Southern Africa', in Carter and

346 *The National Liberation Struggle: Problems and Prospects*

O'Meara (eds) 1982, pp. 128–47. The role of Nigeria is a demonstration of how the Southern African liberation movements have had to contend not only with the international powers, but also with regional powers. Nigeria, Africa's most populous country, has in recent years used its economic muscle, derived from its oil revenue, to secure for itself the status of 'front-line state' in matters relating to the liberation struggles in the sub-continent.

27. Letter dated 20 April 1976, written by Victor Mayekiso to David Sibeko.

28. Interview with BCM-A delegates, Gaborone, Botswana, 10 February 1983.

17. The Enemy: Responses and Capacities

In the decade following the Sharpeville massacre when the South African revolution was 'defeated',[1] analysts concluded that structural change in South Africa could only be effected through external intervention.[2] Various reasons were adduced to support the argument, inter alia, the military might of the South African regime, the effective police controls that had crushed Black resistance and through the medium of such measures as detention and restriction without trial, had successfully curbed extra-legal opposition and criticisms of South Africa's racial policies of apartheid. Psychological reasons were also advanced for the failure of Black revolutionary efforts. Blacks were psychologically not prepared for revolutionary violence,[3] and the failure of the early efforts of the ANC's military wing, Umkhonto we Sizwe, were due to the 'fear of White reprisal'.[4] The US National Security Study Memorandum (NSSM) 39 stated bluntly:

> The whites are here to stay and the only way that constructive change can come about is through them. There is no hope for the Blacks to gain the political rights they seek through violence, which will only lead to chaos and increased opportunities for the communists.[5]

The racism underlying many of the analyses and conclusions on the prospects of the national liberation movements in Southern Africa has been exposed by the successes of the armed liberation struggles waged by the peoples of Guinea-Bissau, Angola, Mozambique and, more recently, Zimbabwe, under the leadership of national liberation movements and by the sustained resistance of the oppressed masses in South Africa, led by their national liberation movements.

The incidence of urban and rural guerrilla warfare in South Africa in the period since the Soweto uprising, sparked off by Black students protesting against a Government decree that certain subjects should be taught in the Afrikaans language, have underscored the fact that the changes that have occurred in the geo-politics of Southern Africa since the collapse of Portuguese colonialism and the defeat of White minority rule in the former Rhodesia, have facilitated the infiltration of liberation forces and equipment into the country. Unlike the situation in the

348   *The National Liberation Struggle: Problems and Prospects*

post-Sharpeville period when trained freedom-fighters had to travel thousands of miles, through unfamiliar terrain, where linguistic differences meant that the freedom-fighers could not merge with the local populations in territories that were ruled by regimes in economic and military alliance with Pretoria, independent Africa is now only a few hours drive by car from the industrial heartland of the Witwatersrand.

Removal of the cordon sanitaire around South Africa's northern borders, however, does not by itself remove all the logistic problems facing the national liberation movements. Given the economic dependence of Mozambique and Zimbabwe, and the peripheral states of Botswana, Lesotho, and Swaziland on South Africa, coupled with their military weakness vis-a-vis their powerful neighbour, they cannot in the foreseeable future permit South African freedom-fighters to operate from their territories. The young Republic of Mozambique, for example, paid a heavy price, economically (through the enforcement of UN mandatory economic sanctions against the Smith regime) and through the loss of life and destruction of property as a result of military aggression committed by the Smith and Smith/Muzorewa regimes in the former British colony of Southern Rhodesia. The newly-independent Republic of Zimbabwe, although sympathetic to the aspirations of the mass of South African people and their national liberation movements, is subject to the same economic and political constraints as Mozambique. Neither of the two countries is in a position to provoke a confrontation with the South African regime by permitting the ANC and PAC to establish military bases from which to launch attacks against the White-ruled Republic. The peripheral states of Botswana, Lesotho, and Swaziland do not permit freedom-fighters to operate from their territories against South Africa. All the countries, however, grant sanctuary to persons fleeing from the brutal repression of apartheid.

Support for the armed liberation struggle in South Africa, overtly or covertly, would expose the African states in the region to pressures and threats of pressures from Pretoria which has already demonstrated its capacity and preparedness to commit acts of aggression against neighbouring states, particularly Angola, Mozambique, Lesotho, Zambia, and Zimbabwe. After South Africa's ill-fated invasion of Angola in 1975–76, the South African regime amended its Defence Act. The legislation now defines South Africa as Africa south of the Sahara. Troops may be committed to any area within this radius without their consent. In addition, the former Prime Minister, B.J. Vorster, as well as his successor, P.W. Botha, repeatedly warned that South Africa will not hesitate to commit aggression against any country in Africa which 'harbours terrorists'.

Pretoria's responses to the changes that have occurred in the subcontinent have been varied. Firstly, P.W. Botha (and the military leadership in the White establishment) mooted the idea of a 'Constellation of Southern African States'. Secondly, Pretoria has engaged in acts

The Enemy: Responses and Capacities 349

of aggression and committed violations of the territorial integrity of the independent states in the region. An examination of the acts of aggression to which these states have been subjected reveals a programme of destabilisation of Southern Africa by Pretoria, particularly of those states which have acceded to independence after years of armed struggle.

The 'Constellation of Southern African States'

The concept of a 'Constellation of Southern African States', was formulated by Pretoria's military strategists as part of their 'total strategy' to counter the 'total onslaught', which, according to the military-politico ideologues, the White minority regime faces. This 'total onslaught' is allegedly political, military, economic and psychological. One of the first explanations of 'total strategy' was made by General Magnus Malan in 1977 while still Chief of the Defence Forces:

> In a mature state the fundamental concepts of conflict entail far more than war. It means the formulation of national objectives in which all the community's resources are mustered and managed on a co-ordinated level to ensure survival. Every activity of the state must be seen and understood as a function of total war.[6]

According to their plans, Pretoria would use its political, economic and military might to establish a grouping of moderate 'anti-Marxist' states in the African sub-continent.

The idea was further propounded by P.W. Botha in the central parliament in April 1979, and subsequently clarified by various National Party spokespersons, academics and analysts. Clearly, Pretoria hoped that the formation of a regional bloc in which it would play the dominant role, would enable it to achieve a number of objectives.

Firstly, in return for certain economic benefits, the independent African states which could be enticed into the alliance would tone down criticisms of the South African regime's racial policies of apartheid, since Botha envisaged the establishment of 'friendly relations with neighbouring states on the basis of non-interference in each other's internal affairs'.[7] By this, Pretoria meant that the countries prepared to join the regional bloc would refrain from criticism of the racial policies of *apartheid* since that would be an internal affair of a legitimate partner in the alliance. The corollary of this would be that the member states of the alliance would also deny support to the ANC and PAC.

Secondly, it was hoped that if the independent African states could be persuaded to join the alliance then international criticisms of *apartheid* would be blunted. Pretoria would be able to point to its co-operation with sovereign and independent African states which are internationally

350 *The National Liberation Struggle: Problems and Prospects*

recognised. The hope was that 'through the adoption of a common approach on matters affecting the region, the Republic would encourage western support in the international community'.[8]

Thirdly, the creation of a regional bloc would have military benefits for the South African regime. In the wake of the independence of Angola and Mozambique, the exodus of thousands of young Blacks after the Soweto uprisings of 1976 and the successes of freedom-fighters in Zimbabwe, there were expressions of concern within the South African military establishment about the 'security threat'.

Having lost the protection of the buffer states, the South African regime hoped that the Bantustans, together with the independent African states prepared to join the alliance, would provide a new cordon sanitaire. Guerrillas of the national liberation movements, if they succeeded in infiltrating from 'hostile' countries, would be contained on the periphery of 'White South Africa' which would assist its partners in the alliance in dealing with the threats to their security. According to Dr. Piet Koornhof, Minister of Co-operation and Development, in a speech in March 1980, the members of the constellation 'would not threaten each other and would present a united front to any external threat'.[9]

The desirability of a regional bloc was emphasised by government as well as White parliamentary opposition spokespersons who pointed out the benefits to South Africa's security and economic development. The idea was enthusiastically supported also by businessmen and industrialists who pointed out that the Southern African region was South Africa's natural hinterland and market for its manufactured goods. It was for this reason that the idea of the 'Constellation of Southern African States' was presented by Botha in November 1979 to a conference of the country's leading businessmen and industrialists with much fanfare.

There was a realisation, however, that progress in the achievement of Pretoria's regional security and economic objectives would be enhanced by changes in internal policy. It was for this reason that Botha's succession to the premiership was accompanied by much rhetoric about 'reform' and 'change'. What was very clear was that the 'reforms' envisaged by the White establishment aimed at creating for Blacks an illusion of 'change', through such measures as desegregation of public amenities and sports facilities, as well as limited access to educational and economic opportunities, while retaining political and economic power firmly in White hands. A knowledgeable journalist who returned to South Africa after an absence of almost five years, to cover the Whites-only general election in April 1981, has written:

> While there is a great ferment in intellectual circles and a continued debate about the need to introduce genuine change — to 'adapt or die', in the dramatic phrase of the Prime Minister — there is neither blueprint nor strategy, nor even some sense of subterranean common purpose on the part of the government to alter the racial underpinnings of South

The Enemy: Responses and Capacities   351

African society. Nor is there, as far as I have been able to discover, an 'explicit commitment' by that government to domestic change in anything other than the vaguest rhetorical terms.[10]

Even the mere rhetoric about the need for change has not been without political cost to the ruling Nationalist Party and to Afrikaner unity. In the general election held in April 1981 the eccentric right-wing Herstigte Nasionale Party (HNP) which has been totally opposed to any liberalisation of *apartheid* increased its share of the popular vote from 2% in 1979 to 13% although it did not win any parliamentary seats. More recently 16 National Party members led by Dr. Andries Treurnicht, former leader of the powerful Transvaal region, were expelled because of their opposition to Botha's acceptance of the idea of limited 'power-sharing' with Coloureds and Indians. Dr. Treurnicht and other expelled MPs formed a new Conservative Party of South Africa. Although, superficially, the splits and divisions within Afrikanerdom may appear to the casual onlooker as a struggle between 'reformists' and 'reactionaries', they manifest shifting class alliances within the White establishment as a whole. What has emerged in recent years as the dominant force is a military-industrial alliance with strong interests in limited domestic reform and an expanded regional role for Pretoria.

Botha's Constitutional Strategy

A cornerstone of the Botha regime's limited domestic reforms has been the new constitution, endorsed by the Whites in a referendum, creating an executive presidency and a parliament of three chambers for Whites, Coloureds and Indians but excluding the 24 million Africans. As a result of the campaign against the new constitutional strategy, spearheaded by the UDF and other organisations, only 30% of the Coloureds and 20% of the Indians voted in the polls in mid-August 1984 to elect representatives to the new tricameral parliament. When the number of eligible voters who did not even bother to register to vote is taken into account, the percentage of votes cast is substantially lower, a mere 10% in the estimates of the UDF. The regime's detention of UDF and AZAPO leaders on the eve of the Coloured and Indian elections failed to stop the boycott. Despite the low voter turn-out Botha declared the results 'acceptable'.

352 *The National Liberation Struggle: Problems and Prospects*

On 14th September 1984 P.W. Botha was sworn in as executive President with powers bestowed upon him by an electoral college of the new tricameral parliament to declare war, veto legislation and to summon and dismiss parliament. On 18 September 1984 Coloureds and Indians sat in the formerly all-White parliament for the first time but their influence in the new constitutional arrangement is circumscribed. The constitution provides for separate chambers for the Coloureds and Indians and they can only make final decisions on their 'own affairs' — like the daily administration of health and educational services — and not on overall policy. The new constitution, rather than being a new dispensation as it has been hailed by the Reagan Administration among others, entrenches racial discrimination, consolidates Afrikaner power and co-opts sections of the Coloured and Indian racial groups as junior partners in the oppression of the majority. The investiture of Botha as President was marked by unrest and police violence in Black townships throughout the country. The world was left in no doubt as to how the vast majority of Black people felt about the 'new political dispensation'.

Larger Regional Role

The idea of a larger regional role in Africa is one that has gripped the imagination of many an Afrikaner, not least among them former Prime Minister, B.J. Vorster, whose policies towards Africa — the 'outward-looking policy', 'dialogue', and finally, 'detente' — were all aimed at achieving legitimacy for White-minority rule in South Africa through economic and technical co-operation with Black Africa. In the mid-1970s Pretoria was even prepared to co-operate with Black Africa in the solution of the 'Rhodesian problem' by using economic pressure to force Ian Smith to negotiate a settlement with the Zimbabwean nationalists. Pretoria hoped thereby that Africa would restrain the national liberation movements fighting for the overthrow of white-minority rule in South Africa and Namibia.

Africa's Response: the Southern African Development Co-ordinating Conference (SADCC)

Pretoria's plans to formalise the creation of a 'Constellation of Southern African States' were predicated upon an independent Zimbabwe under acquiescent Black leadership in the person of Bishop Abel Muzorewa. The Bishop — who succeeded to the premiership following the 'internal settlement' effected by Ian Smith with several Black collaborators — had publicly committed himself (and an independent Zimbabwe under his leadership) to the regional bloc. For this reason, Pretoria invested heavily in the Bishop's election campaign after the Lancaster House

Agreement.[11] P.W. Botha threatened that his country would intervene militarily in Zimbabwe should the elections provided for under the Lancaster House Agreement result in 'chaos' — which was generally assumed to mean election victory by ZANU-PF.

The crucial position of Zimbabwe in Pretoria's schemes to formalise the establishment of the regional bloc has to be understood in terms of that country's strategic location, its economic potential and control of the heart of the communications and transport systems in the region. Zimbabwe has a thriving agricultural sector, often in surplus, and the making of an efficient, mineral, industrial and financially-based economy.

The independence of Zimbabwe under the leadership of Prime Minister Mugabe has dashed to pieces Pretoria's hopes of creating a 'Constellation of Southern African States'. Zimbabwe has joined eight other independent states in the region to establish the Southern African Development Co-ordinating Conference (SADCC) with a view to disengaging themselves from South Africa's economic stranglehold by promoting economic co-operation among themselves.[12] Guy Arnold enumerates two important consequences of Zimbabwe's independence for the region:

> (1) [It gives] new impetus to the surrounding states to search for alternatives to reliance upon the Republic [of South Africa]; and . . .
> (2) Zimbabwe . . . after South Africa has the most sophisticated infrastructure and economy in the region [hence can] replace South Africa, for example, as the source for at least some of the imports countries such as Malawi, Botswana, and Swaziland now take from the Republic.[13]

The co-ordination proposed by SADCC is comprehensive and encompasses the areas of agricultural research, food security, industrial development, technical co-operation and energy and manpower. The first priority of SADCC is the construction of a regional transport and communications infrastructure not dependent on South Africa.[14]

Clearly the task of reducing economic dependence on South Africa is a daunting one. Apart from South Africa being the dominant economic power in the region — a fact recognised and admitted by the SADCC countries — Pretoria will not stand idly by while the nine formulate strategies to lessen their dependence. The task facing the nine has been assessed by Julian Burgess:

> South Africa is the largest trading partner for Zimbabwe, Botswana, Swaziland, Lesotho and Malawi and is a critical source of imports for both Zambia and Mozambique. Zimbabwe's exports to South Africa actually increased for the first four months of 1981, amounting to a quarter of the total. Nor is this the most important of South Africa's services.

354   *The National Liberation Struggle: Problems and Prospects*

South Africa's ports remain vital to all of the SADCC countries, apart from Angola and Tanzania, as well as handling Zairean trade. At the time of its independence, over 90% of Zimbabwe's trade went to or through South Africa and its ports. Though Mozambique now takes about 27% of Zimbabwe's trade, it will be years before it can handle it all. South Africa is now estimated to employ 245,000 workers each year from SADCC states, comprising 40% of the South African mine work force, and these jobs are simply not available at home.[15]

South Africa's punitive economic measures against the newly-independent Zimbabwe (which alone of the SADCC nine has a significant industrial base, hence the potential to rival South Africa's dominance) and its general destabilisation of the region (of which more later) reflect its determination to maintain its economic stranglehold over the independent African states.

A notable feature of the SADCC is the sober realism among the member states, not only of the extent of their economic involvement with South Africa but also of the difficulties and challenges ahead in diminishing that involvement. The realism was reflected in the declaration adopted by the Lusaka summit of SADCC in April 1980: 'Southern Africa is dependent on the Republic of South Africa as a focus of transport and communications, an exporter of goods and services, and as an importer of goods and cheap labour,' The late President Khama of Botswana, in his capacity as Chairman of the Conference warned of the difficulties: 'The struggle for economic liberation will be as bitterly contested as has been the struggle for political independence.'

Rather than embark upon grandiose schemes the SADCC has opted for a modest, achievable programme for economic liberation.

Pretoria's Programme of Destabilisation

The SADCC has not only frustrated South Africa's schemes to formalise the 'Constellation of Southern African States', but also poses a threat to the apartheid regime's hegemony in the region. Should the SADCC succeed in the stated objective of diminishing economic dependence on South Africa, then the nine would be less vulnerable to economic pressures from the White-ruled Republic which has repeatedly threatened retaliation against the independent African states in the region in the event of economic sanctions against the apartheid regime.

Pretoria has, therefore, responded with hostility towards the SADCC and has embarked upon a programme of destabilisation in the region. The programme of destabilisation has several prongs: direct military incursions into neighbouring states; training and supporting of dissident groups in the neighbouring states; assassinations and kidnapping of exiles and refugees; and economic sabotage.

Direct Military Incursions

Angola, Lesotho, Zambia and Mozambique have experienced direct military aggression: border incursions as well as violations of their airspace by South African military forces.

Ever since its accession to independence in November 1975 the People's Republic of Angola has been subjected to repeated acts of aggression by South African Defence Forces. The South African regime has attempted to justify its military aggression against Angola on the grounds of 'hot pursuit' operations against the freedom-fighters of SWAPO.

The Angolan authorities estimated that in the 18-month period June 1979–December 1980 at least 400 civilians and 85 soldiers were killed, 640 civilians wounded. During that same period an untold number of Namibian refugees were killed and wounded. The most gruesome invasion of refugees occurred in May 1978 when South African forces attacked with air and land forces a Namibian refugee camp, at Kassinga, killing almost 800 people, including women and children. The South African regime put out its usual propaganda claiming that its military forces had destroyed a 'terrorist base'. The UNHCR, however, confirmed that the camp attacked was a refugee camp. Western journalists who were taken to the scene of the massacre by Angolan authorities, corroborated this. In southern Angola in particular, the agricultural sector, the industrial, transport and communications infrastructure have suffered extensive damage.

Throughout 1981 South African forces invaded Angola regularly. In August 1981, South African forces from bases in northern Namibia, launched a massive invasion of Angola during which several towns in the southern provinces were overrun and occupied for approximately two weeks. Towns and villages were bombed and strafed by South African jet fighters: what remained was destroyed by columns of armoured carriers, divisions of South African regular forces and a special battalion of mercenaries, called 32 Battalion. Apart from Angolan civilians and soldiers, Namibian guerrillas and refugees who were killed during the invasion, almost 3,000 people were left homeless.

Apart from claiming to have captured tons of 'Soviet-made weapons', South Africa claimed also that its military forces killed Soviet military personnel and captured a Soviet sergeant-major. This was part of South Africa's propaganda campaign that attempted to portray the Namibian nationalists as vassals of the Soviet Union, East Germany and Cuba. The claims stirred little excitement in most capitals. The People's Republic of Angola has consistently asserted its right, as a sovereign state, to seek assistance from any quarter and has never denied the fact that apart from an estimated 15,000 Cuban troops who helped repulse South Africa's invasion in 1975–76, there are also a limited number of Soviet and East German military advisers training the Angolan armed forces. Similarly, the Namibian nationalists have received and continue to receive military and financial aid from a wide range of countries,

356 *The National Liberation Struggle: Problems and Prospects*

including the Soviet Union, as well as humanitarian support from Western countries, non-governmental and religious organisations.

Pretoria's propaganda effort during the invasion suffered a further setback when its military forces attacked a party of Western journalists en route to southern Angola early in September under the escort of Angolan soldiers. The journalists disputed Pretoria's claims that they were accompanied by SWAPO, as well as the claims that South Africa's military operations were directed at SWAPO bases. Based on their investigations, the journalists concluded that the South African military operations seemed to have been aimed more at the Angolan Armed Forces than at SWAPO.[16]

Zambia, which has also provided sanctuary to the Namibians, has also been the victim of frequent acts of aggression by the South African Defence Forces. The Caprivi Strip is a narrow finger of land where the borders of Namibia, Botswana and Zambia meet. That has also been the major point of entry into Zambian territory for South Africa's armed forces who destroyed Zambian lives and property, actions justified on the grounds of 'hot pursuit' of Namibian freedom-fighters. The ANC also has its headquarters in Zambia.

The People's Republic of Mozambique suffered its first significant military incursion in January 1981 when South African commandos raided the houses of South African refugees (associated with the ANC) at Matola, several kilometres away from the capital, Maputo. Eleven refugees and one Mozambican national on his way to work were killed during the attack. Three refugees were kidnapped and taken back to South Africa where they were charged on various counts under the Terrorism Act.

In justifying the incursion into Mozambique, General Constand Viljoen, Commander of the South African Armed Forces, claimed that the ANC residences were a 'springboard for terrorism', where the attacks on the SASOL oil-from-coal plant and the Silverton bank had been planned. The claims were patently untrue in that the Government and Party of Mozambique, while permitting refugees and a number of ANC functionaries to live there have repeatedly stated that they will not allow the ANC either to establish military bases or to use the country as a base for guerrilla attacks against South Africa.

The ease with which the South African commandos penetrated almost 40 miles from the border into Mozambique, passing a Mozambican army base en route, raised serious questions about the loyalty of sections of the armed forces. At a rally in February 1981 eight Mozambican army officers were paraded before the public; President Samora Machel announced that they would be tried by a military tribunal for their complicity in the South African commando raid.

On 4 March 1981 Mozambique announced the expulsion of six US embassy personnel claiming that they were agents of the CIA allegedly responsible for providing intelligence information to the South

The Enemy: Responses and Capacities   357

Africans thus facilitating the raid on Matola. The State Department in Washington denied the allegation, arguing somewhat incredibly that the expulsion of the six had been instigated by two Cuban counter-intelligence officers. Following the expulsion, the Reagan Adminitration announced the suspension of food shipments and a loan of \$5 million to Mozambique for additional grain, pending a 'review of bilateral relations'. US–Mozambican relations are, however, now back on a positive track.

South Africa's commando raid on Matola was followed by the invasion of Phuri, a settlement close to the point where the borders of Mozambique, Zimbabwe and South Africa meet. The invasion was repulsed by the Mozambican armed forces.

Mozambican authorities have since frequently complained about aggression by Pretoria, including violations of air-space and training and supporting subversive elements, of which more later.

In December 1982 South African military forces invaded the mountain kingdom of Lesotho and in an early morning raid on the capital, Maseru, attacked residences occupied by South African refugees and Basotho. The attack left 30 South African refugees (some of whom were ANC members) and 12 Basotho dead. Damage to property was also extensive. In addition to the direct attack by South African military forces, Lesotho authorities have frequently complained about cross border military attacks carried out by the Lesotho Liberation Army (LLA), the military wing of the opposition Basutoland Congress Party of Ntsu Mokhehle.

Training and Supporting Dissident Groups

Coupled with the direct military incursions into neighbouring states, the South African regime has been training and supporting dissident groups from those countries, notably UNITA in Angola, the MNR in Mozambique, the Machala Gang in Zambia, and, according to Prime Minister Mugabe's estimates, some 5,000 Zimbabwean dissidents who are essentially the remnants of Bishop Muzorewa's 'private army' and the Selous Scouts of the former Ian Smith regime. There is, however, also evidence to suggest that Pretoria has exploited the disturbances in Matabeleland; dissidents from the province have been recruited for training in South Africa and re-infiltrated into Zimbabwe where they have engaged in various acts of banditry, including robbery, murder and destruction of government equipment required for development work in the region.[17]

UNITA, led by Jonas Savimbi, has been the recipient of South African support since 1975 when South African military forces invaded Angola in an attempt to prevent the accession to power of the MPLA. Following the withdrawal of the South African military forces and the defeat of UNITA, the latter have continued to operate in southern Angola. Supported by the South African regime, UNITA has engaged in

358   *The National Liberation Struggle: Problems and Prospects*

acts of sabotage in the southern provinces (virtually rendering the Benguela railway inoperative) and in terrorising the civilian population. UNITA has also been used by the South African regime to fight against the freedom-fighters of SWAPO. Savimbi twice admitted in July 1981 during interviews with foreign journalists that UNITA was receiving aid directly from South Africa in the form of diesel fuel, trucks, medical supplies, treatment of the wounded and food.[18] A stock of military equipment impounded by US Federal agents at Houston International Airport in May 1981 was believed to be destined for UNITA via South Africa.[19]

In Mozambique, South Africa has been supporting the 'Mozambican National Resistance Movement' (MNR), a dissident group comprising supporters of the former Portuguese colonial regime, remnants of the Portuguese secret police, PIDE, and, it has been suspected, disaffected FRELIMO troops. Prior to the independence of Zimbabwe, the MNR was created in 1976 by the Rhodesian Security Forces and Central Intelligence Organisation, assisted by the South African Defence Forces, to destabilise Mozambique which provided military bases and other facilities to the Zimbabwean National Liberation Army (ZANLA), the armed wing of Mugabe's ZANU-PF. Its role was to terrorise the civilian population in remote parts of Mozambique so as to create confusion and fear. After the independence of Zimbabwe, the MNR transferred headquarters to South Africa where it broadcasts from a radio station in the northern Transvaal. It has been reported that South African military aircraft regularly dropped supplies to bands of the MNR operating in remote parts of Mozambique.[20]

In December 1980 a South African newspaper listed alleged acts of sabotage committed by the MNR.[21] In February 1981 the Zimbabwean Government announced 'that it has captured 40 "South African armed" members of the MNR inside Zimbabwe'. This followed the signing of a defence pact by Mozambique and Zimbabwe the previous month when the two governments claimed that the MNR was being financed by South Africa to launch attacks against their countries.[22]

In October 1981 Mozambique accused South Africa of direct participation in sabotage operations in central Mozambique, following the killing of at least one White man while he attempted to mine the vital Beira-Mutare railway line.[23] Materials found on the bodies of MNR saboteurs killed by Mozambican armed forces as well as confessions made by others captured by the Mozambicans confirm the claims of a direct role by the South African military forces in the activities of the MNR. In October 1981 when one White man and three Blacks were blown up while trying to sabotage the Beira-Mutare railway, a vital link between Mozambique and Zimbabwe, the Mozambican authorities were unable to identify what was left of the four men, but a page of a handwritten manuscript, a novel about Northern Ireland found next to the bodies, was traced by the London *Observer*.[24] The newspaper reported

The Enemy: Responses and Capacities　359

that the White man was Alan Gingles, 27, a former British army officer who at the time of his death was a lieutenant in the South African army.

Shortly after Gingles' death, army headquarters in Pretoria reported that he had been killed in 'the operational area', a reference to the Namibia war zone. Earlier, the South African regime had called Mozambican charges that the White man was a 'Boer' soldier 'lying propaganda'. Gingles was based at Phalaborwa in the eastern Transvaal, where forces of the dissident MNR are reportedly trained.

Further evidence that South Africa trains and equips the MNR emerged in April 1983 with the murder in South Africa of the dissident group's number-two official, Orlando Cristina.[25] Cristina, a White Portuguese, was fatally shot in a farmhouse north of Pretoria where he had lived for some time. Mozambican officials in Maputo claimed that Cristina was based in South Africa and that he directed the MNR's day-to-day activities, mainly sabotage of power lines, roads, railways and ports. He was reported to have been an agent of the Portuguese secret police, PIDE, in Mozambique prior to the independence of that country. Cristina allegedly helped organise the MNR with the aid of the former Rhodesian Central Intelligence Organisation.[26]

The signing of the Nkomati Accord between Mozambique and South Africa in March 1984 and Pretoria's role in the ceasefire agreement between the Mozambican Government and the MNR in October 1984 have removed all doubts about Pretoria's sponsorship of the MNR. Similarly, the presence of Jonas Savimbi at P.W. Botha's investiture as President in September 1984 was public testimony of Pretoria's support for UNITA.

Spokespersons of the South African regime have attempted to present the apartheid regime's support for dissident and subversive elements from the neighbouring countries as a *response* to the active support for the ANC and other liberation forces by those countries. In November 1982 a South African government spokesperson stated: 'If neighbouring states continue to harbour anti-South African forces, they should not be surprised if South Africa considers doing the same for them.'[27] The Minister of Defence, General Magnus Malan, was even more direct in a speech in parliament in February 1983. The Minister said that if it were necessary in the interests of South Africa, the regime would support movements such as the MNR and UNITA.[28] The fact that these countries have denied military facilities to the ANC and PAC, or do not permit them to carry out military operations against the apartheid state from their territories has not provided immunity from aggression by that regime's military forces.

Allegations that the South African Defence Forces have been training Zambian dissidents in the Caprivi Strip were made as early as 1974. Since then the Zambian Government as well as other leaders of the front-line states have accused South Africa of training and supporting

360   *The National Liberation Struggle: Problems and Prospects*

the Machala Gang with a view to destabilising Zambia so as to overthrow President Kaunda.[29] In October 1983, Zambian authorities announced the arrest of two White South Africans who attempted to enter the country illegally by crossing the Zambesi River in a small boat.[30] At the time of writing neither the motives of the two men in attempting to enter Zambia, nor their identities, had been disclosed. The possibility, however, cannot be excluded that they are part of South Africa's 'dirty tricks' brigade.

Prime Minister Leabua Jonathan of Lesotho has repeatedly charged that South Africa provides facilities to the Lesotho Liberation Army (LLA), the armed wing of Ntsu Mokhehle's Basutoland Congress Party, enabling the forces of that movement to carry out cross-border raids into Lesotho. Political violence in the mountain kingdom has its origins in the 1970 elections when Chief Jonathan, facing defeat at the polls, stopped the elections and suspended the constitution. Mokhehle and other BCP members later fled abroad. In the late 1970s the BCP split into two factions when some of Mokhehle's lieutenants returned to Lesotho, in response to an amnesty offer made by Prime Minister Jonathan. BCP leaders prepared to co-operate with Jonathan were co-opted into the government and announced the 'expulsion' of Mokhehle from the BCP. Mokhele retained a following abroad and in 1979, in the name of the LLA, began armed actions against Prime Minister Jonathan's government.

Prime Minister Jonathan's diplomatic offensive in which he has charged that his country is the object of a destabilisation campaign by Pretoria to pressure him into recognising Bantustans and into surrendering freedom-fighters to the regime's security police has succeeded in winning support, particularly in the OAU. Charges of collusion between the LLA and South Africa are now widely accepted. Following the South African raid on Maseru in December 1982 the ministers of frontline states responsible for defence and security met in Arusha, Tanzania. Lesotho, though not a front-line state, attended the meeting.

Since the independence of Zimbabwe in 1980, Prime Minister Mugabe has repeatedly accused South Africa of training approximately 5,000 Zimbabwean dissidents to destabilise his country. South Africa has also been accused of violating Zimbabwean air-space on a number of occasions.[31] In August 1982 three South African soldiers were killed in Zimbabwe after they had crossed the border. In December 1982 two former members of the Zimbabwe–Rhodesia auxiliary forces were charged in the High Court, Harare, with having undergone military training in South Africa. In their evidence, the two men alleged that they had undergone training in order to reconnoitre ANC bases in South Africa and that members of their group were responsible for the assassination of the ANC representative in Zimbabwe, Joe Gqabi, in August 1981.

There is also evidence that the South African regime exploited and

The Enemy: Responses and Capacities 361

fomented further troubles during the disturbances in Zimbabwe's Matabeleland. Zimbabwean government ministers revealed that South Africa had established a 'Matabele Brigade', comprising Zimbabwean dissidents to infiltrate into the troubled province to carry out acts of sabotage. At the height of the disturbances, radio broadcasts from South Africa, in the Ndebele language, were beamed to Matabeleland fomenting ethnic hostilities. Zimbabwean dissidents captured by the security forces have confirmed the South African role in the training and supporting of anti-government elements.[32]

With the backing of the USA, the South African regime is demanding, as a condition for Namibia's independence, the withdrawal of Cuban troops from Angola. South African forces have occupied part of the southern provinces of Angola since Operation Protea in August 1981. Through a combination of diplomatic manoeuvring, military aggression against Angola and support for the activities of UNITA, the South African regime has successfully kept Namibian independence 'just around the corner', since 1978 when it first indicated its acceptance of the UN plan for Namibia, embodied in UN Security Council Resolution 435. Indications are that the stalemate may continue indefinitely. It is not inconceivable that South Africa, while pursuing its own 'internal settlement' in Namibia, may increase military pressures on Angola and demand the evacuation of SWAPO from Angola. Or launch a 'blitzkrieg' invasion of Mozambique, or Zambia, and demand as a condition for the withdrawal of its forces from either country, the evacuation of ANC personnel. The apartheid regime will not be moved by resolutions of condemnation at the UN or the OAU, or rhetorical speeches. They have endured such condemnations before.

Within one month of the South African commando raid on Maseru and the condemnations of the action at the UN and other forums, 100 ANC members were reportedly leaving Lesotho for Mozambique. They were not deported, but 'for their own security' left voluntarily. That same month, Swaziland authorities, of their own accord, rounded up ANC members in the country. Prior to the bombing by South African jets of targets in Mozambique in May 1983, in retaliation for the ANC's Pretoria car-bomb attack, the South African regime demanded of Mozambique that ANC personnel be removed to the north of the country. In return, Pretoria would restrain the activities of the MNR. In September 1983 Pretoria demanded that the Lesotho authorities expel a number of ANC and PAC members it identified as 'security threats'. The evacuation from the front line under pressure from the apartheid regime of the liberation forces fighting for the overthrow of White supremacy in South Africa and Namibia can no longer be discounted. That is a reality that has to be soberly absorbed by the liberation movements.

In the wake of the South African raid on Maseru in December 1982, the Afrikaans-language newspaper, *Die Transvaler*, declared that all of Southern Africa is now an 'operational area'.[33] In other words, 'the

362 *The National Liberation Struggle: Problems and Prospects*

struggle for political change in South Africa has become a regional war'.[34] By its actions, the regime has demonstrated both the lengths to which it will go and its determination to maintain the status quo in South Africa.

Attacks on Exiles and Refugees

In recent years South Africa's security forces have increased their activities in the independent African states in the region, where they have assassinated and kidnapped representatives of the South African national liberation movements, exiles and refugees. Self-confessed South African spy, Gordon Winter, has revealed that South African intelligence services established an assassination squad in the early 1960s with the aim of killing exiled political leaders considered a threat to the South African regime.

In 1979 a parcel bomb sent to Ms. Phyllis Naidoo, an ANC member who fled to Lesotho, exploded injuring her and a number of others. The Rev. John Osmers, a New Zealand priest working in Lesotho, was among those injured. Apart from facial injuries, he had a hand blown off.

In 1980, a Lesotho national recruited by Pretoria's security police was seriously injured when a bomb he attempted to place under the car of Thembi Hani, an ANC member, exploded.

In August 1981, Joe Gqabi, the 52 year-old representative of the ANC in Zimbabwe, was killed by a hail of bullets from a sub-machine gun as he reversed his car out of the driveway of his home in the formerly all-White suburb of Ashdown Park. Already in March 1981 he had narrowly escaped an assassination attempt when seven kilograms of explosives were found under his car. The Zimbabwean Government blamed South African security agents for the assassination of Gqabi, a view shared by the national liberation movements.

Late in 1981, Napthallie Sidzamba, a PAC member resident in Lesotho, escaped an assassination attempt when the assassin lost courage and confessed his mission. The would-be assassin, a Black South African, revealed that he had been offered a sum of R15,000 (approximately $15,000), an automobile and a house if he succeeded in his mission. He also disclosed that he had been trained by the South African security police in the use of handguns and given a pistol before being despatched on his mission.

Refugees in countries bordering South Africa live in constant fear of kidnapping by Pretoria's security agents. Reference has already been made to the kidnapping in January 1981 of three refugees by South African commandos during the raid on ANC residences in Matola, Mozambique. At that same time, a South African Indian teacher living in Swaziland was kidnapped by four men belonging to the MNR. He was ultimately returned to Swaziland after the authorities there apprehended the MNR band.

In February 1982 South African agents kidnapped Peter Lengene, a former Soweto student leader who had been living as a refugee in Botswana since August 1976. Botswana authorities demanded the return of Lengene: the Foreign Minister, Mr. Archie Mogwe, travelled to Cape Town to discuss the matter with his South African counterpart. Pretoria claimed that Lengene refused to return to Botswana for fear of prosecution for criminal activities.[35] Lengene's colleagues in the South African Youth Revolutionary Council (SAYRCO) are convinced, however, that he was kidnapped and has been held in South Africa against his will.[36] Botswana prosecuted and imprisoned an Angolan and three Black South Africans alleged to have been involved in the kidnapping of Lengene.

In June 1982 two ANC members resident in Swaziland, Petros and Jabu Nzima, were killed when a land mine placed under their car by South African agents exploded. In August 1982, Ruth First, the well-known writer and political activist (she was a member of the ANC and SACP, was killed by a parcel bomb suspectedly sent to her by South African agents. She was killed in her office at the Eduardo Mondlane University where she was Research Director at the Centre for African Studies.

In November 1983, South African agents attacked a house in Manzini, Swaziland, killing two South African refugees and a Swazi national.

Economic Aggression

Pretoria's destabilisation of Southern Africa includes a programme of economic sabotage, particularly against those countries which have achieved liberation after years of armed struggle. Repeated acts of aggression against the People's Republic of Angola, for example, have resulted in destruction of the transport and communications infrastructure in the southern provinces bordering Namibia. South African military aggression, coupled with the subversive activities of UNITA, has created serious economic problems in Angola.

The fledgling state of Zimbabwe has been a target of punitive economic measures by Pretoria ever since independence in 1980. Among some of the measures taken by Pretoria are the following:

Visa Requirements: South Africa now requires visas for Zimbabwean passport-holders, a process that takes up to 14 days. This has had deleterious effects on Zimbabwe's tourist industry since Zimbabwe was forced to reciprocate, thus affecting South Africans who have constituted a significant proportion of tourists. In 1981 the South Africans denied visas to three prominent Zimbabwean White liberals who had planned to encourge Zimbabwean students at universities in South Africa to return to Zimbabwe.

364 *The National Liberation Struggle: Problems and Prospects*

Repatriation of Zimbabwean Workers: South Africa announced in 1981 that the work permits of about 20,000 Zimbabweans working in South Africa would not be renewed when they expired. The repatriation of such a sizeable number of workers would mean that the new government would have to provide jobs for them, or devise means of absorbing them into the economy at a time when the international recession and the prolonged drought had seriously affected the economy.

Lease of Boeing Jets: South Africa in 1981 refused to renew the lease on a Boeing jet for the national airline, Air Zimbabwe.

Withdrawal of Locomotives: In 1981 South Africa Railways withdrew 25 diesel locomotives in service with the National Railways of Zimbabwe when their leases expired even though they were desperately needed, inter alia, to transport Zimbabwe's record maize crop. The South African regime repeatedly stated that it would welcome a ministerial delegation to discuss the matter, obviously an attempt to embarrass the Zimbabwean Government which decided against cabinet contacts as a matter of policy. Even when Zimbabwe offered to submit a written request, signed by a senior civil servant, Pretoria declined, stating that any request for the diesel locomotives would have to be signed by a Cabinet Minister.[37] Suspectedly under pressure from the US, the South African regime subsequently relented and agreed to make the diesel locomotives available.

Preferential Trade Agreement: Initially, the South African regime gave notice that it would not renew the long-standing preferential trade agreement which gave Zimbabwean manufactured goods a guaranteed market in South Africa. The preferential trade agreement covers almost two-thirds of Zimbabwe's export of manufactured goods to South Africa. Termination of the agreement would thus have serious and far-reaching effects on Zimbabwe's manufacturing industry. In 1982, South Africa renewed the trade agreement; many Western diplomats expressed the view that Pretoria's change of heart was due to pressure from the Reagan Administration.[38]

In recent months, South Africa's strategy appears to be aimed at making difficult the achievement of the objectives of SADCC. This is not difficult to understand, since the success of SADCC would close avenues to South Africa's economic and political expansion in the region. The Johannesburg *Star* was fairly blunt in linking internal destabilisation of Mozambique, the SADCC, and South African support for the MNR:

> The [MNR] are also threatening important facets of the plan for a constellation of Black states to rival the one mooted by the South African

> Prime Minister, P.W. Botha. The rival plan is particularly vulnerable to the activities of the [MNR] because its success hangs largely on smooth transport and communication.[39]

The truth of the observation was evident in two acts of sabotage carried out by the MNR in October and November 1981. At the end of October 1981 they destroyed strategic bridges at Pungwe, cutting the vital Beira-Mutare road and rail link between Mozambique and Zimbabwe. The effect was the interruption of a project sponsored by the World Food Programme under which Zimbabwean maize was shipped via Beira to other African countries desperately short of grain. In mid-November 1981, navigational buoys in Beira harbour were destroyed by saboteurs making the port inaccessible until the completion of repairs.

In an analysis of South Africa's destabilisation of the region, the political editor of the London *Economist* wrote of the MNR:

> [The MNR] can disrupt the country's main communications at will — including the Beira railway and oil pipeline to Zimbabwe in the north and the coast road from Beira to Maputo, on which traffic must now go in armed convoy . . . In 1980 and 1981 it blew up the main Cabora Bassa power line and it makes frequent attacks on other government and economic targets. The railway into South Africa from Mozambique is relatively safe, but for obvious reasons: it carries some 17% of South Africa's overseas trade.[40]

In 1982 Zimbabwe and Mozambique were reportedly growing increasingly concerned about the intensified sabotage efforts of the South African-sponsored MNR. The main targets of the MNR were road and rail links between Mozambique and Zimbabwe, and between Zimbabwe and Malawi, which pass through Mozambique. As a result of the frequent attacks on the two railway routes from landlocked Zimbabwe to the Mozambican ports, Zimbabwean businessmen were reluctant to ship their goods through Beira and Maputo. Trucks using the road between Zimbabwe and Malawi were ambushed several times by the MNR forces. As a result road transport companies used the more circuitous route through Zambia, doubling freight rates.[41] Pretoria's aim seems to be to ensure that the neighbouring countries, particularly Zimbabwe, remain dependent on South Africa's transportation network.

In Mozambique, the MNR has also attacked foreign aid projects, in some instances kidnapping experts assisting in reconstructing the economy.

In December 1982, at the same time as the South African raid into Lesotho, South African commandos (believed to be former Rhodesian SAS) sabotaged the oil depot at Beira. The oil, almost 2 months' supply and valued at $12 million, was destined for Zimbabwe. The political editor of *The Economist* explains:

366 *The National Liberation Struggle: Problems and Prospects*

The alternative rail route for oil was from Maputo via Chicualacuala, but this too was conveniently sabotaged. This left South Africa with a grip on all of Zimbabwe's oil supplies, whether purchased direct or from Maputo by the (unsabotaged) Komatipoort rail link. South Africa suddenly announced that there was an industrial dispute on this line and wagon turn-rounds would be long delayed. *It was the big squeeze, far worse than any UDI sanctions.*[42] (Emphasis added.)

The resultant fuel crisis in Zimbabwe had a serious effect on the economy. The fuel crisis, with its crippling effects, followed six months after the destruction of two-thirds of the Zimbabwean air force at Thornhill Air Force Base in Gweru by saboteurs using South African equipment.[43]

Conclusion

This examination of the South African regime's response to the geopolitical changes that have occurred in Southern Africa since the coup in Lisbon in April 1974 which resulted in the withdrawal of the Portuguese from Angola and Mozambique, and the independence of Zimbabwe in 1980, shows that the balance of forces has shifted in favour of the forces of liberation. Two pillars of White minority rule in Southern Africa have been knocked away, leaving South Africa (which also occupies Namibia illegally) as the last bastion of White domination. The national liberation movements, however, still have enormous logistic problems. The ANC and PAC are still predominantly externally-based. The independent African countries in the region, because of the military and economic dominance of South Africa, are unable to provide the military facilities and support to the two liberation movements that would enable them to sustain a military challenge against the apartheid regime. Coupled with the logistic problems, has been the problem of security, evidenced by the assassinations and kidnappings of exiles and refugees associated with the liberation movements in the neighbouring countries.

Pretoria has embarked upon a programme of destabilisation of the independent countries in the region to deter them from providing sanctuary for the freedom-fighters of the liberation movements. The destabilisation programme has been accelerated since the independence of Zimbabwe, which dashed Pretoria's hopes of creating a 'Constellation of Southern African states'. Several prongs are discernible: direct military incursions into the independent African countries in the region; training and supporting dissident groups in individual countries; assassination and kidnapping of political exiles and refugees; and economic sabotage. The programme of destabilisation is aimed at making difficult the task of national reconstruction, particularly in those

The Enemy: Responses and Capacities 367

countries that have achieved liberation after years of armed struggle. Human and financial resources that could be utilised in social and economic development are being diverted to defence expenditure.

The success of the SADCC in decreasing economic dependence on South Africa simultaneously with promoting regional economic co-operation among the independent African states, poses a threat to Pretoria's regional military, economic and political ambitions. For that reason, Pretoria's response to the SADCC has been one of hostility, evidenced by the war of attrition against Zimbabwe and the sabotage of the transport communications network in Mozambique by the Pretoria-sponsored MNR.

Despite these difficulties, the liberation movements, notably the ANC, have succeeded in recent years, in infiltrating trained freedom-fighters and equipment into South Africa, surreptitiously transiting through the independent states in the region. Much of the guerrilla activity, as we have already demonstrated, has been attributed to the ANC's military wing, Umkhonto we Sizwe. These freedom-fighters have successfully penetrated the borders of South Africa, created arms caches in various parts of the country and carried out acts of sabotage of economic and strategic installations. There have also been clashes with security patrols in the border areas; in many cases, guerrilla activities are reported by the military authorities as 'cattle theft', or 'poaching', or incidents involving 'FRELIMO soldiers' from neighbouring Mozambique.

Pretoria's proposed land deal with Swaziland, under which the South African regime would cede to that country, the territory of KaNgwane as well as the strip of land known as Ingwavuma, was aimed at securing the co-operation of the Swazi authorities in preventing incursions into South Africa by ANC freedom-fighters.[44] The land deal, opposed by the ANC and resisted by the people of KaNgwane and the Kwazulu regime of Chief Gatsha Buthelezi, would have provided Swaziland with an outlet to the sea. Following a South African Appeal Court decision setting aside the Botha regime's decision to cede the territory to Swaziland and the anticipated negative recommendation of the government-appointed Rumpff Commission of Inquiry, the land deal was abandoned in 1984.

A stark reality of Pretoria's regional strategy is its determination and capacity to achieve, through military and economic pressures, the evacuation of South African freedom-fighters from the front line. The challenge facing the national liberation movements, therefore, is one of transferring the locus of their activities back into the country so as to lessen their dependence on external sanctuary for execution of the liberation war. This has assumed an added urgency in the wake of the Nkomati Accord.

Implications of the Nkomati Accord

On 16 March 1984, following three months of intense diplomatic activity, South Africa and Mozambique signed a non-aggression pact, the Nkomati Accord, under which each party to the Accord undertook to prevent its territory from being used as a springboard for acts of aggression against the other. In effect this meant that South Africa would withdraw support for the MNR while Mozambique would withdraw support for the ANC. This represented a compromise by FRELIMO because it placed on a par the ANC, a genuine nationalist organisation with over 70 years' history of legitimate struggle and popular support in South Africa, and the MNR, a group sponsored initially by the Rhodesian security forces and subsequently by the Pretoria regime to destabilise a progressive government in Mozambique that supported the liberation struggles in Zimbabwe and South Africa.

Following the signing of the Accord, the Mozambican authorities demonstrated that they took seriously their obligations under the pact. Police and armed units were deployed to search the homes of ANC members and supporters in the capital, Maputo. ANC members in Mozambique were ordered to leave the country after they refused to be herded into refugee camps under the aegis of the UNHCR where they feared they would be sitting targets for South African commandos or bomb attacks. Henceforth, the ANC would be permitted a presence of only four persons in its office to perform functions related to information and publicity. A number of ANC cadres who escaped from Mozambique at the time of the police raid, fled to neighbouring Swaziland which disclosed that it had secretly signed a non-aggression pact with Pretoria in 1982. In armed clashes between the Swazi police and ANC cadres there were casualties on both sides.

Pretoria has secured a number of objectives. Firstly, the ANC has been driven out of Lesotho, Swaziland and Mozambique; South Africa's foreign minister, Pik Botha, had told a *New York Times* correspondent in October 1983 that his government was determined to drive the ANC out of the region. Secondly, it has caused a rift between the African front-line states and the national liberation movements, principally the ANC and SWAPO. At the SADCC economic summit in Lusaka, Zambia in February 1984 the communique referred to a decrease in Pretoria's acts of aggression, a view challenged by the ANC. According to the ANC's unofficial representatives at the meeting, there had been no let-up in Pretoria's destabilisation. South Africa still occupied southern Angola, trained and supported dissident groups and refused to relinquish control of Namibia. Following the signing of the Lusaka Agreement between South Africa and Angola and the establishment of a Joint Military Commission (JMC) there were persistent but unconfirmed reports of clashes between SWAPO guerrillas and Angolan forces. In Mozambique, FRELIMO repeatedly pledged its

The Enemy: Responses and Capacities 369

continued moral, diplomatic and humanitarian support for the ANC but nevertheless expelled its members from the country. Various Mozambican officials privately expressed anger at the ANC's public condemnation of the Nkomati Accord.

Even though the leaders of the Front-line states at their summit in the northern Tanzanian town of Arusha in April 1984 reaffirmed their support for the liberation struggles in Namibia and South Africa, the ANC and SWAPO have been under pressure to accept the 'new realities'.

Thirdly, it has caused a rift within the OAU between the Front-line states and certain other countries. The OAU Council of Ministers, meeting in Addis Ababa in February 1984, failed to endorse a resolution tabled by the Angola and Mozambican delegations, supporting the rapprochement with Pretoria even after almost a dozen countries publicly expressed support for Angola and Mozambique at the meeting. Instead, the OAU policy of isolating South Africa until apartheid is dismantled was re-affirmed. Morocco, probably because Mozambique supports the Polisario Front and recognises the Saharawi Arab Democratic Republic in the disputed Western Sahara, condemned the Nkomati Accord. Ghana, in a statement to commemorate the Sharpeville Massacre of March 1960, similarly described the Nkomati Accord as undermining the liberation struggles in Southern Africa. In October 1984, Nigeria's new High Commissioner to Zambia condemned the Nkomati Accord when he presented his credentials to President Kaunda.

Aware of the confusion and criticism sparked off by their signing of the non-aggression pact with South Africa, Mozambican leaders have gone to great lengths to explain their position to the world. President Samora Machel visited Zaire and the Congo (Brazzaville) where he secured the support of those countries for his actions in Southern Africa. The Mozambican foreign minister, in Tokyo at the invitation of his Japanese counterpart, similarly explained his government's position. Mozambique also hosted a summit meeting of the leaders of the former Portuguese colonies in April 1984 at which the leaders expressed support for Angola and Mozambique. At the Arusha summit of the African Front-line states in April 1984 President Machel gave a lengthy explanation for his government's actions, obtaining the support of his colleagues.

Fourthly, it has exacerbated divisions within and rivalry among SADCC member states. Following the signing of the Nkomati Accord, South African industrialists and businessmen are poised to return to Mozambique to restore South African economic involvement in that country to pre-independence levels. Yet, one of the major reasons for the formation of SADCC was to decrease dependence on and economic involvement with South Africa while the system of apartheid is maintained.

Fifthly, Pretoria used the signing of the Nkomati Accord to launch a

370   *The National Liberation Struggle: Problems and Prospects*

diplomatic offensive. P.W. Botha's eight-nation European tour in June 1984, the first in more than 20 years by a South African Prime Minister, was part of the diplomatic offensive begun with the signing of the accords with Angola in February 1984 and Mozambique in March. European leaders attempted to justify their meetings with Botha by pointing to the meetings between Botha and African leaders and the resultant co-operation between South Africa and Angola, South Africa and Mozambique and South Africa and Zambia. Botha failed to secure the eviction of the ANC and SWAPO from London and Bonn, one of his principal objectives during his European tour and his offer to surrender control of Namibia to the Western contact group aroused little enthusiasm. His major success was in creating the perception among South Africa's Whites that after years of isolation, he had gained acceptance in the Western capitals for his regime. For this reason, Botha's tour received massive publicity in the South African media, especially in the state-owned radio and television services.

The Nkomati Accord has brought little tangible benefit to Mozambique in the field of security. In the period immediately after the signing of the Accord, the Mozambican authorities announced the capture and/or surrender of 'hundreds of MNR bandits'. The MNR continued, however, to attack convoys of trucks travelling between Zimbabwe and Malawi. There was speculation among political observers in Southern Africa that prior to the signing of the Nkomati Accord, Pretoria had provided the MNR with equipment to sustain its bandits for several years and that rather than stop outright support for the group, Pretoria had facilitated the transfer of their operations to the Bantustans. Should Mozambique then complain that South Africa was not upholding its part of the Accord, South Africa would then argue that the MNR was not operating from South African territory but from the 'independent national states'. In this way Pretoria could pressurise Mozambique to deal directly with the Bantustans thus conferring on them a degree of legitimacy. In the late 1970s South Africa engineered several border incidents with Lesotho in an attempt to force that country to recognise the Transkei, but without success.

Initially the Mozambican authorities claimed that the signing of the Accord had resulted in diminished attacks by the MNR, but at the beginning of October 1984, prior to negotiations in Pretoria on a ceasefire with the MNR, Mozambican government officials called on the South Africans to honour their obligations under the Accord and expressed the view that it was in jeopardy. Soon thereafter Pretoria announced a ceasefire between the Mozambican Government and the MNR. The cessation of hostilities was to have been followed by the inclusion of the MNR in a government of national unity but immediately after the announcement of the ceasefire agreement there were denials by both sides. The Mozambicans stressed the priority of the military struggle against the MNR. The FRELIMO youth wing staged a demonstration calling for the MNR 'bandits' to be wiped out on the battlefield. During Machel's state visit to Malawi at the end of October 1984 he called upon the Malawian Government to cooperate in the elimination of banditry; he pointed out further that the MNR (which used Malawian territory for its attacks against Mozambique) affected Malawi's trade through his country. As if to underline the fact that the Nkomati Accord did not decrease attacks by the MNR, the group attacked a bus 5 kilometres north of Maputo, killing 27 people, while Machel was in Malawi.

Lessons for South African Revolutionaries

If Mozambique's signing of the Nkomati Accord and the resultant evacuation of the ANC from that country presents a challenge to the South African Liberation movement, it is also rich in lessons for South African revolutionaries. Rather than beat their breasts in moral indignation and cry betrayal of the struggle, they must examine critically and learn from the Mozambican experience. While the Mozambican economy was brought to the brink of collapse as a result of the country's imposition of economic sanctions against the Smith regime, repeated acts of aggression by the Smith and Smith/Muzorewa regimes during the liberation struggle in Zimbabwe, South Africa's 'undeclared war' and natural disasters, including three successive years of drought and the devastation of Cyclone 'Domoina' in early 1984, FRELIMO also made mistakes in the post-liberation period. It was a combination of objective and subjective factors that ultimately led to the Nkomati Accord. Among these was the abandonment, after independence, of the feature that was the strength of FRELIMO during the armed struggle for liberation, the politicisation and mobilisation of the masses. The masses must not only be mobilised during the struggle for liberation but thereafter they must be mobilised to defend their revolutionary gains. Because the rural poor had not been politicised as to the threat posed by the MNR and the half-hearted manner in which FRELIMO had embarked upon the training of the people's militia, the MNR was able to operate with little resistance in most of the country's ten provinces. It was only after FRELIMO's Fourth Congress in April 1983 at which the rural poor were represented that some of the mistakes that were made were addressed and the decision taken to recall the veterans of the armed struggle.[45]

If the Nkomati Accord which has been a temporary setback for the liberation struggle in South Africa results in serious debate and discussion, honest criticism and self-criticism among South African revolutionaries who must chart a way forward, then the Mozambican plight will in the final analysis have positive side effects.

372 *The National Liberation Struggle: Problems and Prospects*

Notes

1. Johnson 1977, p. 22, puts forward the view that the South African revolution was defeated at Sharpeville: 'The revolution had been routed, not stalemated.'

2. Adam 1971, p. 119.

3. Ibid., p. 115.

4. Ibid., p. 116.

5. Quoted by Lockwood 1974.

6. Quoted by Caryle Murphy, 'South African Military exert greater influence on policy', *Washington Post*, 30 May 1981.

7. See South African Institute of Race Relations 1980, p. 643.

8. Ibid., p. 647.

9. Ibid., p. 627.

10. De St. Jorre 1981, p. 106. A very perceptive and incisive analysis of the nature of and motives for the much-heralded 'changes' in South Africa on which the Reagan Administration's policy of 'constructive engagement' has been based.

11. *The Voice*, 12 December 1979, reported that the South African regime and industrialists invested an amount of R17 million in Bishop Muzorewa's election campaign, as well as providing a number of motor vehicles.

12. The eight other members of SADCC are: Tanzania, Zambia, Malawi, Botswana, Angola, Mozambique, Lesotho and Swaziland. Provision has been made for an independent Namibia to join the alliance.

13. Arnold 1980, p. 40.

14. See Alan Cowell, 'Cutting the links to Pretoria', *New York Times*, International Economic Survey, 14 February 1982.

15. Julian Burgess, 'South Africa's Campaign Against SADCC', *African Business*, January 1982, p. 12.

16. Quoted in *Southern Africa*, September–October, 1981 (Southern Africa Collective, New York), p. 21.

17. *The Herald*, 7 October 1983; *Sunday Mail*, 9 October 1983.

18. *The Star* (Johannesburg), 24 July 1981; and interview with *The Scotsman*, broadcast by the BBC on 23 July 1981.

19. *The Star*, 18 May 1981; *Sunday Tribune*, 17 May 1981.

20. *The Star*, 17 December 1980.

21. Ibid.

22. *Sunday Times*, 8 August 1981.

23. *The Guardian* (London), 26 October 1981.

24. *The Observer*, 20 February 1983.

25. *The Times* (London), 22 and 23 April 1983.

26. Ibid.

27. Quoted in 'Destabilisation in Southern Africa', *The Economist*, 16 July 1983.

28. South African Press Association, 3 February 1983.

29. Machala, a former game warden, fell out with President Kaunda after he was overlooked for appointment to a higher post that he sought. After years of banditry, Machala was ultimately killed by Zambian security forces in 1981.

30. *The Herald*, 14 October 1983.

31. *Focus*, Special Issue, No. 2, IDAF (London), April 1981.

The Enemy: Responses and Capacities 373

32. *The Herald*, 7 October 1983.
33. Quoted in *Work in Progress* — 27, 1983, Johannesburg, p. 14.
34. Ibid.
35. *The Star*, 20 February 1983.
36. Communicated to the author by SAYRCO members based in Lagos, Nigeria.
37. See Caryle Murphy, 'South Africa Waves Aid Carrot, Stick at Mugabe', in *Washington Post*, 2 November 1981; also Jenny Cargill, 'Zimbabwe: A War of Attrition begins', *Africa Now*, October 1981.
38. *Financial Times* (London), 19 March 1982.
39. *The Star*, 7 July 1981.
40. *The Economist*, 16 July 1983.
41. *The Star*, 17 July 1982.
42. *The Economist*, 16 July 1983.
43. Ibid.
44. See 'Swaziland: South Africa's Willing Captive', in *Work in Progress*, 27, 1983, p. 14.
45. See Campbell, H., 'War, Reconstruction and Dependence in Mozambique', *Journal of African Marxists*, 6, 1984, p. 53.

18. The Home Front: What Is To Be Done?

The Growth of the Black Labour Movement

Coupled with the resurgence of the ANC and the increase in military operations in South Africa, the other notable development has been the increase in working class militancy. Official figures released by South Africa's Department of Manpower indicate that in 1982 there were 394 strikes and work stoppages, more than in any year in recent South African labour history.[1] The figure of 394 compares with 342 in 1981. This means that, on average, approximately 1,000 workers were on strike each calendar day in 1982 when incipient recession and the effects of the prolonged drought which seriously affected Blacks, notably in the rural areas, was expected to dampen worker militancy.

Saul and Gelb have analysed the deepening of the economic crisis in South Africa in the 1970s into organic crisis and the responses of both the dominant and dominated classes to the crisis.[2] This provides a clear framework for understanding not only the much-vaunted 'reforms' in South African capitalism, but more importantly, the resurgence in Black resistance, particularly Black working-class resistance.

As in most developed economies there has been a major turnaround in South Africa since the boom years of the 1960s and early 1970s. Foreign capital was readily available to South Africa during the world economic boom of the 1960s and the unprecedented rise in the price of gold in the early 1970s (from $35 per ounce to almost $200 per ounce) prolonged the period of economic growth. From a situation of a large balance of payments surplus in 1972, however, South Africa moved to a huge balance of payments deficit in 1976. This was brought about partly by excessive government expenditure on the future development and enforcement of its apartheid policies (e.g. Bantustans) and on the boosting of the social and economic position of the Afrikaaners within the White racial grouping. In addition, government expenditures on munitions and fuel soared: the radical changes in the Southern African political situation in 1974 and 1975 precipitated stockpiling of fuel and weapons. The dramatic rise in the price of oil, following the 1973 Arab–Israeli war, contributed to this problem.

By May 1976, inflation was running at an average annual rate of 13%;

The high inflation rate hit the Black population particularly hard.[3] The Finance Minister, Senator Horwood, claimed that Black wages had risen faster than inflation.[4] Independent researchers, however, found that Blacks' actual buying power was falling.[5]

there were predictions of an absolute decline in the country's Gross Domestic Product for the first time since World War II; the balance of payments deficit was increasing with continued high levels of imports; gold reserves were declining and the treasury had to resort to raising loans of increasingly shorter maturity periods abroad in order to cover the deficit. By March 1976, outstanding foreign loans totalled R1,005 million, double that of a year previously, of which almost 25% had to be repaid during the 1976–77 fiscal year.

The high inflation rate hit the Black population particularly hard.[3] The Finance Minister, Senator Horwood, claimed that Black wages had risen faster than inflation.[4] Independent researchers, however, found that Blacks' actual buying power was falling.[5]

Deflationary measures introduced by the government in an attempt to restore the economy, caused a sharp rise in unemployment. This, too, was largely borne by the Blacks. The Federated Chamber of Commerce reported that in mid-1976, 30,000 Africans were losing their jobs each month.[6] African unemployment was expected to be close to 2 million by the end of 1976, equivalent to 20% of the economically active African population. The government-created Bantustans are not economically viable; they cannot support their own populations, let alone absorb such a large army of unemployed. The conditions in the Bantustans, combined with rising unemployment in the urban areas and high inflation, heightened Black critical consciousness — this was what undoubtedly made the Black urban townships explosive (a factor in the rapid spread of the uprisings in 1976) and resulted in the high success rate of the workers' strikes. *The Economist* observed:

> The Blacks of South Africa want better jobs, more pay and better education — this was what the Soweto [uprisings] were about. But they can no longer be bought off with bread-and-butter concessions. *More and more they are demanding a transformation of the whole system.*[7] (Emphasis added.)

One of the most significant developments in South Africa in the last decade has been the resurgence of the labour movement, following the strikes that rocked the country in 1973 and 1974. In 1974 alone there were, almost 374 strikes involving approximately 75,000 workers. The strikes were largely spontaneous, without any recognisable leaders (the workers themselves refused to expose individuals to retribution by the regime) and largely centred around demands for higher wages and better working conditions. In 1980, there were 207 strikes, involving close to 62,000 workers.[8]

There are a number of significant differences between the strikes that rocked the country in 1973 and 1974, and the more recent wave of strikes. Firstly, they have in most cases been better organised and have been backed by a 'young but vigorous Black trade union movement'.[9] Secondly,

376 *The National Liberation Struggle: Problems and Prospects*

the demands of workers have not been restricted to economic issues; they have included demands for the reinstatement of dismissed fellow-workers and for the recognition of trade unions.

Membership of the trade unions has grown rapidly. The biggest grouping of Black trade unions (though non-racial) the Federation of South African Trade Unions (FOSATU), claimed a membership increase in its eleven unions of 59,000 in 1981 to over 105,000 by the end of 1982.[10] It had also signed 173 recognition agreements with companies, with almost 45 under negotiation, and had more than 1,500 highly-trained shop stewards. FOSATU has adopted a cautious approach, concentrating on building an 'effective organisational base for workers to play a major role as workers'.[11]

The Council of Unions of South Africa (CUSA), another umbrella body of eleven unions, recorded an increase in membership from 28,000 in 1980 to 41,000 (paid up) in 1982.[12] CUSA, like FOSATU, has stressed the need for the building of strong organisational structures and stresses the workers' struggle purely in economic terms. CUSA has been strongly influenced by the philosophy of Black consciousness; it emphasised the need to build Black trade union leadership.

Militant trade unions that stress that trade unionism must be linked with wider political and community issues are the East London-based South African Allied Workers' Union (SAAWU) which in 1982 claimed membership in the region of 75,000, and the Motor Assembly Components' Workers' Unions of South Africa (MACWUSA) which is Port Elizabeth-based but has expanded to the Sigma plant in Pretoria. Another is the Media Workers' Association of South Africa (MWASA) which exerts an influence out of proportion to its membership of 400. SAAWU and MWASA were later affected by splits that reflect the ongoing ideological struggles between Black Consciousness-oriented organisations and those subscribing to an all-inclusive South African nationalism.

Amendments to the industrial legislation in 1979, following the recommendations of the Wiehahn Commission, permit the registration of trade unions under stringent conditions, including the approval of the constitutions and elected officials of the unions seeking registration. Subsequent amendments to the legislation in 1979 permitted membership of registered unions by migrant workers and frontier commuters, but excluded foreign Blacks (for example, migrant workers from Lesotho and Mozambique). New trade unions seeking registration under the new dispensation had to be racially separate, unless an exemption from the requirement was approved by the Minister of Manpower. In many instances, particularly where White trade unions applied for exemption in order to grant membership to Black workers, such approval was granted. In other instances, the minister was less amenable and refused applications by FOSATU when it sought to recruit White members. In 1983 FOSATU won a two-year battle with the

The Home Front: What Is To Be Done? 377

government on the question of racial registration when the Natal Supreme Court ruled that race was not an industrial interest.[13] Whether the ruling would apply to other trade unions which have accepted racial registration, however, was not clear.

In 1981 the legislation was amended further. Foreign Blacks were permitted to join trade unions seeking registration. The 1981 Labour Relations Act expunged all references to race; the trade unions were granted autonomy in deciding upon their racial composition, that is whether or not they would be uni-racial.[14]

Despite the changes in the industrial legislation, a number of trade unions refused to apply for registration, arguing that registration subjects the trade unions to controls by the government, controls that are the prerogative of the members of the trade unions. In 1982 there were almost 20 unregistered unaffiliated trade unions.[15] Apart from FOSATU and CUSA, with a combined total of 22 registered trade unions, the Trade Union Council of South Africa (TUCSA) had 57 affiliates; there were also 107 registered unaffiliated unions in 1982.[16]

Several attempts in 1981 and 1982 to unify the emergent Black trade unions failed as a result of differences over policy towards registration, political involvement by trade unions, and the role of White leadership in the trade unions, among other things. In April 1983, however, a summit meeting attended by almost 200 delegates from virtually the entire Black trade union movement was held in Cape Town. Discussions centred around the need for a national federation of trade unions, a forum through which to fight legislation hostile to workers as well as to fight intransigent employers. The move came at a time when the unions were in a weaker negotiating position because of the economic recession. Unions were unable to prevent widespread retrenchment of workers and the harassment of trade union leaders by the regime's security police.[17]

Government Repression

In an attempt to crush the burgeoning Black trade union movement, the South African regime, as well as stooge administrations in the Bantustans, embarked upon a campaign of repression. Black trade unionists have been detained indefinitely, others have been banned and banished. In the aftermath of an effective strike by Black municipal workers in Johannesburg in August 1980, a number of trade union leaders were detained and charged under the Sabotage Act even though not a single physical act of sabotage had either been committed or alleged. But the regime hoped that the use of such draconian legislation as the Sabotage Act, which provides for a minimum sentence of five years' imprisonment and a maximum penalty of death, would cow Black workers. The President of the South African Allied Workers' Union (SAAWU), an unregistered unaffiliated union that has recorded a rapid growth in the Eastern Cape, was detained five times in less than

378   *The National Liberation Struggle: Problems and Prospects*

a year and then detained and charged under the Terrorism Act in 1982. He was acquitted on charges of furthering the aims of the ANC. In February 1982 Dr. Neil Aggett, Secretary of the African Food and Canning Workers' Union, died in police custody.

Police and management intensified the harassment of workers. In February 1981, 188 Black bus drivers were arrested by police after their pay negotiations broke down, and were charged under the Black Labour Regulations Act (which was due to be repealed). All but twelve of the drivers pleaded guilty to taking part in an illegal strike and were sentenced to twelve months' imprisonment, suspended for five years, on condition that they returned to work. The tough action against the bus drivers coincided with a speech in parliament by the Defence Minister, General Magnus Malan, who accused the trade unions of being 'front organisations' for the banned liberation movements.

In September 1981, 205 trade union members affiliated with the SAAWU were detained by the Ciskeian security police when they returned to Mdantsane township outside East London after attending a meeting of the union in the city. The Ciskeian authorities virtually declared war on the labour movement, particularly SAAWU which has a strong base of support in the Eastern Cape and which expressed strong opposition to Ciskei's 'independence' in 1980. After a long battle with SAAWU and its leadership the Ciskeian administration eventually banned the union early in 1983.

The detention of the 205 SAAWU members was preceded in June 1981 by the arrest of some 60 workers from Wilson-Rowntree. Fifty-seven of the workers were subsequently charged, 21 of them with violating the Riotous Assemblies Act. The workers were part of the 350 workers dismissed by Wilson-Rowntree, an East London-based subsidiary of a British company, following a strike by the workers in sympathy with three fellow-workers whom they felt had been unfairly treated. In addition, they demanded the recognition of their trade union and the right to join the trade union of their choice. Management recognised the Sweet Workers' Union which is affiliated to the White-controlled Trade Union Council of South Africa (TUCSA), while the majority of workers supported SAAWU. Initially, the head office of the company refused to intervene on behalf of the workers; instead, the leadership of SAAWU was accused of escalating unrest at the factory. As a result of a country-wide boycott of Wilson-Rowntree products called by SAAWU, the company ultimately relented and reinstated all the dismissed workers in November 1981.[18]

The use of the boycott has also been one of the effective weapons used by the Black trade union movement in recent years. The boycott of Wilson-Rowntree products followed similar boycotts of red meat in the Western Cape, following the dismissal of Black meat-workers and the demands of their union both for the reinstatement of all the dismissed workers and the recognition of their union. The year before, there was a

The Home Front: What Is To Be Done? 379

boycott of Fatti's and Moni's products, following the dismissal of workers by the company and the refusal to reinstate them. In instances where the trade unions have called for the boycott of the products of specific companies, they have been supported by the Black community.

Victimisation and the harassment of trade union leaders (the state tried but failed to secure convictions for criminal offences against 20 trade union leaders in an 18-month period between June 1981 and December 1982), the dismissal and deportation of workers to the Bantustans (as occurred in Johannesburg in August 1980 following the strike by Black municipal workers), and police brutality (such as the killing of eight Black miners during a strike in 1981), have not succeeded in preventing the growth of the labour movement and in preventing strike acion by workers. According to figures released by the regime in February 1982, there was a 65% increase in strikes and work stoppages in 1981 in comparison to 1980. The number of workers involved in strikes and the number of shifts lost by industry in 1981 were far greater than in any year for more than a decade. Statistics show that there were 342 strikes and work stoppages in 1981, compared to 207 in 1980, considered a year of labour turmoil. A total of 92,842 Black workers were involved in strikes and work stoppages in 1981, of whom 84,706 were Africans, and the rest Coloureds and Indians, a 50% increase over 1980 figures.[19] The figures did not take into account go-slows, overtime bans or other forms of worker pressure which would not be reported to officials of the regime. Official strike figures for 1982 show an even greater increase over figures for 1981.

The Recession

The economic boom precipitated by the rise in the price of gold in 1979 and 1980 did not benefit the Black majority whose depressed wages have not kept up with inflation. In his new year message for 1982, the President of the Azanian People's Organisation (AZAPO) referred to the economic hardship experienced by the Black population. He said that Black people found it difficult to subsist on their meagre incomes, which were continuously eroded by arbitrary increases in rents, hikes in the costs of transport and ever-increasing costs of such basic necessities as bread, milk and maize.[20]

The economic recession in South Africa and the severe drought in 1982 and 1983 had a devastating impact upon the Black population, particularly in the rural areas. The South African Reserve Bank, in its annual economic report in 1982 attributed the economic problems to the world-wide recession. The international economic recession had resulted in a steep decline in the price of gold from an average of $613 per ounce in 1980 to $460 in 1981 and $346 by August 1982. The international recession had also decreased demand for South Africa's other mineral exports.[21]

Inflation amounted to 14.4% between July 1981 and July 1982, almost

380 *The National Liberation Struggle: Problems and Prospects*

double the average rate of inflation of South Africa's major trading partners.[22] Unemployment was estimated to be around 2.5 million to 3 million, or 24% of the economically active population, and Africans constituted the vast majority of the unemployed.[23]

The downward cycle continued through 1983, characterised by regressing output and rising unemployment.[24] In its annual economic report for 1983, the Reserve Bank stated that during 1982 and the first half of 1983, the South African economy made progress in adjusting to the changed circumstances brought about by the international recession.[25] However, the rate of inflation remained high and inflationary expectations firmly entrenched. Measured over a twelve-month period, consumer prices increased by 12.4% in June 1983, about 2½ times the average for South Africa's major trading partners.

The severe drought affecting the Southern African region, led to a sharp drop in South Africa's GDP. According to the South African Reserve Bank, the decline 'clearly reflected both the primary and the secondary effects of the marked drop of 34% in real agricultural output'. The drought has had a devastating impact upon the country's poor Blacks, particularly in the rural areas. Subsistence farmers in the Bantustans were scarcely able to plant, let alone grow, maize, the staple diet. In the commercial sector, maize production was expected to be about 4 million tonnes in 1983, compared with 8.4 million tonnes in 1982 and 14 million tonnes in 1981. It was estimated that South Africa would have to import about 2 million tonnes of maize.

The Future

It is very clear that industrial action by Black workers, coupled with increasing organisation among the workers, will be one of the major focal points of the struggle for national liberation in the 1980s. At the present time, approximately 2% of urban Black workers are unionised, but it has been shown that the pace of unionisation is increasing, as is organisation. Coupled with that has been the increasing interest among workers and unionists in Marxism and class analysis, in an effort to understand better the complexity of the South African revolution.[26] One of the features of the growth in membership of the trade unions is that the militant trade unions, like SAAWU, which have stressed the need for the trade unions to define for themselves a political role, have experienced a rapid expansion, but the danger is that unless trade unions have a strong organisational infrastructure and ideologically-clear leadership, they will not be able to withstand sustained attacks from the state, an inevitability if they continue to register the same growth in membership and influence within the community. That has been the problem with other populist organisations in the past which showed phenomenal growth, the Industrial and Commercial Workers'

Union (ICU) led by Clements Kadalie in the 1920s and the Port Elizabeth Black Civic Organisation (PEBCO), led by Thozamile Botha, in the late 1970s being but two examples. The reasons for the decline of the ICU have already been briefly mentioned earlier, namely government action, lack of organisation, financial mismanagement, personality conflict, lack of analysis and strategy, to mention a few.[27] PEBCO, a newer organisation with much potential, as was demonstrated by the community support in Port Elizabeth for the Ford workers, had simply not had sufficient time to consolidate its leadership and to formulate its strategy and tactics. As a consequence, the harassment of its leaders, notably Thozamile Botha who was banned and forced to flee the country to Lesotho where he joined the ANC, resulted in the collapse of the organisation.

In this regard, the approach of those trade unions that are investing time and effort in the building of strong organisational bases among the workers, is the one that is likely to enable them in the long term to play a significant revolutionary role in challenging the capitalist system of exploitation. The danger, however, exists that the cautious professional approach to trade unionism, represented by FOSATU, may nurture a class of 'bourgeois union leaders' whose interests may conflict with those of the workers on the shop floor. That is a danger that has to be pre-empted; this can only be done through the politicisation of the workers, and the emergence from among the workers themselves, of a leadership. This is precisely where the liberation movements will face the test.

The militancy of the urban Black working class, together with guerrilla warfare, both increasing in extent, intensity and sophistication, will lead to the gradual undermining of the system of capitalist exploitation, rather than there being any sudden upheaval in South Africa. One of the significant differences between the current resistance in South Africa and the mass popular struggles of the 1950s is precisely the combination of a growing Black labour movement which, by all indications, is likely to increase in strength and organisation in future, and guerrilla warfare by the National Liberation Movements, which is also likely to increase. After the defeat of the African Mineworkers' strike in 1946, organised by the African Mineworkers' Union, led by J.B. Marks, the Black labour movement went into decline so that by 1950, trade union membership had dropped to a paltry 38,000 and the government was able to report gleefully that 36 trade unions had ceased to function.[28] When the trade union movement was revived in 1955 with the formation of the South African Congress of Trade Unions (SACTU), the regime had substantially increased its battery of repressive legislation which it used against organisations as well as individuals, both in the national political organisations and the labour movement. The point is that at the height of the Defiance Campaign of 1952 and the subsequent campaigns of the 1950s, the ANC did not have the added support of a powerful organised labour movement. The situation in the

382 The National Liberation Struggle: Problems and Prospects

1980s is totally different; apart from the resurgence of the ANC, the other singular spectacular political development in South Africa is the resurgence of the labour movement.

The national liberation struggle in South Africa is being waged, or must be waged, for *political* objectives which will create the necessary conditions and framework upon which a socialist economic system will be established. The initial objective of the liberation struggle is the seizure of state power and the use of such state power for the creation of a socialist mode of production. The military activities of the liberation movements are a means to *political*, and consequently, *economic* ends. This has to be so, not simply in theory or slogans, but in the programmes of the liberation movements, the allocation of resources, attitudes, etc. For example, at the present time, rather than recruit workers to undergo military training abroad, the liberation movement should devise ways and means of assisting workers to sustain their strike action, by providing the necessary logistical support; in exactly the same way, the military training for self-defence and to increase the combat-readiness of the workers and other sections of the population, has to be provided *inside the country*.

The internally-based resistance in South Africa is in urgent need of effective revolutionary party machinery to centralise experiences and to ensure the continuity of the revolutionary actions of workers, peasants, students and other strata of the dominated classes. Such an internally-based revolutionary vanguard would have to initiate, broaden and generalise experiences, actions and consciousness of workers, peasants, and other strata of the oppressed masses. To say this is not to belittle the attempts and sacrifices that are being made by the liberation movements, or to under-estimate the enormous difficulties which the suggested course of action entails. But, the greatest weakness of the South African liberation movements has been due to their predominantly external operations and lack of well-organised and internally-based revolutionary organisational machinery and network in control of the tempo and directions of the liberation struggle, with the exiled organisations serving in a supportive capacity. This has led to a lack of continuity in the mass resistance; the liberation struggle has been characterised by episodic (and monumental) battles — the Defiance Campaign, Anti-Pass Law campaigns, Sharpeville, Pondoland, Soweto — primarily because there is no internally-based organisational machinery responsible for planning, motivating the masses for greater sacrifices, directing the struggle, co-ordination of actions and activities and the control of the revolutionary actions based on the concrete but ever-changing revolutionary conditions. The convening of the National Forum, attended by 800 delegates at Hammanskraal, in June 1983 at which a manifesto was adopted identifying 'racial capitalism' as the real enemy of the people of South Africa and pledging to work for the establishment of an 'anti-racist, socialist Republic', and the formation of the United Democratic Front, constituting some 400 different organisations, to oppose the Botha regime's constitutional proposals, are reflective of the search for cohesion, for leadership and direction in the internal resistance. Rather than being indicative of the 'unity of the oppressed masses', as some exiled optimists have attempted to portray the emergence of the two coalitions, they indicate the ideological struggles taking place in the country among the forces of resistance as they attempt to define the real enemy, the class content of the required unity and the ultimate objectives of the liberation struggle.[29]

The political struggles within the country in 1984 highlighted the difficulties confronting those involved in resistance internally in South Africa and re-emphasised the challenge facing the liberation movement. From the time of its formation in August 1983 following months of preparation, the UDF began a painstaking campaign to mobilise mass opposition to the Botha regime's constitutional strategy. By mid-1984 almost 600 different organisations, representing a membership of 2 million drawn from trade unions, sporting and cultural organisations, student organisations, women's groups, Christian and Moslem bodies, were affiliated to the UDF. The UDF had two immediate problems: how to build a viable mass movement that would survive government action against its most able leadership and how to link up national issues with the local issues of the affiliated grassroots organisations so as to establish sustained political involvement through mass movements. What was to be the fate of the UDF beyond the new constitution and creation of the President's Council? There were considerations of short-term and long-term objectives, a need constantly to assess strategy and tactics. Despite fears of a government ban in 1984 following ministerial attacks labelling the UDF a 'front for the ANC', the UDF successfully mobilised opposition to the constitutional strategy. In the process it had to overcome obstacles posed by the ban on meetings, constant security police surveillance and harassment and, in Natal, disruptions of UDF meetings by Chief Gatsha Buthelezi's Inkatha. Inkatha tribal warriors physically assaulted UDF leaders at several meetings, at one of them viciously assaulting the UDF's Natal President, Archie Gumede. These obstacles notwithstanding, the mass mobilisation resulted in the effective boycott of the Coloureds' and Indians' elections in August 1984. Six leaders of the UDF and Natal Indian Congress (out of a total of 17 political activists detained on the eve of the elections) were ordered released by a Natal Supreme Court judge only for the Minister of Law and Order to amend their detention orders whereupon they sought sanctuary in the British consulate in Durban, much to the embarrassment of Her Majesty's government. The consulate sit-in and the re-arrest of three activists when they left the consulate focused international attention on the repression in South Africa at a time when P.W. Botha was trying to project an image of reform, and of his regime as a 'peace broker' in Southern Africa. But, in a more important sense, it also

384 *The National Liberation Struggle: Problems and Prospects*

provided the UDF with an issue and postponed debate of the strategic issues which would have to be addressed once it was clear that the regime would disregard the broad consensus of opposition to its constitutional proposals.

The UDF combined with the labour movement and the student movement to make a list of democratic demands for the release of political prisoners and detainees, improvement of living conditions including affordable rents for all and higher wages, and a universal system of education for all South Africans. The demands were backed by a 2-day strike on 5 and 6 November that was 70% effective, achieved in the face of police brutality and repression. Following the national strike, about 22 trade union and student leaders were detained. The Detainees Parents' Support Committee estimated that about 1000 persons had been detained in 1984 — the highest total since 1977. Months of continual unrest in the Black townships was fueled by the deployment of thousands of police and armed units who sealed off entire townships of Daveyton, Boipeng, Sharpeville and Tembisa, conducted house-to-house searches and arrested hundreds of people. By the end of November 1984 close to 200 persons had been killed by police and armed units since February in demonstrations and protests that the regime admitted were more broadly based than the uprisings in 1976–77 since they had a strong worker involvement. But in the end, despite their heroism, the masses, unarmed and defenceless, were no nearer seizing state power than they were in 1976–77. The struggles of 1984, like the struggles of 1980 and 1976 demonstrate the need for internally-based revolutionary organisational machinery to plan, initiate, direct and control the struggle to overthrow the system, not to demand certain changes. The autonomous actions of the masses have to be fused and integrated into programmed actions against the status quo through the deliberate and conscious intervention of an internally-based revolutionary vanguard with a clear ideology and co-ordinated revolutionary programme.

Spontaneous movements and actions, doomed onslaughts and military skirmishes, aimed at demonstrating to financiers of the liberation movement that 'we are doing something at least', are incapable of destroying the apartheid-colonial capitalist system which has the tenacious support of Western imperialism, led by the US. As the US becomes increasingly involved in South Africa, the apartheid-colonial capitalist system will become highly flexible with the capacity to absorb any unplanned onslaught against it. It will be made to absorb all demands except those that threaten the logic of its existence.

Dangers of Increased US Involvement

The report of the Rockefeller Commission Study on US Policy towards South Africa, entitled *Time Running Out*, provides a basis for increased US

The Home Front: What Is To Be Done? 385

involvement in South Africa.[30] The report identifies five US interests which are at stake in South Africa, with emphasis upon the protection of US military and strategic interests and minimising Soviet influence in the sub-continent, and maintaining adequate supplies of strategic minerals that are available in South Africa.

The US, through direct investments by corporations in the South African economy where the main attraction is the high rate of returns on investments made possible by the super-exploitation of Black labour, and through the transfer of military, nuclear, scientific and industrial technology, through the provision of bank loans, has nurtured a relationship with the apartheid regime which militates against the interests of the mass of the population.[31] The authors of the report, *mindful of the interests of the US*, argue that US interests lie in *change*, but *not revolutionary change*. They present a broad range of actions which can be pursued by the US administration and US corporations in South Africa.

They recommend that the pressure of the Carter Administration should be maintained; but the pressure of that administration upon the Pretoria regime was purely rhetorical, consisting of condemnations of the human rights violations of the apartheid regime. The Reagan Administration, of course, abandoned that approach in favour of 'constructive engagement' and 'quiet diplomacy'. They recommend the adoption and implementation by US corporations in South Africa of the 'Sullivan principles', which provide for fair employment practices, equal pay for equal work, training of Blacks in skills development, etc. The measures that have been demanded by the national liberation movements, such as the withdrawal of all foreign (including American) investments, the imposition of mandatory economic sanctions under Chapter seven of the UN Charter, have been unequivocally rejected. The report recommends that US administrations should maintain contact with Black leaders — and significantly, in the list of such leaders, the representatives of the national liberation movements feature at the very end. What is, or should be of concern to the national liberation movements is the recommendation that the US Government and private institutions should 'support organisations inside South Africa working for change, assist the development of Black leadership, and promote Black welfare'.

While certain initiatives ought to be supported inside the country, it is obvious that the initiatives which the masses are permitted to undertake in the country are those that are approved by the regime. Worthy efforts very often run the risk of serving merely to perpetuate the status quo, or at best, to ameliorate the conditions of the masses so that they live comfortably in their oppression. This recommendation is one that is most convenient for those forces which seek to undermine the national liberation movements, while claiming to be supportive of the efforts of the 'people inside' to bring about change. US corporations investing in

386 *The National Liberation Struggle: Problems and Prospects*

South Africa, in response to demands for their withdrawal, are now building schools (modern and well-equipped) in Soweto and providing financial assistance for their Black employees to purchase their own homes in exclusive suburbs — aptly named Selection Park, for instance. Scholarships are provided for South Africans to study in the US: as a result of the educational programme, co-ordinated with a selection committee comprising prominent Black South Africans, educational programmes for South African refugees were affected by a serious shortage of funds in 1981 and 1982. Organisations which have traditionally provided scholarships for South African refugees had to compete for funds with organisations providing scholarships for South Africans selected in the country. US colleges, under pressure from students and faculty to sell their stocks and shares in corporations which have investments in South Africa, are able to rationalise the retention of their stocks and shares by arguing that they can perform a better function by offering tuition waivers and other scholarships to Black South African students under such programmes.

The motives of US business are patent: in sponsoring such educational and training programmes they hope to build a Black comprador class, or, alternatively a Black bourgeoisie which would have strong interests in capitalism and thus serve and promote US business interests. The liberation movements must be alert to attempts, continuously, to divide the forces of resistance into the 'forces of the interior' and the 'forces of the exterior', but should work towards a harmonisation of effort. In addition, the liberation movements and South Africans generally, should resist the temptation to dismiss persons coming out of South Africa under such educational and training programmes as 'sell-outs'. Regardless of the motives of the sponsors, there is also the 'unintended result' factor to consider. That is, *organisational skills* acquired in the process of such educational and training programmes can be used for many ends, including political ends. Also, *scientific skills*, denied to the masses in South Africa, can be utilised to further the revolutionary effort. Already, contrary to the expectations of US business, there is evidence that some of the returnees who have benefited from educational and training programmes abroad, have gone into education and community-based work in South Africa.

The African–American Labour Centre (AALC), an affiliate of the American Federation of Labour-Congress of Industrial Organisations (AFL-CIO), has expressed an interest in the labour movement in South Africa, the motivation being to 'protect' the workers from communist seduction. As Irving Brown, former executive director of the AALC warned the US Congress in 1973: 'Unless we of the "free world" can condemn and fight African [sic] apartheid, there is real danger that liberal and anticommunist forces will be unable to cope in the future with the situation through lack of support and may be superseded completely by the totalitarian forces of both sides.'[32]

The Home Front: What Is To Be Done? 387

Fortunately, the emergent Black trade unions have rejected the overtures of the AALC.[33]

The apartheid regime welcomes such external intervention in support of Black efforts because they do not challenge the status quo. Under the Reagan Administration, there can be expected an increase in US involvment in South Africa in the economic, political, social and cultural spheres.

All Quiet on the Rural Front?

Most of the Black resistance to White supremacy in South Africa over the past decade has been concentrated in the urban areas, where the most notable feature has been the resurgence of Black working class resistance. Apart from a few skirmishes between guerrillas of Umkhonto we Sizwe and the South African regime's security forces in the Eastern Transvaal and northern Natal border areas, as well as attacks on police stations in Venda and Bophuthatswana, there has been little, if any organisation in the rural areas. This is anomalous because almost half the Black population lives in the rural areas, including 3.1 million who live on White-owned farms. The conditions of abject poverty and pressures on the land in the rural areas have already been amply documented and do not have to be repeated here. Moreover, resistance such as that demonstrated by the people of Driefontein, led by Saul Mkhize who was fatally shot by a young White police constable in April 1983, who refused to move from their land shows that the rural areas are not unaffected by the general mood of resistance among the Black population generally.

Although both the ANC and PAC committed themselves in the early 1970s to a strategy of organising and mobilising for guerrilla warfare in the rural areas, in the process greatly romanticising the revolutionary potential of the South African 'peasantry', they have so far failed to do so. The stooge administrations in the rural backwaters of South Africa have shown themselves to be as brutal as, if not worse than their masters. The war declared by the autocracy on the trade unions in the Ciskei Bantustan, the torture and murder in detention of Lutheran clergymen in the Venda Bantustan, and the brutality and corruption of the Matanzimas in the Transkei Bantustan, all point to Pretoria's success in creating a class of collaborators who have assumed responsibility for exercising control over the Black masses.

Difficult as it is, there is a need for the National Liberation Movement to organise and mobilise the masses in the rural areas, especially the sizeable agricultural working class. The Afrikaner historian and political analyst, Hermann Giliomee, has already pointed out the vulnerability of the rural areas which, he observes, in the light of the Zimbabwean experience, can be destabilised by a determined cadre of

388   *The National Liberation Struggle: Problems and Prospects*

guerrillas.[34] He points out that gradual economic and social liberalisation by the Smith and Smith/Muzorewa regimes failed to satisfy the aspirations of the urban 'insiders', many of whom turned to organising the Black masses in the rural areas. Giliomee warns the South African regime against trying to stave off Black revolution solely by trying to co-opt a Black urban middle class, and argues that it should simultaneously implement a massive development programme in the underdeveloped rural areas where poverty and pressure on the land have reached critical proportions. The importance of the points made by Giliomee is that it indicates an awareness that the situation in the rural areas has security implications. Undoubtedly, others in the White establishment share his view and many would heed his warning that one of the lessons of the peasants' revolt in Pondoland in the 1960s is that a rural area, once destabilised, is very costly to bring under control.

The rural areas must become an area of focus and a theatre of struggle for the National Liberation Movement. The same degree of organisation and levels of political consciousness that are evident among the Black urban proletariat must be developed among the masses in the rural areas. In other words, the worker-peasant alliance so often referred to by theorists in the National Liberation Movement, but be turned into a reality rather than a mere political slogan.

Conclusion

There is a need for the South African National Liberation Movement to monitor and assess realistically the changes going on in South Africa and outside. The propensity is to assume the status quo, to remember things as they were and to feel threatened by changed circumstances. Tolerance of the unknown, or shifting circumstances, is vital to effective action.

The labour area is one that has changed and continues to change. An independent Black labour movement has come into its own in South Africa, a fact that has to be recognised by the National Liberation Movement. Rather than be tempted to claim credit for the increasing organisation among and militancy of the workers, the National Liberation Movement should recognise that new momentum leads to a new set of realities.

Education is another area that has implications for the liberation struggle. The number of Black students at high schools is increasing; the students also have *rising expectations*, they expect that upon graduating from high school they will secure either university places or better jobs. The economic recession and rising unemployment, however, mean that their expectations may not be fulfilled. In 1976, Black youths faced similar bleak prospects, a contributory factor in the student revolt.

Exposure of Black students to external education may similarly result

The Home Front: What Is To Be Done? 389

in a challenge to the status quo in that skills acquired abroad will not necessarily be used to promote the system. While studying abroad, many such students come into contact with fresh ideas, they acquire analytical, organisational and scientific skills that they would not otherwise have acquired. The important issue is the use to which such skills are put. While many of the students who have studied abroad have done so with a view to personal advancement and are capable of playing an anti-revolutionary role as the liberation struggle progresses, there are many more students who have returned from studying abroad to work in the community.

Coupled with Black revolutionary efforts, or perhaps because of such efforts, there is increasing polarisation within White politics in South Africa. The National Liberation Movement has to develop skill and sophistication in exploiting the contradictions within the White establishment so as to widen the fissures.

In recent years, the South African military has exerted a great influence over policy, so that even Afrikaner academics have expressed concern over what they have termed a military dictatorship. Some analysts have argued that P.W. Botha, backed by the military, has embarked upon the path of an executive presidency so that, de Gaulle-like, he can initiate unpopular reforms. Advocates of this argument cite the example of the Armed Forces Movement in Portugal, which overthrew the Caetano dictatorship, to support their thesis that the military can play a 'progressive' role. But, the South African military forces are not soldiers fighting in distant colonies; like the White population generally, they have no country to which to return. Moreover, the liberation struggle in South Africa has not reached the same level of development and intensity that it reached in Guinea-Bissau, Angola and Mozambique where the national liberation movements, with popular support, scored military victories against the colonial armies. As the liberation movements increased their political and military strength, inflicting greater casualties upon the colonial armies, there was increasing doubt among the soldiers (like General Spinola who had seen duty in Guinea-Bissau where he was outfought and outsmarted by the PAIGC leaders) about the wisdom of continuing the wars when there was no victory in sight. The South African military forces are confident that they are able to hold their own, not only against the South African freedom-fighters, but also against the military forces of the African states in the region. The escalating military actions against African countries in the sub-continent, like the raid on Maseru in December 1982, the bombing raid into Mozambique in May 1983 and the raid by South African commandos who destroyed ANC offices in Maputo in October 1983, reflect not only the confidence of the South African military, but also their choice of military, as opposed to political and economic options (such as the 'Constellation of Southern African States') in their regional strategy.

390 *The National Liberation Struggle: Problems and Prospects*

The spectrum of internal and external factors require ongoing, absolutely frank assessment by the National Liberation Movement, in the best meaning of *intelligence*. A national liberation movement needs to be informed, to have its own intelligence capacity; it should not depend on any single internal source and needs to protect itself from wishful thinking and self-interested blindness. That is especially difficult in circumstances of exile.

Another difficulty for the South African National Liberation Movement is that the moral issues in the struggle are so overpowering, so evocative, that they provoke *emotional* responses. This results in rhetorical gestures and appeals, it makes it harder to think in cold terms of interests, power, strategy, and dissimulated action. The moral issues can drown out what cold, rational analysis suggests is necessary and makes what may work pragmatically unacceptable. It makes people *feel good* (as one person once said, it feels good to feel bad about apartheid), but results in no change. The South African National Liberation Movement thus has a choice between the blinding quality of self-righteousness and a needed capacity for objective analysis and action in line with consciously set and held political goals.

Notes

1. *Rand Daily Mail*, 8 April 1983.
2. Saul and Gelb, supra.
3. *International Currency Review* (ICR), 8, 5, 1976.
4. ICR, 8, 4, 1976.
5. South African Institute of Race Relations 1977.
6. ICR, 8, 5, 1976.
7. *The Economist*, 1 January 1977.
8. Kane-Berman, J., 'Black South Africans Strengthen Unions', *South*, August 1981.
9. South African Institute of Race Relations 1982, p. 208.
10. South African Institute of Race Relations 1983, p. 147.
11. *The Sowetan*, 8, 14, 15 April 1982; *The Guardian*, 16 April 1982.
12. South African Institute of Race Relations 1983, p. 149.
13. *The Sowetan*, 20 April 1983; *The Star*, 23 April 1983.
14. Jones 1982, p. 33.
15. South African Institute of Race Relations 1983, pp. 146–58.
16. Ibid.
17. *The Sowetan*, 8 April 1983.
18. South African Institute of Race Relations 1982, p. 212.
19. *Rand Daily Mail*, 5 February 1982.
20. *The Sowetan*, 6 January 1982.
21. South African Institute of Race Relations 1983, p. 49.
22. Ibid.
23. Ibid., p. 73.

The Home Front: What Is To Be Done? 391

24. South African Reserve Bank annual economic report, summarised in Business Section, *The Herald*, 25 August 1983.

25. Ibid.

26. See South African Institute of Race Relations 1982, pp. 77–81 for evidence in Berger-Pillay ANC trial, also evidence in Hogan trial.

27. See Bonner, P., 'The Decline and Fall of the ICU-A Case of Self-Destruction?' in Webster, E. (ed), pp. 114–20.

28. See Harsch 1980, p. 230.

29. In an article entitled 'The importance of the National Forum', (*The Herald*, 23 August 1983) Gora Ebrahim, the PAC's observer at the UN, argued that the National Forum was indicative of the unity of the oppressed masses. If the argument was correct, there would have been no need for the formation of a new coalition two months later, in the form of the United Democratic Front. The National Forum and the United Democratic Front represent two ideological positions that have crystallised in the country, largely centred around the issues of race and class.

30. Rockefeller Commission 1981, University of California : South African Institute of Race Relations 1982, p. 208 has a summary of the major recommendations of the Commission.

31. See Lockwood. Numerous studies have been done which show that the net effect of foreign, including US, corporate involvement in South Africa has been to strengthen the industrial-military complex of the apartheid regime. See First, Steele and Gurney 1973; Suckling, Weiss and Innes 1975; also Schmidt 1980.

32. Quoted by Cohen, B. 'The CIA and African Trade Unions', in Ray, Schaap, Van Meter and Wof (eds.) 1979, p. 770.

33. South African Institute of Race Relations 1983, p. 160.

34. Giliomee 1982, pp. 28–33.

ACRONYMS

AALC	African–American Labour Centre
AFL-CIO	American Federation of Labour – Congress of Industrial Organisations
ANC	African National Congress (of South Africa)
APRP	Azanian People's Revolutionary Party
AZAPO	Azanian People's Organisation
AZASO	Azanian Students' Organisation
BAWU	Black Allied Workers' Union
BCM	Black Consciousness Movement
BCAM-A	Black Consciousness Movement of Azania
BPC	Black People's Convention
BCP	Basutoland Congress Party
COREMO	Revolutionary Committee of Mozambique
CPSA	Communist Party of South Africa
CUSA	Council of Unions of South Africa
CYL	Congress Youth League (of the ANC)
Fofatusa	Federation of Free African Trade Unions of South Africa
FOSATU	Federation of South African Trade Unions
FNLA	National Front For the Liberation of Angola
FRELIMO	Front for the Liberation of Mozambique
FROLIZI	Front for the Liberation of Zimbabwe
ICU	Industrial and Commercial Workers' Union of Africa
IDAF	International Defence and Aid Fund for Southern Africa
ILO	International Labour Organisation
IUEF	International University Exchange Fund
LLA	Lesotho Liberation Army
MNR	Mozambique National Resistance Movement
MPLA	Popular Movement for the Liberation of Angola
MWASA	Media Workers' Association of South Africa
MWU	Mineworkers' Union
NIC	Natal Indian Congress
NIS	National Intelligence Service
NP	National Party

Acronyms 393

OAU	Organisation of African Unity
OAU (ALC)	Co-ordinating Committee for the Liberation of Africa (commonly referred to as the Liberation Committee)
PAC	Pan-Africanist Congress of Azania
PAIGC	African Party for the Independence of Guinea and Cape Verde
PEBCO	Port Elizabeth Black Civic Organisation
SAAWU	South African Allied Workers' Union
SACP	South African Communist Party
SACTU	South African Congress of Trade Unions
SADCC	Southern African Development Co-ordination Conference
SAIC	South African Indian Council
SAIRR	South African Institute of Race Relations
SASO	South African Students' Organisation
SASOL	South African Coal, Oil and Gas Corporation
SAYRCO	South African Youth Revolutionary Council
SOWETO	South Western Townships
SWANU	South West Africa National Union
SWAPO	South West Africa People's Organisation
UDF	United Democratic Front
UMSA	Unity Movement of South Africa
UN	United Nations
UNDP	United Nations Development Programme
UNESCO	United Nations Educational, Scientific and Cultural Organisation
UNITA	Union for the Total Independence of Angola
WHO	World Health Organisation
ZANU (PF)	Zimbabwe African National Union (Patriotic Front)
ZAPU	Zimbabwe African People's Union

BIBLIOGRAPHY

Adam, H. (ed.), *South African Sociological Perspectives*, London, Oxford University Press, 1971.
——, *Modernising Racial Domination*, Berkeley, University of California Press, 1971.
Adam, H. and Giliomee, H., *Ethnic Power Mobilised*, New Haven, Connecticut, Yale University Press, 1979.
Africa Information Service, *Return to the Source: Selected Speeches of Amilcar Cabral*, New York, Monthly Review Press, 1973.
Ahmad, E., 'How to tell when the Rebels have won', *The Nation*, 30 August 1965.
——, 'Revolutionary Warfare and Counter-Insurgency', in Miller and Aya (eds.) 1971.
Arnold, M. (ed.), *Steve Biko: Black Consciousness in South Africa*, New York, Vintage Books, 1979.
Aylesworth, L.S., Ossorio, P.G. and Osaki, L.T., 'Stress and Mental Health Among Vietnamese in the US', in Endo, Sue and Wagner (eds.) 1978.
Barber, J., *South Africa's Foreign Policy, 1945–1970*, London, Oxford University Press, 1973.
Benson, M., *South Africa: The Struggle for a Birthright*, Harmondsworth, Penguin Books, 1966.
Bonner, P., 'The Decline and Fall of the ICU – A Case of Self-Destruction?' in Webster, E. (ed.) 1978.
Bratton, M., 'Structural Transformation in Zimbabwe: Some Comparative Notes from the Neo-Colonisation of Kenya', in Wiley, D. and Isaacman, A. (eds.) 1982.
Brooks, A. and Brickhill, J., *The Whirlwind before the Storm*, London, International Defence and Aid Fund for Southern Africa, 1980.
Brooks, H.C. and El-Ayouty (eds.), *Refugees South of the Sahara: An African Dilemma*, Westport, Connecticut, Negro Universities Press, 1970.
Burchett, W., *Southern Africa Stands Up*, New York, Urizen Books, 1978.
Burgess, J., 'South Africa's Campaign Against SADCC', *African Business*, January 1982.

Bibliography 395

Callinicos, A., *Southern Africa After Zimbabwe*, London, Pluto Press, 1981.

Carter, G., *The Politics of Inequality*, London, Thames and Hudson, 1958.

Carter, G. and O'Meara, P. (eds.), *International Politics in Southern Africa*, Bloomington, Indiana, Indiana University Press, 1982.

Catholic Institute for International Relations, *Southern Africa under Attack*, London, 1983.

Cohon, J.D. Jr., 'Psychological Adaptation and Dysfunction Among Refugees', *International Migration Review*, 15, I, 1981.

Couzens, T. and Patel, E. (eds.), *The Return of the Amasi Bird: Black South African Poetry*, Johannesburg, Ravan Press, 1982.

Cowell, A., 'Cutting the Links to Pretoria', *New York Times*, 14 February 1982.

Davidson, B., Slovo, J. and Wilkinson, A.R., *Southern Africa: The New Politics of Revolution*, Harmondsworth, Penguin Books, 1976.

Davis, J.A. and Baker, J.K. (eds.), *Southern Africa in Transition*, New York, Praeger, 1966.

De. St. Jorre, J., 'South Africa: Is Change Coming?', *Foreign Affairs*, New York, Council on Foreign Relations, 1981.

Dobb, M., *Studies in the Development of Capitalism*, New York, International Publishers, 1963.

Dreyer, P., *Martyrs and Fanatics*, New York, Simon and Schuster, 1980.

Dube, E.M., 'Relations between the Liberation Movements and the OAU', in Shamuyarira, N. (ed.) 1975.

Feit, E., *South Africa: The Dynamics of the African National Congress*, London, Oxford University Press, 1962.

——, *Urban Revolt in South Africa, 1960–1964*, Illinois, Northwestern University Press, 1971.

First, R., Steele, J. and Gurney, G., *The South African Connection*, Harmondsworth, Penguin, 1973.

Gerhart, G., *Black Power in South Africa: Evolution of an Ideology*, Berkeley, University of California Press, 1978.

Gibson, R., *African Liberation Movements: Contemporary Struggles against White Minority rule*, London, Oxford University Press, 1972.

Giliomee, H., *The Parting of the Ways: South African Politics 1976–1982*, Cape Town, David Phillip, 1982.

Halberstam, D., *The Best and the Brightest*, New York, Fawcett Crest, 1969.

Hamrell, S. (ed.), *Refugee Problems in Africa*, Uppsala, Scandinavian Institute of African Studies, 1967.

Harsch, E., *South Africa: White Rule, Black Revolt*, New York, Monad Press, 1980.

Herbstein, D., *White Man, We Want to Talk to You*, Harmondsworth, Penguin, 1978.

396　*Struggles within the Struggle*

Hilgard, E.R. and Atkinson, R.C., *Introduction to Psychology*, New York, Harcourt, Brace and World, Inc., 1967.

Hirson, B., *Year of Fire, Year of Ash. The Soweto Revolt: Roots of a Revolution?*, London, Zed Books, 1979.

Hoagland, J., *South Africa: Civilisations in Conflict*, London, George Allen and Unwin, 1973.

Holborn, L.W., *Refugees: A Problem of our Time*, Metuchen, New Jersey, Scarecrow Press, Inc., 1975 (Vol. 2).

Hommel, M., *Capricorn Blues: The Struggle for Human Rights in South Africa*, Toronto, Culturama, 1981.

Janis, I.L. et al. (eds.), *Personality Dynamics, Development and Assessment*, New York, Harcourt, Brace and World, Inc., 1969.

Johns, S., 'Obstacles to Guerrilla Warfare – A South African Case Study', *Journal of Modern African Studies*, 11, 2, 1973.

Johnson, C.,*Autopsy on People's War*, Berkeley, University of California Press, 1973.

Johnson, R.W., *How Long Will South Africa Survive?*, London, Oxford University Press, 1977.

Jones, R.A., *Collective Bargaining in South Africa*, Johannesburg, Macmillan's Publishers (S.A.), 1982.

Kalb, M., *The Congo Cables*, New York, Macmillan Publishing Co., 1982.

Kane-Berman, J., 'Black South Africans Strengthen Unions', *South*, August 1981.

——, *South Africa: Method in the Madness*, London, Pluto Press, 1979.

Karis, T. and Carter, G. (eds.),*From Protest to Challenge: A Documentary History of African Politics in South Africa, 1882–1964* (4 vols), Stanford, Hoover, Institution Press, 1972–77.

Krasin, Y., *Lenin, Revolution and the Third World Today*, Moscow, Progress Publishers, 1971.

El-Khawas, M.A. and Cohen, B. (eds.), *The Kissinger Study of Southern Africa NSSM 39*, Westport, Lawrence Hill, 1976.

Laurence, P., *The Transkei: South Africa's Politics of Partition*, Johannesburg, Ravan Press, 1976.

Lenin, V.I., *Left-wing Communism: An Infantile Disorder*, Moscow, Foreign Language Publishing House, n.d.

——, *Imperialism, The Highest Stage of Capitalism*, in Tucker, R.C. (ed.) 1978.

Leonard, R.,*South Africa at War: White Power and The Crisis in Southern Africa*, Lawrence Hill, Westport, 1983.

Lodge, T.,*Black Politics in South Africa since 1945*, Johannesburg, Ravan Press, 1983.

Lodge, T., 'The Resurgence of the ANC: 1976–81', *Reality* (Pietermaritzburg), March 1982.

——, 'The African National Congress in South Africa: 1976–82: Guerrilla War and Armed Propaganda', (Paper delivered at the

Bibliography 397

annual conference of the African Studies Association, Washington, D.C. October 1982).

Lockwood, E., 'National Security Study Memorandum 39 and the Future of U.S. Policy towards Southern Africa', *Issue*, IV, 3, 1974.

Machel, S., *The Tasks Ahead*, New York, Afro-American Information Service, 1975.

Magubane, B.M., *The Political Economy of Race and Class in South Africa*, New York, Monthly Review Press, 1979.

Mao-Tse-Tung, *Selected Readings from Mao-Tse-Tung*, Peking, Foreign Languages Press, 1971.

Marcum, J., *The Angolan Revolution: Anatomy of an Explosion (1950–62)*, Cambridge, Mass., M.I.T. Press, 1969, vol. I.

——, *The Angolan Revolution: Exile Politics and Guerrilla Warfare (1962–76)*, Cambridge, Mass., M.I.T. Press, 1978, vol. II.

——, 'The Exile Condition and Revolutionary Effectiveness: Southern African Liberation Movements', in Potholm and Dale (eds.) 1972.

Mbeki, G., *The Peasants' Revolt*, Harmondsworth, Penguin, 1964.

O'Meara, D., 'Muldergate and the Politics of Afrikaner Nationalism', *Work in Progress*, 22, 1982.

Miller, N. and Arya, R. (eds.), *National Liberation: Revolution in the Third World*, New York, The Free Press, 1971.

Mondlane, E., *The Struggle for Mozambique*, Baltimore, Penguin, 1969.

Moss, G., *The Wheels Turn: South African Political Trials, 1976–79*, Geneva, IUEF, 1979.

——, 'Total Strategy', *Work in Progress*, 11, 1980.

Mphahlele, E., *The Wanderer*, New York, Macmillan, 1971.

——, *Chirundu*, Westport, Lawrence Hill, 1979.

——, 'Africa In Exile', *Daedalus*, Spring 1982.

Murphy, C., 'Military exert greater influence on Policy', *Washington Post*, 30 May 1981.

——, 'South Africa Waves Aid Carrot, Stick at Mugabe', *Washington Post*, 30 November 1981.

Nkoana, M., *Crisis in the Revolution*, London, Mafube Publications, 1968.

No Sizwe, *One Azania, One Nation: The National Question in South Africa*, London, Zed Books, 1979.

Nzongola-Ntalaja, 'Internal Settlement, Neo-Colonialism and the Liberation of Southern Africa', *Journal of Southern African Studies* (College Park, University of Maryland), 4, 2, April 1979.

Padilla, A.M. (ed.), *Acculturation: Theories, Models and Some New Findings*, Colorado, West View Press, 1980.

Plaut, M., Unterhalter, E. and Ward, D., *The Struggle for Southern Africa*, London, War On Want, 1981.

Price, R. and Rosberg, C. (eds.), *The Apartheid Regime: Political Power and Racial Domination*, Cape Town, David Phillip, 1980.

398 *Struggles within the Struggle*

Potholm, C.P. and Dale, R. (eds.), *Southern Africa in Perspective: Essays in Regional Politics*, New York, The Free Press, 1972.

Rhoodie, N. (ed.), *South African Dialogue*, Johannesburg, McGraw Hill Book Co., 1970.

Rive, R., *Writing Black*, Johannesburg, Ravan Press, 1981.

Rotberg, R.I. and Barratt, J. (eds.), *Conflict and Compromise in South Africa*, Cape Town, David Phillip, 1981.

Rubin, N., 'Africa and Refugees', *African Affairs*, 73, 22, 1974.

Saul, J. and Gelb, T., *The Crisis in South Africa*, New York, Monthly Review Press, 1981.

Schmidt, E., *Decoding Corporate Camouflage: U.S. Business Support for Apartheid*, Washington, D.C., Institute for Policy Studies, 1980.

Shabalala, S.R., *Tribute to Sobukwe (1924–1978)*, mimeo., March 1978.

Shamuyarira, N. (ed.), *Essays on the Liberation of Southern Africa*, Dar-es-Salaam, Tanzania Publishing House, 1975.

Simpson, H., *The Social Origins of Afrikaner Fascism and its Apartheid Policy*, Stockholm, Almqvist and Wiksell, 1980.

Smither, R., 'Psychological Study of Refugee Acculturation: A Review of the Literature', *Journal of Refugee Settlement*, 2, March 1981.

South African Institute of Race Relations, *Laws Affecting Race Relations in South Africa* (to the end of 1976), Johannesburg, SAIRR, 1978.

——, *Survey of Race Relations in South Africa* (annual to end of 1983), Johannesburg, SAIRR.

Stalin, J.V., *The Foundations of Leninism*, Peking, Foreign Languages Press, 1970.

Steinbridge, R., 'Black Political Organisations in South Africa', in Price and Rosberg (eds.) 1980.

Stockwell, J., *In Search of Enemies*, New York, W.W. Norton & Co., 1978.

Stubbs, A. (ed.), *Steve Biko: I Write What I Like*, London, Bowendean Press, 1978.

Suckling, J., Weiss, R. and Innes, D., *The Economic Factor*, Uppsala, Scandinavian Institute of African Studies, 1975.

Tandon, Y., 'The Organisation of African Unity', in Potholm and Dale (eds.) 1972.

Thompson, L. and Butler, J. (eds.), *Change in Contemporary South Africa*, Berkeley, University of California Press, 1975.

Tucker, R.C. (ed.), *The Lenin Anthology*, New York, Norton and Co., 1978.

Turok, B., *Strategic Problems in South Africa's Liberation Struggle: A Critical Analysis*, Richmond, LSM Information Centre, 1974.

——, (ed.), *Revolutionary Thought in the Twentieth Century*, London, Zed Books, 1980.

Walshe, P., *The Rise of African Nationalism in South Africa*, London, Hurst, 1970.

Webster, E. (ed.), *Essays in Southern African Labour History*, Johannes burg, Ravan Press, 1978.

Wiley, D. and Isaacman, A. (eds.), *Southern Africa: Society, Economy and Liberation*, Lansing, Michigan State University, 1982.

Wilson, A., *The Developmental Psychology of the Black Child*, New York, Africana Research Publications, 1978.

Wilson, M. and Thompson, L. (eds.), *The Oxford History of South Africa*, London, Oxford University Press, 1969, 2 vols.

Wolpe, H., 'Capitalism and Cheap Labour Power: From Segregation to Apartheid', *Economy and Society*, I, 4, 1972.

——, 'Apartheid's Deepening Crisis', *Marxism Today*, 23, I, 1983.

Woods, D., *Biko*, London, Paddington Press, 1978.

Index

African American Labour Centre (AALC) 388
Afro-Asian People's Solidarity Organisation 72, 339
African Liberation Committee 9, 69, 70, 71
African Nationalism 17, 254
African National Congress: alliance with ZAPU 54; driven out of Lesotho Swaziland and Mozambique 370; experienced a resurgence in South Africa 206; formed 1912 17; growth in influence of 310; military activities 6; publications produced regularly 275; undergone a resurgence 309; unity with PAC 329
African Resistance Movement 41
Aggett, Dr Neil 380
Alexander, Dr Neville 41
All Blacks Rugby Tour, 1976 2
Anti-Apartheid Movement: 2; British 67; Irish 67; New Zealand 68
Assassination of South African exiles 6
Azania Komite 67, 247
Azanian People's Organisation 309, 324, 381

Ben Bella Strategy 53
Biko, Steve 2, 45, 147
Black Consciousness Movement: 1, 31, 44-6; conglomeration of organisations 45
Black Consciousness Movement of Azania: 344-6; & ANC 345
Black Labour Movement 310
Black Trade Union Movement: summit meeting 379; use of boycott by 380
Botha, P.W.: 53; declared results "acceptable" 353; & "Consellation of Southern African States" 350; as Executive President 354
Botha, Thozamile 324, 383
bourgeois movements 9
bourgeois nationalists: 9; reformist tactics 10
Breytenbach, Breyten 325
Buthelezi, Chief Gatsha: 6; Kwazulu regime of 369

Chama Cha Mapinduzi 103, 133, 152
China, People's Republic of: 72; & the PAC 73
Congress of Democrats 27
Congress of the People 27
Congress Youth League 23-7, 254
Constellation of Southern African States 350ff
"Constructive Engagement" 331
Council of Unions of South Africa 378

Defiance Campaign 26
destabilisation: by South Africa 6; programme of 350, 356, 368
Dube, Harrison 323
Du Bois, W.E.B. 19

Ebrahim, Gora: 96; Director of Publicity and Information 256, 274, 276, 291; failed to follow through on negotiations 276; member of PAC Central Committee 95; quest for power and influence 283; representative to Zimbabwe 232; schemed and manoeuvred 260
Education: inferior system for Blacks 6
Ethiopianism 20
exile: politics of 63; frustration of 76

Federation of South African Trade Unions 378-9
First, Ruth: 36; killed by parcel bomb 365

Struggles Within the Struggle

Freedom Charter: adoption of 18; & general conference of the SACC 324
FRELIMO: 4, 169, 360, 373; compromise by 370; pro-Frelimo rallies 2

Ganya, John 145
Garveyism 23
Gola, Thobile: Chief Representative to Tanzania 128, 169; escapee from the camp 169
Gqabi, Joe: assassination of 282, 364
Gqobose, Mfanyaseka Pearce: 109, 122; & PAC 288
Gqweta, Sabelo Victor: appointment as Secretary for Defence in the Central Committee 294-5
Gumede, Tshepiso 147-8

Halberstam, David 11
Harris, John 41
High Command: 118, 126, 133, 135, 142, 157-65; & Central Committee, exclusion from 118; Justice Nkonyane & other members 171; & Leballo 119

Industrial and Commercial Workers' Union 20
Inkatha 6
International University Exchange Fund 65, 325, 342

June 16 Azania Institute 287

Keke, Hamilton 294, 343
Kennedy, President John F. 11
Kgosana, Phillip: & march on Cape Town 33
Kissinger, Henry 12
Koeberg nuclear power station 315

Leballo faction 102, 111, 114
Leballo, Potlako Kitchener: 90; alliance with Victor Mayekiso 123; arbitrary actions of 136; departed for London 164; deported from Sierra Leone 220; duplicity 161; expulsion 197; & Military Commission 145; press conference, Lagos 200; isolated within leadership 142; relationship with Amin 338; self-styled "Chancellor" 267; state witness in Treason Trial 269; summoned reinforcements from among his loyalists 153; violated principles established at Arusha 144
Lembede, Anton Muziwakhe 33
Lesotho Liberation Army 299, 359, 362
Liberalism 14
Luthuli, Abert 33

Machala Gang 359, 362
Mafole, Molefe Ike: 178, 212, 224; appointment rescinded 264; report on "New York situation" 265; representative to USA & Caribbean 292
Make, Vusumi: appointed Administrative Secretary 125; appointed deputy chairman only 257; Central Committee, Chairman 176; Lesotho visit 191; Nkonyane's warning 162; & PAC: leader 197/chief representative, West Africa 106; Pan-African Affairs, Director 108; Presidential Council, Chairman 195; & Sibeko, murder of 172; Tolbert (President), political adviser on Southern Africa to 109; willing to step down 253
Makhanda, Leasoana Sam: 187, 212, 221, 225-7, 236-7; implicated in a criminal act 259; problems, personal and domestic 227; & Sibeko, Elizabeth 224
Makoti, Edwin: abduction of 134; appointed Secretary for Defence 114; Director of Publicity and Information 276; Leballo faction, member of 102; Secretary for Defence 151-2 185
Mandela, Nelson: 36; ANC, Transvaal President of 26; arrest, warrant for 36; campaign for release of 323; left the country 40
Mantshontsho, Douglas D.D.: Administrative Secretary 197, 278; charges against 238; concern for safety of 134; deported from Botswana 130; dismissal of 240; joined Sibeko/Makhanda coalition 242; PAC representative to Botswana 127
Mayekiso, Victor: 106-8; Central Committee, appointment to 114; Leballo alliance with 123; Military Commission, resignation from 124
Mbeki, Govan 41
Mboko, P.Z.: alias Dimitrov 112; "Japie Belgeveer" 113; political commissar 102
Mdluli, Dan: 105; PAC's representative to Canada 249, 292
Mgweba, Temba Lawrence: 109-10; Director of Finance 256
Mkwanazi, Joe: 97, 113; Administrative Secretary 256; deportation 105; Director of Labour and Social Affairs 241; representative in Swaziland 104
Mngaza, Vuyani 111-12
Moabi, Joe 104-5
Mokgakala, Esrom: 114, 134-5, 151;

Index

Central Committee, expulsion from 197

Mokgoatsane, Mogale Jimmy: appointed Administrative Secretary 114; absence from headquarters 121; & Leballo, rewarded for support 137; vulnerable to pressure and blackmail 121

Molotsi, Dr Peter 298

Mothopeng, Zephaniah: 94; on trial at Bethal 116

Mozambique National Resistance Movement (MNR): a dissident group 360; acts of sabotage by 360, 361, 363, 367, 369-70, 372-3

Mphahlele, Es'kia 63, 76-7

Muendance, Ngila Michael: appointed Director of Labour and Social Affairs 256; called for Leballo's expulsion 194; chief representative to UK 232; Make loyalist 256; Mgweba's appointment, opposition to 264; PAC representative at a conference 340; provoked intense anger and bitterness 261

Mugabe, Robert: 89; Prime Minister 281; ZANU-PF, leadership of 278, 340

Mxenge, Griffiths 323

National Forum 384

National Liberation Movement: alienated from political developments in South Africa 52; demands for unity 18; democratic debate 4; military activities, initiation of 5; problems 4

national liberation movements: & class struggles 13; characteristics of 9; conscientisation 10; humanitarian assistance to 65; infiltration by enemy 15; not governments 71; oppressed masses in South Africa led by 369; problems within 13

national liberation struggles Vietnam, Laos, Cambodia 1

nationalist movements 9 *see also* bourgeois movements

Natives' Land Act 21

New Zealand University Students' Association 2

Nhlapo, Fezile 116

Nkoana, Matthew 268

Nkomati Accord: 321; ANC's public condemnation of 371; & Mozambique 372; signing of 361

Nkonyane, Justice: arrest 129; APLA, deputy commander of 146; awarded

non-existent "Lembede Medal" 148; escaped from police custody 147 *see also* High Command

Nqotjane, Mzwandile (alias Zwai Maglas, alias Zola Zymba): chief representative to Nigeria 126, 143; deputy political commissar 118, 128

Ntantala faction 102, 108-9, 111

Ntantala, Templeton M.: 90, 104, 106, 268-9; deputy chairman 90; military leadership 108; PAC members led by 171; reinstatement of 252

Ntloedibe, Elias: 90, 150-1, 155, 159; Botswana, returned to 243; Central Committee: appointed to 114/cadres demand dismissal from 237; charges against 238; Director of Publicity & Information 114, 118; dismissal of 237; letter by 244; Presidential Council, nomination to 157

Ntuli, Cohen: 182; brutally victimized 271

Ntuli, Pitika 105, 129, 182

Nujoma, Sam: President of SWAPO 279

Okhela 325

opportunism 13

Organisation of African Unity (OAU): 3, 5, 18, 59, 65, 67, 77, 95-7, 185-7, 201, 205, 209, 240; Article II of Charter 68; & OAU Liberation Committee 217; & Co-ordinating Committee for Liberation of Africa 69; material and financial assistance from 76; liberation, strategy for 68; Summit meeting, Nairobi 279

PAIGC 4, 10

Pan-Africanist Congress (PAC): alliance with COREMO 54; anti-pass campaign 32; & BCM, unity with 345; Bethal 18 Trial 96, 145; & Biafra, support for 338; & Black resistance, escalation 97; cadres, militarily trained 4; & CIA, finance from 335; the Congo, facilities in 336; consultative conference 101, 106; decline in strength 89; factions, power struggle 90; 'falling to pieces' 281; formation 29; infiltration: 145/vulnerability to 295; internal strife 183; mediocrity, problem of 211; military programme, immobilized 284; organizationally ill-equipped 286; a potential FNLA or UNITA 98; problems 184; publicity & information, failure in 274; & reactionary & discredited movements 335; rear bases & supply lines 95; rerecognition bid,

Struggles Within the Struggle

survival of 187; recruitment minimal 321; the Shah, financial support from 339; split 181; theoretical formulations, weakness 31; underground, fiction of 246; united front, favoured 329; & ZANU-PF 282

Pityana, Hyameko Barney 2, 324

Phiri, Edgar (Alias Lancelot Dube): APLA, commander 119; Botswana, refused entry 127; fatal road accident 135

Pokela, John Nyati: & Iraq, support for 279; manipulated & misled 260; PAC, leader 256; peasant stock 254; & POQO activities 255; pressures on 266

POQO 42, 43, 255

Presidential Council: appointed 156-7; dissolution of 197

Programme of Action: adopted by 1949 Conference 25

Radebe, Erret: appointed Director of Finance 114, 232; forced by high command 118; resignation 252

Reagan Administration 331-2

Rivonia Trial 41

Robben Island 41, 255

Rockefeller Commission study 386

SASOL 310, 314

Seme, Pixley Ka 20

Sharpeville: massacre 33, 349; economic consequences 35; significance 36

Sibeko, David: 90, 166; appointed Director of Foreign Affairs 114; assassination 172, 174; commission of inquiry, proposal 143; & FNLA & UNITA 338; gunshot wound 170; 'strongly pro-Leballo' 178

Sibeko, Elizabeth: & Central Committee, appointment & dismissal 114, 258; disruptive activities 224; & Make 175; & the murder 188; & PAC, effect on 176

Sidzamba, Napthallie: & assassination attempt 364; de facto representative 192; removed from position 299

Sino-Soviet rivalry 5

Sisulu, Albertina 323

Sisulu, Walter 26, 41

Sobukwe, Mangaliso Robert: death 33, 91; imprisonment 33; presidential address 29; solitary confinement 44; struggle for his successor 116 imprisonment of 33

South African Allied Workers' Union (SAAWU) 379

South African Communist Party (SACP): 20; indirect impact 24

South African Students' Organisation (SASO) 2, 45, 324

Southern African Development Co-ordinating Conference (SADCC) 355

South African United Front 50

South African Youth Revolutionary Council (SAYRCO) 344, 365

Soviet Union: support to ANC 72; & SACP 72

Soweto uprisings 1, 102

Tambo, Oliver: ANC president 279; news conference in Nairobi 319; visit to India 97

Thloloe, Joe 94

Trades Union Council of South Africa (TUCSA) 379-80

tribalism 14, 103-4

United Democratic Front (UDF): campaign spearheaded by 353; fate of, rationale for 323

Umkhonto We Sizwe: ANC's military wing 310; founders 37; guerrilla activities 311

Union of South Africa 21

United Nations (UN): assistance: agencies 60/negative effects 63; observer status granted 56; Security Council 58; Special Committee Against Apartheid 57

United States of America (USA) 11, 334

Victoria University of Wellington 2

Viljoen, General Constand 317-18, 358

Washington, Booker T. 19

Wiehahn Commission 378

Williamson, Craig 65, 325, 342

World Council of Churches (WCC): & national liberation movements 67; programme to combat racism 66, 249

World Peace Council (WPC) 72

Xoxelelo, Reginald 115, 142, 166

Xusa, Mzonke 176-8

Yu Chi Chan Club 41

Zimbabwe African National Union (ZANU-PF): 55-6, 119, 278, 281-4; victory of 323

Zimbabwe: APLA cadres arrested in 282; Republic of 350; PAC in 281; Pretoria's punitive economic measures 365

Zulu, Enoch (alias John Mvelase): appointed

Index

Director of Operations 206, 291;
arrested for currency offence 282;
defended Gora Ebrahim 293; & Mafole,
supported appointment 292; & Make
232, 253; pre-Arusha Central Committee member 194; vituperous attacks
219

HELEN JOSEPH
SIDE BY SIDE

Helen Joseph is perhaps one of the most famous South African women to campaign against apartheid. Her autobiography is being published on her 81st birthday and is a deeply moving account of her 30 years' involvement in the struggle of the South African people. As the people of the black townships continue to confront the South African police and armed forces, this book is a contribution to their courageous history by a woman who is herself a part of that history.

Hb 086232 564 1   £18.95
Pb 086232 565 X   £6.95

VUKANI MAKHOSIKAZI COLLECTIVE
SOUTH AFRICAN WOMEN ON THE MOVE

Women in South Africa suffer a triple oppression – from racial discrimination, exploitation as workers, and sexual inequality. In this remarkable book they describe in their own words the harsh realities of living under apartheid.

Hb 0946848 81 5   £14.95
Pb 0946848 80 7   £5.95

NEW FROM ZED

AFRICA TITLES FROM ZED

Dan Nabudere
IMPERIALISM IN EAST AFRICA
Vol. I: Imperialism and Exploitation
Vol. II: Imperialism and Integration
Hb

Elenga M'Buyinga
PAN AFRICANISM OR NEO
COLONIALISM?
The Bankruptcy of the OAU
Hb and Pb

Bade Onimode
IMPERIALISM AND
UNDERDEVELOPMENT IN
NIGERIA
The Dialectics of Mass Poverty
Hb and Pb

Michael Wolfers and Jane Bergerol
ANGOLA IN THE FRONTLINE
Hb and Pb

Mohamed Babu
AFRICAN SOCIALISM OR
SOCIALIST AFRICA?
Hb and Pb

Anonymous
INDEPENDENT KENYA
Hb and Pb

Yolamu Barongo (Editor)
POLITICAL SCIENCE IN AFRICA:
A RADICAL CRITIQUE
Hb and Pb

Okwudiba Nnoli (Editor)
PATH TO NIGERIAN
DEVELOPMENT
Pb

Emile Vercruijsse
THE PENETRATION OF
CAPITALISM
A West African Case Study
Hb

Fatima Babikir Mahmoud
THE SUDANESE BOURGEOISIE
— Vanguard of Development?
Hb and Pb

No Sizwe
ONE AZANIA, ONE NATION
The National Question in South
Africa
Hb and Pb

Ben Turok (Editor)
DEVELOPMENT IN ZAMBIA
A Reader
Pb

J. F Rweyemamu (Editor)
INDUSTRIALIZATION AND
INCOME DISTRIBUTION IN
AFRICA
Hb and Pb

Claude Ake
REVOLUTIONARY PRESSURES
IN AFRICA
Hb and Pb

Anne Seidman and Neva Makgetla
OUTPOSTS OF MONOPOLY
CAPITALISM
Southern Africa in the Changing
Global Economy
Hb and Pb

Peter Rigby
PERSISTENT PASTORALISTS
Nomadic Societies in Transition
Hb and Pb

Edwin Madunagu
PROBLEMS OF SOCIALISM: THE
NIGERIAN CHALLENGE
Pb

Mai Palmberg
THE STRUGGLE FOR AFRICA
Hb and Pb

Chris Searle
WE'RE BUILDING THE NEW SCHOOL!
Diary of a Teacher in Mozambique
Hb (at Pb price)

Cedric Robinson
BLACK MARXISM
The Making of the Black Radical Tradition
Hb and Pb

Eduardo Mondlane
THE STRUGGLE FOR MOZAMBIQUE
Pb

Basil Davidson
NO FIST IS BIG ENOUGH TO HIDE THE SKY
The Liberation of Guinea Bissau and Cape Verde:
Aspects of the African Revolution
Hb and Pb

Baruch Hirson
YEAR OF FIRE, YEAR OF ASH
The Soweto Revolt: Roots of a Revolution?
Hb and Pb

SWAPO Department of Information and Publicity
TO BE BORN A NATION
The Liberation Struggle for Namibia
Pb

Peder Gouwenius
POWER OF THE PEOPLE
South Africa in Struggle: A Pictorial History
Pb

Gillian Walt and Angela Melamed (Editors)
MOZAMBIQUE: TOWARDS A PEOPLE'S HEALTH SERVICE
Pb

Horst Drechsler
LET US DIE FIGHTING
The Struggle of the Herero and Nama Against German Imperialism (1884-1915)
Hb and Pb

Andre Astrow
ZIMBABWE: A REVOLUTION THAT LOST ITS WAY?
Hb and Pb

Rene Lefort
ETHIOPIA: AN HERETICAL REVOLUTION?
Hb and Pb

Robert H. Davies, Dan O'Meara and Sipho Dlamini
THE STRUGGLE FOR SOUTH AFRICA
A Reference Guide to Movements, Organizations and Institutions
Hb and Pb

Joseph Hanlon
MOZAMBIQUE: THE REVOLUTION UNDER FIRE
Hb and Pb

Henry Isaacs
LIBERATION MOVEMENTS IN CRISIS
The PAC of South Africa
Hb and Pb

Toyin Falola and Julius Ihonvbere
THE RISE AND FALL OF NIGERIA'S SECOND REPUBLIC, 1979-83
Hb and Pb

Dianne Bolton
NATIONALIZATION: A ROAD TO SOCIALISM?
The Case of Tanzania
Pb

A.T. Nzula, I.I. Potekhin and A.Z. Zusmanovich
FORCED LABOUR IN COLONIAL AFRICA
Hb and Pb

Jeff Crisp
THE STORY OF AN AFRICAN WORKING CLASS
— Ghanaian Miners' Struggles, 1870-1980
Hb and Pb

Aquino de Braganca and Immanuel Wallerstein (Editors)
THE AFRICAN LIBERATION READER
Documents of the National Liberation Movements
Vol I: The Anatomy of Colonialism
Vol II: The National Liberation Movements
Vol III: The Strategy of Liberation
Hb and Pb

Faarax M.J. Cawl
IGNORANCE IS THE ENEMY OF LOVE
Pb

Kinfe Abraham
FROM RACE TO CLASS
Links and Parallels in African and Black American Protest Expression
Pb

Robert Mshengu Kavanagh
THEATRE AND CULTURAL STRUGGLE IN SOUTH AFRICA
A Study in Cultural Hegemony and Social Conflict
Hb and Pb

A. Temu and B. Swai
HISTORIANS AND AFRICANIST HISTORY: A CRITIQUE
Hb and Pb

Robert Archer and Antoine Bouillon
THE SOUTH AFRICAN GAME
Sport and Racism
Hb and Pb

Ray et al.
DIRTY WORK 2
The CIA in Africa
Pb

Raqiya Haji Dualeh Abdalla
SISTERS IN AFFLICTION
Circumcision and Infibulation of Women in Africa
Hb and Pb

Christine Obbo
AFRICAN WOMEN
Their Struggle for Economic Independence
Pb

Maria Rose Cutrufelli
WOMEN OF AFRICA
Roots of Oppression
Hb and Pb

Asma El Dareer
WOMAN, WHY DO YOU WEEP?
Circumcision and Its Consequences
Hb and Pb

Miranda Davies (Editor)
THIRD WORLD — SECOND SEX
Women's Struggles and National Liberation
Hb and Pb

Organization of Angolan Women
ANGOLAN WOMEN BUILDING THE FUTURE
From National Liberation to Women's Emancipation
Hb and Pb

Zed Books' titles cover Africa, Asia, Latin America and the Middle East, as well as general issues affecting the Third World's relations with the rest of the world. Our Series embrace: Imperialism, Women, Political Economy, History, Labour, Voices of Struggle, Human Rights and other areas pertinent to the Third World.

You can order Zed titles direct from Zed Books Ltd., 57 Caledonian Road, London N1 9BU, UK.